# Ambition
## and
### Identity

# Ambition
## and
### Identity

# Ambition and Identity

## Chinese Merchant Elites in Colonial Manila, 1880–1916

ANDREW R. WILSON

UNIVERSITY OF HAWAI'I PRESS
Honolulu

**Library of Congress Cataloging-in-Publication Data**

Wilson, Andrew R.
  Ambition and identity : Chinese merchant elites in colonial Manila,
1880–1916 / Andrew R. Wilson.
     p.   cm.
Includes bibliographical references and index.
  ISBN 0-8248-2650-7 (hardcover : alk. paper)
1. Chinese—Philippines—Manila—History.   2. Elite (Social
science)—Philippines—Manila—History.   3. Manila
(Philippines)—History.   I. Title.
DS689.M2W55 2004
305.895'1059916'09034—dc22

                                                      2003020643

Designed by University of Hawai'i Press production staff

Printed by The Maple-Vail Book Manufacturing Group

*For Don and Julie*

# Contents

# Acknowledgments

IN MY FIRST YEAR of graduate school, I took a course on the history of United States–East Asia relations with Akira Iriye. In our discussion of the Spanish-American War, I asked a question about China's response to the American annexation of the Philippines. Professor Iriye admitted that he did not know how Beijing had responded and that the topic might be worthy of a research paper. The rest, if you pardon the pun, is history. From that first project I developed a keen interest in Sino-Philippine relations and in the Chinese community in the colonial Philippines. Throughout the rest of my graduate career my interest was encouraged by dedicated faculty mentors. William Kirby not only guided the project as my dissertation adviser, he also made it possible for me to travel and conduct research overseas. I was also fortunate to share a nascent interest in Chinese overseas with Philip Kuhn. To journey together with a historian of Kuhn's caliber through the complexities of Chinese migration history was both a privilege and an invaluable learning experience. Finally, Peter Bol not only trusted me to teach premodern Chinese history but forced me to look farther back into the history of the Chinese in colonial Manila in search of larger patterns of community development. To all of these mentors I am deeply indebted.

A good deal of published material was available for this project in the United States, and thus I am grateful to the staffs of the Harvard-Yenching Library, the Naval War College Library, and the National Archives II for all of their assistance. My various research trips in the United States and overseas would not have been possible without financial and spiritual aid. I would like to thank the Foreign Language and Area Studies Fellowship, the Sawyer Fellowship, and the Naval War College Foundation for making these numerous excursions possible. In Taiwan, I am grateful to Chang Jui-te, Li Hsiao-t'i, and Chang Tsun-wu, as well as the library and archive staffs at the Academia Sinica for facilitating my research there and at the Guomindang Party Archives. In Mainland China, Nanjing University's Chen Hongmin and Zhang Xianwen were of enormous help. In both Taipei and Nanjing I was dependent on the hospitality of my good friend Nowell Chernick, who spared no generosity in supplementing the meager prebend of a poor graduate student. With equal kindness Jason and Elizabeth Copeland hosted me on my foray into the wilds of the National Archives. In the Philippines, I was housed and fed by the Sievers family, Lynn, Ulf, and Katherine, who never failed to amaze me with their generosity. I regret that Ulf is not around to see the final result, but I hope he knew how important his friendship was to me. My research in Manila was further aided by Karen Gollin and David Keck, Teresita Ang See, and the staff of the Kaisa Para Sa Kaularan, as well as the staffs of the University of the Philippines, the Records Management and Archives Office, and Ateneo de Manila.

Many friends and colleagues at Harvard, Wellesley, the Naval War College, and elsewhere have not only helped this project along, but also made the process enjoyable and collegial. Analytical, interpretive, archival, editing, and translation advice came from numerous sources. Elaine Mossman, Chen Shiwei, David Pietz, Jon Rosenberg, Richard Horowitz, Chang Li, Chu Ping-tzu, Karl Gerth, Caroline Reeves, Pat Giersch, Chen Hsi-yuan, Mike Montesano, and Carsey Yee all contributed to various drafts of this work in the dissertation phase, and for that I am deeply grateful. Financial support for travel and writing came also from my employers in Boston, Bob Fraser and Sari Abul-Jubein. More recently, the manuscript was read and critiqued by colleagues who not only exposed flaws but also found hidden strengths. For this aid, I am thankful to Wang Gungwu, Edgar Wickberg, Adam McKeown, Richard Chu, Evelyn Hu-DeHart, Sally Paine, Bruce Elleman, Tom Mahnken, David Kaiser, George Baer, Melanie Johnson, Steve Ross, Steve Forand, Tom Nichols, Brad Lee, Bill Fuller, John Maurer, and Pamela Kelley, my editor at Hawai'i. Most of all I must thank John Carroll and Andy Meyer, who have provided the greatest help to me in this project by balancing brilliant minds with unerring friendship.

As if this were not enough, there are the many people who have aided this project in subtle ways. I am indebted to Peter and Sarah, John and Daniella, Tony Davlin, Dave Gelfman, Don, Audrey and Bruce Wood, Craig, Bernie, Jen, Deni and Jason, Art Palmer, Brian, Julie and Warner, Dwight, Marieke and Rose, the folks at the Red Rock, and the many others whom I have forgotten to name.

Finally, my family has been a constant source of inspiration, support, and love. I am blessed with such a large family that it might be possible to forget some of them. My thanks go to Don and Julie (my parents); Dave, Mimi, and Coleen (my in-laws); Aunt Amy, Uncle Roger, and Aunt Ruth; Dave and Ann Gray (my godparents); Suze, Gwyneth, Jeanie, Katie, Bryan, and Sean (my brothers and sisters); Philip, Dennis, Dave, Amy, and Kim (their significant others); and Michael, Sara, Gerald, Willie, Rachel, Zoe, Zach, Aisha, Mikayla, Maya, Zeke, Tyler, Sebastian, and Rhiannon (my nieces and nephews). Kelly, my wonderful wife, is deserving of the greatest praise and the deepest apologies. She has endured this process for more than a decade now and has been both my best editor and my best friend. And last, there is my greatest joy, McKeon, for when he smiles it is as if a light switch has been thrown in my soul.

MAP 1. The major ports and sending counties of Fujian Province.

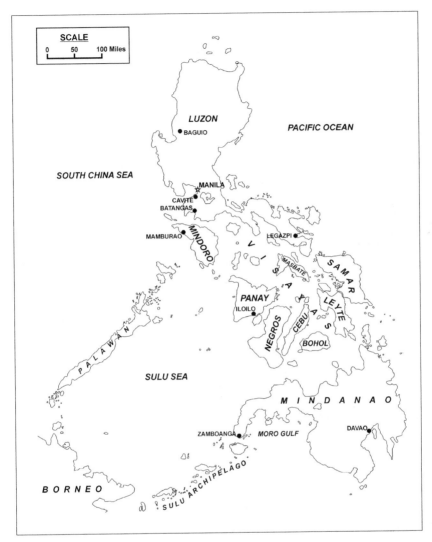

MAP 2. The main islands and major ports of the Spanish Philippines.

MAP 3. The provinces of Luzon in the late nineteenth century.

# Introduction

On May 9, 1912, the *Manila Times* reported that the Manila Chinese General Chamber of Commerce, the leading voice of the local Chinese community, had formally recognized the new Republic of China and had received official greetings from China's new president, Yuan Shikai. Many in Manila's Chinese community responded enthusiastically to the overthrow of the moribund Qing dynasty by a modern Chinese republic. Some young Chinese patriots even had a celebratory photo taken unfurling the new republican flag. Given that the leaders of the 1911 Revolution, especially Dr. Sun Yat-sen, would later give great credit to Chinese overseas for their role in the fall of the dynasty, such overt support for the new republic either by the dour heads of the chamber or by the younger generation was completely understandable. Only six years earlier, however, the Chinese Chamber of Commerce had been founded with the direct support of the Qing government and had welcomed the Qing consul general as an honorary member. Moreover, the Chinese merchant elite, who controlled the Chamber of Commerce, had been aggressively emphasizing their loyalty and personal ties to the dynasty for over thirty years. These loyal overtures were reciprocated. In the last four decades of its rule, the dynasty had reoriented its foreign policy agenda to emphasize the protection of Chinese overseas through the establishment of consulates and embassies in major nodes of Chinese emigration—allowing Beijing to develop institutional linkages with its expatriate subjects—and had reformulated its national development strategy to capitalize on the wealth and talent of Chinese overseas. Manila's Chinese merchant elite had been significant players in

1

FIGURE 1. Local Tongmenghui members unfurling the new national and party flags in Manila, 1911. Courtesy of Guomindang Party Archives, Jinshan, Taiwan.

this process, but all these efforts were insufficient to save the faltering dynasty or to guarantee the loyalty of the Chinese overseas.[1]

The reorientation of Beijing's foreign policy agenda had been rapid. Throughout most of the Qing dynasty (1644–1911), the imperial court had problematic relations with Chinese overseas. Various forces loyal to the Ming dynasty (1368–1644) had taken refuge in Southeast Asia in the late seventeenth century and harassed the South China coast in the name of restoring the Ming. Taiwan, once a Dutch outpost, fell to the pirate Koxinga, the most notorious Ming loyalist, whose family held the island until it fell to a massive Manchu-Chinese expedition in 1683. Other Ming loyalists found refuge in Vietnam and Thailand, often blending with established Chinese communities. Ethnic Chinese interaction with the region was therefore suspect in the eyes of the Manchu court. In the eighteenth century, Beijing took various measures to ban emigration for any purpose; while these laws were often relaxed in the case of merchants, it remained illegal for Chinese to travel abroad without official permission. In the late nineteenth century, however, the massive and largely uncontrollable flow of Chinese into Southeast Asia and the Americas as well as the dynasty's pressing need for talent and money forced a reappraisal of Qing emigration policy. A series of accords with Britain and France in the 1850s and 1860s sought to regulate labor recruitment in China's treaty ports. The 1868 Burlingame Treaty, between China and the United States, recognized the right of Chinese to emigrate freely and heralded a new official attitude toward the Chinese overseas.[2] Emigration laws were constantly revised, and the connections between Beijing and the Chinese overseas were continuously enhanced up until the dynasty's final collapse.

Institutional innovation accompanied this policy reorientation. In the 1870s and 1880s, the Qing established consulates and embassies throughout the world, charged to protect Chinese subjects and thereby improve the dynasty's international image. Investigative missions sent to Peru and Cuba in 1874 resulted in treaties that promised better treatment of Chinese laborers. Beijing successfully pressured foreign governments to end the abominable coolie trade and made the protection of Chinese overseas the first priority of China's new ambassadors to the United States, Spain, Peru, and Great Britain. In an era when China's international position was worsening daily, the Qing dynasty managed to enjoy a few foreign relations successes in the area of overseas Chinese affairs.

Beijing also courted the money and talent of the Chinese overseas for its self-strengthening program. In a reversal of the Confucian hierarchy that placed commercial activity near the bottom of the professions, merchants in the late Qing found their status elevated by a government that needed their skills. Successful Chinese were encouraged to return to China and invest in industrial and infrastructure projects. Zhang Bishi, a wealthy Straits Chinese from Penang, parlayed his overseas accomplishments into official position. His skills as a manager and his cash donations to government enterprises won him an imperial audience, and he was promoted to Director of the Court of the Imperial Stud and a place in the first rank of Qing officialdom.[3] Another Straits Chinese, Wu Tingfang, was trained in English law and later became the Qing ambassador to the United States, Spain, and Peru. Chinese students, trained overseas, also returned to China to take up posts in the imperial government, in state-run enterprises, in the military, and in the foreign service. Those who did not return were still encouraged to invest in China and to send aid in times of distress, while others were called upon to render service as consular officials overseas. The Qing rewarded its loyal and generous subjects with honorary titles and imperial emoluments, and imperial seals and charters were granted to the benevolent associations and economic institutions founded by Chinese overseas. The establishment of Chinese chambers of commerce, which were at once local but also chartered by the Qing government, further enhanced the linkage. To symbolize these formal and informal ties, the dynasty introduced a new word into its official vocabulary, *"huaqiao"* or "Chinese sojourner," a term that emphasized membership in a larger cultural-ethnic Chinese community *(hua)* and directed loyalty toward the homeland as "sojourners" *(qiao)* rather than immigrants. Finally, the Qing Nationality Law of 1909 declared, by the principle of consanguinity, that all Chinese, everywhere, were subjects of the emperor.[4] By the beginning of the last century, Chinese sojourners enjoyed a central place in Beijing's consciousness that they had never known before, and they had access to institutions and the protection of laws that would lead them to identify themselves more readily with the dynasty and as Chinese.

The Qing government, however, was not the only political entity that took an interest in the Chinese overseas. Chinese reformers and revolutionaries also set their sights on Chinese expatriates. The leading constitutional reformers, Kang Youwei and Liang Qichao, were well received throughout Southeast Asia (Nanyang) and the Americas after their exile following the failed "Hundred Days Reform" in 1898. Kang and Liang collected donations and established numerous branches of their Protect the Emperor Society (Baohuanghui). Sun Yat-sen, the "Father of the Chinese Republic," spent most of his life outside of China as both a student and an exile. In 1894, with the help of local Chinese, Sun founded the Revive China Society (Xingzhonghui) in Honolulu. In Tokyo, in 1905, Sun became head of the Revolutionary Alliance (Tongmenghui), which brought together the various Chinese student and political groups, and was later reorganized into China's first political party, the Guomindang. In many ways, Chinese communities overseas, especially student communities, were the birthplace of Chinese republicanism and the place where many ethnic Chinese first began to identify with the Chinese nation.

In the Philippines, local Chinese were not immune to these developments. Branches of both Kang Youwei's and Sun Yat-sen's groups were founded in the islands, but these movements developed slowly in the years before 1911. Instead of reformist or revolutionary affiliations, the local Chinese elite usually sided with the dynasty, and Beijing offered them awards and dispensations in exchange for this ostensible loyalty. The merchant elite lobbied successfully for the establishment of a consulate, purchased mandarin titles, dressed themselves in the style of Chinese officials, won imperial honors, and, in 1906, founded the Manila Chinese General Chamber of Commerce. The chamber, chartered in accord with the regulations of the new Ministry of Agriculture, Industry, and Commerce, granted an official Qing seal and, enjoying initially close ties to the imperial consul general, institutionalized the link between the local elite and the dynasty.

The Chamber of Commerce became the dominant Chinese institution in the American Philippines, and its directors took the lead in organizing Chinese community events. The chamber's members held annual celebrations for the emperor's and the empress dowager's birthdays, prepared lavish receptions for visiting imperial dignitaries, and collected funds for relief projects in China. As a reward, the chamber was allowed to select a delegate to represent the Philippine Chinese in China's new Constitutional Assembly. In every way, these merchants proved themselves to be loyal subjects of the Qing dynasty. How then could they so easily throw their support to a new government and a new president?

In pursuing the answer to this question, it became clear that understanding the dynamics of Chinese expatriate communities is central to understanding the social, economic, and political history of China in modern times. In the late nineteenth and early twentieth centuries, Manila's Chinese community underwent dramatic changes. These changes reflected the evolution of colonial Southeast Asia and the dynamics of the global economy. Change among the Chinese in the Philippines also reflected the revolutionary developments taking place in China: a growing sense of Chinese nationalism, simultaneous with a growing regionalism, politicization of Chinese merchants, anti-Manchu revolutionary activity, intellectual and cultural experimentation, as well as a host of social and institutional innovations. In the Philippines, and particularly in Manila, these developments prompted the reorientation of the Chinese community's social structure, the adoption of new institutional forms, and the aggressive promotion of community and individual identity as Chinese.

Perhaps the most revolutionary event for all Chinese, both at home and abroad, was the end of China's dynastic history and the establishment of a Chinese republic in 1912. With the exception of Yuan Shikai's unsuccessful attempt to found a constitutional monarchy in 1915–1916, the Chinese entered a prolonged era of experimentation with various forms of republican government. This was a fundamentally new historical experience for the Chinese people. By evaluating the overseas response to the Qing collapse within numerous discrete communities, one can go on to better illuminate the patterns of China's modern history by looking at this seminal event within the broader history of a transnational migrant community.[5] This Chinese community's response to the 1911 Revolution did not represent disloyalty to the fallen dynasty, nor did it embody the inherent revolutionary or patriotic consciousness or even the appearance of a new generation of Chinese leaders. Such conclusions are either insufficient or simplistic. Dynastic collapse was both a crisis and an opportunity for Manila's Chinese merchant elite. They seized on this opportunity by identifying with the new government of China in an informed and logical manner that best suited their socioeconomic ambitions. Identifying with the Chinese government, whether imperial or republican, reinforced the community's Chinese identity, legitimized the elite, and promoted community cohesion: factors essential to the social and economic success of the Chinese in the past and presumably in the future.

Prasenjit Duara has provided a persuasive explanation for this phenomenon. By exploring the ways in which three factions of nationalist emissaries to Southeast Asia sought to create a sense of identification with China by establishing hard boundaries that distanced ethnic Chinese from their host environments, Duara finds that the first two factions—imperial officials and constitutional reformers—were the most successful among the Chinese in Southeast Asia. Chinese merchants in the region responded enthusiastically to the sale of imperial titles and the Qing empire's "effort to construct a Confucian nationalism."[6] Kang Youwei and Liang Qichao's reformist Baohuanghui employed a "hybrid philosophy" to recruit overseas Chinese to the cause of constitutional monarchy for China and furthered their efforts through business activities that both enhanced the prestige of Chinese entrepreneurs and appealed to them as a symbol of a prosperous future.[7] Revolutionary nationalism, in contrast, was less successful before 1911, because participation in Sun Yat-sen's Tongmenghui had fewer social and economic benefits. After the fall of the Qing, however, the first generation of republican historians, responding to Sun's claim that Chinese overseas were the progenitors of the new China, sought to locate revolutionary activism in overseas Chinese communities where little actually existed. The subsequent politicization of *huaqiao* historiography is what Duara sought to correct and part of what this current work aims to evaluate.[8]

Among the Chinese merchant elite in the Philippines, the overwhelming appeal of constructing linkages to the Qing government relegated the reformist and revolutionary options to the status of minor political movements. Official certification by the Qing had more currency for a merchant community that was struggling to survive in an often hostile environment and that needed good relations with established authority than the potentially disruptive cause of an anti-Manchu revolution. When the dynasty ceased to be a viable political entity, however, the elite did not hesitate to shift its loyalty to the republic. Since it has been read as indicative of inherent revolutionary spirit among the Nanyang Chinese, this rapid—and opportunistic—shift has subsequently obscured the complexity of the relations between the Chinese overseas and the governments of China. Only by examining how the social and economic ambitions of the Chinese merchant elite in Manila informed their shift in loyalty from imperial to republican China—with little change in personnel or strategies—is it possible to salvage the history of the Manila Chinese community from the nationalist historiography of both China and the Philippines. Moreover, the reorientation of elite political loyalty was part of a greater pattern of skillful handling of shifts in the local and regional environment. Therefore, one must look farther back in time for the origins of merchant-elite strategies.

The subsequent chapters will show that 1911 was not the first time that local Chinese had faced a major crisis or had seized on a historic opportunity. For centuries, the Chinese migrants who traveled to Manila had been aggressively and opportunistically responding to changes within the host community and within China itself. In the nineteenth and twentieth centuries these changes were both more dramatic and more rapid. To meet these challenges, the most skillful and successful Chinese employed a complex web of strategies and identities, some of which could be appropriated or dispensed with at will. The Chinese discussed in this work are simultaneously "traditional" and "modern," monarchists and revolutionaries, merchants and mercenaries, self-serving and community-minded, Confucian and Catholic, Philippine and Chinese. The rapidly shifting matrix of identities is responsible for the success of the Chinese in Southeast Asia, which, in the words of G. William Skinner, "has yielded a wondrous array of adaptive, acculturative, and assimilative phenomena."[9] Whereas by the mid–twentieth century the distinctions between all of these categories had become much starker, the three and one-half decades that are the subject of this book were an age in which the totalizing narratives of modernity and nation were still being written. Hence, once we recognize the fluidity that characterized this era, it becomes impossible for scholars of this period to apply Manichean labels to our subjects. Much of this fluidity, in turn, was a product of the place we are examining.

## The Philippines as a Historical Setting

Perhaps the greatest appeal of this topic is that the Philippines in general and Manila in particular provide unique historical environments in which to study Chinese community dynamics and the development of Chinese identity that can serve as a comparative case for other Nanyang Chinese communities. The Philippine Islands have enjoyed a long history of intercourse with China because of both their proximity and the value of the Manila trade to the Chinese economy. There has been a distinct and documented Chinese community in the Philippines since the late sixteenth century, and therefore, the evolution of community institutions and socioeconomic strategies can be observed over a much longer period than Chinese communities elsewhere, notably enclaves in the United States, the Caribbean, or Singapore, that appeared only in the nineteenth century. Perhaps the best comparison can be made between Manila's Chinese and the Chinese in the Dutch East Indies. Those familiar with Leonard Blussé's *Strange Company: Chinese Settlers, Mestizo Women and the Dutch in VOC Batavia* will see many similarities between the two communities. Both colonies were centered on major entrepôt ports, Manila and Batavia, and both were established early in the history of Asian colonization, 1571 and 1619 respectively. In each case, the Chinese were essential collaborators in the colonial exploitation of regional trade but at the same time had uneasy relations with their European hosts, which resulted in uprisings and massacres. In an attempt to stabilize these alien enclaves, Dutch and Spanish colonial policy initially encouraged Chinese intermarriage with the indigenes and the creation of a creole elite (Chinese *mestizos* in the Philippines and Peranakans in Java), but in the nineteenth and twentieth centuries social and economic changes served to encourage the reassertion of Chinese identity. Finally, both colonies underwent a profound economic restructuring in the course of the nineteenth century from entrepôt economies to an agricultural and raw material export focus. This restructuring attracted a new influx of Chinese immigrants, who were recruited and employed through migration networks dominated by "Chinese" elites, but whereas the community superstructure in Java was constructed and maintained by locally born Peranakans, it was almost exclusively China-born elites who controlled these critical institutions in colonial Manila.[10]

By looking farther back into the nineteenth century for the origins of Chinese adaptability, I am also answering a challenge raised by Claudine Salmon's work on the reassertion of Chinese identity among Java's Peranakans. In a departure from the work of earlier scholars,[11] Salmon locates the origins of this movement farther back in the nineteenth century and argues that the establishment of various Chinese temples, funeral, and marriage associations in the mid–nineteenth century were part of an attempt to revive Chinese cultural identity in the face of social and economic challenges. Salmon raises the possibility that "resinicization" was a direct result of Dutch colonial policy, which offered both the institutional forms and the economic incentives for the creation of distinct (and self-consciously) Chinese communities in Java.[12] The evolution of a distinct ethnic-national identity among the Chinese in the Philippines followed a similarly complex course, being a product of intracommunity dynamics, external forces, and elite ambitions. Yet despite these numerous similarities, there were significant differences in the development of the two Chinese communities. This work will employ comparisons to other Chinese enclaves in Southeast Asia, in particular to Batavia, to highlight the uniqueness of the Manila-Chinese experience and to assess the impact of geographic, economic, religious, and policy factors on the history of Sino–Southeast Asian interaction.

A case study of a Chinese migrant community becomes all the more significant when one can observe how the Chinese respond to dramatic social, economic, and political changes in the host environment. Focusing on the late nineteenth and early twentieth centuries offers several revolutionary developments: the reorientation of the Philippine economy in the 1800s, the commodification of Philippine agriculture, the emergence of Filipino nationalism, a prolonged turn-of-the-century crisis, and a change in colonial rule in 1898. Beyond the significance of colonial transitions, the economic reorientation of Chinese overseas in this era also coincided with a period of monumental change in Chinese society and politics, and with a dynamic period in the history of Southeast Asia. Change in the host environment, the regional economy, and changes in Chinese politics and society combined to create the unique history of this Chinese community. These factors justify the unique periodization of this study, to which I shall return shortly.

Social and economic conditions in late colonial Manila encouraged the local Chinese elite to construct a distinctive Chinese ethnic identity. The assertion of this Chinese identity abroad through appeals to the government of China were manipulated by that elite to establish and maintain its control over the ethnic enclave and to expand its influence with external sources of authority. Access to external sources of authority, specifically the Chinese government and the colonial administrations, buttressed the power of the Chinese elite and allowed them to respond aggressively and successfully to opportunities in the Philippines. As a result, competition for power and resources within the Chinese community invariably involved appeals to these external actors through the agency of Chinese community institutions.[13] This was a common pattern among Chinese communities throughout colonial Southeast Asia and in China itself. The matrices of trust—native-place associations, surname groups, kinship organizations, guilds, secret societies, and chambers of commerce—that were the sinews of Chinese urban communities required points of connection with external sources of authority to legitimate their functions within those communities. Each venue, however, differed in the number and nature of these points of contact and therefore resulted in unique patterns of state-society relations and elite dynamics. A close examination of this process of adaptation in colonial Manila is not only enlightening in and of itself, but can also form the basis of later studies of the local Chinese responses to life under the American-tutored Philippine Commonwealth, during the Japanese occupation, and in the Republic of the Philippines. By limiting this study primarily to Manila, I am neglecting other Philippine-Chinese communities, but the limitation is justified by the fact that the Manila community was the largest, the most influential, and the best documented. In the period under examination, other Philippine-Chinese enclaves were still quite small and only developed to significant size and influence later in the American period; therefore, they left much less of an archival imprint. So far, only a handful of other Chinese communities, such as in Iloilo and Negros Oriental, have been the subject of book-length monographs.[14] What is known about these other communities, however, will be used to complement my examination of the Chinese in colonial Manila.

Transnational Chinese communities are inseparable from and central to the histories of China and Southeast Asia. Therefore, by observing the evolution of the Manila-Chinese community as an expression of what it meant to be Chinese in a period of revolutionary social, economic, and political change, one gains new insights into the complexities of Chinese community dynamics, national identity formation, and institutional and social change in the era of European imperialism, ethnic nationalism, and dynastic decline.

## Periodization

Philippine studies, as well as more specific works on the Chinese, usually choose 1898 as their dividing point.[15] Antonio S. Tan's *The Chinese in the Philippines, 1898–1935: A Study of Their National Awakening* and Edgar Wickberg's *The Chinese in Philippine Life, 1850–1898* are two illustrative examples of this common periodization. Wickberg's thesis is that the structure of the Chinese community and the roles played by the Chinese in the Philippine economy and Philippine society in the 1960s were "shaped in large part by the developments of the period 1850–1898."[16] While Wickberg does not deny that other periodizations are possible, 1898 is for him both a convenient and an appropriate watershed. After that date, community evolution followed paths established in the closing years of Spanish dominion. Tan, in contrast, argues that it was only with the advent of American rule, which he argues differed radically from that of Spain, that conditions in the colonial Philippines allowed the local Chinese to awaken to their Chinese identity and to forge closer ties with China as a nation. Of the two, Tan's argument is the more problematic because he is too wedded to Manichean notions of nation and identity. But even Wickberg's overwhelmingly valuable work pays insufficient attention to critical events in the early American period. If anything, the foundations of the community that were laid in the late nineteenth century were only solidified by choices made and institutional innovations undertaken in the early years of the twentieth. As for Tan, he pays insufficient attention to continuities across the 1898 divide. These included continuities in community leadership, institutions, and strategies. Moreover, even though the advent of American rule brought with it dramatic changes in law and colonial policy, and certainly witnessed the expansion of institutional linkages between local Chinese and the Chinese state, the American colonial enterprise manifested significant similarities to that of Spain.

The year 1898 is certainly a critical watershed that changed much of the course of Philippine history—not least because the settlement of the Spanish-American War fixed the nation-space of the modern Philippines—but it does not represent a neat divide between the old and the new. Imperial Spain undertook significant modernizing reforms in the nineteenth century that, although imperfectly applied, echoed many of the rationalizing and "modernizing" actions of the Americans. The United States, for its part, stumbled into empire and into its role as colonial ruler. The gaps in Washington's attempts to apply law, order, and good government to the Philippines, exacerbated by ignorance of the locality, allowed significant elements of the pre-1898 colonial dynamic to survive throughout the American era. While Wickberg would likely agree with this characterization, there were still sufficiently dramatic changes both in colonial rule and in the larger region following 1898 that required local Chinese to alter and in some cases displace earlier strategies and institutions. The primary weakness with 1898 is that it is a nationcentric date representing a major turning point in the histories of three nations—the United States, Spain, and the Philippines—and to a lesser extent China, marking the failure of the Hundred Days Reform. Furthermore, while nations are significant actors in this study, to be primarily nationcentric would ignore the communities and localities whose rhythms defy such facile periodization.

In addition to the significant continuities across the 1898 divide, the Philippines, and especially Luzon, were suffering through a prolonged crisis, beginning in the 1890s and only abating toward the end of the first decade of American rule. This crisis was produced by the cumulative effects of peasant immiseration (arising from long-term changes in rural society and economy), crime, urbanization, rebellion, cholera and rinderpest epidemics, market forces, and a host of other factors. No single event, not even one as dramatic as a change in colonial regime, could solely determine the course of Philippine

history. Manila too had its own rhythms, which defy simple periodization. Ever since the Spanish conquest in the sixteenth century,
Manila has been a critical node in the global economy. And yet, while
it was the center of colonial administration, Manila was, for much of
its history, isolated from the rest of the archipelago and remote even
from its immediate hinterland. Until the late nineteenth century
Manila was "closer" to China, Mexico, and Spain than to the northern Luzon province of Isabela or Nueva Vizcaya. Even when Manila
became integrated into the rapidly developing Philippine agro-ex-
port economy in the nineteenth century, it was still not completely
"of" the Philippines. Thus, even though the change in regime was felt
most acutely in Manila, the history of the city was still as much determined by the actions of the metropole as it was shaped by global market forces and the movements of people. This study does not reject
the notion of 1898 as an appropriate divide and uses it where applicable, but by examining the Chinese community over a thirty-five-
year period that crosses that divide and encompasses several larger
trends and critical watersheds, I hope to show how the history of a
community and a locality corresponds to and/or transcends this particular national narrative.

Within the field of Chinese overseas history, the fall of the Qing
dynasty in 1911–1912 is the event usually chosen to begin or end a
study. While this is certainly an appropriate choice, it is likewise insufficient in that such an approach threatens to elide significant continuities across the empire-republic divide. The changes in Beijing's attitudes and policies toward Chinese overseas that began in the 1800s
long survived the Qing's fall. Perhaps even more important, the institutional innovations undertaken by the Qing, especially in the consular movement of the late nineteenth century and the founding of
chambers of commerce in the 1900s, created a formal linkage
through which all subsequent Chinese governments could (and
would) communicate with *huaqiao*.[17] Choosing the period 1880–1916,
in addition to accounting for longer-term developments across the
1898 divide, also corresponds to a clearly defined stage in China-
*huaqiao* relations. Although attempts to formalize ties between Beijing and the Manila Chinese were made earlier, it was only in the
1880s that the opportunity and motivations were present to consti-
tute a real beginning to the relationship between a sufficiently attentive Chinese state and a motivated local elite. At the other end of this
period is the collapse of the Yuan Shikai government and with it the

end of the centralized authority of a Chinese state and Beijing's ability to confer authority on its consuls and to offer Chinese expatriates much of value.[18]

The two governments that ruled China during the period under study (the Qing and the early republic) were weak, but they were both centrally located and enjoyed, albeit briefly, sufficient domestic legitimacy and international recognition to give them a reasonable amount of leverage over Chinese communities overseas. This recognition was in turn reflected in the relative value and influence that formal ties to Beijing carried for Chinese elite who cultivated such linkages. While the relations between the various Chinese institutions in the Philippines and the local consul general were often acrimonious, that relationship was nonetheless significant during the period when the Chinese state was unified and attentive to its expatriate subjects and when it could satisfy the ambitions of the local Chinese. Since this is a work about the ways in which Chinese in the Philippines began to think of themselves as members of a larger entity, "China," and to build formal linkages with the Chinese state, it is therefore appropriate to study the period from 1880 to 1916, when these processes began in earnest, peaked, and then receded for a significant period. These dates are themselves nationcentric, but by superimposing a Chinese narrative on colonial Manila it is possible to reconcile the story of a specific ethnic community in a specific location with the numerous national, regional, global, and market narratives that converged at that point. Each of these narratives has its own benchmarks and its own value, but when taken in isolation they are each insufficient and, in some cases, deceptive. Only by negotiating the boundaries of these multiple histories at the points where they converge, as the Chinese merchant elite negotiated the landscape of colonial Manila, can one rescue their history from those who would place them exclusively within one of these narratives.[19]

## A Note on Sources

One appeal of this topic is the wealth and diversity of archival material. When pursuing the study of Chinese overseas, a historian has access to material from numerous sources: the Chinese community itself, the Chinese government, and the local authorities. Chinese materials on the two attempts to found a Qing consulate general in Manila are abundant, as is correspondence between Beijing and the local Chinese elite. These materials are contained in the Zongli Ya-men (the Qing dynasty's first foreign office) and Waiwubu (Board of Foreign Affairs) archives at the Academia Sinica in Taiwan and at the Number One Historical Archives in Beijing. Other relevant documents have been compiled in the Academia Sinica's *Zhongmei guanxi shiliao* (Historical sources on Chinese-American relations). Also in Taiwan, the Guomindang Party Archives stores early documents on Tongmenghui activities in Southeast Asia. The published collections of leading Qing officials likewise contain references to the Philippines and the local Chinese. Among the luminaries who took an interest in the islands were Li Hongzhang, Zhang Zhidong, Zhang Yinhuan, Yang Ru, Wu Tingfang, and Liang Qichao.

Despite decades of war and revolution, a wealth of material has also survived in the Philippines. The leading Chinese community institutions have published histories, and the archival material from the Spanish era, in particular from the Gobernadorcillo de los Sangleyes, the Chinese headman, is extensive, although much of it is in poor condition and often difficult to access. The main repositories of primary sources in Manila are the Records Management and Archives Office and, to a lesser extent, the Archives of the Archdiocese of Manila. Microfilm, yearbooks, newspapers, and personal accounts of the period discussed in this book are also held in the libraries of Ateneo de Manila, the University of the Philippines, and the Kaisa Para Sa Kaunlaran. The Kaisa's library is perhaps the best single resource for the study of the Chinese in the Philippines.[20]

Records for the American period, stored at the National Archives II facility in College Park, Maryland, are also excellent and give great attention to the Manila Chinese community in a time when the United States government was wrestling with the issues of Chinese immigration to North America.[21] Published collections, such as E. H. Blair and J. A. Robertson's massive *The Philippine Islands* and Gregorio Zaide's recent *Documentary Sources of Philippine History*, are frequently mined but never exhausted.

## A Review of the Existing Scholarship

The history of the Chinese community under Spanish rule is best chronicled in Edgar Wickberg's seminal work *The Chinese in Philippine Life, 1850–1898*.[22] Produced in the years following G. William Skinner and Maurice Freedman's pioneering works on other Chinese

communities in Southeast Asia, *The Chinese in Philippine Life* and
Wickberg's earlier article "The Chinese Mestizo in Philippine History" have had a similarly important impact on Philippine-Chinese
studies and all subsequent research is beholden to and measured
against that of Wickberg.[23] The present work is equally indebted to
Professor Wickberg, and one purpose of this book is to build on his
extensive research and cogent analysis by extending the temporal focus into the twentieth century through the use of source materials
that were not available in the 1960s.[24]

The strengths of Wickberg's contributions notwithstanding, he
remains tied to the 1898 divide, which fails to recognize and illuminate the ways in which local dynamics were and were not affected by
events on the larger historical stage. Wickberg further emphasizes
that community cohesion and a shared Chinese identity were the
product of two countervailing forces. The first were those exoge-
nous factors that set the Chinese apart from the other groups in the
colonial Philippines—*indios, mestizos,* and Spaniards—that is, discrimination, prejudice, legal distinctions, and imposed institutions.
Complementing this external "othering" were the internal—or endogenous—forces of shared language, native-place ties, and the patron-client relations that were so critical to Chinese success in the
retail trade and that exercised a kind of cultural gravity on the Chinese community. These were certainly powerful forces shaping the
structure and consciousness of the Chinese community in colonial
Manila, but they are an insufficient explanation for the relative cohesion of the enclave. The present study introduces a third force that
shaped Chinese identity, the Chinese merchant elite, who straddled
the divide between the Chinese community and the local environment and who manipulated colonial aspirations and prejudices to
satisfy their personal ambitions and further the security and prosperity of those under their leadership. Rather than having institutions
and ethnic distinctions thrust upon them by the colonial regime or
simply replicating strategies from their native places, these Chinese
*cabecillas* (as the merchant elite were known locally) demonstrated a
subtle hand and what I call a "liminal virtuosity" in creating the institutions and constructing the identities that largely defined what it
was to be "Chinese" in colonial Manila. As Wickberg shows, this was a
process begun in the closing years of Spanish rule, but as this work
demonstrates, it was only solidified during and after the change in
colonial regime. Ironically, the flexibility and virtuosity of the Chi-

nese merchant elite, which had allowed them to manipulate both colonials and mandarins, would later be lost as the institutions and "identities" that their ambitions had created bounded and constrained the Chinese as an ethnic enclave within an increasingly nationalistic Philippines. With the advent of the totalizing tropes of national identity in the twentieth century, the divide between Chinese and Filipino became more stark and served to obscure the more fluid identities that obtained at the turn of the century.

Antonio Tan's *The Chinese in the Philippines, 1898–1935: A Study of Their National Awakening* is a prime example of how these reified definitions of nation and identity can color a community history and obscure the varied ways in which local Chinese thought of themselves and viewed their place in the colonial milieu. Tan contends that community cohesion arose from a shared set of grievances over discrimination and anti-Chinese hostility. He concludes, however, that communality only manifested as "Chinese" political consciousness under the far more benevolent and rational American rule, which added as well to Chinese cohesion by applying the Chinese exclusion laws to the Philippines.[25] "Before the turn of the present century, the Chinese residents in the Philippines, like their compatriots at home, lacked the spirit of national and political consciousness. . . . The Chinese were, if we may use the term, apolitical, or better still, parochial: political sleepwalkers. They had neither knowledge of nor interest in politics and government."[26] Chinese political activism and direct linkages to the Chinese state did increase under American rule, but to characterize the Manila Chinese in the nineteenth century, and especially the merchant elite, as "political sleepwalkers" is wholly inaccurate. The fact that the Chinese were successful local and international merchants as well as the managers of complex recruitment and migration networks demanded tremendous sensitivity to local politics in both China and the Philippines as well as to the politics of the region.

Beginning in the 1880s Chinese *cabecillas* consistently demonstrated not merely an awareness of China as a political identity but quite detailed knowledge of Qing foreign relations, domestic politics, bureaucratic personnel, and the bureaucratic process. The elite also showed a keen interest in and knowledge of politics, government, and law in the Spanish Philippines and used that knowledge to protect and enrich the community. Tan's argument is circular: the manifestations of Chinese national consciousness—measured in membership in Chinese political parties (which begin to appear only very late in the 1890s), opposition to Chinese exclusion laws (applied by the United States), regular contact with the Chinese state (via the Consulate General or Chamber of Commerce, founded in 1898 and 1905, respectively), Chinese newspapers, Chinese schools, and so on—were only possible under the conditions and timing of American rule. By his criteria, one will inevitably look in vain for Chinese political consciousness in the Spanish Philippines.[27] If anything, national consciousness was present among the Chinese elite in colonial Manila, but it was complemented by numerous other identities that were gradually lost. Ultimately the options were reduced to two: either Filipino or Chinese, and by the middle of the twentieth century, ethnic Chinese rarely had a choice in the matter of identity.

Tan's emphasis on a major break occurring in 1898 seems logical but is nonetheless analytically flawed for several reasons. Much of the way Chinese identity was constructed and directed in the colonial Philippines involved institutions. One of the most important of these institutions was the Qing Imperial Consulate, founded at the end of a protracted negotiation that began in the 1880s and culminated only in 1899. Therefore, to use the founding of the consulate as a watershed in the emergence of national consciousness ignores the fact that the local elite had been trying to get Beijing's attention for nearly two decades. Moreover, even though the consulate was a Qing institution, it ultimately replicated many of the functions of its predecessor, the Spanish office of Gobernadorcillo de los Sangleyes, and thus change in institutional form and name did not represent a dramatic change in strategies or identities after 1898.

Tan's contention that there was a significant generational change in the early 1900s is equally forced. He argues that generational change was reflected in new institutional developments, specifically the replacement of the apical Gobernadorcillo with a dyarchy of consul general and chamber of commerce. His evidence is that the dominant figure of the late Spanish period, Carlos Palanca Chen Qianshan, was replaced by a broader leadership cadre of politically conscious and much more strictly "Chinese" leaders. By Tan's calculus, Chen had compromised his "national" consciousness. As the last Gobernadorcillo Chen was a subject of both the Spanish king and the Qing emperor as well as both a practicing Catholic and a Confucian. Tan argues from the perspective that Philippine Chinese are first and foremost Chinese and thus have only one natural locus of national identity: the Chinese state. Therefore, such a multiplicity of identities would have invalidated Chen as a community leader in the twentieth century.[28] But for Chen, his peers, and his protégés—many of whom continued to lead the community well into the American era—multidirectional loyalties were part and parcel of their socioeconomic strategies and a key ingredient of their financial success. While the advent of American rule certainly altered the landscape of colonial Manila, the effects were not nearly as dramatic or rapid as Tan concludes. Generational change occurred far more gradually and did not begin to affect the Chinese community significantly until the 1910s. Likewise, it was not until the passage of the Payne-Aldrich Act in 1909 that the Philippine economy began to recover from the prolonged crisis that had begun in the closing years of Spanish rule.[29] Therefore, in terms of both community leadership and economic activity, a complete turnover only came to fruition a full decade after American annexation, and thus continuities in community leadership and business strategies across the 1898 divide were more significant than Tan admits.

With regard to the inability of Chinese to assimilate into *indio* (native Filipino) society, Tan concludes that this was a result of a powerful "culturalism" among the migrants. These factors in turn explain the familialism of local Chinese, their consistent use of the Chinese language, failure to learn the local languages, retention of Chinese styles of dress, and so on.[30] In this assertion he shares many of the culturalist biases of Chinese *huaqiao* historians, but he is also echoing the conclusions of Jacques Amyot, John Omohundro, and more recently S. Gordon Redding. These writers explain the successes and the structures of Chinese communities as products of powerful cultural forms and, most important, a unique Chinese business culture. While a culture as varied and rich as China's does have tremendous power, the endurance of uniquely "Chinese" ways of dressing, speaking, and conducting commerce was also a function of the utility of these cultural forms to the type of business the Chinese did in the Philippines. The cultural forms practiced by Manila's Chinese merchants were the product of commercially sophisticated coastal Fujian, which had long been sending its sons to trade in the cities of China and Southeast Asia, and therefore many (but not all) of these "Chinese" attributes—which were essentially commercial common sense—were readily transplantable to Luzon. Here it is important also to keep in mind that, with the exception of a small Can-

tonese population, to be "Chinese"—or *chino* or Chinaman—in colonial Manila meant that one was Hokkien, that is, from one of the
counties around the port city of Xiamen on the southern Fujian
coast.[31] And even narrower native-place distinctions were in play, as
many of the Chinese in Manila were from a handful of villages.
Hence, while these migrants were "Chinese," because of their origin
within the geographical entity known as China and the fact that they
spoke a dialect of the Chinese language, it would be problematic to
conflate the much narrower identity of Hokkien with the broader
category of Chinese, and yet that is exactly what colonials and the
Chinese merchant elite did. To be "Chinese" in colonial Manila differed in many subtle (and a few not-so-subtle) ways from what it
meant to be "Chinese" in Chicago, San Francisco, or Havana. Nor
should the Chinese in Manila be viewed as a "group-apart," isolated
from *indio* or colonial society. Every Chinese in Manila, from the
wealthiest *cabecilla* to the poorest coolie, interacted with *indios,* Europeans, Japanese, and Americans on a daily basis.[32]

Tan's work demonstrates the limitations of trying to fix the
Philippine Chinese as exclusively "Chinese"—with only one natural
locus of identity—and to characterize the post-1898 Philippines as
uniquely American. He is resorting to overly determined views of cultures and identities. Yet he is not alone in this shortcoming. Despite
the trend toward challenging these totalizing tropes of nation, especially in colonial studies, much of the scholarship on the Chinese in
the Philippines continues to be dominated by individual national
narratives. Given the biases within Philippine historiography, those
who have studied the Philippine Chinese in the archipelago are often constrained to massage the community's history into that of the
nation. To tell the story of the Chinese in this context, one must often demonstrate how the Chinese shared the sufferings and achievements of the Filipinos, for example, as fellow victims of Spanish discrimination or as coparticipants in the Philippine Insurrection or in
the anti-Japanese resistance.[33]

Showing the Chinese as fellow victims also explains away the cohesiveness of the Chinese community. Similar to much of the scholarship on the Chinese in America written by Chinese Americans, the
literature on the Philippine Chinese produced by Philippine Chinese has located the causes of Chinese community cohesion in the
hostility of the host environment, rather than emphasizing the continuities of particular migrant strategies and the obvious utility of com-

munity cohesion in exploiting the export economy of the late colonial Philippines.[34] Absent the hostility of the local environment, the Chinese are portrayed as being exemplary Philippine citizens. A heightened sense of historical self-consciousness among contemporary Philippine-Chinese community leaders and historians is entirely understandable. Chinese in the Republic of the Philippines are alternately praised and damned in the chaotic political environment of that country. The implication that prosperous Chinese are sojourning parasites or the willing lackeys of corrupt regimes haunts the Chinese community. Therefore, while not dismissing their distinct cultural background, the primary locus of loyalty of the Philippine Chinese emphasized by these authors is to the Philippines as nation-state. This characterization therefore ignores the far more fluid environment in which the Chinese moved in the late nineteenth and early twentieth centuries, a time before the Philippines was a fully constituted nation-state and a time when, in the words of Adam McKeown, a Chinese immigrant could be both "here and there."[35] And yet it was the eminently practical and practicable pattern of sojourning in the Philippines that was the cornerstone of Chinese economic success in the late Spanish and early American periods. Being both "here and there" was how Chinese recruited talent, moved money, researched markets, sired heirs, and invested in real estate. Before the nation-spaces of both China and the Philippines became so reified in the twentieth century, steaming from Xiamen to Manila was perhaps as mundane as my morning commute and probably carried about as much political consequence. Yet in the twentieth century—and even now—to show the local Chinese as possessing divided loyalties and divergent localities was suspect. The key is therefore to show the Chinese as "Chinese" but essentially "of" the Philippines—which satisfies local Chinese advocates—and to avoid showing them as essentially "of" their motherland.[36]

A notable exception to this trend is the work of Richard Chu, himself a Philippine Chinese, whose exploration of late–Spanish era legal documents has shown a significant degree of interaction between Chinese and non-*paisanos*—people of other nationalities—including business partnerships. Thus, he challenges the notions of hard boundaries between Chinese and others in colonial Manila and the familial exclusiveness often attributed to the Chinese.[37] In addition, Chu shows that the *chino-mestizo* dichotomy, so often pointed to as indicative of the divergence between Filipinos and Chinese, is equally overplayed. In fact there were numerous Chinese *mestizos* who were very much part of the "Chinese" community, as well as Spanish- and Tagalog-speaking *chinos* who were part of *indio* and *mestizo* society, all of whom could move across ethnic boundaries with considerable ease. Chu has made a major contribution to our understanding of both the fluidity of colonial Manila and the contingent nature of ethnic identity in this period.[38]

The Chinese community was indeed dominated by the *cabecillas* who controlled the majority of the critical external linkages, but given the nature of the *tienda de sari-sari* system, which sent young Chinese alone out into the provinces as retailers and agricultural purchasing agents, not to mention the streets of Manila, where individual Chinese could fight, fornicate, gamble, and trade with locals and colonials, the Chinese elite could not possibly exercise total control over the community. Clearly, there were numerous contacts between Chinese and non-*paisanos*, and there were numerous opportunities to forge such linkages, either with *cabecilla* blessing or without. Thus, the construction of Chinese identity and the perceived insularity of the Chinese community were more the product of migration strategies, community institutions, and elite ambitions than they were the result of spontaneous ethnocultural affinity or innate "Chineseness." The ambitions of Chinese *cabecillas* led them to construct an institutional superstructure for the Chinese community as a distinct ethnic enclave, and although the Chinese, even the transients *(invernados)*, could never be completely isolated from local society, that superstructure had a great, but not quite hegemonic, influence on the ways in which they interacted with that society.

Gregory Bankoff's *Crime, Society, and the State in the Nineteenth-Century Philippines* demonstrates that, while the Spanish were hard-pressed to reform the colonial legal system systematically—lacking the means and personnel to do so—they nonetheless endeavored to implement a series of egalitarian and rationalizing measures in the late nineteenth century that echoed many of the legal reforms implemented in the American period. Thus, there were numerous continuities in the legal realm that have been heretofore ignored. Taken in tandem with Chu's work, Bankoff's study provides a clearer picture of the juridical environment of the late Spanish Philippines and the place of the Chinese within that system. One of the most significant revelations in this book, probably because of its broader treatment of criminality and justice in a multiethnic setting, is that the Chinese had a varied intercourse with *indios, mestizos,* and Spaniards that was both licit and illicit. These relations show again that, while the Chinese community was relatively cohesive, it was far from insular. Furthermore, the Chinese litigiousness of the American period, which seemed to be a new phenomenon, in fact had its origins in the 1880s. Finally Bankoff's evocative descriptions of the various and varied neighborhoods of Manila, their denizens, and their attractions exposes that the Chinese were distinguished within the mix not simply by their language, their features, or their dress, but by their "characteristic" appetites for opium, cards, and prostitutes.[39]

The aforementioned works on the Philippines are but a small sample of the recent flood of works that address the history of the Chinese overseas. David Ownby and Mary Somers Heidhues' *Secret Societies Reconsidered* was one of the first works to draw together a cadre of talented Chinese and Southeast Asian historians who emphasized the interconnectedness of Chinese and Southeast Asian history and offered up a wealth of comparative case studies. Equally valuable is *Sojourners and Settlers: Histories of Southeast Asia and the Chinese,* edited by Anthony Reid, which gives needed attention to the diversity and vigor of Chinese interactions with the peoples and polities of the region. Three of the essays in this volume deserve special note: Wang Gungwu manages to rescue "sojourning" from its twentieth-century pejorative and political connotations and restores it as a valid analytical device for understanding the ways in which Chinese did business, recruited talent, and moved through Southeast Asia. G. William Skinner's comparison of creolized Chinese demonstrates the ways in which colonial policy, demographics, and economic opportunity influenced the construction and assertion of ethnic identity in colonial Southeast Asia. Finally, Anthony Reid takes a macrohistorical approach to Chinese emigration and shows the critical role that migration networks—active even in times of significantly reduced emigration—played in directing and shaping the massive outflow of Chinese in the nineteenth and twentieth centuries.[40] This macrohistorical approach provides a much better picture of the extent of Sino–Southeast Asian interaction and the degree of China's connection to the global economy before the so-called "opening" of China in the middle of the nineteenth century.

One academic discipline that has taken an increasing interest in the Chinese overseas are postmodern historians and social scientists. They generally critique much of the earlier scholarship on Chinese overseas as trapped within the dominant narrative of republican Chinese historiography and cultural determinism, or informed by the "metanarratives" of highly nationalistic postcolonial host societies. Aihwa Ong and Donald Nonini's *Ungrounded Empires: The Cultural Politics of Modern Chinese Transnationalism* aims to link the flexible repertoire of Chinese sojourner strategies of the early modern world, such as the period that is the subject of this work, to those employed by the transnational diaspora of ethnic Chinese in the contemporary era of globalization. These strategies are transnational—also read transregional—linkages, mobility, diversification, adept role playing, manipulation, and adaptability. While I would not say that there is a perfect resonance between my subjects and today's ethnic Chinese, the critical emphasis of postmodernism, especially in challenging the totalizing tropes of nationality and ethnicity, is a necessary tool in the study of both historical and contemporary Chinese migration and adaptive strategies. In this work I seek to employ these recent contributions judiciously in concert with the classic works of Wickberg, Freedman, and Skinner.[41]

Christine Dobbin's comparative study of five "conjoint communities," Chinese *mestizos* in the Philippines, Peranakan Chinese in Java, the Parsi in Bombay and China, the Ismaili in East Africa, and the Nattukottai Chettiars in Burma, is yet another important addition to the field. Dobbin emphasizes the centrality of Chinese and South Asian capital and talent in the development of the world economy in the early modern era. Although trade may have been facilitated by European entrance into Asia, it was the preadaptation and flexibility of the local entrepreneurial minorities that provided the talent necessary for the colonial enterprise. At the root of this entrepreneurial success has been the ability of these middleman minorities to construct or appropriate multiple identities while at the same time maintaining a link to a unifying spiritual source that, in turn, is fundamental to their economic advancement.[42] The significance of this approach is the revelation, corroborated by both Skinner and Salmon, of the contingent nature of ethnic identity in the early modern era, especially on the fluid peripheries of empire.[43]

Thanks to these comparative and postmodernist volumes, the concept of transnationalism has recently gained currency in the study of Chinese overseas.[44] As much as Chinese migrants overseas are physically transnational, moving back and forth from one nation-space to another and relying on familial and commercial linkages that cross boundaries, they are also historically transnational, because their individual and community histories transcend and interconnect numerous national histories. Adam McKeown has provided, to date, the best application of the transnational concept in his study of three Chinese enclaves, Peru, Chicago, and Hawai'i, which were each situated at the nexus of various global, regional, national, local, and individual histories. In *Chinese Migrant Networks and Cultural Change*, McKeown demonstrates how the value and utility of transnational linkages (especially of migration networks), the type and relative power of community institutions, and the construction of ethnic identity all varied from one community to another depending on the nature of the local economy, the political scene, elite ambition, and even the physical environment. This comparative and local approach is an important corrective to more essentialized and totalizing portrayals of Chinese migrations and Chinese communities. The present work provides yet another local history of a distinct Chinese community that in some ways challenges but in other ways corroborates McKeown's conclusions.

To date, few of these new trends in scholarship have been able to penetrate the field of *huaqiao* studies as it is practiced in China. As has been thoroughly discussed in other works on the Chinese overseas, much of the scholarship on *huaqiao* produced in Taiwan and mainland China has been highly politicized and highly problematic from a scholarly perspective in that it has placed disproportionate emphasis on the natural affinity of Chinese overseas for the motherland.[45] In the twentieth century the essentialist rhetoric of ethnic commonality and cultural affinity demonstrated its utility in casting a unifying national veneer over competing and complementary local, regional, and national interests and identities. Thus, it has been nearly impossible for Chinese scholars, either on Taiwan or on the mainland, to extricate their studies of *huaqiao* from historiographical biases that portray Chinese overseas as instinctively and overwhelmingly "Chinese" and only assimilating into local society when all bonds to China—be they new migrants, mail, or family—are completely severed.[46] The reality, as I will show, was far more contentious and contingent.

Finally, in pursuing the present study, I have also benefited from the high caliber of contemporary scholarship on local elite and merchant communities in late imperial and republican China.[47] Such works, especially those concerned with regional "sojourner" communities within China, such as Shanxi bankers in the great commercial nodes of Hankou and Shanghai, provide an analytical platform from which to view Chinese migration history. Given the sophistication and diversity of China's domestic economy, it should not be surprising to discover that many of the commercial strategies employed in China's cities worked equally well in overseas entrepôts. Moreover, one should also expect to find that the increasing levels of social mobilization and political sophistication that characterized elites in late imperial and republican China were reflected among Chinese elites in colonial Southeast Asia.[48] As more recent works, such as those of Prasenjit Duara and others—all formally trained as historians of China—attest, this foundation of local and elite histories of communities in China can be applied profitably to the study of Chinese communities overseas.

The breadth of scholarship and historical disciplines that are applicable to this topic should by now be readily apparent. In fact they are as diverse and yet as complementary as the historical forces that converged on colonial Manila. Therefore, as impossible as it is to confine the history of a place as unique as Manila within a single national or even regional history, it is equally impossible to shoe-horn the story of Manila's Chinese community conveniently into a linear narrative. Likewise, to limit the analytical tools that one applies to this task to a single historical discipline or a particular historiographical epistemology does an injustice to one's subjects. The Chinese merchant elite of colonial Manila survived and thrived in an era of war, revolution, and economic upheaval because they were able to deploy a flexible web of identities and employ a complex repertoire of social, economic, and political strategies. The remarkable degree of virtuosity that they demonstrated at this liminal point—the place where numerous global, regional, market, national, and personal histories converged—demands a multidisciplinary approach that is as flexible and complex as the historical actors to whom it is applied.

# 1
# Origins and Evolution of the Manila-Chinese Community, 1571–1898

Two MAIN FACTORS conditioned the evolution of the Manila-Chinese community between 1571 and 1898. First, the nature of Spanish colonial rule was well suited to certain forms of Chinese social and economic organization prevalent in the migrants' place of origin, namely, the commercially sophisticated southern Fujian prefectures of Zhangzhou and Quanzhou.[1] The preadaptation to a commercial economy based on wholesale-retail networks and export allowed the southern Fujianese, or Hokkiens,[2] to exploit quickly the opportunities made available by the Spanish presence in Southeast Asia.[3] Second, the specific Chinese legislation enacted by the Spanish and the economic and political development of the Philippines over the course of Spanish rule first promoted and then discouraged Chinese assimilation with native *indios*.

The political, social, and economic landscape of the Philippines under Spanish rule developed through three distinct time periods, which in turn shaped the evolution of the Chinese community. During the initial surge of Chinese in-migration, when the newly conquered Spanish Philippines were suddenly plugged into the massive Chinese economy, the Spanish had tremendous difficulties reconciling their commercial interests with their fear of being overwhelmed by the Chinese. After a tumultuous first century, the Spanish developed policies, designed to limit the size and mobility of the community, that promoted the growth of a distinct Sino-Philippine minority of *mestizos*. During the nineteenth century, dramatic changes in the economic and political landscape combined to attract Chinese who once again poured in from the Hokkien region and to a limited extent from Guangdong. Unlike that of the preceding era, this new wave of Chinese immigration increasingly formed an institutionally cohesive and self-consciously Chinese enclave and began to displace *mestizos* from the retail trade in Luzon. Whereas it made good economic sense to "assimilate" into *indio* society in the early Spanish eras, it made equally good economic sense not to assimilate in the late nineteenth century. Yet even with the new socioeconomic environment of the late Spanish Philippines, local Chinese continued to draw on the wide variety of mechanical and commercial skills present in their native places and to adapt them to better exploit economic opportunities in colonial Manila. That the Chinese were able to do this so consistently and so successfully is indicative not only of the sophistication of the Chinese coastal economy but of some critical similarities between late imperial China and the Spanish Philippines.

## The Nature of Spanish Colonial Rule

Although they were products of two completely different cultural and historical milieux, the similarities between imperial China and imperial Spain point to a deep resonance between the nature of state-society relations and economic policies of the two empires.[4] Beyond their geographic breadth, flexible borders, and ethnic and environmental diversity, the Qing and Spanish empires of the seventeenth to twentieth centuries deployed universal cultural values and the common quest for moral transformation to overcome the rifts and parochialisms common to all such empires. On the more mundane level, both empires had the same administrative and revenue priorities and employed many of the same methods to achieve their goals. Critical limitations in manpower and the reach of the state allowed for a high degree of local autonomy. While the Qing state was a good deal more elaborate and integrated than imperial Spain, Chinese immigrants could nonetheless directly import tested Chinese economic strategies and institutional forms that were exceptionally well suited to the Spanish Philippines.

These similarities did not make Manila a mirror image of a Chinese port city.[5] The Philippines themselves had numerous unique characteristics that required adaptation or innovation, and the Spanish imposed all manner of alien organizational and cultural requirements on the local Chinese. These, in turn, had to be incorporated into community dynamics. Nonetheless, considering the centrality of the Chinese to the development of the economy, Manila was as much a Chinese city as it was Spanish or *indio*. Therefore, understanding the resonance between China and the colonial Philippines is essential to understanding why the Manila-Chinese community, as a unique social, economic, and political unit, developed the way it did.

According to Charles Tilly, "Spain produced a sixteenth-century spurt of state-making which, if continued, could easily have brought her to Europe's highest level of centralization, differentiation, autonomy and coordination; the process slowed, and sometimes reversed, in the seventeenth and eighteenth centuries. As a result, Spain entered the age of industry and empire with one of the least stately governmental structures on the continent."[6] This initial spurt of activity provided the Spanish empire with the means to extract resources from its colonies with remarkable effectiveness. This capability was best represented by Madrid's command over precious metals production in Mexico and Central America. This wealth of precious metals had a "trickle-down effect" for the entire Hispanic world. American gold and silver provided the motor for the Manila economy, which in turn supplied the empire with Chinese luxury goods and enriched Spanish officials. Such a windfall, however, had its costs. In the case of Mexico, fiscal rationalization and economic development were hindered by the colonial state's obsession with bullion. In short, Spain's addiction to silver stifled development.[7]

The effectiveness of the colonial state in extracting resources was achieved by means of laws, institutions and policies that imposed constraints on colonial economic activity. The principal constraints may be summarized under two headings: (1) the system of socioethnic adscription that defined a separate legal status for Europeans *(peninsulares* and *criollos), castas* (persons of mixed race) and Indians and, (2) the myriad interventions of the state for fiscal purposes, including not only the tax system itself but also a complex set of regulations, concessions, permits, privileges and state monopolies that supported and supplemented it. The first of these served to facilitate and to legitimate fiscal extractions. The second served directly to define and enforce the extraction process. Together these constraints made economic organization inefficient and thus reduced the productivity of the economy.[8]

The Spanish empire was fiscally and administratively premodern. The two main functions of government were tax collection and social control. This system of priorities coupled with the immense breadth of the empire and its severely limited administrative resources rendered the colonies of the empire "primitive nation states,"[9] in which colonial governors were granted vice-regal authority. However, since the colonial governments did not have the bureaucratic manpower to administer the entire social control and tax collection systems, they had to coopt the local elite into state service. In exchange for this service, the state granted certain privileges to the elite, including exemption from taxation and capital punishment and "ex post facto payments to overlook irregularities and criminal activities."[10]

The Chinese state had long before learned the value of coopting the local elite to provide services that the state had neither the manpower nor the resources to perform. The Chinese local elite assisted in tax collection, organized disaster relief, and founded hospitals, orphanages, cemeteries, and schools. They mediated local disputes in the absence of an extensive legal system,[11] financed local temples and religious festivals, and played the leading role in local community life. By the end of the imperial period, these activities were no longer just the responsibility of the local elite but had come to define elite status in local society.[12] The limited reach of the state in the Spanish Philippines and that state's willingness to farm out government services to local notables allowed the elite, among them wealthy Chinese merchants, to form an intermediary layer between the state and local society. Among the primary functions of this local elite was tax farming.

Imperial Spain was never well staffed, and in the Philippine archipelago, on the far edge of the empire, the bureaucratic manpower shortage was even more acute. Spanish officials were a minuscule proportion of the population, and the reach of the state was limited by poor communications and little or no transportation infrastructure. The state, therefore, delegated the majority of tax collection to the local elite. In rural areas, taxes and fees were collected by the Dominican, Franciscan, and Augustinian friars and the plantation owners who had de facto control of the majority of the colony. In the cities, despite the higher bureaucratic concentration, most tax collection was done by Chinese merchants and Chinese *mestizos*. Spanish bureaucrats focused their attentions on galleon trade profits.

In the colonial Philippines, the taxes collected by this local elite were numerous, but the fiscal cornerstone was the direct, or capitation, taxes. As Gabriel Ardant has argued, this placed Spain and her colonies at the elementary stage of state development.[13] The capitation tax was based on the "socioethnic adscription" described by John Coatsworth, in which classes and ethnic groups were taxed according to the state's perception of their ability to shoulder the burden of taxation regardless of the individual taxpayer's income.[14] In the Philippines, Chinese *mestizos,* emerging as a semi-elite in the seventeenth and eighteenth centuries, were taxed at twice the rate of the *indios* (natives), and the Chinese were taxed on a per capita basis that was at least four times the rate for the native population.[15] Since the Chinese population hovered around twenty thousand for most of the seventeenth century, the Chinese must have provided a substantial contribution to the colonial budget. In the Dutch East Indies, the capitation taxes on only three thousand resident Chinese provided nearly half of the colonial government's income in the seventeenth century.[16] In addition to capitation, the state employed a myriad special taxes, customary fees, levies, and "voluntary donations" to meet extraordinary expenses. Charged with collecting these sums (in essence a quota or "gross levy"), the local elite tax farmer could act in the interests of local society by seeking to minimize the burden on his community, or he could act in his own interest by skewing collection to favor relatives or allies, or by collecting in excess of the state quota to keep the surplus for himself or hold as a communal fund for lean years.[17]

Government monopolies and revenue farms supplemented taxation. Until the nineteenth century, the Philippine colonial government held a lucrative, but regressive, monopoly on tobacco, and the provincial governors monopolized interprovincial trade.[18] The important revenue farms included opium, gambling, salt, and local markets. These were initially contracted out to local Spaniards and *mestizos* but were opened to foreigners in 1857.[19] Recently arrived Chinese would have been very familiar with the practice of state monopolies and tax farming. The Chinese government had employed government monopolies on salt and iron since the second century B.C.E., and, by the Ming and Qing dynasties, the state was farming out tax and monopoly collection to local merchants. Many of these state contractors, like the Yangzhou salt merchants, were some of the wealthiest men in the empire. Hokkien migrants would have been intimately familiar with the *yanghang* monopoly of the Qing. The *yanghang*, or "ocean guild," authorized a select group of merchants to take responsibility for all foreign trade. The most famous example of the foreign trade monopoly was the *cohong* that dealt with European traders in Canton from 1754–1842. Hokkien ports, from whence the majority of the Manila Chinese originated, had their own *yanghang*. Fujian was also home to huge government porcelain contractors. Chinese migrants were therefore preadapted to monopoly systems and Spanish revenue strategy, and could enter the market with skills drawn from the Chinese milieu.[20]

In the realm of social control, the Spanish lacked the resources to handle many of the day-to-day issues of public order. To meet this challenge, Spain used two main strategies: promoting cultural and moral consensus, and delegating judicial and police functions. The application of normative standards through the agency of the Catholic Church was an attempt to integrate the empire through cultural consensus and shared values. The basic assumption was that a good Catholic was also a good—and law-abiding—subject. The Chinese state had a similar method of promoting cultural consensus, through the emphasis on Confucian precepts of hierarchy and the respect for elders and social superiors. These could be very effective means of minimizing socially disruptive forces. The Chinese state also controlled the avenues of social mobility via the imperial examination system, which required the memorization of state-sanctioned Confucian and Neo-Confucian texts that emphasized these same socially integrative values. Even religious practices were directed toward the goals of the state. Prasenjit Duara and James Watson have both demonstrated the state's ability to coopt local elites through local patron deity cults that were appropriated into the state-sponsored pantheon.[21] The Chinese elite as well as aspirants to elite status were therefore conditioned to view state-sanctioned activities as the most effective avenues of social mobility. This view directed private ambitions toward the public good. In both milieux, however, the cultural consensus was flexible and was negotiated with local religious sensibilities and indigenous customs. Within the Spanish empire, in exchange for proclamations of loyalty to the church and His Catholic Majesty, and in the interests of imperial integration, both crown and church were willing to tolerate a significant degree of regional variation in Catholic ritual and practice. The same can be said of activities in local temples in China. The Filipino church that evolved in the Spanish era incorporated existing *indio* folk beliefs and revolved around the pageantry of Catholic festivals,[22] and the Hokkien Chinese who converted to Catholicism in the Philippines coopted the Virgin of Antipolo as an incarnation of Mazu, the patron deity of Hokkien travelers.[23]

In both late imperial China and Spanish colonies, delegating judicial and police authority to the local elite was the answer to the state's inability to respond systematically to criminality and socially deviant behavior. Since each state lacked the manpower and funds to field a pervasive and effective police force or judiciary, "it did not go out, in most cases, searching for criminality but rather adjudicated when asked to by one or more inferior bodies."[24] Again, the state relied on the local elite to mediate disputes and handle lower-order criminal behavior. The state only intervened in extreme cases, such as revolts and conflicts between two or more of its agents. It was only in the late nineteenth century that the Spanish attempted to reform the colonial legal system. Despite the best egalitarian and rational intentions, the limitations of this later reform and church hostility to the extension of colonial authority left a great deal of police and juridical authority in the hands of friars and local elites.[25] Among the Chinese in colonial Manila, the delegation of this authority was apparent both in the importance of Chinese secret societies, which recent scholarship has shown were central to mutual aid and local order in the unstable environment of South China,[26] and the semiautonomous nature of the community; the Chinese had their own court (the Tribunal de los Sangleyes) and their own governor (Gobernadorcillo de los Sangleyes).[27] These agencies were the main instruments of social control within the community. Such a delegation of the primary tasks of governance represented a tacit acceptance that the state did not have a monopoly on coercive force and was willing to tolerate "high levels of illicit violence" in exchange for maintenance of the status quo.[28] Using Chinese secret societies for revenue collection and occasionally social control was not unique to the Spanish Philippines. In the Straits Settlement, the British relied heavily on secret societies to collect opium revenues and to control the unruly population of recent Chinese arrivals in the early nineteenth century but were ultimately forced to suppress them.[29] Even in the United States, Chinese secret societies or sworn brotherhoods, like Chicago's On Leong Tong, demonstrated a degree of organizational flexibility that allowed them to evolve from protection/intimidation rackets into overarching community institutions.[30] While the Philippine societies never eclipsed the "legitimate" Chinese institutions, both colonials and Chinese elites used secret societies up until the very end of the Spanish colonial enterprise. Moreover, Spanish authorities applied a double standard when it came to certain vices, notably opium, gambling, and visiting prostitutes, which were legally prohibited for *indios* but were tacitly accepted for Chinese both because they provided revenue and because they were thought to keep the *chinos* quiescent.[31]

For recent Chinese arrivals, this probably seemed a natural response to vice and violence. Chinese from southeastern China, where stockaded villages were a common sight, were very familiar with "high levels of illicit violence." Throughout the late eighteenth and nineteenth centuries, in particular, clan feuds, peasant rebellions, and organized criminal activity had become endemic in China. In the absence of an effective state response, organizing militias in the defense of hearth, home, and lineage was a common response, as was the use of violent tactics as part of social and economic strategies. Merchants were well aware of the dangers posed by criminal predators. Furthermore, clan feuds, or *xiedou,* and "secret societies" were especially prominent in Fujian and Taiwan.[32] For the Hokkien merchants in the Philippines, carrying lucrative cargoes and huge amounts of silver and lacking official protection from either the Spanish or Chinese governments, it was natural that they take responsibility for defending themselves against economic rivals and criminal predators. Chinese traders in the Nanyang had learned the dangers of piracy, and they armed themselves in response. Since many traders joined secret societies for protection, armed merchants frequently blurred the line between piracy and commerce.[33] It comes as little surprise that the first encounter between Spanish troops and Chinese merchants resulted in an armed clash.[34] Rulers of the Philippines would find it difficult to make the distinction between law-abiding Chinese and the criminal element.

Although the essential nature of Spanish rule was consistent for most of the pre-nineteenth-century era, there were sufficient changes in the economic environment, colonial policy, and Sino-Spanish relations to allow for periodization. The history of the Chinese community can be divided roughly into three periods, 1571–1686, 1686–1834, and 1834–1898. I refer to these as the "period of crisis," the "period of stasis and assimilation," and the "period of diversification and expansion." These divisions are necessary, because each era was marked by a distinct relationship between the Spanish and the Chinese, and different strategies and dynamics within the Chinese community. The nature of Spanish rule and the Chinese ability to respond flexibly and import tested strategies and institutions from southern Fujian allowed the community to survive through centuries of discrimination and exploitation and to come to dominate critical segments of the colonial economy in the closing years of Spanish rule.

## Period of Crisis: The Chinese during the Early Spanish Period, 1571–1686

The first century of Spanish rule was a time of tremendous economic growth in the Philippines, and the Chinese population increased to take advantage of these new opportunities. Relations between the Spanish and the Chinese, however, although initially friendly, soon soured and created an environment of distrust and periodic violence. Even though this was the apogee of their imperial expansion, the Spanish were intimidated by and suspicious of the Chinese, and they implemented a series of policies to focus Chinese social and economic activity toward desired ends. But formulating an effective system of colonial rule proved difficult, and for most of this period the Philippines was in a near constant state of upheaval.

Although Chinese had been traveling to the Philippines for centuries, it was not until the arrival of the Spanish that large numbers were attracted to the islands. In 1570, there were only about 150 Chinese in Manila; by 1603 there were more than 20,000. In 1636 there were 30,000 Chinese compared to only 230 Spaniards.[35] This population expansion coincided with Manila's growth as the administrative and trading center of Spain's Pacific empire and the end to the Ming dynasty's ban on Chinese overseas trade. The Spanish arrival in 1571 opened many opportunities for the Chinese and attracted them to the new city; the large number of Chinese, however, unnerved the Spanish.

The galleon trade was so lucrative for the Spanish and the Chinese that neither side saw the need to diversify the Manila trade to include Southeast Asian commerce. As a result, Manila trade remained essentially one-dimensional and seasonal for the next 250 years.

Their role as transshippers and the seasonal nature of the Manila trade also meant that most Chinese during this period lived in Manila for only part of the year. This characteristic of the ethnic Chinese (*chino* or *sangley*) community persisted into the early nineteenth century and conditioned the Spanish colonial enterprise in the Philippines.[36] With few exceptions, the Chinese merchants in Manila traveled back and forth between the Fujian coast and Luzon, funneling Mexican silver into the Amoy (Xiamen) trade network; they did not pursue multidirectional commerce outward from Manila. This was not necessary, because Xiamen was internally integrated into the massive Chinese economy and externally connected to regional marketing systems. With the exception of spice imports from Molucca and cloth from India, Manila never became part of an articulated trade network until the nineteenth century. Almost everything that the Spanish consumed was brought from Mexico, China, and, in some cases, India—via Armenian merchants—or was produced locally. The only desirable Spanish product was silver, which was shipped directly to China. For most of the Spanish era, therefore, the Philippines was poorly integrated into the East Asian economy and remained at one remove from the Chinese market. Ironically, it was Mexican silver flowing into Manila that in turn fueled development throughout the region.

In addition to being its best suppliers, the Chinese contributed to the success of the galleon trade in other ways. Many of the galleons plying the Pacific were built with the aid of Chinese shipwrights in Manila and Cavite. Some of these ships displaced as much as two thousand tons and required massive amounts of hardware, rigging, and sails produced either in China or by local Chinese craftsmen.[37] Of all the peoples of East Asia, the Chinese probably had the most experience as shipwrights, especially for transoceanic vessels (*yangchuan*) of the size required by the Spanish.[38] The Chinese also provisioned the galleons. On the return voyage to Acapulco, the hundreds of crew and passengers dined on Chinese rice and fowl, including pressed duck; drank tea; and ate mandarin oranges to prevent scurvy.[39]

Free of competition from indigenous craftsmen and practitioners, the Chinese became the principal professional class in Manila and were in high demand for their skills as physicians, masons, and printers. Transient (*invernado*) Chinese worked as tailors, shoemakers, metal smiths, sculptors, painters, and locksmiths and were responsible for most of the material culture of early colonial Manila. The various religious orders also benefited from Chinese skills. Early churches were almost exclusively built by Chinese masons, and the first books printed in the Philippines (bibles and apologia) were the product of Chinese craftsmen.[40] Whatever colonial Manila needed, either materially or as manpower, China could provide. While the most consistently important group were Hokkien merchants and their clerks, both during the galleon trade and especially during the nineteenth-century commercial boom, at other times agriculturists (both truck gardeners for urban areas and rural farmers), stevedores, masons, and other skilled craftsmen could migrate from China to fill market demand. Such practitioners existed in the millions in China, and since China also possessed the largest and most complex economy in the world, where trade in skills was as important as trade in goods, there was a preexisting system of internal migration of labor. If a Southeast Asian colony (especially one as close as the Philippines) could "plug in" to this massive economy, it would almost immediately be flooded with desirable (and undesirable) Chinese labor. This in turn meant that *indios* (given also the nature of the colonial regime) were nearly always at a skill disadvantage compared to the Chinese. Lacking as they did the specific talents that the colonial regime wanted in the short term, they were therefore unlikely to fill anything but the most menial jobs and consequently were less likely to develop either the craftsmanship or the commercial acumen necessary to compete with the Chinese in the long term. The exception to this pattern was the later appearance of a rural elite of *caciques* (chiefs) many of whom could trace their ancestry to the Chinese agriculturists that the colonial state had imported to meet labor demands earlier.[41]

Chinese contributions to the economy and the galleon trade were numerous, but Sino-Spanish relations quickly soured. Violent incidents and tragic misunderstandings created a tense environment. The first incident was the attack by the Chinese pirate Lin Feng on Manila in 1574. During the attack, the Spanish were barely able to defend Manila from the pirates and from a simultaneous local rebellion. Then again in 1603 an ill-conceived Chinese embassy to Manila—looking for a legendary mountain of gold and silver—sparked a Chinese riot that frightened the Spanish so much that they slaughtered thousands of Chinese. Throughout this period the Spanish were understandably suspicious of *sangleyes* (as they called the Chinese), and relations between the two groups were often marked by violence. For much of the late sixteenth and early seventeenth centuries, the Spanish feared a Chinese invasion. Furthermore, some critiques claimed that the Manila trade was draining the empire's silver reserves, and the colony itself was a budgetary burden for the throne. Chinese merchants were the frequent target of Spanish governors-general sent to correct these problems. Since the governors-general were invariably military men, they needed to balance their personal desire for profit against the security of the archipelago. Consequently, colonial officials were critical of the Chinese and enacted legislation to severely limit their numbers, mobility, and economic opportunities, while at the same time endeavoring to extract more money from them.

## Chinese Policy in the Early Colonial Philippines

In the opinion of some Spaniards, a Chinese enclave was a necessary evil. Colonial officials wanted to attract Chinese to Manila in order to exploit their industriousness, skills, and wealth, and to buy their silks, porcelain, and other luxuries. But, at the same time, they feared the economic power of the Chinese and the threat posed by a large population of inscrutable aliens in close proximity to their home empire—an empire that was imposing in its size and wealth. The strategic anxieties of the governors-general were reasonable. Although the total number of *chinos* was relatively small, compared to the numbers of Chinese in Thailand, Vietnam, and Malaya, they still outnumbered the Spanish. Their wealth and numbers disquieted the colonialists at a time when Spanish control was tenuous. Local Chinese and pirates like Lin Feng could organize effectively and assault the Spanish, and the Spanish were unclear about the Ming dynasty's intentions toward Southeast Asia. Manila's distance from the metropole meant that reinforcements would be long in coming.

In order to balance economic necessity and colonial security, the Spanish conceived of an ideal number of Chinese. Other colonials made similar calculations. When the Dutch founded Batavia as a base for their East India Company, they too wanted to attract the Chinese. As in the Philippines, the natives of Java did not have the economic sophistication or valuable commodities to support the kind of trading enclave that the Dutch envisioned. But they were also concerned that the Chinese would overwhelm them. As a result, the Dutch decided in 1742 that 5,934 Chinese were needed to maintain Batavia's economy.[42] In Manila, perhaps because of the numerous early conflicts with the Chinese, the ideal number of *chinos* was smaller, roughly four thousand.

Colonial officials, however, found it difficult to regulate the size of the Chinese community, especially when the Chinese heard about the profits to be made in European colonies. Attaining a "magic" number of Chinese was an elusive goal at the height of the galleon trade in the early seventeenth century, when the Chinese flooded into Manila for both licit and illicit purposes. Wholesale expulsion, therefore, was periodically employed. Expulsion followed Chinese tax or labor riots, which were then followed by reassessments of the "ideal" Chinese population. The 1742 assessment in Batavia came on the heels of the Chinese revolt in 1740 in which ten thousand Chinese were killed, and the population fell to the Spaniards' magic four thousand when a riot in 1686 prompted their expulsion.[43]

While colonial officials could not effectively control the exact Chinese population or separate good Chinese from bad, they could pursue other policies to mitigate the Chinese threat. Unlike multicultural Java, the Chinese in the Philippines were a hazard to the Spanish *mission civilatrice*. Not even the Spanish were blind to the fact that the Chinese possessed attractive alternatives to Catholicism and European culture. Both church and state were concerned that the evangelical mission in the Philippines would be hindered if the natives were exposed to Chinese belief systems. The Spanish faced a similar problem with the Muslims in the Sulu archipelago as they had with the Moors and Jews on the Iberian peninsula, and their attempts to control the Chinese were conditioned by these experiences.[44]

The Chinese policy that evolved was designed to limit the size, geographic extent, and professions of the *chinos/sangleyes*. It also represented the "traditional concept of recognition of cultural differences within the empire" and "revealed the basic compromise between religious-cultural ideals and economic interest."[45] The overwhelming emphasis placed on the galleon trade during the sixteenth, seventeenth, and eighteenth centuries meant that the Spanish felt they had little need for *chinos* beyond their role as importers, artisans, and retailers in the environs of Manila; consequently they restricted the Chinese to activities that were beneficial to both the colony and its mission. The main instruments of control used by the Spanish were taxation, segregation, and conversion.

As mentioned earlier, the Spanish empire was a classic premodern state. The main purposes of government were extraction of wealth and elemental social control. Under Spanish rule, Philippine taxation was rudimentary, and the Chinese, as the wealthiest non-Spaniards, were a cornerstone of the Spanish fisc. They were subject to a wide variety of residence, capitation, commercial, and labor service taxes. In addition to these official exactions, the Spanish employed numerous extralegal fees. Individual magistrates and bureaucrats were paid a fixed sum (prebend) that was significantly less than was required to cover living expenses or the administrative costs of a staff and the administration of a jurisdiction. A similar prebendal system prevailed in imperial China. As a result, officials in both China and colonial Spain were forced to supplement their meager prebends through extraordinary means, such as collecting excess taxes and keeping them, at the lower administrative level, or assessing myriad fees and fines on all the licit and illicit activities of their charges. The line could easily be crossed into personal pocket lining.[46] Since this characteristic was common to both the Hispanic Philippines and late imperial China, the local response was similar.

Local Chinese generally accepted the extractive characteristics of Spanish rule and readily adapted to the system. The Chinese in Batavia were equally adaptable and would periodically provide extraordinary funds for the construction of major public works projects, such as canals and city walls. The same Chinese who provided these funds also stood to benefit from their role as contractors and materiel suppliers for these projects, especially given the existing Chinese expertise in large-scale civil engineering.[47] The Spanish also needed Chinese labor and capital to build and fortify Manila. When taxes and service levies were seen as excessive, however, the Chinese responded with popular protests and occasionally violence, but local officials rarely knew what would spark an uprising. This pattern dominated the early years of Spanish dominion—when the Spanish were still fine-tuning the colony's revenue system—and was most clearly demonstrated in the Chinese riot in 1639.[48] A combination of corvée labor demands and new taxes in a particularly lean trade year provoked a Chinese rebellion, which was brutally suppressed. Recent migrants, unaccustomed to Spanish rule and lacking a stake in the status quo, were frequently the catalyst for such riots; consequently, violence followed spikes in immigration, as had occurred in the 1630s. The colonial administration eventually balanced revenue needs with Chinese financial constraints but only after a century of experimentation. When the corvée levy for Chinese was abolished, conditions did improve, but by that time the numbers of resident Chinese and new arrivals had declined dramatically. The tax structure remained regressive and, until the nineteenth century, was consistently prejudiced against the Chinese.

Spanish controls on the Chinese also included mobility restrictions and strict residence requirements. Mobility restrictions were designed to keep interaction between the Chinese and the native population at a minimum. Only Catholic Chinese were allowed outside the immediate hinterland of the main Spanish settlements. Cultural pollution would hinder the Hispanization and catholicization of the archipelago. The Spanish may also have been concerned that the Chinese would compete in provincial trade, which would cut into gubernatorial profits. The few Chinese who moved into the provinces were restricted to agricultural pursuits, and trade was forbidden.[49]

In addition to a prohibition against traveling beyond the environs of Manila, the Chinese were required to reside in a combination market and barracks, known as the Parian, located outside the walls of Manila but within range of the city's cannon. The Parian system segregated the Chinese from the Spanish enclave within the walled city *(intramuros)*, from the *indios,* and from the recently converted Chinese. Described as a commercial jewel by some, incorporating hundreds of stores and thousands of residents, the Parian was actually a shoddily constructed, disease-ridden firetrap. Periodic fires in the ghetto cost the lives and property of numerous resident Chinese.[50] Yet to the amazement of many, the Parian—in its numerous incarnations—was a thriving commercial center. Its narrow streets contained apothecaries, butcher shops, bakeries, food stands, bookbinderies, tailor and cobbler shops (which copied all the latest Spanish fashions), as well as artist studios, smithies, and tack shops. Built on marshy ground to the north of the *intramuros,* the Parian was fronted by a shallow pond that filled at high tide to allow the on-loading and off-loading of goods.[51] In spite of the liveliness of the Parian, it was still an enclave of Chinese bachelors trading with but kept apart from the Spanish and the *indios.* Catholic Chinese, however, could avoid segregation in the Parian. Various religious orders sponsored enclaves for converts, notably in Tondo and Binondo just across the Pasig River from the walled city, where they could settle with *india* brides.[52] When non-Catholic Chinese merchants were finally allowed to reside outside the Parian in the late eighteenth century, they moved into the former *mestizo* suburbs and created the thriving, cosmopolitan Manila Chinatown that exists today.[53]

The third means of Spanish control was conversion. According to Edgar Wickberg, "Spanish religious policy with respect to the Chinese had three objectives: extension of the Faith, inculcation of loyalty, and encouragement of eventual assimilation."[54] The use of conversion to promote loyalty was prefaced on the belief that an open (if not always sincere) acceptance of the Catholic faith also represented a declaration of fealty to God's chosen agent, the king of Spain. The goal of assimilating the Chinese was also an effort to eliminate any cultural or religious alternatives that might pollute the native population. Extension of the faith involved not only the catholicization of the Philippines, but also the ultimate goal of expanding the missionary enterprise to China. As a result, church authorities were often at odds with colonial officials over the treatment of the Chinese.[55] The clergy urged moderation in the hopes that word of the enlightened nature of Spanish rule would filter back into China and thereby assist the spread of the faith, while colonial authorities were faced with the more immediate task of controlling the physical and economic threat posed by the Chinese.[56]

Restrictive economic and social control policies were a product of the early Spanish era, a time of frequent violence and conflict, but they remained the framework for Sino-Spanish interaction even when violence between the Chinese and the Spanish was on the wane. Furthermore, the three aspects of Chinese policy—extension of the faith, inculcation of loyalty, and encouragement of eventual assimilation—created socioeconomic incentives for Chinese intermarriage with *indias*. The use of mobility restrictions and skewed taxation was an expedient and inexpensive way to encourage the overwhelmingly male *chinos* to marry local women. Although the Spanish feared the alien Chinese, they also wanted to exploit their skills and invigorate what they perceived as an unskilled native population. Miscegenation, it was hoped, would create a stable minority, loyal to church and crown but also possessing Chinese industry, capital, and agricultural skills.[57]

For the Chinese, conversion to Catholicism had tangible benefits. It was a prerequisite for marriage into *indio* families and therefore had both personal and social rewards. Conversion was also a shrewd economic strategy. Marriage into an *indio* family changed the convert's tax status from that of *chino* to the legally distinct *mestizo* category. Although *mestizo* taxes were higher than those levied on *indios*, they were still well below those for unconverted *chinos*. Recent converts were also exempt from the head tax for a period of ten years.[58] Conversion under a Spanish or local elite patron *(padrino)*, gave the Chinese Catholic access to the personal connections of his patron and to sources of credit provided by the various orders and the *obras pias*, or charitable foundations.[59] Socioethnic adscription also served to attract brides for Chinese and *mestizo* men. The wealth and status attributed to the *mestizo* class made these men attractive mates. The children of *mestiza* or *india* women and Chinese or *mestizo* men were automatically *mestizo*, whereas if a *mestiza* woman married an *indio*, her children lost their *mestizo* status.[60]

Hokkien Chinese were aggressive retailers and naturally sought to extend trade networks into the surrounding provinces, a role the Spanish saw as demeaning, and there were numerous commercial opportunities even in the early Spanish Philippines. Colonial officials preferred prebends, revenue from the galleons, gold mining, and spice production to the less lucrative and more pedestrian retail trade. Since the Spanish saw no need to provide for greater economic integration, colonial officials paid little attention to the provinces and left the ruling of areas outside of the trading ports to Dominican and Franciscan friars. In fact, many *conquistadores* had originally been granted large estates on Luzon, but these were gradually handed over to clerical control as the Spanish aristocrats gravitated to Manila. The Chinese, therefore, had an opportunity to fill a void in the metropolitan economy, but access to areas outside of Manila was limited to Catholic Chinese.

Since conversion and intermarriage were the prerequisites for exploiting Luzon's markets, economic opportunity was a key factor in the origin of the Chinese *mestizo*. While some Spaniards were critical of the opportunistic conversion of the Chinese, citing the wholesale apostasy reported on the junks returning to China (an early example of the Chinese merchant's opportunistic appropriation of identity), the growth of a Sino-Philippine merchant class proceeded apace.[61] *Mestizo* merchants bought imports from Chinese shops in Manila and exchanged them for local commodities at periodic rural markets; they thereby provided Manila and the Spanish with the necessities of daily life, and, to a limited extent, helped to integrate the Sino-Spanish and nascent native economies. In contrast to commerce, very few Chinese *mestizos* initially went into agriculture—the farming population that emigrated from Fujian in this period tended more toward settlement on Taiwan, where there were greater incentives to agricultural migration. The Chinese in the Philippines, predominantly originating from the trading communities of the Amoy network, were predisposed to commercial activity. *Mestizos* eventually became a landed elite, but the process was gradual and had its roots in their role as provincial retailers. They would ultimately be displaced from the retail trade by Chinese shopkeepers *(tenderos)*.[62]

Conversion also allowed some Chinese to become naturalized Spanish subjects and to have greater access to office holding and royal encomiums. The advantages of conversion were many, but in spite of the numerous Chinese conversions in the Philippines, Catholicism never gained a significant foothold in southeast China. Initially, conversion was more prevalent among the locally married Chinese, so most of the transient Chinese returning home had not converted. For those wealthy Chinese Catholics who periodically returned to China, their new faith, although a boon to their careers in the Philippines, could be a hindrance to business relations on the mainland. But in the Philippines early Spanish efforts at converting the Chinese and encouraging intermarriage with the *indios* were very successful and led to the creation of a large and dynamic *mestizo* population.

In the scholarship on Chinese overseas, considerable attention has been paid to the role of local religion as a help or a hindrance to Chinese assimilation. G. William Skinner, as a pioneer of this field, has offered some of the most convincing analysis. His work on the Chinese in Thailand emphasizes the importance of Theravada Buddhism, as the dominant indigenous religion, in easing the assimilation of the Thai Chinese into Thai culture.[63] In other places he has described a more complex religious milieu that hindered or promoted Chinese assimilation.

> Islam and Christianity are exclusivist, monotheistic religions requiring the renunciation of false gods, whereas Theravada Buddhism is not only more permissive and pantheistic in spirit but also remarkably tolerant, in practice, of animistic survivals. In spirit and form, then, the folk religion carried by Chinese immigrants—polytheistic, eclectic, pervaded by animism—is relatively congenial to the total religious system of Theravada Buddhists but antithetical to that of

orthodox Christians and Muslims. . . . Closely related is the fact that becoming a Muslim or Christian entails at an early stage abrupt discontinuities of behaviour . . . which are not lightly countenanced by the Chinese.[64]

Although I agree with most of Skinner's conclusions, the experience of the Chinese in the Philippines defies his interpretation of the barrier presented by Christianity. Although the opposite may be true for Protestantism, Roman Catholicism, as practiced in the Spanish empire, was both "permissive" and "pantheistic." Throughout the Catholic world, the church accommodated a great deal of regional variety and local beliefs. The development of the syncretic religions of Santería in the Caribbean and the Cao Dai sect in southern Vietnam are just two extreme examples of regional variation. For the eclectic merchants of Hokkien, two of their three main deities, Mazu (guardian of seafarers) and Guanyin (goddess of mercy), are benevolent females who were easily superscribed onto various incarnations of the Virgin Mary. Furthermore, the emphasis on the ritual aspects of religion, in particular feast days, fit well with Chinese patterns of religious observance. Catholic conversion, therefore, did not initially represent a major barrier or lead to significant behavioral discontinuities.[65] In China, the main barrier to Christianization has generally been assumed to have been ancestor worship, which many missionaries found idolatrous and prohibited among converts. This conflict is best illustrated in the extended Rites Controversy between Jesuits (on the side of accommodation with Chinese civic rituals) and Franciscans and Dominicans (who viewed ancestor worship as adoration that should be reserved for God), which occurred in the seventeenth and eighteenth centuries. This controversy, however, seemed to have little impact on the Catholic enterprise in the Philippines. I have found very little in the sources that refers to Chinese ancestor worship as an impediment to conversion. Although unconverted Chinese were referred to as superstitious and "idolatrous infidels," the major complaints against the Chinese were their spendthrift ways and their sexual promiscuity with both women and young men and boys.[66] The lack of attention to ancestor worship may be attributable to the fact that ancestor tablets (the objects of veneration) are usually kept in the family home in the native place. The young Chinese bachelors who traveled to the Philippines did not carry these objects of worship with them. Among the Chinese overseas, it was clan associations, such as those that appeared in the Straits Settlements in the nineteenth century, that funded ancestral temples and held large-scale ancestor worship ceremonies.[67] Major clan associations and similarly conspicuous Chinese religious rites were not evident in the early colonial Philippines. As a result, the "idolatry" that had so incensed Franciscan and Dominican missionaries would have been substantially less evident among the Chinese in Manila. *Chinos* and *mestizos* gradually diverged, and the mutual animosity that appeared in the late nineteenth century and sharpened in the twentieth was more a product of economic competition and political aspirations than religious conflict. As the subsequent discussion will demonstrate, even in the late Spanish period, when battle lines had begun to be drawn between Chinese and European culture and between *chinos* and *mestizos* or *Filipinos,* the local Chinese elite frequently converted to Catholicism as a socioeconomic strategy, while at the same time emphasizing their Chinese identity.

## Period of Stasis and Assimilation, 1686–1834

After the last major Chinese riot in 1686, the Spanish finally had a Chinese community close to their perceived ideal of four thousand. Over the next century and a half, the relations between the Spanish and the Chinese fell into a routine, and, although there were sporadic conflicts, there were no violent incidents on the scale of those in the early seventeenth century. During the century between the last serious piracy threat in 1662 and the British occupation of Manila in 1762–1764, the population of Chinese in Manila remained essentially constant, and their participation in the economy was static, mainly as galleon trade middlemen, artisans, and urban retailers.[68] Stasis, in turn, provided the stable environment for the Chinese *mestizos'* evolution as a dynamic economic force.

In the late seventeenth century, the number of Chinese traveling to the Philippines declined. Furthermore, although the Philippines was generally isolated from the East Asian economy, both suffered a downturn in the seventeenth century followed by a gradual recovery in the eighteenth. Throughout this period the Philippines was in decline, and therefore was a less attractive destination for new Chinese migrations. The Acapulco galleon trade, while lucrative, was one-dimensional and offered only limited opportunities and little real growth. In fact, the Chinese and the Armenians were the only foreign traders in the Philippines, because non-Spanish Westerners were forbidden from Philippine ports and the Japanese had disappeared from Manila after the Tokugawa closed-door policy prohibited overseas trade. Manila's decline was also due to contraction in the world economy that had widespread impact on both China and the Philippines. The Philippines' "seventeenth-century crisis," which included climatic changes and economic depression, caused a sharp downturn in agricultural production and the registered population of the islands.[69]

The Manila economy was also hurt by events in China. Chinese overseas trade was hampered by the maritime prohibitions enacted by the Kangxi emperor in the 1660s and 1670s.[70] In an effort to cut off supplies and personnel to the various Ming loyalist movements, the Qing ordered all coastal residents to move inland and forbade them from taking to the seas for fishing or commerce. The destructive war of the Three Feudatories, between the Qing and the powerful generals enfeoffed in southern China, disrupted commerce throughout the region, and the efforts to suppress the remnants of the Zheng family on Taiwan wrecked the maritime economy. After Taiwan fell to the Qing in 1683, the various maritime bans were lifted, but China's trade with the Philippines went into an extended decline.

In spite of the crisis, the Chinese continued to dominate the galleon trade and the retail trade of Manila, but they were still a target for the Spanish control policies mentioned above. Critics argued that the Chinese were draining the wealth of the empire by trading nonessential luxuries for Mexican silver. Over the course of the eighteenth century, frequent attempts were made to expel the Chinese from Manila, but they were just as frequently rescinded.[71] During this century, an uneasy balance was struck between the Chinese and the Spanish, but the regressive nature of this balance meant that there was little real development in the galleon trade or diversification in the Chinese enclave.

In stark contrast to the stagnation of the Sino-Spanish economy, this interim period witnessed the remarkable growth of the *mestizos* as an economic force in the Philippines. The relative peace achieved in the aftermath of that first tumultuous century was central to the *mestizo* rise. Although the origins of their rise corresponded to the decline of the *chino* population, which fell to only a few thousand after 1686, the growth of the *mestizo* community relied on a steady, albeit limited, stream of fresh immigrants from China. Over the course of the eighteenth and nineteenth centuries, the *mestizo* population enjoyed remarkable growth. A steady inflow of Chinese males, the attractiveness of *mestizo* and Chinese men as spouses, and the disincentives for *mestiza* women to marry *indios* focused the breeding potential of the minority group. Stability and *mestizo* identity were also promoted by Spanish laws that distinguished *mestizos* from both *chinos* and *indios*. From a few hundred Chinese Catholics in the late sixteenth century, the Chinese *mestizo* population reached a quarter of a million by the end of the nineteenth century.[72]

Partial assimilation may also have been encouraged by the Philippines' relative isolation from China in this period. The period of stasis was marked by a significant decline in Chinese migration, which attenuated personal and cultural linkages to the homeland, and by a near total absence of Chinese imperial involvement in the region.[73] The social and economic importance of maintaining transnational ties to their native places, which were central in the preceding and subsequent periods, probably declined in the interim.

Originally concentrated in the immediate environs of Manila, Binondo, and Tondo, *mestizos* naturally pursued commerce and crafts. At this time they were still closely linked to the Sino-Spanish economy and helped to retail Chinese imports in Manila and beyond.[74] The foundation of *mestizo* ventures was assisted by credit allocation from religious orders and *obras pias,* and their success relied on imported Chinese merchant skills. The establishment of distinct *mestizo gremios,* which were similar to Chinese merchant and craft guilds *(hang),* also helped to focus economic activity.[75] As the subsequent discussion will show, *gremios* were both community organizations and professional associations, and were central to community coordination and the channeling of manpower and economic resources. With a sharp reduction in *chino* competition especially in the eighteenth century, the maintenance of socioeconomic incentives for assimilation, and the lingering Spanish distaste for commerce, the door was open for the *mestizo*.

Dominican friars also encouraged the expansion of the *mestizos* into the hinterland. Initially as farmers and then as merchants, the *mestizos* spread into the central Luzon provinces of Tondo, Bulacan, Pampanga, Cavite, and Bataan. *Mestizos* sold Chinese and European imports at periodic local markets and used the profits to buy commodities for export or sale in Manila. As their trade networks and wealth expanded, so too did the *mestizos'* interest in other ventures.

Retail profits soon funded a diversification into the sugar market. By 1700 the Chinese *mestizos* outside of Manila had extensive interests in the sugar industry; for example, they controlled the purchase of raw cane and owned refining facilities for low-grade sugar.[76] Various scholars have emphasized the importance of Hokkien expertise in the sugar trade that arose out of involvement in sugar production on Taiwan and was later transplanted to the Philippines.[77] This is an early indication that the migrant-sending communities of southern Fujian were already deeply attuned to the labor demands in the colonial Philippines and adjusted their labor exports accordingly. Diversification into production marked the beginning of the *mestizos'* transition to an agricultural elite, but this transition was gradual, and the *mestizos* continued to dominate retail trade. By 1800, the entire retail network of Luzon, although limted in extent and sophistication, was firmly under *mestizo* control.[78] Over the subsequent century, changes in Spanish policy and the economic environment changed the role of the *mestizos* and encouraged them to reorient their identity. This environmental change began in the late eighteenth century and accelerated rapidly in the nineteenth.

The major cataclysmic event during the period of stasis was the British occupation of Manila between 1762 and 1764. During the brief occupation, many Manila Chinese—but not *mestizos*—collaborated enthusiastically with the British. The Chinese responded aggressively to the economic opportunities created by the British liberalization of the Manila economy, particularly in the export sector. A British conquest may have heralded a new era in commerce, an era in which moribund Spanish rule was replaced by a thriving British mercantile spirit. Unfortunately for the Chinese, the British did not stay, and the occupation's most significant consequence was not Chinese prosperity but the reassertion and expansion of anti-Chinese legislation. When the Spanish returned in 1764, they implemented a widespread crackdown on the Chinese. In a move reminiscent of the seventeenth-century tensions, Governor Simon de Anda y Salazar ordered the execution of all Chinese. This plan was not carried out, but the Spanish government did order the expulsion of all Chinese who had collaborated with the British and placed severe restrictions on those remaining.[79]

During the 1750s and 1760s the colonial authorities seized on anti-Chinese sentiment to wrest control of Manila's retail trade from the Chinese and attempted to staunch the silver drain that accompanied the galleon system.[80] Efforts were made to reorient the galleon trade by replacing Chinese imports with locally produced goods for export to Mexico. By the early nineteenth century, the combination of anti-Chinese legislation and a general economic depression had reduced the resident Chinese population to below six thousand, and of those, more than 90 percent were concentrated in Manila.[81] Manila's decline as an entrepôt for Asian trade accelerated with the end of the Acapulco galleon's annual visit in 1815, which had proved too expensive for the Spanish to maintain.[82] With the empire crumbling, the Spanish government was forced to rethink its colonial strategy and to attract those it had previously expelled.

In the late eighteenth century, the Spanish took some tentative steps toward reversing anti-Chinese legislation. Strict anti-Chinese policies began to be relaxed when the Spanish realized that a dramatic fall in Chinese population was detrimental to the colonial economy. The Spanish lifted the restrictions on Chinese residence following the destruction of Manila's Parian in 1790. Chinese were allowed to settle in the nearby provinces of Tondo and Cavite—mixing freely with the *mestizo* and *indio* population—and were granted access to the outlying provinces if they restricted themselves to agriculture, although such self-restraint was unlikely given the commercial inclination of the Hokkiens.[83] Related to the lifting of mobility restrictions, the new Spanish taxation laws also recognized that the Chinese population comprised two elements: those with a long-term approach and those with a short-term approach, with the former dominating and being held accountable for the good behavior of the latter. The Spanish classified the Chinese as either *invernado* (transient) or *radicado* (resident) and taxed them accordingly. Late in the Spanish era, the distinction would help to distinguish a local Chinese elite when there was a sharp increase in both kinds of Chinese.[84]

Mexican independence in 1821 cut deep into the empire's revenue, and following the disasters of the Napoleonic Wars, Madrid was under tremendous pressure to make its remaining colonies profitable. Over several decades the Spanish gradually liberalized their policies toward Chinese immigration. Not until the middle of the nineteenth century, however, did the Chinese return in significant numbers.[85] The final period of Spanish rule was marked by a fundamentally new approach to colonial rule, by greater diversification and articulation of the Chinese community, as well as by a greater degree of community cohesion. But this era was also characterized by enduring and, in many ways, growing anti-Chinese sentiment.

## Period of Diversification and Expansion, 1834–1898

In the early 1800s, a small number of *chinos* were concentrated in the environs of Manila, where they engaged in retail trade, handicraft production, and labor brokerage. Except for smaller populations in some of the other major ports, the Chinese had limited contact with the provinces outside of the immediate hinterland of Manila.[86] In contrast, over 100,000 *mestizos* had spread throughout Luzon and established enclaves in the port cities. In the 1830s, for example, Cebu, the main Visayan port, had 1,200 Chinese *mestizos* and only six Chinese.[87] This demographic phenomenon was a result of the new laws that allowed the Chinese in Manila to choose their occupations freely, while non-Catholic Chinese living in the provinces could only engage in less lucrative agricultural work.[88] At the beginning of the nineteenth century, it seemed that the Chinese would remain a minor component in the Philippine economy.

These conditions changed dramatically after 1834 and especially after 1850. In fact, between 1875 and 1896 more than 200,000 Chinese arrived in the Philippines, and the resident Chinese population increased from a few thousand in the early 1800s to 100,000 in the 1890s.[89] In the course of the nineteenth century, the Chinese community was transformed from a small transient enclave into a cohesive, aggressive, and efficient mercantile community with complex transnational linkages back to China. Ultimately, the Chinese would displace *mestizos* from the retail trade and then dramatically expand the market systems of Luzon to meet the growing demand for Philippine agricultural products. In the last decades of Spanish rule, international market forces began to affect Philippine agriculture directly. For the most part it was the Chinese who facilitated the commodification of agriculture, but it was the *mestizos* who capitalized on the increasing value of land and thus became a landed elite holding key local offices in rural Luzon.[90] The two, therefore, were complementary agents of the same process, but the success of each planted the seeds of later acrimony.

As with most migrant communities this expansion of immigration and alien residence was the result of both "push and pull" factors. Pushing the Chinese out of China were population pressure, increasing unrest at home, particularly the Taiping rebellion and other antidynastic uprisings, the opening of treaty ports, and the search for economic opportunities in the wider world.[91] The "pull" factors included improvements in transportation, specifically steamship service from Hong Kong and Xiamen to the Philippines, the now active encouragement of Chinese immigration by the Spanish authorities, and the easing of restrictive residence and occupation laws for Chinese, including those in the provinces. Most important, a spectacular restructuring of the Philippine economy by the Spanish attracted Chinese to the islands by offering great opportunities to get rich. And yet the proximity of China and the Philippines and the importance of transnational migration networks for both recruiting labor and directing commercial activities blurs the distinction between "push" and "pull." The Chinese were not the atomistic or passive subjects of mechanical "push" or "pull" forces; they played a major role in the process. A migration network might begin as a straightforward way to meet a labor demand and/or export a labor surplus, but the network can evolve in such a way as to skew the sending society toward labor specialization and at the other end can create a demand in the receiving society's economy for that product.[92] The dialectical and transnational relationship between sending and receiving societies is in turn managed by those elites who control the network and who straddle both localities. As I shall demonstrate in chapter 2, the ways in which Chinese migrated to the Philippines shaped the evolution of the Philippine economy, which in turn conditioned the strategies that the Chinese would employ to move talent and exploit opportunities in the colony.

## Social and Economic Change in the Nineteenth-Century Chinese Community

The most important change in the Philippine economy in the nineteenth century was its conversion to an agricultural export economy.[93] Although the Spanish had experimented with free trade in the eighteenth century, it was only in 1834 that they made Manila a free port and dissolved the monopolistic Royal Philippine Company.[94] Improvements in nautical technology and the expansion of the world economy provided a broad market for Philippine products, specifically abaca, coffee, sugar, tobacco, and wood products, while the opening of the Philippines' largest port simultaneously facilitated the export of these commodities.[95] The origin of this transformation was twofold: the Spanish empire's hunger for revenue to supplement its dwindling resources and the changes in the global economy. These factors had a dramatic impact on both *chinos* and *mestizos*.[96]

The economic reforms implemented by the Spanish in the nineteenth century were a desperate attempt to put the colony on a profitable basis and to take advantage of the growing global demand for Southeast Asian products. The reforms were sweeping and well-intentioned, but the lack of funds and bureaucrats to implement the new policies meant that a fundamental restructuring of the fiscal apparatus or of the general approach to colonial rule was unlikely. Their primary goal was to expand the revenue base of an empire that was struggling to compete with its more fiscally rational and industrially advanced neighbors. As a result, the reforms did not preclude the use of prereform socioeconomic strategies and may in fact have enhanced their efficacy. These limitations notwithstanding, the impact of the reforms on the Philippines and on the Chinese community was spectacular.

While the Spanish government did eliminate government monopolies, most notably on tobacco in 1880, and rescinded the trading privileges formerly granted to provincial governors, it did not seek to reassert central control over the fiscal infrastructure of the Philippines. The state actually increased the number of tax- and revenue-farming opportunities for non-Spanish and promoted the in-migration of economic actors who would fill these brokerage roles or otherwise work to expand the colony's tax base. These policy changes encouraged Chinese *mestizos* to move into landholding and sugar production, and opened the revenue farms to a new wave of Chinese immigrants.

The eleventh-hour Spanish economic reforms were unencumbered by substantive political reform. While the economy grew exponentially and with it the economic and educational opportunities for new social groups, in particular native *indios, mestizos,* and *criollos* (Philippine-born Spaniards, sometimes called *filipinos*), these were limited to the major cities, and there was no corresponding increase in access to the political arena. In the same period numerous political experiments were being tried in Spain, but clerical paranoia and the need for colonial revenue prohibited wholesale political innovation in the Philippines. Despite the best intentions of Spanish liberals to bring egalitarian rule of law and political reform to Cuba and the Philippines, the colonial governments and the church became increasingly conservative and authoritarian.[97] When economic revolution outpaced political reform, the result was often popular dissent and rebellion. In its desire for revenue, the state had released social forces that were beyond its limited abilities to control. Policy changes also contributed to the emergence of a new Filipino elite, the *ilustrados,* who were an amalgam of wealthy *indio* and *mestizo* families.[98] Although an extremely narrow segment of Philippine society at the time, this wealthy and educated—sometimes European-educated—elite began to see themselves at odds with the Spanish, the religious orders, and the rising Chinese merchant elite.[99] *Ilustrado* hostility toward the friars and the *chinos* was partly conditioned by *mestizo* competition with these two groups but would only achieve its full exposition as Filipino nationalism under American rule.[100]

Before the nineteenth century, Manila was primarily a way station in the exchange of Acapulco silver for silks and Chinese luxury goods exported from Quanzhou and Xiamen. The Spanish consciously transformed the one-dimensional nature of Philippine trade. In the 1800s, the Spanish, particularly the Royal Philippine Company, displaced a portion of the junk-carrying trade, entered into the Canton system, and attempted to transform Manila into a major regional trade center that was better integrated into the world economy. The Spanish were attempting to expand their revenue base by linkages to the world economy; this change was particularly needed after Mexican independence. Early in the century, the Spanish opened the Central Luzon Plain to wet-rice farming, transforming the swamps and jungles of this sparsely populated region into endless paddies. For the five decades between the 1820s and the 1870s, Luzon rice was a valuable export to the China market. Competition from French Indochina, however, ultimately captured the China market, and while Luzon remained a major domestic rice producer, colonial officials looked to develop other commodities for export.[101]

Liberalization of the laws pertaining to foreign residence in the Philippines and a modest supply of unemployed Spaniards led to a substantial increase in the number of traders in the port cities, and the relaxation of mobility restrictions for foreigners allowed larger numbers of foreign merchants access to the provinces where they could exploit the agricultural sector and sell European factory goods and other imports. The Spanish also eliminated the gubernatorial trade privileges in the hope that this would increase internal trade.[102] The goal was to make the Philippines a financial asset, rather than a drain, and the Spanish recognized the importance of attracting foreign capital and talent—in particular Chinese—to achieve this end.

The increasingly liberal economic policies of the Spanish authorities had the greatest impact on Chinese immigration. The effect was not, however, immediate, as it took about twenty years from the opening of the Philippines in 1834 for the Chinese population to show a substantial increase. The Spaniards ultimately realized that a crop export economy required skilled agriculturists, and importing Chinese labor appeared a simple and inexpensive way to expand crop production. They encouraged Chinese to enter the islands to work on plantations.[103] A similar scheme was implemented in Cuba with some success, but in the Philippines the commercial inclinations of the Hokkiens and the fact that this commercial elite managed their own migration networks meant that Chinese arriving in Manila were destined for either retail or the urban labor market. The results, therefore, were not what the Spanish had envisioned. Since the new legislation did not bind the Chinese to contracts, once they entered the Philippines, they were free to engage in any sort of business even though they had entered under the pretext of becoming farmers. As a result, the number of Chinese directly engaged in agriculture remained very small, but their impact on the agricultural sector was nonetheless significant. Chinese occupational freedom was further enhanced by a law of 1863 that "allowed all foreigners to practice whatever occupations they wished, and gave them rights of land ownership and inheritance in the Philippines."[104] Coincident with the Spanish-led economic reforms, American and British capital began to flow into the Philippines. Foreign capital attracted Chinese entrepreneurs, who, given the absence of an expansive European elite, rapidly filled key middleman roles in the economy and the colonial enterprise. The nineteenth-century flood of Chinese into the Philippines was also a part of the larger pattern of Chinese emigration. Throughout Southeast Asia and the Americas, local governments actively recruited Chinese labor and talent for economic development. Overpopulation and domestic disorder in China made emigration all the more attractive for the Chinese, and the intersection of these two historical phenomena had dramatic results for both the regional and global economies. Nonetheless the dialectical relationship between specific sending and receiving societies, for example, between the Xiamen region and Manila, means that it is difficult to generalize about Chinese migrations at this point. Each relationship was the product of a unique convergence between localities and global market forces.

The most important Chinese contribution to growth in the Philippine export economy came as a result of their role as middlemen and moneylenders. With the opening of Cebu and Iloilo to trade in the 1850s, the pacification of once dangerous areas in the archipelago by the Spanish,[105] and their new freedom of movement and occupation, the Chinese spread throughout the islands.[106] In the provinces, the Chinese retailed imported products, purchased and shipped agricultural products for domestic use, and sold these commodities to foreign merchants for export.[107] For example, in the tobacco industry the government initially monopolized and limited its cultivation, but the Chinese controlled its transport. With the end of government control, the Chinese sidestepped into a virtual monopoly. Although the Chinese owned some tobacco land, they rarely worked it themselves. Instead, they rented it out to *indios* and concentrated on shipping high-grade tobacco to manufactories in Manila for export and on processing the lower-grade product for consumption in the domestic market. This was essentially what the government had tried to do with the monopoly, but their limitations on cultivation and markets had stifled growth. When those restrictions were lifted, there was a spike in tobacco production. The Chinese were poised to direct this supply toward local and global demand. The Chinese also boosted production by introducing much-needed credit into what was still a rudimentary barter economy.[108] Chinese made loans to tobacco producers who posted their now-valuable farm land as collateral; the Chinese thus gained control of landholdings when, for various reasons—be they downturns in demand, poor harvests, or personal dissolution—the farmer was unable to make his payments.[109]

The other major financial opportunity for *chinos* at this time was work as tax and revenue farmers. Hungry for income but with a limited number of officials, the Spanish employed Chinese as monopoly contractors for the main revenue farms. In the nineteenth century, the Spanish tried to expand their extractive capabilities and allowed foreigners to bid on revenue-farm contracts. As the preceding discussion of Hokkien preadaptation to Spanish revenue strategy has shown, the Chinese were well suited to this role and fully exploited the opportunity. In fact, by the 1880s Chinese tax farmers controlled as much as 80 percent of the municipal tax contracts. The Chinese were particularly important in municipal and provincial tax collection, and collected fees for weights and measures, livestock slaughter, opium, and gambling. Opium was a key source of revenue for European colonies in Southeast Asia. In Malaya, Singapore, the Dutch East Indies, and the Spanish Philippines, wealthy local Chinese bid on state contracts and took charge of opium sales. For the Europeans, opium was not only a source of revenue, but was also important in keeping Chinese labor quiescent. The main problem with the opium farm throughout the region was the threat of smuggling. As a result, Chinese opium farmers had to provide their own police forces. A similar phenomenon characterized legalized prostitution and gambling, which were also farmed out to Chinese contractors. In the Philippines, the position of tax and fee collector entitled Chinese revenue brokers to employ armed troops to protect themselves and their monopoly rights and to facilitate collection.[110] Ultimately, this access to coercive force gave Chinese revenue contractors an added dimension of authority and personal power.

Over time colonial authorities made concessions to the Chinese in recognition of their value as administrative agents. In the hopes of guaranteeing the loyalty of the Chinese, special dispensations were granted for Catholic Chinese to become naturalized Spanish subjects and to have access to government posts.[111] Extraordinary Chinese generosity in times of fiscal emergency was rewarded with encomiums and emoluments from the Spanish throne. Thus, the informal contract between the state and the Chinese elite offered benefits to both sides. At the same time that the Spanish were inclined to hand over authority to local Chinese in exchange for peace and prosperity, the Qing dynasty was reaching out to overseas elites. These overtures would create a unique contest between Beijing and Madrid for the loyalties of the local Chinese.

Growing opportunities for the Chinese in the provinces dramatically increased the proportion of Chinese living outside of Manila, from around 8 percent in 1849 to a high of 52 percent in 1894.[112] Therefore, although the largest concentration of Chinese still lived in Manila, as many as fifty thousand were in the provinces in the waning years of Spanish rule. The Chinese dominated mining, which was widespread throughout coastal China; riverine and coastal shipping, which was the stock in trade of the Hokkien region; agricultural brokerage; and "had a true monopoly of the sale of all staples consumed in the Philippines, whether locally produced or imported from Europe."[113] The relaxation of mobility restrictions in the nineteenth century also let Chinese engage in rural tax farming. This brought Chinese into increasing contact with Chinese *mestizos* who had shifted to a provincial base during the preceding century.

While the new wave of Chinese immigration spread into the provinces, the *mestizos* were reorienting their social and economic strategies. World demand for Philippine products dramatically increased the value of agricultural enterprise and the value of land, and Chinese *mestizos* were well positioned to take advantage of these opportunities. After more than a century of retail expansion and diversification into sugar and later into indigo, cotton, and tobacco, not to mention extensive intermarriage with the local *indio* elite in agricultural areas, the *mestizos* were on their way to becoming a landed provincial elite. This process was accelerated by the entry of highly efficient Chinese retail networks into the provinces. Existing *mestizo* commercial operations could not compete and were quickly displaced by *chinos*.

Several prominent Philippine historians have pointed to this development as the origin of potent anti-Chinese sentiment among the Filipinos. They argue that although *mestizo* landholdings proved very lucrative, retail competition engendered animosity between the Chinese and the *mestizos*. Competition over control of agricultural exports and the growing *chino* importance in Spanish revenue extraction exacerbated this animosity.[114] To assume that anti-Chinese sentiment among the Filipino elite was an inevitable result of nineteenth-century trends, however, ignores the critical role that later decisions by the Americans, particularly in the legislative system, would play in shaping the evolution of a Filipino national elite. Moreover, in the nineteenth century the *chinos* that the majority of *indios* and *mestizos* interacted with were *tenderos de sari sari*, who slept on the dirt floors of their *nipa*-hut *tiendas* and who were scarcely better off than the farmers with whom they did business.[115] That a *mestizo hacendado*, the owner of a large estate, would feel threatened by competition from a *tendero* seems a stretch. In fact, it was the complementary effects of Chinese retailing/agricultural brokerage and *mestizo* landholding that allowed both groups to prosper. It was not until the American period, when a significant number of the provincial elite began sojourning in Manila, where they came in direct contact and competition with wealthy and powerful *chinos,* that they began to see that this "alien" elite posed a threat to their collective interests.

Perhaps the most disruptive aspect of the Philippine agricultural revolution was the unintended consequences of prosperity. While opening to the world market was a boon to the Philippine economy, it also brought market forces to bear in rural Luzon. Downturns in global demand, such as the industrial depression of 1893, could have catastrophic consequences in the nascent rural economy. Moreover, the massive ecological violence done to the forests and river systems of Luzon dangerously affected the environmental balance. The intense exploitation of land for ranching, wet rice, abaca, tobacco, and sugarcane increased the economy's vulnerability to weather and disease. The commercialization of agriculture and the rise in population also led to the consolidation of large estates or haciendas, and with it wealth and power in the hands of a few local elites, which included friars, Spaniards and *mestizos español,* some *indios,* and Chinese *mestizos.* As would be expected, there was a concomitant rise in land tenancy and peasant immiseration. All of these forces converged in the 1880s and 1890s to spur a major crisis in Luzon. Locusts and army worms were legion, rinderpest and hoof-and-mouth epidemics in the 1880s devastated livestock, while cholera and smallpox struck the tenant farming population in 1882 and 1894 respectively.[116] These in turn led to banditry, endemic feuds, and ultimately massive social upheavals, particularly on the friar haciendas in the Manila hinterland, which culminated in the insurrections of 1896–1901, which did even more to depress the rural economy. The Chinese were directly involved in these forces, as progenitors of the *mestizo* elite, as retailers and creditors, as agents of change and the intrusion of the market, as supporters of insurrections, and also as targets and victims of increasingly violent peasant and elite dissatisfaction with colonial rule. The massive socioeconomic crisis lasted well into the first decade of American rule and therefore demands a more encompassing periodization.

As rural provinces were opened to world trade and the landscape of the rural Philippines was remade, metropolitan Manila was also being transformed. Liberal Spanish policies, the growth of global markets, and the entrance of numerous foreign merchants changed the city from a minor entrepôt and sleepy colonial capital into a major crossroads of Pacific trade with a significant import-export market. The metropolis itself spread far beyond the confines of the original walled city, and Manila Bay, one of the best natural harbors in Asia, began to fill with merchant vessels.[117] Foreign enterprises were "the main nexus between the Philippine economy and the currents of world trade."[118] The colonial government, for its part, tried to facilitate trade through government-sponsored infrastructure improvements, most notably in rail, steamship lines, telegraphy, and mail, and through state-sponsored banks.[119] Despite severe limitations, the Spanish and their economic reforms laid the foundation that the Americans would build on.

As more and more *indios* migrated to Manila in search of work in the manufacturing and service industries, the urban population surged from 93,000 in 1814 to over 300,000 by 1896. Outside the walls of Spanish *intramuros* were the multiethnic and cosmopolitan districts of Binondo and Tondo. Binondo was a bustling center of trade, manufacturing, and entertainment. Here a mix of races and classes, from coolies and *india* prostitutes to Chinese *cabecillas* and aristocratic *peninsulares,* intermingled in theaters, restaurants, casinos, brothels, and opium dens. Beyond Binondo was Tondo, where traditional *nipa* huts doubled as smithies, livestock markets, and low-rent gambling dens. Here the working classes of Manila lived, ate, drank, shopped, gambled, and fought.[120]

In the burgeoning metropolis of late colonial Manila, the Chinese flourished. While they continued to import goods from China, run small retail operations, and engage in handicrafts, particularly woodworking and printing, the Manila Chinese also expanded into new fields. They purchased foreign cargoes for sale in Manila and the provinces, brokered agricultural products to export firms, smuggled silver, engaged in moneylending, coolie-labor brokerage (essential for off-loading and transporting cargo and for public works projects),[121] ran the main urban revenue farms (tax collection, cockfighting, and opium), and were beginning to participate in liquor distilling and cigar manufacturing.[122]

However, in spite of these increased opportunities and the active encouragement of immigration, conditions were far from ideal for the Chinese. In addition to the epidemics and crises that all residents of the Manila were prey to, the Chinese with their growing numbers and prominence in the economy were increasingly singled out as victims, and restrictive legislation that remained on the books was a potential threat to their interests. Crimes against the Chinese were on the rise in the 1880s and 1890s: it was "not infrequent above all in Tondo to see shopkeepers and especially Chinese shopkeepers being importuned by soldiers and other natives."[123] Moreover, pure predation was not the only motivation for crimes against Chinese and their property. Some viewed the Chinese with suspicion, and the few but increasingly shrill voices of Filipino nationalism saw them as parasitic aliens and colonial collaborators. In the late nineteenth century, the wealth of this new *ilustrado* class gave them access to education in Manila and Europe, thus exposing them to the doctrines of anticolonialism and nationalism, and to the various republican experiments in Spain. Filipino nationalism, engendered in part by economic competition between *chinos* and *mestizos,* would later prove dangerous for the Chinese community. Moreover, the same economic changes that had created opportunities for the Chinese, in an anti-Chinese environment destabilized conditions within the community. This instability was exacerbated by the arrival of new Chinese migrants, particularly Cantonese, into a community that had been nearly uniformly Hokkien for centuries.

With increased competition, social mobility, and status volatility, Manila's Chinese sought new strategies to establish and protect social status and economic interests in an unstable environment. These strategies contributed to the expansion of the Chinese role in the economy, and this expansion, in turn, enhanced the importance of specific strategies for maintaining and justifying dominance within the Chinese community. Elite strategies and institutions also served to reinforce Chinese identity and ethnic solidarity. Community cohesion was effective not just for responding to external threats, but it also shaped the economy of the colonial Philippines as well as dictated the ways in which established Chinese merchants and new arrivals exploited that economy.

# 2
# Patterns of Chinese Elite Dominance in Spanish Manila

IN THEIR CONCLUDING REMARKS to *Chinese Local Elites and Patterns of Dominance,* Joseph Esherick and Mary Rankin raised the following challenge: "By examining elites in their local contexts, we can work from the bottom up to identify the resources and strategies they employed to maintain their dominance. To understand this flexible elite repertoire we must look more closely at the nature of the late imperial elite and the resources and strategies it employed."[1] The same methodology can be applied profitably to a discussion of the dynamics and institutions of elite leadership in the Manila-Chinese community during the late nineteenth century not just because the Chinese elite replicated or adapted various "Chinese" strategies within the colonial milieu, but also because state-society relations and economic policy in the Spanish Philippines allowed the elite to export a significant amount of their cultural arsenal to the islands. The strategies they pursued and the institutions either imposed on or adopted by this Chinese elite to attain, maintain, and justify their position at the top both promoted community cohesion and largely determined what it meant to be Chinese in colonial Manila. These elite dynamics both paralleled and differed from those employed by local elites in China and those that appeared in the Chinese communities of Malaya and Java. A comparison is in order to highlight what was unique about the Chinese merchant elite in colonial Manila and what might be common to all Chinese merchant communities in the same period. That this merchant elite survived and thrived in an era of war, revolution, and economic upheaval is a testament to the strength of their institutions and their ability to deploy a flexible web of identities and to employ a complex repertoire of social, economic, and political strategies. This superstructure of strategies, identities, and institutions would in turn affect the relations between the Manila Chinese and the colonial authorities, and between the merchant elite and the Qing government.

## Institutions of the Chinese Community

As the Chinese community grew in numbers, geographic extent, wealth, and visibility, so too did its need for organizations to protect and promote community identity and interests. The Chinese used a wide array of social organizations to handle conflicts with forces outside the community, to mediate internal rivalries, and to focus collective action. These social organizations showed rapid growth and structural diversification in the late nineteenth century. For the sake of convenience I divide these organizations into specialized associations—those with a relatively narrow membership base—and those that had the authority to represent the entire Chinese community.

## Specialized Associations

As in many Chinese communities, social institutions are one of the key integrative components for community solidarity and mutual aid. In sojourner or migrant communities, the need for these institutions is even greater. In her work on the Chinese in the United States, L. Eve Armentrout Ma has divided Chinese community institutions on the basis of membership: those with "restrictive entrance requirements" and those whose membership was "based primarily on occupation or personal choice."[2] The same dual classification can be applied to those of Manila's Chinese institutions with narrow membership bases.

The three main types of institutions with restrictive criteria were native-place *(tongxianghui* and *huiguan)*, dialect, and surname associations. Because the smaller size and transient nature of the Chinese community in the Philippines inhibited the establishment of strong lineage organizations in that there were insufficient members of the same lineage to give a surname association significant numerical clout, the most prominent of these restrictive associations were the Quanzhou and Zhangzhou *huiguan* (a native-place associations for all immigrants from the various villages of Zhangzhou and Quanzhou prefectures), the Minnan dialect organization (a broader institution for all Hokkien speakers), and the Guangdong *huiguan* (Cantonese association) founded in the mid–nineteenth century.[3] The Cantonese association had less restrictive membership criteria because there were significantly fewer immigrants from Guangdong. These social organizations were headed by prominent merchants and engaged in mutual aid. Frequently, they were responsible for the housing and employment of new arrivals and also extended loans to their members to establish or expand businesses. The organizations with open membership criteria also included trade and merchant guilds (referred to by both the Spanish term *"gremios"* and the Chinese, *"hang"*), as well as secret societies, patron deity cults, athletic and music clubs, and a Confucian temple.[4]

Secret societies are one of the most important, yet frequently the least documented and thus least understood, organizations in Chinese society. In the Philippines, Chinese secret societies served essential social functions and, in the early years of the nineteenth century, "were the main institutions of internal control" in the Chinese community.[5] These societies, the Langjunhui and the Changheshe, were dominated by wealthy merchants and served as mutual aid societies for newly arrived immigrants. They were also the leading social organization among coolie laborers, and each had a armed component that was used to solve conflicts between the societies and to intimidate individual Chinese.[6] The significant growth in the Chinese population after 1850 also led to the founding of branches of the more famous Hongmenhui and the Tiandihui in the islands.[7] In fact, one of the generals in Emilio Aguinaldo's rebel army was the leader of the Manila branch of the Tiandihui. General José Ignacio Paua, a Hokkien, brought with him three thousand of his Chinese brethren to fight in the rebellion, a powerful testament to the size of these organizations in the late nineteenth century.[8] Paua's support for the rebellion also indicates that, as social order decayed in the late Spanish Philippines, Chinese secret societies could readily join up with the forces of disorder and that many Chinese did not see their aspirations as being at odds with those of Filipinos.

It is likely that the growth of secret societies was a direct result of greater diversification within the Chinese community. Before the nineteenth century, the community was composed almost entirely of traders and artisans who shared the same interests and had the same relative status; furthermore, most of the migrants were from the same area in Fujian and were usually recruited and employed through family and village networks. There was, therefore, little cause for class conflict and internecine rivalry. In the late 1800s, the importation of tens of thousands of Chinese coolies to meet the labor demand of Manila, however, introduced a group with different priorities and one that lacked internal cohesion. This huge influx required instruments of control to direct manpower and to minimize conflicts within the community, which was showing an increase in income, status, and native-place disparities. Here secret societies, with their semimystical rituals and fictive bonds of sworn brotherhood, were critical in overcoming the fissiparous forces within a rapidly growing community. Thus secret societies could be both a means of internal control and a way to direct migrant energies toward elite objectives.

The British experience in Malaya shows a direct correlation between Chinese labor imports and the growth of secret societies.[9] The expansion of Chinese involvement in the leading revenue farms also required the cooperation of secret societies. Yen Ching-hwang, Carl Trocki, and James Rush have all shown that European colonial governments relied on Chinese revenue farmers and their secret society allies to maintain social order, suppress opium smuggling, and crack down on unlicensed gambling and prostitution.[10] As long as the colonial governments relied on Chinese-operated revenue farms, extortion and intimidation by Chinese secret societies were a necessary evil. When the opium farms were abolished, however, many socially disruptive elements that had previously been coopted by the colonial state were able to pursue these now criminal enterprises free from elite and state control. A similar dynamic obtained in the Spanish Philippines, where secret societies were used to facilitate tax and revenue farming and to police the opium and gambling monopolies held by the Chinese merchant elite.

Yet in spite of the numerous similarities to other colonial environments and to merchant communities in China, many of the most important institutions were unique to the Spanish Philippines. The Chinese ability to adapt to these institutional forms goes a long way toward explaining their success in the local environment. In all the major towns and cities in the Philippines, the three non-Spanish socioethnic classes—*chinos*, *mestizos*, and *indios*—were organized into distinct social and professional *gremios*, which were in turn divided into major occupations and commercial fields. The most important *gremios* encompassed the Chinese involved in the textile, lumber, sugar, and tobacco industries. These organizations expanded Chinese purchasing power and also provided a forum for collective action. *Gremios* were also important to social organization in the Philippines, because they provided services, credit, and mutual aid to their members, beyond their function as professional associations, and served as the institutional framework for the most important integrative Chinese institution, the *cabecilla*-agent system.[11]

The Chinese *cabecilla*-agent system, although not a formal organization, provided the matrix of personal and professional linkages for the Chinese and was the foundation of community cohesion. It encompassed vertical networking and patronage relationships that manifested many similarities with networking strategies of Chinese on the mainland.[12] The system consisted of a small number of wealthy merchants and manufacturers whose wealth and social connections defined them as *cabecillas* (literally "little head," referring to their leadership of subordinate organizations). Under these wealthy patrons were a much larger number of Chinese who were tightly bound to the *cabecillas* by kinship, loyalty, and obligation. The relations of paternalism and reciprocity between the *cabecilla*/patron and his apprentices and agents provided the man in the inferior position access to the *cabecilla*'s financial and legal assistance as well as personal connections. For the *cabecilla,* an extensive network of clients and connections enhanced his own prestige, emphasized his superior status, and expanded his business opportunities.

It is difficult to overstate the importance of *cabecillas* to community cohesion and the success of the Chinese in the Philippines. While there may have been the occasional "rags to riches" tale among the Chinese, few of these meteoric rises would have been possible without the patronage of a well-connected and economically skilled *cabecilla.* An illustrative comparison can be drawn to Cuba, where there was no analogous Chinese elite to manage migration networks or direct migrants into upwardly mobile ventures. As a result, the Chinese in Cuba were scattered across dispersed plantations and had no substantive corporate influence, and few were able to break out of the ranks of workers and petty retailers or service providers. The "successful" and wealthy Cuban Chinese interviewed by the Cuba Commission in the 1870s were lottery winners rather than self-made men.[13] The experience of the Chinese in the Philippines was very different from their compatriots in Cuba. Their migration was not the violent "uprooting" that severed most ties to their native place as was the case with many Chinese in Cuba. In fact, migration to and employment in Manila were carefully managed by a Chinese elite.[14] Moreover, the manager of the migration network was often a relative of the migrant, rather than one of the foreign labor brokers who hired coolies *en masse* from migrations to the Caribbean. To facilitate the movement of talent and labor, members of the Chinese elite were co-located in the sending communities and in Manila and therefore managed both ends of the migration network. They matched labor supply from the native place to market demand in colonial Manila and "soft-landed" the migrants' arrival in the Philippines. As such, a robust corporate structure and linkages between native place and receiving society were built into the community. Migration networks not only fed Chinese labor into the colonial milieu and managed the remittance of earnings to the *qiaoxiang*, but also allowed the *cabecillas* to cultivate talented protégés for accession into the ranks of the elite. In the absence of structured corporations and legal contracts, it was the *cabecilla*-agent system that provided the fluid matrix for Chinese economic activity. In the Philippines, the Chinese *cabecilla* functioned in two distinct but interrelated realms: first, by his participation in trade throughout the archipelago and, second, through his socioeconomic status in Manila, specifically his leadership role in the largest Chinese community.

## The *Cabecilla* in Interprovincial Trade

The Chinese *cabecilla* has been productively compared to the Peranakan *towkay* and the *cabang atas* of Java. Both were a recognized "Chinese" elite in their respective colonies, and both sat at the apex of a complex set of patron-client relations. The *cabecilla* and the *cabang atas/towkay* were also essential collaborators in the colonial endeavor—serving as tax farmers and government contractors—and were closely linked to the Chinese and colonial governments. Leonard Blussé's research on Jan Con, a seventeenth-century *towkay*, and Lin Kunhe, a nineteenth-century ocean guild (*yanghang*) merchant, and James Rush's descriptions of the *cabang atas'* role in the Dutch opium farm offer valuable comparative studies of these colonial middlemen who, because of their wealth and transregional connections, enjoyed semiofficial status.[15] The gap between the practical reach of the colonial state and its revenue needs opened a realm for elite "Chinese" middlemen. A similar dynamic is visible in nine-

teenth-century Peru and Hawai'i, where it was facilitated by a gulf between the rulers and the ruled and by "clear-cut social stratification . . . that produced many notable migrant success stories" for
Chinese intermediaries.[16] In the Philippines, a *cabecilla* facilitated
the late-Spanish economic reforms as the "wholesaler of imported
goods and export produce."[17] The main Philippine exports were
abaca, tobacco, lumber, and a variety of tropical fruits, and the primary Chinese imports were tea, silk, porcelain, lacquerware, and
coolie labor, in addition to Western manufactures. Alternately, the
term *"cabecilla"* could also refer to the leader of one of the various occupational *gremios,* such as lumber, distilling, tobacco, and textiles,
which as corporate entities managed the commercialization of
Philippine agriculture. There was significant overlap between these
two roles, as *cabecillas* were both merchants and manufacturers. The
*cabecilla* was the primary guarantor and financier for a network of
merchants, agents, and apprentices, and, by including a variety of
occupations, the *cabecilla*-agent system provided the means by which
the Chinese gained control of nearly all of the retail trade in the islands and began to monopolize key export sectors.[18] It was in these
two roles that the Chinese *cabecillas* had the largest impact on the
Philippine economy.

The nineteenth-century increase in the Chinese population and
the economic opportunities open to the new arrivals were intimately
linked with the *cabecilla*-agent system. A *cabecilla* constructed his patronage network by either hiring apprentices from among recent immigrants, often through local Chinese community associations such
as *huiguan,* or more likely by recruiting directly from his family or native place.[19] The *cabecillas* were the pivot of Chinese migration networks to the Philippines, and controlling a migration network became a primary criterion for *cabecilla* status. Scholars have already
described the importance of kinship, dialect, and native place to the
migration networks and the role of the elite in managing these networks within China, particularly in regard to the importance of kin
and native-place networks both in the opening of new agricultural
lands, notably in Sichuan and Taiwan, and in filling key market/ser-
vice niches in China's merchant cities, such as the great market
nexus of Hankou.[20] The mechanics of Chinese migration networks
between South China and the Philippines bore a greater resem-
blance to the latter and thus can be seen as a subset of the larger pat-

tern of merchant migrations, but they were themselves a unique result of the dialectical relationship between the merchant communities of southern Fujian and the colonial Philippines.

Fe Caces and Douglas Gurak's discussion of the mechanics of migration networks underscores their importance to understanding both the "sending" and the "receiving" societies and the dialectical relationship between the two. Rather than representing a break between "here and there," there is a constant two-way exchange of information, people, wealth, and credit through the migration network that both shapes the "sending society" and determines migrant strategies in the "receiving society."[21] The proximity of the Philippines to China's southeast coast as well as the expansion of steam service in the late nineteenth century made sojourning or "commuter migration" (distant residence punctuated by regular, if not frequent, return to the native place) both feasible and profitable in the Philippines. The young, ambitious men in the towns and villages surrounding the maritime cities of Fujian Province were an easily tapped, skilled manpower reserve to staff the warehouses and *tiendas* of the Chinese *cabecillas*. Therefore, most of the elite of the Chinese community maintained strong ties to their *qiaoxiang*, their native places or points of emigration, including maintaining households, educating children (even those born of foreign mothers), and preparing their Chinese sons for the imperial civil service examinations.[22] These ties carried over to the host community, where native-place associations, *tongxiang huiguan*, played a central role—as the institutional superstructure for discrete migration networks—in maintaining community cohesion and in directing young recruits into profitable enterprise.

Such a strong identification with the native place was not, therefore, solely an expression of a powerful sense of cultural superiority or of an exclusively Chinese identity that steadfastly resisted assimilation into the host environment, as much mainland and Taiwan scholarship would have people believe.[23] Rather, the importance of *qiaoxiang* ties and the transnational migration networks that were built on them were the result of numerous factors. Obviously the desire for familiarity in an often-hostile environment promoted cohesion, as did the need for help in settlement and employment. But of equal importance was the long history of Hokkien villages as sending societies for merchants, clerks, and craftsmen. Similar to the more famous sending societies, such as Taishan County in the Pearl River

Delta region of Guangdong, which exported tens of thousands of laborers to the Americas, Zhangzhou and Quanzhou prefectures thrived by sending sons to trade in Chinese merchant cities and overseas. To paraphrase Adam McKeown, Xiamen was a hub from which rays spread out in one direction to Hokkien villages, and in the other to locations around the world, further branching out from secondary nodes in places like Manila and Batavia.[24] This is not to say, however, that these contemporaneous migration systems were identical parts of the same "Chinese diaspora." Rather, the unique migrations from southern Fujian and Guangdong were dictated by distinct local systems and regional economic developments and only converged as part of the same larger historical process at the global level.

Ultimately Hokkien success in the colonial Philippines lay not only in their ability to adapt personally to local environments, but equally in their ability to adapt their migration networks (all the way back to the *qiaoxiang*) to enhance their competitiveness. Also critical were the unique patterns of patron-client business relations (often familial) that conditioned recruitment in the native place and employment in the Philippines. Finally, the management of the migration network itself both defined the Chinese elite and furthered their ambitions.[25] One might be tempted to conclude that migration networks exercised a narrowing if not hegemonic influence on Chinese migrants, where only "a few elite were able to travel freely across these rays."[26] As I will show, however, individual migrants, even those well below the elite stratum, could step away from a migration network "groove."

In fact, the most important characteristics of the *cabecilla*-agent system were its remarkable flexibility and its numerous external points of contact that gave *cabecillas* and their protégés the ability to respond to dramatic changes in the colonial economic environment. Some generalizations, however, can be made about the system. Most new arrivals entered into a bond of indentured servitude with a *cabecilla*. The contract offered guaranteed employment and credit and eased the transition to an alien environment. For a set period thereafter, the new arrivals worked in the patron's stores and warehouses in Manila or as assistants to the *cabecilla's* purchase and marketing agents in the provinces. Job placement was probably based on a number of factors: commercial experience, literacy, and personal relation to the patron.

Later, if the client had proven his worth, he would act as a senior agent or set up his own retail operations. In many cases, the agent was both an agricultural purchaser and the operator of a *tienda de sari-sari*.[27] The *sari-sari* store is a ubiquitous phenomenon in the Philippines. *Tiendas* were usually housed in easily constructed *nipa* huts, which kept start-up costs low. From these huts the shopkeeper (*tendero*) sold all manner of goods, down to individual cigarettes and single matches, at a low overhead. In a currency-poor economy, credit and barter frequently stood in for cash. In spite of its humble appearance, therefore, the *tienda de sari-sari* was essential to Chinese commercial success in the late Spanish Philippines. These small retail operations, a sort of nineteenth-century convenience store, provided all manner of daily necessities and were open on a daily basis. The *sari-sari* store was therefore more efficient than *mestizo* retail operations—which only opened at periodic rural markets—and rapidly displaced them from the trade.[28] *Tiendas* were strategically located in the major agricultural export producing regions and on all the large haciendas, and retail profits and barter were used to collect sugar, tobacco, abaca, and indigo for sale in Manila.[29]

The *cabecilla*-agent system provided a ready-made structure for the Chinese commercial expansion in the late nineteenth century. Since he was the patron and supplier for all of his dependent *tenderos,* the Manila merchant/*cabecilla* had an extensive marketing system and information-gathering network established throughout Luzon, and thus he could readily develop a macropicture of the market. *Tiendas de sari-sari* were also a particularly efficient way to exploit the talents and energies of new arrivals. Because most migrants wanted to earn money quickly and then return home to marry, go into business for themselves, and/or retire, the *sari-sari* system, where the wealthy patron covered the start-up costs and provided an existing trade network, proved beneficial to both patron and client.[30]

The *cabecilla* system had a number of built-in commercial advantages. To avoid the taxes on large commercial ventures, the various outlets of a *cabecilla's* network would be registered under the names of his agents, thus spreading risk. Moreover, if any single *tienda* failed, the *cabecilla's* role remained secret, and only the agent was held liable for debts. The high level of trust required to maintain this level of secrecy meant that the *cabecilla* and the agent were very closely bound. As Norbert Dannhaeuser has found, this trust improved the efficiency of Chinese retail and served to protect it from outside competitors.[31] The close bonds between the *cabecilla* and his provincial agents created a highly efficient force that displaced almost all local competition and allowed the Chinese to dominate much of the retail trade in the provinces as well as corner the market in several major export commodities.[32] The Chinese *cabecilla*-agent system, having predated the midcentury economic reforms, put the Chinese merchants in a very advantageous position when the Spanish colonial authorities actively promoted economic development.[33]

## The *Cabecilla* and the Manila-Chinese Community

With few exceptions, the majority of Chinese *cabecillas* lived in Manila, and most had their business headquarters in the Binondo district.[34] Since virtually all the Luzon import-export trade was carried through Manila, this choice of location was obvious. As heads of leading industries and merchant houses, the Manila *cabecillas* had access to market information that was not as readily available in the provinces. It also provided them with more convenient access to those commodities most in demand. Chinese merchants were able to buy goods directly from foreign importers who had neither the means nor the desire to compete with Chinese retail networks. Manila was also the site of Chinese manufacturing enterprises, most notably distilleries and cigar and cigarette factories. In addition, European and American firms hired Chinese *cabecillas* to act as middlemen so as to avoid certain discriminatory policies of the Spanish government and to take advantage of the *cabecillas'* networks. The *cabecilla* system also replicated key aspects of the comprador system then dominant in China's treaty ports, and, as a result, some of the strategies employed by Manila's *cabecillas* were similar to those used by the compradors of Shanghai, Guangzhou, Xiamen, and Hong Kong.[35] These similarities are evident in the fact that some Hong Kong trading houses, like Russel and Co., brought their own compradors with them to Manila, and these Cantonese agents were able to join the ranks of the *cabecillas*.[36]

One of the most valuable Chinese imports, for which the *cabecilla* system was the main broker, was coolie labor. Since the Spanish considered the Filipinos to be unindustrious, Chinese labor was needed both in the provinces and in Manila. In the 1840s, the colonial authorities recognized a need to encourage Chinese labor migration and employed a more open entrance policy and tax incentives for Chinese who engaged in farming. But, as discussed previously, very few Chinese were directly engaged in farming; instead, their labor was used to facilitate the movement of goods through cartage and infrastructure improvements.

In Manila, coolie laborers and their *cabecilla* contractors controlled much of the port's transportation of goods, including the on- and off-loading of vessels in the harbor, the movement of goods within the city, and transshipment onto railroads and onto steamers plying the sea lanes between Manila and the provinces. In addition, the Spanish relied almost exclusively on Chinese labor for public works projects. Contractors would purchase the contracts of Chinese laborers upon their arrival in Manila and then hold the laborers in indentured servitude until the purchase cost was remitted.[37] During that time, the contractor would hire out his coolie gangs to Chinese, Filipino, Spanish, and foreign merchants and would collect the wages himself. *Cabecillas* were able to control the coolies through the agency of the secret societies and thereby to dominate the majority of the Chinese labor force.[38]

In addition to their control of Chinese labor and much of the provincial retail trade, Chinese *cabecillas* held key revenue-farming contracts. Besides monopoly rights granted to naturalized Spanish subjects for spice, cocoa, cotton, and tobacco production, the Spanish authorities contracted out lucrative revenue farms to Chinese *cabecillas,* among them municipal and provincial taxation, weights and measures, livestock slaughtering, opium, and cockfighting. Revenue farming was also conducive to absorbing new immigrants as collection agents and guards. Chinese secret societies provided the manpower for revenue collection by Chinese tax farmers. Skinner has emphasized the importance of the opium monopoly in facilitating the expansion of Chinese enterprise into the countryside, which accelerated the decline of *mestizo* retail interests.[39] The expansion of these contractual relations also gave the *cabecilla* elite a greater sense of official legitimacy and coincided with Spanish efforts to win Chinese elite support through the award of medals and titles for loyalty and service to Spain and the granting of special dispensations for Catholic Chinese to become Spanish citizens.[40] These Spanish efforts may have been the result of the Qing dynasty's growing interest in the Chinese in the archipelago. If the local Chinese became too China-oriented, it might undermine the colonial enterprise. As subsequent chapters show, the colonial office and Malacañang resisted Beijing's attempts to found a Chinese consulate in Manila.[41] For their part, the *cabecillas* naturally diversified their contacts and cultivated relations with both sets of political power holders.

Because of their wealth, control of migration networks and the coolie trade, and privileged access to Spanish authorities, the *cabecillas* dominated the Manila-Chinese community. *Cabecilla* status coincided with leadership of surname groups, *huiguan* and *tongxianghui*, in addition to the various *gremios*, secret societies, athletic, musical, and benevolent associations.[42] Not only did this status lend them prestige and socioeconomic power in the host community, leadership of native-place associations was crucial to a *cabecilla*'s continuing success. Formal and informal links to the *qiaoxiang* guaranteed a supply of new arrivals to serve as trustworthy subordinates, and key institutions facilitated elite control of the rapidly expanding Chinese population.

The personalistic and kinship orientation of the *cabecilla*-agent system and the migration networks through which it was implemented encouraged community cohesion and tended to prevent the types of assimilation that had characterized the earlier period when the creolized *mestizo* class appeared. Tilly and Brown have argued that the more personalistic and narrowly defined—native place, kinship, profession—a migration network is, the slower the rate of migrant assimilation into the receiving society.[43] S. Gordon Redding has applied a similar approach to his work on Chinese capitalism. Redding finds that the overwhelming emphasis on trust *(xinyong)*, client obligation, and networking *(guanxi)* within Chinese communities overseas contributes greatly to their economic efficiency but alienates them from external actors, who are viewed with distrust.[44] While Redding's argument is a bit too reductionist when it comes to describing traditional "Chinese" ways of doing business and ignores the ties that successful Chinese must cultivate with non-Chinese, he is correct to point out that within the "traditional" arsenal of tested practices of exploiting economic opportunities are cohesive systems of trust built on preexisting kin and native-place ties. The utility of these systems, however, will vary dramatically depending on the nature of the receiving society, and they therefore are limited in their explanatory value. These limitations notwithstanding, the Chinese merchant elite in both the late Spanish and American Philippines relied heavily on cohesive networks of kinship and trust. The Chinese community was relatively cohesive and did not tend to assimilate, in the sense of moving sharply away from the core community, because it made good economic sense.

In explaining the difference between the earlier era of assimilation with the later era of Chinese insularity, an informative comparison can be drawn between the Chinese experience in the nineteenth-century Philippines and their contemporaries in Java.[45] Both host environments were in the midst of an agricultural export boom, were ruled by European colonials who relied on socioethnic adscription to organize society and were seeking to expand their revenue, and witnessed a late-nineteenth-century surge in Chinese immigration. The new arrivals in both areas, numbering several hundred thousand, were still primarily Hokkien but were accompanied by a growing number of Cantonese and Hakka. In the Philippines, new Hokkien arrivals were incorporated into the Chinese economy through the agency of the *radicado* (resident) Chinese elite, not the *mestizos*. In Java, new Hokkien arrivals joined the Peranakan (products of Chinese and non-Muslim Javan marriages) economy under the patronage of creolized Peranakan *towkays*. The reasons for the different outcomes goes a long way toward explaining the origin of Chinese community identity in the Philippines.

The explanation lies in the socioeconomic environment. In the Philippines, creolized *mestizos* were physically, economically, and increasingly socially isolated from the new arrivals, whereas the *radicado cabecillas* and Java's Peranakan *towkays* were not. As they expanded their interests into landholding, the *mestizo* power base moved into the countryside and away from the major port cities where the *chino cabecillas* reigned supreme and into which Chinese arrivals were funneled. This *mestizo* diversification into agriculture had taken decades and required long-term economic strategies. Long-term interaction with the native population and their role as a landed elite encouraged *mestizos* to identify themselves much more closely with the *indios*. When the Spanish abolished the legal distinction between *mestizos* and *indios* in 1880, the bond was strengthened.[46] While Chinese *tenderos* interacted with the provincial elite and *indio* tenant farmers, and while all played complementary roles in the market revolution, *tenderos* and *mestizos* operated at the furthest margins of discrete economies, the provincial and the metropolitan, and thus their economic roles and identities tended to diverge. The socioeconomic crises of the late Spanish and early

American era widened the social rift between *chinos* and *mestizos* but did not create an unbridgeable divide.

In contrast to the Philippines, the Peranakans of Java were physically, economically, and socially proximal to the new arrivals. The highly extractive Cultivation System that the Dutch employed in the early 1800s created disincentives for Peranakan diversification into agriculture, and in 1870 the Dutch prohibited Peranakans from owning land.[47] As a result, their economic activity and residence remained centered on the major port cities into which new immigrants were channeled. Peranakan retail operations and revenue farm activities paralleled Luzon's Chinese economy and could readily absorb new immigrants from commercially oriented Zhangzhou and Quanzhou. Socially, the Peranakans maintained their interests in Chinese deities and local temples, which formed a convenient point of convergence between new arrivals and established Peranakan merchants.[48] "Talent and enterprise found its best outlet by assimilating to *peranakan* culture and achieving social and economic mobility within it."[49] Large numbers of Cantonese and Hakka, who arrived in the late nineteenth century, were not as easily incorporated into the Peranakan economy. Their decision to compete with the Peranakans by emphasizing their pure Chinese *(totok)* identity was a response to the specific social and economic circumstances.[50] In colonial Southeast Asia, the competition for scarce resources encouraged local Chinese to emphasize their cultural identity in the pursuit of social and economic advantage.

Early in the colonial enterprise, the Spanish had created social and economic incentives for creolization. The removal of these incentives in the nineteenth century—reinforced by the pattern of Chinese sojourning described by Amyot and the nature of Chinese economic activity—created disincentives against the scale of assimilation that had characterized the earlier period and encouraged the construction of a more coherent and less ambiguous Chinese community identity. This is not to say, however, that the identity categories of *chino* and *mestizo* had become reified by the late Spanish period. As Richard Chu's examination of court records, wills, and other legal documents demonstrates, there were numerous *mestizos* and *mestizas* who had strong links back to their ancestral native places in China and who were active within the Chinese community as well as Spanish- and Tagalog-speaking *chinos* who were integral parts of Spanish, *indio,* and *mestizo* society.[51] A multiplicity of identities was practicable, and in fact essential, in the multiethnic terrain of Manila where these embryonic identities converged and were negotiated. It would be ahistorical therefore to argue that the later melding of *indios* and *mestizos* into Filipinos and the hostility between Chinese and Filipinos were either a natural results of or predetermined by economic competition between these groups in the nineteenth century. Nonetheless, there were sufficient economic and legal motivations present in the 1880s and 1890s to encourage the local Chinese elite to adopt a more cohesive, but not exclusive, Chinese identity. The apparent homogeneity of the Chinese was imposed on the community by colonial policy, but it was also something that *cabecillas* manipulated to perpetuate their social and economic status. It was in the *cabecillas'* best interest to maintain the cohesion of the recruitment apparatus, because it offered the best opportunity to exploit the talent and energies of the new migrants and to defend against rivals.[52] Changes in immigration law and the economy during American rule actually enhanced the utility of Chinese migration networks and buttressed the power of the Chinese merchant elite, but even in the Spanish period *cabecilla* power was impressive.

Chinese *cabecillas* had a virtual monopoly on the financial and social capital within the community, and they had five main mechanisms for attaining and justifying their dominance: *cabecilla*-agent networks; tax brokerage and control of important revenue farms; leadership of the various Chinese social and business organizations and the official institutions of the Chinese community; control of credit and capital allocation, and acts of conspicuous consumption and conspicuous charity that served to distinguish them as a Chinese elite; and a monopoly on coercive force through the Chinese secret societies and the troops provided during their revenue collection services.

John T. Omohundro has described the Chinese community that emerged in the port city of Iloilo in this period as a "closed ethnic community under tight rein."[53] This description cannot easily be applied to the larger Chinese community in Manila. The *invernado* (transient) Chinese were dominated by the *cabecillas,* but that control could never be absolute. The Chinese community was a well (but not perfectly) integrated system of patron-client and both real and fictive kin relations, but it was far from "closed" or "airtight."[54] Neither the wealthy *cabecilla* nor the lowly *tendero* could afford to be isolated from local society and still be successful. Colonial policy and overarching community institutions as well as "Chinese" ways of doing business gave the community a recognizable structure and "Chinese" identity, but that structure needed to have numerous contact points with both the rural and the urban dimensions of the socioeconomic landscape. In general, the community might be likened to a complex puzzle piece or an integrated circuit that was a distinct entity but also an integral part of the whole. In Manila it was the *cabecillas* who controlled the majority of linkages, but the *tienda* system out in the provinces meant that the individual *tendero* had responsibility for managing his own external linkages.

Yet even in Manila, the urban landscape prohibited isolation. It would have been impossible to have a completely insular Chinese community; moreover, it did not make good economic sense to attenuate linkages to local society. In addition to business contacts, external linkages could be romantic as well as strategic, culminating in marriage to an *india* or *mestiza;* sexual, for example, frequenting the prostitutes who were a regular (and tolerated) fixture in Binondo; recreational, including gambling and public entertainments; or criminal, as a smuggler or fence, and as a victim of a racially or economically motivated crime. The ways in which the Chinese interacted with local society were legion, yet the community itself was still distinct and "insular." While factors such as physical appearance, cultural differences, sojourning, and language played key roles in defining Chinese identity, other factors made them distinct. Even with institutional and legal reforms, Malacañang tended to treat the Chinese as a distinct corporate entity, and there were certain occupations, such as shopkeepers or stevedores, that were thought of as typically "Chinese." The Chinese were moreover distinguished not only by their dress, language, and occupations, but also by their vices: their characteristic predilections for opium, gambling (especially cards), and prostitutes.[55] While these vices are synonymous with those of bachelors nearly everywhere,[56] they became a defining measure of Chinese identity in the colonial Philippines: "If the Indios are inclined to gamble, it is not so much a vice as a means of occupying their minds or for the pleasure it affords them, but this is not the case with the Chinese living in these Islands. With them it is a true vice, and one that is so serious, that it is not only their own fortunes that they risk; it is well known that through their means other people's fortunes are jeopardized."[57]

Nor could the *cabecillas* afford to be isolated. *Radicado cabecillas* had to have a commitment to long-term, if not lifetime, residence in the Philippines punctuated by periodic pilgrimages to if not parallel residence in the *qiaoxiang*, and to participation in the civic life of Manila to achieve their positions of prominence. *Cabecillas* had to be both "here and there." Prominent merchant elites maintained households in both China and the Philippines, drawing young male relatives from the native place to work for them as shopkeepers and managers as well as returning to the native place to father children, while at the same time fathering *mestizo* children with *indias* and *mestizas*. This practice created problems for the Spanish and later American courts. When a wealthy *cabecilla* died intestate, the Chinese side of the family could sue the estate.[58] Both the Spanish and later American courts tended to favor local families' claims, either because the marriage involved conversion to Catholicism and thus legally annulled all previous marriages or because a marriage in China was more difficult to prove than one in the Philippines. Here the Chinese wife found herself in the status of secondary wife rather than the primary wife that Chinese cultural practices had convinced her she was. Unlike in the Philippines, where the latest wife was the only legal wife, in China it was the first wife that maintained the patriline in the native place. Wives in the *qiaoxiang* endured long separation from their spouses in exchange for the security gained from marriage to a consistent breadwinner and stable family lineage, and it was expected that a portion of the wealth generated overseas would be invested at home.[59] These various legal cases, moreover, demonstrate the fluidity of identities and the extent of transnational ties. What might have been morally shocking to a contemporary Spanish or American jurist and suspect from the nationcentric perspective of a mid-twentieth-century Chinese or Philippine nationalist was standard operating procedure for a turn-of-the-century *cabecilla*.

Furthermore, *cabecillas* could only hope to compete with the agents of the major foreign trading houses by establishing their reputations as reliable and committed to the local economy.[60] Their position as a Chinese elite was defined by their control of a distinct Chinese community, but it was strengthened by extracommunity linkages. The Chinese elite therefore competed for external resources to secure and enhance their elite status. Catholic conversion, often a prerequisite for marriage, was particularly useful, especially if it was under the sponsorship of a Spanish *padrino*. Conversion had both economic and social benefits, notably an expanded realm of action, connections to the Spanish power structure, opportunities for office holding, and the chance to become a naturalized Spanish subject. But conversion in the late Spanish period did not make a *chino* into a *mestizo*.[61] Reforms in the late Spanish legal system further facilitated extracommunity linkages. In contravention to what some assume to be a traditional Chinese strategy of relying almost exclusively on "trust" in business dealing, Chinese merchants in the Spanish Philippines had increasingly to resort to legal devices, such as powers-of-attorney and limited liability corporations, to facilitate their dealings both with fellow Chinese and with non-*paisanos*, that is non-Chinese.[62] The extension of the Spanish penal and civil codes to the islands in the late 1880s expanded the legal options open to Chinese, but even before then "there was no shortage of lawyers in Manila."[63] As early as the 1860s Chinese resorted to Spanish legal representation in criminal and legal suits against non-*paisanos* and fellow Chinese. This was a trend that continued and in some ways escalated in the American era.

Chinese vertical networking to the Spanish community was also enhanced through bribery and gift-giving to Spanish officials. This practice was encouraged by the low salaries of Spanish officials and their tendency to supplement their meager resources through kickbacks and irregular fees. This strategy could be pursued either on a personal level, with an individual merchant seeking the protection and patronage of a single official, or on a community level, in which Chinese *cabecillas* pooled resources to purchase the protection of an important official, such as a provincial governor or even the Spanish governor-general. In one telling example, the Chinese are reputed to have provided Governor-General Valeriano Weyler with all his household furnishings and 80,000 pesos to secure his good intentions toward the Chinese community.[64]

The *cabecilla* elite also sought recognition from the Qing government through the purchase of imperial titles and the education of sons for the examinations. The small size of the Chinese community limited the chances that a successful candidate could rise from among their ranks, but mere participation in examination culture and purchased titles had great social significance in the local context. Purchased titles, mandarin robes, and Confucian-educated sons were de rigueur for an elite whose Chinese identity was the foundation of their economic success. Logically, *cabecillas* pursued imperial recognition for their institutions and emphasized their elite status through the affectation of Qing bureaucratic form and language and by their correspondence with the Chinese authorities.[65] This correspondence included petitions to Qing officials in Beijing, the coastal provinces, and Chinese diplomats overseas. The economic and social prominence of the *cabecillas* among the Chinese placed the responsibility for extracommunity activism on them. Since the *cabecillas* were the primary mediators between Spanish authorities and the community and because they engaged in correspondence with Beijing, they dominated every major institution, both narrow and communitywide, and established the linkages between them. It was through the agency of communitywide institutions that they defined themselves as a distinct community, pursued closer relations with China, and largely defined what it meant to be Chinese in colonial Manila.

Chinese *cabecillas* were one manifestation of a type of Chinese elite that appeared throughout colonial southeast Asia. I have already mentioned the comparisons that can be made between *cabecillas* and the *cabang atas* and *towkays* of the Dutch East Indies. The Straits Settlement government was equally beholden to wealthy Chinese. The merchant elite, especially Chinese from the commercially sophisticated environment of South China, were essential collaborators in the European colonial enterprise. A grounded Chinese elite brought the economic wherewithal to these previously underexploited environments and served as a stabilizing force in volatile regional economies, and it was from among the ranks of this Chinese merchant elite that the official representatives of the Chinese community were chosen. The most successful of these colonial middlemen walked a fine line between their Chinese identity and their colonial masters. They aggressively pursued closer ties with the European authorities and took great pride in official recognition. At the same time, these elite played a leading role in cultivating closer ties to China and, especially in the late nineteenth century, supplemented their colonial encomiums with titles and ranks purchased from or awarded by the Qing empire. Chinese *kapitans* and even some Qing consuls were drawn from the wealthiest and most prominent Chinese. These men were wealthy because they had succeeded in commercial enterprises, and they were prominent because they played a highly visible role in community activism and charity, and because they dominated the main Chinese community institutions.

Their official recognition was an outgrowth of their tacitly accepted role as organizers of and spokesmen for the enclave. In the Dutch East Indies and the Straits Settlement, Chinese *kapitans* were charged with handling intracommunity affairs and mediating disputes that were beyond the abilities and inclinations of the colonial authorities to address.[66] The Spanish employed a similar system of Chinese self-governance.

## Communitywide Institutions

The arrival of so many new immigrants in the late nineteenth century made it imperative that the Chinese community have organizations to provide for them. Of the two institutions that arose to speak for the Chinese community in this period, the first was a spontaneous creation of the local elite, and the second was imposed on them by the colonial government but was nonetheless manipulated by the elite to serve the community and to define Chinese identity.

As with many Chinese communities overseas, charitable associations became the main instrument of community cohesion and elite activism. Hong Kong's Tung Wah Hospital (Donghua Yiyuan), provided not only medical services and rudimentary welfare, but also served to coordinate local elite activity and to communicate with the government in Beijing. In Manila, the local Chinese elite founded the Huaqiao Shanju Gongsuo, commonly referred to in English as the "Chinese Guild" or "Chinese Community," or in Spanish as the "Communidad de Chinos." Founded in 1870, the Chinese Guild engaged in general acts of charity and eventually came to administer the Chinese cemetery. The guild also managed and funded the Chinese hospital, known as the Chongren Yiyuan. Structurally, the Shanju Gongsuo was dominated by the wealthiest *cabecillas* and was formally chaired by the senior member of the Chinese community. The Shanju Gongsuo's leadership also promoted education and was instrumental in founding the Anglo-Chinese School in 1899.[67] Beyond these charitable functions, the guild was essential to community solidarity, and it "became the principal formal instrument for handling internal affairs" of the Chinese community and engaged in correspondence with the Qing authorities.[68] It was the Manila Chinese who initially employed the term *"huaqiao"* to describe themselves, even before it became part of the Qing dynasty's official lexicon. There are numerous possible reasons for the choice: perhaps it was indicative of self-conscious transnational status, or it explicitly declared a link between themselves and the Qing dynasty, a government that was increasingly interested in patronizing overseas Chinese for its own political and economic purposes and whose patronage satisfied the ambitions of the Chinese elite in Manila. The use of "*hua*," Chinese, might have been more in line with the emerging preference among the Spanish for national categories, *chinos* vice *sangleyes*. It is also reasonable to speculate that by choosing the largest feasible identity category, *hua* vice Hokkien, for example, the elite was preempting any possible rival organization, a Cantonese one, perhaps, that would claim the right to speak for all Manila Chinese. As such, an all-encompassing institution could not only claim authority to speak for the whole community but would in turn enjoy privileged access to Malacañang, Beijing, and provincial authorities in Fujian.[69]

The institutions created by the Chinese Guild symbolically emphasized the Chinese identity of the community. It was logical that the *cabecilla* elite, who benefited from community cohesion, would seek to promote a greater sense of ethnic identity. The founding of the Anglo-Chinese School (Zhongxi Xuexiao), modeled on a similar school in Xiamen, was also linked to the promotion of a more coherent Chinese identity. Founded by the Chinese Guild and the first Qing consul (the son of a local *cabecilla*), the school was a product of Chinese elite activism and can be seen as part of a broader trend among Chinese overseas to promote identification with Chinese culture and values. Throughout Southeast Asia, local Chinese, both creolized and pure-blooded, were promoting Chinese-language newspapers and Chinese schools. These schools taught standard Mandarin as a way to overcome dialect boundaries between different native-place groups and to create a unified Chinese culture.[70] Since the lack of Chinese women in the nineteenth-century Philippines limited the number of local-born Chinese children, the initial target for the Anglo-Chinese School was *mestizo* children. While it may be tempting to conclude, as does Skinner, that this was a vain attempt to recapture *mestizo* children as "Chinese," such a conclusion is difficult to substantiate given both the fluidity of ethnic categories at this point and the long-standing practice of sending local-born children, both *chino* and *mestizo*, to the *qiaoxiang* for schooling.[71] The school combined "Confucian learning and practical commercial instruction" and therefore replicated many of the roles of a *qiaoxiang* school, and since it was a joint local community–imperial effort, it seemed to offer the dual benefits of proximity and transnational utility.[72]

In addition to associations founded by the Chinese elite, the community was distinguished by organizational forms imposed by the colonial authorities. Unlike their contemporaries in China, the Manila Chinese enjoyed recognition as a distinct corporate and legal entity. The social and economic transformation of the Philippines, despite the best efforts of liberal reformers, limited Malacañang's effective reach.[73] Early on, the Spanish had recognized and encouraged Chinese autonomy, and they responded to the growth in the size and economic power of the Chinese community by granting them even more autonomy and official recognition, a trend that would continue in modified form under the Americans. The end result was an essentially autonomous Chinese enclave that the Spanish could not afford to do without but were unable and disinclined to administer directly.[74] The institution the Spanish relied on in these relations was the Gremio de Chinos and its leader the Gobernadorcillo de los Sangleyes.[75]

## The Gremio de Chinos and the Gobernadorcillo de los Sangleyes

According to Wickberg, the term "Gremio de Chinos" (Huarenqu Gonghui) referred to "a kind of vaguely defined, supramunicipal corporate organization of the Chinese in the Manila area."[76] In other words, the Gremio served as a semiautonomous government for the Chinese in the islands and fulfilled an organizational function that was very similar to the Chinese Kongkoan (*gongguan*) in Semarang.[77] The Gremio and its subordinate agencies recorded births and deaths, reported arrivals and departures, assisted in criminal investigations, deported vagrants, issued various permits and passports to local Chinese, and collected taxes.[78] As such, this organization was beneficial to the Spaniards, because it saved them from having to deal with the Chinese alien minority on an individual basis. The Spanish only became involved in Chinese affairs in exceptional cases. The Chinese could, in turn, use the Gremio as an instrument for collective action to pressure the Spanish authorities and appeal to the Qing. The Gremio de Chinos, like the other Chinese institutions, was dominated by the wealthiest *cabecillas*, who selected and served as the Gobernadorcillo de los Sangleyes.[79]

The office of Gobernadorcillo (*jiabidan,* a loose translation lifted from the Dutch and British "Kapitan") had a long history and beyond the ease of translation demonstrated several significant similarities to the Chinese *kapitan* system employed throughout Southeast Asia, but for most of the eighteenth and early nineteenth centuries the position had little real influence in the Chinese community, because power resided with the Cabecilla Principal. This situation changed, however, in the late nineteenth century, as both the Chinese and the Spanish recognized the need for a single, elected, and officially recognized headman.[80] By the 1860s, the post of Gobernadorcillo was more attractive and more powerful, and the Spanish decision to allow the *cabecillas* to elect the Gobernadorcillo gave the Chinese elite an additional stake in the office.

The Gobernadorcillo elections in the 1870s saw a substantial increase in the power associated with that office. The most important criteria in voting for or serving as Gobernadorcillo was wealth. Only those Catholic, Spanish-speaking Chinese *cabecillas* who paid at least 60 pesos in taxes could legally run for this position, and only slightly more than 1 percent of the Chinese community paid enough in taxes to vote for the Gobernadorcillo. The Gobernadorcillo was assisted in his duties by a first lieutenant, a comptroller, and a chief constable, all of whom were drawn from the pool of Chinese *cabecillas*.[81] Since it was under the complete control of the Chinese elite, the office of Gobernadorcillo could better serve elite interests in maintaining a cohesive and hierarchical Chinese community.

Headquartered in a large office building in the Binondo district, the Gobernadorcillo's jurisdiction technically covered the entire Chinese population residing in the archipelago, although his functional reach probably did not extend beyond Luzon. He was the apical spokesman for the Chinese community in relations with the Spanish government, petitioning the authorities on matters such as the issuance of passports for Chinese, visa extensions, and changes in residency status, and requesting permits for Chinese to live in the provinces. Given the importance of migration networks and market access, this role potentially gave the Gobernadorcillo tremendous leverage over his *cabecilla* peers. In addition to deporting undesirable or insolvent Chinese, the Gobernadorcillo also collected passport and other administrative fees and imposed various fines.[82] The Gobernadorcillo oversaw all *chino* taxes and collected funds for the Chinese hospital, and he was held financially responsible for any shortfalls.[83] Actual tax collection was handled by the Chinese *cabezas de barangay* (neighborhood headmen), who sent tax revenues to the Gobernadorcillo. In their role as tax collectors, the Gobernadorcillo and the *cabezas de barangay* were filling a brokerage role that enhanced their social prestige and expanded their networks.[84] Since the Gobernadorcillo was the tax farmer for the entire community, he could use this position to his own advantage to secure favors or to mitigate Spanish demands on the community. While the Spanish employed a capitation tax based on the registered Chinese population and required that the Gobernadorcillo turn over a fixed amount, the nature of the collection procedure was left to the Gobernadorcillo's discretion, as was the dispensation of any surplus. Therefore, the Chinese headman had the ability to exempt certain individuals from taxation, place a heavier burden on others, or spread the burden as he saw fit.[85]

The Gobernadorcillo housed new arrivals, collected landing fees, and was officially recognized as the chief mediator of the Chinese community, all duties that could be very lucrative. Included in his jurisdiction was the Tribunal de los Sangleyes, the Chinese small claims court. Controlling the Tribunal made the Gobernadorcillo the supreme jurist in the economic relations of the Chinese community.[86] The cases handled by the Tribunal included small business claims, domicile licenses, indebtedness, and the expulsion of undesirables.[87] The Tribunal also provided translators and legal advice for Chinese brought before the Spanish courts.[88] Such extensive official sanction for judicial and mediation activities was often denied to the Chinese elite in the late imperial period, but many of the Gobernadorcillo's duties echoed those of local luminaries in China.[89] In addition to his official post, the Gobernadorcillo also chaired the Chinese Guild; hence, he managed the major charitable and educational institutions and was both the main mediator within the community and the chief delegate to the outside.[90]

Given the administrative, taxation, juridical and law enforcement jobs of the Gobernadorcillo de los Sangleyes, the office replicated many of the functions of a county magistrate back in China. The fact that the elites who held the post also affected mandarin dress and Chinese bureaucratic style in their official correspondence is a clear indicator that this parallel was not lost on them. There was, however, one critical difference between a Chinese Gobernadorcillo and a Qing magistrate. Because of the "rule of avoidance" that prevented

Qing officials from serving in their home provinces, a Chinese magistrate was a stranger to his charges, whereas the Gobernadorcillo shared linguistic, native-place, and affinal ties to the local Chinese community. Whether these ties created greater or lesser solidarity within the community is unclear, but it did give the Gobernadorcillo a remarkable degree of internal and external authority. Those who served as Gobernadorcillo were the supreme *cabecillas,* men who had mastered the dynamics of intracommunity status and extracommunity networking and who acted in the interests of an elite that defined the Chinese community.

## Conclusion

The Chinese merchant elite had a sophisticated and well-articulated system for establishing and maintaining its dominant position within the community. The origins of some of these strategies and institutions lay in familiar Chinese elite practices that were appropriate to the Philippines owing to the nature of Spanish colonial rule. The limited reach of the colonial state left a vacuum into which institutions could successfully be inserted between state and local society. The local Chinese elite could fill these interstices with institutional forms exported from China, among them guilds, charitable institutions, native-place associations, and secret societies, but they could also appropriate institutions imposed on them by the colonial state, the Gremio de Chinos in particular, to perform the functions expected of a "Chinese" elite and a merchant enclave. The fluid boundaries on the periphery of the Chinese and Spanish empires encouraged the flexible use of numerous strategies, networks, and institutions. The Chinese, therefore, were not constrained by Chinese institutional forms. But as they would have in China, the merchant elite took the lead in organizing community celebrations, financed and directed charitable institutions, founded schools and temples, mediated conflicts, organized self-defense, affected elite lifestyles, and interacted with external sources of authority. In Xiamen, Quanzhou, Hankou, and Manila, the economic and social base of the local elite was essentially the same. Commercial enterprises, staffed though migration networks, provided the wealth; charity and community leadership defined elite status; and formal institutions provided the external connections that enhanced their power. In China and throughout colonial Southeast Asia, local Chinese elites cultivated close ties to political power hold-

ers. These ties were facilitated by the elite's role as agent for the state
in revenue collection, mediation, and local defense, and by the state's
conferring of lucrative revenue farms and its monopoly on avenues of
social mobility. A pro-state inclination among the local elite was, however, tempered by a distinctly local bias. When the state's interests
contradicted those of the local community, particularly in matters of
revenue extraction, the local elite could, and did, hinder and sabotage
the state's efforts or seek support from an alternate source of power
and legitimation, such as Beijing, to further its interests.

The one area in which Chinese *cabecillas* differed from their elite
brethren on the mainland was the greater range of choices they had
when it came to cultural orientation. Existing on the physical and cultural boundary between two empires that claimed a historic mission
of moral transformation, Chinese *cabecillas* had two distinct cultural
agendas to satisfy. The Chinese cultural agenda was characterized by
participation in local patron deity cults (deemed essential for good
fortune) and the emphasis on Confucian family rituals and education. The Spanish agenda involved conversion to Catholicism and
loyalty to the Spanish monarch. Skillful negotiation of fluid boundaries allowed the Chinese elite to satisfy both of these cultural agendas. The fact that local Chinese duplicated Qing imperial forms in
their bureaucratic documents, going so far as to substitute *"wang,"* referring to the Spanish king, for *"huang,"* the Qing emperor, and even
going so far as to elevate *"wang"* in the same way that *"huang"* was traditionally elevated above the line, demonstrates both the flexibility of
indigenous Chinese forms of local-state relations and the fact that divided loyalties were both practicable and practical. It should be
noted, however, that this liminal virtuosity was exercised at a time
when neither state could demand the total loyalty of the Chinese elite
or make absolute claims to their cultural orientation. *Cabecillas* were
valuable to both states, because they were fundamentally and instinctively transnational.

With the increased competition, regional diversity, social mobility, and status volatility that characterized the late nineteenth century, the Manila Chinese sought new strategies and reworked older
methods to establish and protect social status in an unstable environment. Employing stable institutions and reliable strategies meant
that, even though elite personnel might change, the criteria for elite
status was well defined; consequently, this system was relatively flexible when it came to social mobility, while avoiding excessive struc-

tural instability. The central strategy was to maintain community cohesion and the close bonds of loyalty and obligation between *radicado* and *invernado,* while at the same time cultivating profitable external linkages that were responsible for Chinese economic success in the late Spanish era and that guaranteed the perpetuation of the *cabecilla* elite. The integrative institutions—migration networks, native-place associations, sworn brotherhoods, and the Gremio de Chinos—established, maintained, and managed by the elite were the cornerstone of community solidarity.

There were times, however, when even the elite perceived existing institutions as inadequate to respond to emergent crises. This occurred when forces outside the direct control or network integration of the *cabecillas* (and beyond the control of their informal allies, the Spanish and later the American authorities) threatened the physical or economic well-being of the community or its leaders. These forces included the fundamental problems presented by the turn-of-the-century crisis; the physical dangers inherent in the 1896 revolt, and later The Philippine Insurrection and the Spanish-American War; and key changes in colonial policy after 1898. When the Qing dynasty's eleventh-hour reorientation of emigration and economic policy offered new institutional forms that could protect the Chinese from these forces, reinforce community cohesion, strengthen their identification with China, and strengthen their hand vis-à-vis their colonial rulers, the local elite immediately sought to coopt them. It is not surprising that rival forces within the Chinese community competed for control of these new institutions. The Chinese experience in the late nineteenth century made it clear that social and economic power rested with those who not only controlled the institutions that defined Chinese identity in the colonial Philippines, but also had the greatest rapport with and institutional linkages to external sources of authority.

# 3
# China and the Philippines, 1571–1889

THE SOUTHERN CHINESE have lived and traded in the Philippine Islands for more than a thousand years. Consequently, the Philippines and the Manila Chinese have periodically played a central role in Chinese history. During the Ming dynasty (1368–1644), that role arose predominantly from the material consequences of Sino-Philippine trade. Mexican silver, New World crops, and the opening of markets for Chinese commodities and manufactures radically altered mainland China's economy and society. New crops changed China's demographic history, while export markets and imported silver commercialized and monetized the Chinese economy on an unprecedented scale, linking late imperial China into the global economy. Yet for all of their importance to the Chinese economy (and their proximity to China), the Philippines and the Chinese merchants residing there remained peripheral to China's official consciousness. Before the late nineteenth century, only sporadic mention of the Philippines is found in the official records of the Ming and Qing dynasties. Yet these dynasties were a period of significant economic intercourse between China and the Philippines.

Owing to the absence of a Spanish trading base on the Chinese coast or on Taiwan as the Portuguese had at Macao or the Dutch at Zeelandia, Manila was the major entrepôt for Sino-Spanish trade for the two centuries after its founding in 1571. Of all the Chinese products brought to Manila, silks and porcelains were the most sought after. To pay for Chinese manufactures, the Spanish exported huge amounts of silver from their Mexican and Peruvian mines. In 1597, for example, it was estimated that 345,000 kilograms of silver entered

China via Manila. This exceeded the total amount of silver produced by China's domestic mines in the preceding fifty years.[1] Even in the twentieth century, the Mexican silver dollar was still the dominant, albeit unofficial, means of exchange on the Chinese coast.

For China the material consequences of the Manila trade were spectacular. The discovery and exploitation of overseas markets for Chinese products catalyzed commercial expansion along the southeast coast. Demand created a boom in the trade networks of coastal China as suppliers scrambled to provide Fujianese and Cantonese merchants with exports. Demand raised prices and created fortunes for the ambitious, talented, and lucky, leading to a significant change in Chinese culture and society in the late Ming era. The great prosperity traveled through China's river systems and marketing networks, resulting in a general increase in wealth. The importance of household putting-out industries, especially in tea harvesting and sericulture, commercialized the rural economy and raised the value of domestic labor, particularly the value of female labor. These developments had wide-ranging consequences for Chinese society and the economy.

The key ingredient for this boom was foreign silver. Beginning in the sixteenth century and lasting until the 1820s, China was the largest and most aggressive silver consumer in the world.[2] The massive importation of silver, however, created new problems, among them inflation, growing income disparities, and official corruption. Moreover, a drop in the silver supply was a triple threat: it depressed the economy; caused economic hardship, unemployment, and popular unrest; and, at the same time, decreased the state's revenue and hindered its ability to respond to crises.[3] In addition to vast quantities of silver, the Manila trade also introduced New World crops to China, including sweet potatoes, peanuts, corn, and tobacco; these had an enormous impact on Chinese agriculture and demographic development not the least of which was fueling the dramatic spike in Chinese population that began in the seventeenth century. From this brief overview, the centrality of Sino-Spanish trade to the economic and social history of late imperial China should be apparent, but the question remains as to why this critical trade relationship was not reflected in a more substantive state-to-state relationship. Moreover, given that the Chinese merchants who traveled back and forth to Manila were such critical intermediaries in this trade, it might seem surprising that they are also largely absent from the historical record.

The reason for these lacunae becomes clear when one understands the dynamics of China's foreign relations in the late imperial period.

## Patterns of Foreign Interaction in Late Imperial China

Throughout the late imperial period, the Chinese and their rulers interacted with Southeast Asia within two spheres. The first sphere comprised the sporadic relations between officials at the center of the Chinese empire and the rulers of the periphery. During the Ming and Qing, official relations with Southeast Asia were prioritized on the basis of the tribute system. The tribute system was a complex network of symbolic and ritual relations in which local rulers declared fealty and submission to the supreme ruler, the emperor of China, in exchange for ritual benefits and the friendship of the region's superpower. History, ritual, and the frequency of tribute missions determined a country's position within the hierarchy. The tribute hierarchy, therefore, did not consistently reflect the relative economic or geostrategic importance of certain countries. As a result, the tiny Ryukyu Islands, which were closer to the apex of China's tributary hierarchy, enjoyed much more attention in the Chinese historical record than the Philippines, which, despite having a greater impact on the course of Chinese history, occupied an insignificant place in the tribute system.

Also affecting the first sphere of Sino-Spanish relations was the restrictive nature of China's official policy regarding Chinese overseas. As far as the emigration of Chinese to Southeast Asia was concerned, the official line condemned overseas settlement as traitorous and unfilial, a policy that reflected the conservative moral stance taken by China's rulers. The Qing dynasty also considered émigré Chinese, many of whom were pirates and Ming loyalists, a threat to coastal security.[4] The Manchu court officially disavowed any responsibility for Chinese subjects residing overseas, and during the Qing dynasty, the court went so far as to refuse them the right to return to China on pain of death.

After the conquest of Taiwan in 1683, the Qing turned its attention inward, toward consolidation. Although they took great interest in pacifying Taiwan and the southeast coast, the main priorities of Manchu foreign policy involved the consolidation of the empire's western frontiers. The Qing considered maritime trade less important than central and northern Asia and continued to view Southeast Asia as a haven for potentially dangerous Ming loyalists. The Manchus, therefore, made a conscious effort to attenuate the linkages between China, Southeast Asia, and the maritime economy.

These were difficult policies to enforce, especially considering the revenue still being collected from Chinese merchants trading with Southeast Asia.[5] Neither the "myth of superiority" explicit in the tribute system, nor anticommercial rhetoric represented the total reality of China's interaction with the outside world.[6] Recent scholarship has shown that China's foreign relations apparatus was significantly more flexible than the preceding description would indicate. Officials in Beijing could and did interact with foreign powers outside of the ritual hierarchy of the tribute system, and overseas residence was tacitly accepted long before the bans on emigration were lifted in the late nineteenth century, but to document a reality that did not jibe with the moral absolutes promulgated by the court ran the risk of challenging the moral authority of the emperor. Moreover, the majority of China's foreign relations took place on the fluid frontiers of the empire, far from the moralizing center, and for the most part were too mundane to be noticed in Beijing.

The second sphere of China's Southeast Asian relations, the realm of the rarely documented informal relations between China and maritime Asia, was more constant and more localized than the first sphere. It was also less constrained by ritual and bureaucracy although it regularly involved China's coastal governors, governors-general, and military officials as well as the pirates, merchants, colonials, and indigenous peoples of Southeast Asia. At times, events in this realm could intrude on the consciousness of the imperial court, as in pirate suppression or in the search for extraordinary sources of revenue, but for the most part the international relations of this second sphere were conducted by and in the interests of local officials and the region's residents. Unlike the Canton system, which limited European maritime traders to a small enclave in Guangdong, this larger realm offered more natural and more varied points of contact between China and the regional and global economies. Yet because the Canton system was overseen by the Imperial Household and was therefore within the first sphere of Qing foreign relations, its paper trail is disproportionately large. Thus, the documentary lacunae and emphasis on Canton mask a more sustained, robust, and significant interaction—within the second sphere—between late imperial China and maritime Southeast Asia. In the case of the Spanish Philippines, while Beijing was generally disinterested in the Manila trade, it was likely an issue of significant interest for the governor, magistrates, and *daotai* of Fujian, and verged on an obsession for the residents of Zhangzhou and Quanzhou. Xiamen, the leading Fujian port, was known as a "city of silver" *(yincheng)*, a point of connection between the vast Chinese market and the global economy, where foreign silver flowed in—as remittances from Hokkiens overseas and in exchange for Chinese commodities and manufactures—and from which commercial talent flowed out from the villages crowded into this narrow coastal belt.[7]

Official proscriptions and a decline in trade could not completely sever China's links to maritime Asia. Nonetheless, the Qing dynasty's initial antipathy to maritime trade did contribute to a general decline in Sino-Spanish trade in the seventeenth century. This decline was hastened by the destruction involved in the suppression of Ming loyalists (especially in Fujian province) and by the fact that the galleon system, which had been so spectacularly influential in the century before, had already begun its long decline. In consequence, the quantity and total value of Sino-Spanish trade—and the number of Chinese in Manila—declined even after the regional recovery that began in the 1680s. The relative importance of Manila was further reduced by the growing trade between China and Vietnam, Siam, and especially the Dutch East Indies. The opening of Canton to foreign trade in 1685 shifted China's mercantile center of gravity southward toward the Pearl River, and while this location created more points of contact between China and the global economy, it also served to eclipse, but not eliminate, Sino-Spanish trade through Fujian.[8] Thus, while Qing maritime policy initially succeeded in relegating this trade and the Chinese merchants who plied the East and South China Seas, to the far periphery of Beijing's consciousness, coastal officials continued to deal with maritime issues as long as the southeast provinces enjoyed healthy and prosperous trading relations with the outside world.[9]

## Late Qing Relations with the Chinese Overseas

The Qing dynasty's relations with the Chinese in Southeast Asia have traditionally been characterized as distrustful and apathetic, and, as discussed above, there is some validity to this view. Ming loyalist activities in Southeast Asia and a Manchu propensity to focus on the land frontiers meant that little attention was given to the Chinese in Southeast Asia, despite their critical contributions to the Chinese economy. Moreover, migrations of Chinese within the region were relatively small—numbering in the tens of thousands—and were generally limited to the major trading cities of Asia.[10] However, with the opening of the treaty ports in the aftermath of China's midcentury defeats in the first and second Opium Wars, compounded by rising social disorder and growing population pressure, large numbers of Chinese males began to emigrate to both Southeast Asia and the Americas. Improvements in nautical technology contributed to the globalization of markets, and the Industrial Revolution required vast quantities of raw materials for fuel, but demand for these materials also made labor shortages acute across the globe. With the California gold rush, the expansion of guano mining, and the growth of the American, Caribbean, and Southeast Asian agricultural industries, a steady supply of cheap, efficient labor became essential. When these regional economies were able to plug into the Chinese economy through treaty ports and move hundred of thousands of laborers by sail and steam, China, especially the Pearl River Delta and southern Fujian, became the major labor supplier for the Pacific and Caribbean markets.[11] The dynasty's traditional attitudes had obviously changed when the affairs of Chinese in places as remote as Cuba began to interest not just provincial officials but Beijing as well. Even then, it would prove difficult to reconcile the center-periphery dichotomy or to develop a coherent policy that satisfied local, provincial, and imperial interests.

China's forced opening and the huge outflow of Chinese migrants in the mid–nineteenth century made Chinese immigration an international issue. While a significant number of these migrants were merchants, students, and artisans, it was the thousands of Chinese laborers (coolies) that attracted the most attention. Whereas cheap Chinese labor regularly incited labor tensions, in the American west, for example, it was the inhumanity of the coolie system that became a cause célèbre in international relations in the mid–nineteenth century. In the Caribbean especially, where Chinese were brought in as indentured laborers either to replace African slaves or to work alongside freed blacks, there seemed to be little difference between the coolie system and slavery. As a result, the Qing government was under pressure both to control the outflow of Chinese labor as well as to build an international coalition to halt the coolie trade and thus salvage some of the dynasty's prestige. Despite the maintenance of the legal ban on emigration, the Chinese government was neither immune nor indifferent to the plight of its subjects overseas.[12] The court and its leading ministers pursued a pragmatic policy that, despite the hindrances of internal rebellion and systemic flaws in the imperial system, was eventually able to use international law and pressure to bring the coolie trade to an end in 1874.[13]

The apex of China's battle to suppress the coolie trade coincided with the dispatch of a commission to investigate conditions among Chinese coolies in Cuba.[14] Because Qing officials had heard disturbing accounts of the mistreatment of Chinese laborers in Cuba in 1873, Beijing's Foreign Office, the Zongli Yamen, prohibited Spanish labor recruiters from hiring coolies to supply the Cuban sugar industry with much-needed manpower. The court's refusal was met with a countersuit for damages by the Spanish minister, and the result was the dispatch of a commission to verify the rumors. The investigative team was headed by the Special Commissioner of the Chinese Education Mission to the United States, Chen Lanbin, who was assisted by one French and one British member of the Imperial Maritime Customs Service.[15]

Arriving in Cuba in the spring of 1874, the commission spent six weeks taking depositions from Chinese laborers, investigating conditions, and receiving petitions from groups of coolies. The commission found that mistreatment of Chinese coolies was rampant in Cuba. In some cases the laborers were treated as slaves, tortured, branded, and often beaten to death for minor infractions. The committee's findings were made public early in 1875, and the Zongli Yamen was able to capitalize on the bad press that this generated to force Spain to make concessions. The Sino-Spanish treaty, finally signed in November 1877, was a minor victory for Qing foreign policy.[16] The treaty guaranteed the protection and freedom of the Chinese residing in Cuba and set limits on the recruitment of Chinese laborers. In addition, the Chinese government agreed to establish a consulate general in Cuba to guarantee adherence to the treaty and give the Cuban Chinese a venue to express their grievances.[17] This minor diplomatic achievement also established a precedent for Chinese consular representation in a Spanish colony, a fact that later Qing statesmen and Manila's Chinese merchants would try to use in their campaign for a Philippine consulate.

Whereas the dominant issue from the 1850s to the 1870s had been the coolie trade, the notion of constructing a more mutually beneficial relationship between Chinese overseas—especially wealthy Chinese merchants—and the motherland began to gain currency among some capital bureaucrats, but especially among those governing China's coastal provinces.[18] After the midcentury rebellions, the Qing state was far more willing to sell titles and grant symbols of legitimacy to local elites, even those overseas, both to earn revenue and to minimize the problems of ruling and financing a vast, populous, and varied empire. Qing officials had come to realize that Chinese expatriates could be a valuable resource for their attempts at economic and military strengthening and for disaster relief.[19] If properly mobilized, Chinese overseas could provide the talent and essential financing for China's military and industrial modernization. Consulates could offer the Chinese overseas legal protection in foreign countries, which would encourage Chinese merchants to increase their business activities.[20] That trade would strengthen China in two ways: first, by improving its balance of trade and, second, by enriching the empire's citizens who would then, out of loyalty, support China's modernization.

Due to the efforts of the Qing's first minister to Great Britain, Guo Songtao, a Chinese consulate was established in Singapore in October 1877.[21] The Singapore endeavor was the most convenient because of the size and wealth of the Singapore Chinese community, because of the availability of a qualified member of the local elite to serve as consul, and because Guo Songtao was able to focus a great deal of energy during his early days in London on the consular negotiations. Guo saw a direct correlation between trade and national power, arguing that China should expand its trading potential and access to foreign markets by encouraging Chinese merchants to travel overseas. The means of encouragement was to be a series of Chinese consulates throughout the world, similar to those maintained by the Western powers, that would afford legal protection to overseas Chinese traders through diplomatic representation. The founding of the consulates would thus benefit both parties: the merchants' livelihood would be protected, and the empire would be strengthened by an improved balance of trade. For the post of consul, Guo recommended a wealthy and respected member of the local Chinese community, Hu Xuanze (Hoo Ah Kay or Whampoa).[22]

By choosing a member of the local elite, Beijing might have been better able to coopt the local Chinese by giving them the hitherto unknown prestige of members in the imperial bureaucracy. Guo had met Hu in 1876 during a stop in Singapore on his way to England. At that time Hu had already been granted a Qing title, and he had been serving as "honorary consul for China" since 1870. In addition, Hu was also serving as the Singapore consul for both Japan and imperial Russia. Such broad experience made Hu a likely choice for consul but also raises an interesting conundrum. That Hu could wear so many hats, including occupying a seat on Singapore's Legislative Council and receiving awards from Queen Victoria, would seem to indicate that his interests and loyalties were firmly grounded in the British colony, and this would make him a problematic choice for Qing consul. But if the main purpose of a consulate in a place like Singapore was to funnel overseas talent and wealth back to China, then Hu was an excellent choice. The same would not have been true for Havana, where a Qing consul would have needed to be a more formal diplomatic representative tasked to protect Chinese in a hostile environment and therefore would likely be dispatched directly from Beijing. The dynasty seemed thus to be pursuing a pragmatic program for staffing consulates, choosing prestigious local figures for the less taxing posts and dispatching professional bureaucrats to the more challenging locales. Nonetheless, this practical approach threatened to blur the distinction between local and imperial interests, and likewise set a problematic precedent for a Qing consulate in Manila, where numerous prominent local elites wanted to and could be called on to serve as consul. The local environment, however, was increasingly volatile and thus seemed to demand professional representation.

The establishment of the Singapore consulate began China's first phase of consular expansion. Between 1878 and 1883 consulates general were founded in Yokohama, San Francisco, Havana, and New York, and a commercial directorate was also set up in Honolulu.[23] After 1883, however, the consular expansion movement was hindered by financial constraints. The overextended Qing court was hard-pressed to divert more customs funds to pay for new legations while it was faced with the prospects of war with France over Annam and before the initial consulates had proved their viability and value.[24]

The initial call to establish a Chinese consulate general in the Philippines came in 1880, when Li Hongzhang received a petition from a group of prominent Manila-Chinese merchants. Apparently hoping to capitalize on China's success in negotiations with the Spanish and the recent founding of consulates in Singapore and Yokohama, the merchants complained of unfair taxation and economic exploitation by the Spanish government in Manila.[25] Li responded by suggesting to the Zongli Yamen that an investigative commission, similar to the one sent to Cuba, be dispatched to the Philippines to verify the charges.[26] The Zongli Yamen in turn instructed the Chinese ambassador to Spain, the United States, and Peru, Chen Lanbin, to raise the subject with the Spanish foreign ministry.[27] The Qing government was not forceful in its demands, and Chen was handicapped by the fact that his diplomatic jurisdiction covered three continents. Thus sustained, or even consistent, negotiations were likely to prove difficult. The Spanish government managed to evade the issue of allowing Beijing to investigate conditions in the Philippines until the spring of 1885, when it refused the request.[28]

## Zhang Zhidong and the Manila Consulate General

After these initial frustrations, the campaign for a Manila consulate took an encouraging turn later that summer. At that point Beijing appointed a new ambassador to Spain, Peru, and the United States, Zhang Yinhuan. But, more important, the consular issue attracted the attention of one of the brightest stars in the Qing bureaucracy, Zhang Zhidong, recognized as a leader of China's late-nineteenth-century attempts at "self-strengthening."[29] Zhang Zhidong's early career was marked by stunning success and controversy as he climbed rapidly within the Qing bureaucracy. He first came to national prominence as a practitioner of *qingyi* (pure discourse), a type of strict Confucian policy critique.[30] It was especially in the arena of foreign affairs that Zhang, as an ambitious midlevel bureaucrat, used his rhetorical skills to criticize policies and officials seen as "soft" on foreign powers and to further his own career.[31] This hawkish bent landed Zhang the critical post of governor-general of Guangdong and Guangxi provinces (Liangguang) in 1884, on the eve of war with France.

As the growing Sino-French controversy was the most pressing matter at the beginning of Zhang's six years in Liangguang, the new governor-general's time was consumed by preparations for war and defense against a technologically advanced adversary. At this point

Zhang began to appreciate the potential value that Chinese overseas might have in these efforts. Not only were many Annam Chinese from Guangdong, but there were significant Cantonese communities throughout Indochina—the presumed theater of conflict. These Chinese patriots might be called on to aid the war effort with their money and talent, or they might also be drafted into the war itself. In September of 1884, Zhang proposed that Chinese be called upon to prove their loyalty to the dynasty by sabotaging French vessels in Annam and elsewhere in Southeast Asia.[32]

The Sino-French War, however, was a disaster for the Qing, and Zhang was never able to test the loyalties of the Chinese overseas accurately. Nonetheless, his interest in these communities continued, not in the least because their contributions to provincial coffers allowed him to pursue an ambitious program of reform and industrialization. From his seat in Guangzhou, Zhang had come to realize that the *huaqiao* could prove a valuable resource for his attempts at economic and military strengthening. If properly mobilized, the overseas Chinese, through donations and remittances, could provide essential financing for the military and industrial modernization of South China. In October 1885, Zhang Zhidong recommended to the throne that the Chinese overseas be called on to finance the construction of a fleet of warships that would not only defend China, but would also protect Chinese merchants and promote the expansion of China's overseas trade. Zhang also suggested that the sale of imperial titles be expanded among the *huaqiao*, presumably to raise funds and to promote identification with the dynasty among the overseas Chinese.[33]

As the governor-general of Guangdong and Guangxi, Zhang Zhidong was a regional official operating within a long history of *huaqiao* policy, a policy that was undergoing important changes and one in which China's coastal governors had begun to play a prominent role. Not merely because of his post as Liangguang governor-general, but also because of his recent advocacy of overseas migration issues, Zhang Zhidong suddenly became a prominent figure in this particular national debate. Therefore, when Zhang Yinhuan, the new ambassador to Spain, Peru, and the United States, departed Beijing—after meeting with the Spanish ambassador—he proceeded to Guangzhou to meet with Zhang Zhidong. The new ambassador, a native of Guangdong, probably had some reservations about the meeting, having himself been removed from an earlier office after a particularly harsh *qingyi* critique in which Zhang Zhidong participated.[34] However, Zhang Zhidong's sensitivity to the changing political climate and his abrupt volte-face in foreign affairs now made him and Zhang Yinhuan nominal allies.

While in Guangdong, Zhang Yinhuan received another petition from four Manila-Chinese merchants, among them Carlos Palanca Chen Qianshan, the Gobernadorcillo de los Sangleyes in Manila, requesting the establishment of a consulate general in Manila. Zhang Yinhuan traveled to Hong Kong to meet with the petitioners and to discuss conditions in the islands. The meeting was arranged by the directors of Hong Kong's Tung Wah Hospital. While ostensibly a local charity, Tung Wah served a secondary role as an information source and intermediary between imperial officials and Chinese overseas.[35] Contrary to Antonio Tan's portrayal of the Manila Chinese as ignorant of Chinese politics, the Tung Wah, as well as other transnational institutions, not only provided the Chinese merchant elite overseas critical information about affairs in China, but also enabled them to meet or communicate directly with senior mandarins. The Manila delegation knew who the ambassador was, when he was going to be in Guangzhou, and how best to get his attention. Moreover, the fact that these merchants were primarily Hokkiens yet went to Hong Kong to petition a Cantonese ambassador and a Liangguang governor-general demonstrates a remarkable ability, even at this early stage, to expand—when it served their interests—their range of connections far beyond the confines of either their native place or their host environment.

In the same memorial in which they reported the receipt of the petition and the meeting with the *cabecillas,* the governor-general and the ambassador jointly recommended that, in addition to the Singapore consulate general, the throne establish another consular office in Manila.[36] Considering the size, wealth, and proximity to China of the Chinese community in Manila and the empire's recent relations with Spain, a Manila consulate seemed to be the next logical step in Beijing's expansion of its diplomatic presence in Southeast Asia. Basing their calculations for the Manila office on the Singapore model, where local Chinese elites financed and staffed the consulate, the joint memorialists also recommended that the first step toward establishing the office be the dispatch of an investigative commission along the lines of the earlier mission to Cuba. The memorialists were thus relying on a proven procedure and one that had been advo-

cated earlier by the powerful Li Hongzhang. Since the majority of
the local Chinese were Hokkiens, Zhang Zhidong thought it appropriate that the commission be headed by Brigade-General Wang
Yonghe, a Fujianese, who would be better able to communicate with
the local Chinese.[37] As Wang's assistant the memorialist suggested Yu
Qiong, a Guangdong native who had served as Chinese consul in
Japan.[38]

The commission's itinerary was not limited to the Philippines.
Over a period of eight months in 1886–1887, the investigators were
to travel to several major ports in Southeast Asia and Australia to investigate conditions in a variety of Chinese communities.[39] Although
the memorialists advocated a broad scope for the inquiry, they were
careful to assure the throne that consular expansion would move
ahead gradually and not to suggest that consulates be immediately established in all the places the commission was to visit. Zhang Zhidong
was thus making a sophisticated political move to portray himself as a
reformer but not one so extreme as to advocate overtaxing the dynasty's limited consular legation budget. The Philippines consulate
would serve as a test case not only for China's second phase of consular expansion but for Zhang's new stance on foreign relations. The
governor-general was careful not to jeopardize the project by being
overly enthusiastic.[40]

The establishment of Chinese consulates would serve the same
purpose as Zhang Zhidong's other proposals, such as the sale of titles
and the collection of overseas funds for naval construction. Chinese
legations offered Chinese subjects legal protection in foreign countries and encouraged Chinese merchants to increase their business
activities.[41] Increased commercial activity would in turn strengthen
China by improving its balance of trade and enriching the empire's
subjects, who would then, out of loyalty, support China's modernization. The Philippines was an attractive location for this new policy.
Beijing had legal justification and treaty precedent for establishing a
consulate general. The 1864 Sino-Spanish treaty guaranteed Chinese
merchants "most-favored-nation" treatment, which, according to the
petitioners, they were not receiving. Furthermore, despite the failure
of the first round of consular negotiations, Zhang Yinhuan may have
been encouraged by the ease with which his predecessor, Chen Lanbin, had succeeded in establishing a consulate in Havana.[42] Propos-
ing the establishment of the Philippines consulate general therefore

seemed a safe project through which Zhang Zhidong could test his new role as advocate for Chinese overseas.

The plan to send the investigative mission was granted imperial sanction, and the committee departed from China in August 1886. Zhang Zhidong had initially requested that the commission travel aboard Chinese warships to add force to their mission and to emphasize Zhang's pet project of using overseas donations to fund naval construction, and perhaps to practice a bit of "gunboat diplomacy" with the Spanish.[43] With a show of force, Beijing might be able to persuade the Spanish to concede, given their increasingly weak position among the imperial powers. The gunboat plan, however, was immediately rejected by Li Hongzhang, and the investigators traveled by ordinary steamship lines.[44]

Wang Yonghe's commission remained in the Philippines, where it was warmly received by the local Chinese, for one month, before spending the rest of the year traveling throughout Asia. The investigators reported that conditions in the Philippines were as deplorable as described in the earlier petitions—a finding that lent support to the project of consular expansion.[45] The accuracy of these findings, however, may be questionable. Without trivializing the mistreatment of the Chinese in the Philippines, the main purpose of the mission was to provide evidence for the proposals of Zhang Zhidong and Zhang Yinhuan. Given that Wang Yonghe and Yu Qiong were sensitive to the wishes of their immediate superiors, they may have tailored their findings to fit a larger purpose. Furthermore, the dispatch of the mission coincided with the imperial command to Zhang Yinhuan to begin negotiations with the Spanish foreign ministry on the subject of the consulate. In these talks the ambassador required documentation that the Spanish were not adequately protecting the Chinese living in the islands so that he might better press his case.[46]

Meanwhile in Guangzhou, Zhang Zhidong had been directed by the Zongli Yamen to determine the structure and financing of the Philippine consulate general based on preliminary reports.[47] In a memorial dated December 8, 1887, Zhang laid out a complete plan for the Manila consulate general. As before, Zhang planned to base the legation on the Singapore model of using imperial customs funds for the initial costs of founding and staffing the office, which were then to be covered through consular fees and donations from the local Chinese.[48] The post of consul was to be filled by Wang Yonghe, whose Fujian background and experience abroad—and as the head of the investigative commission—made him an obvious choice. To gain further support for the project in the islands, members of the local Chinese elite would be recruited to fill the subordinate offices and to provide staff for future consulates outside Manila. Coopting local Chinese into the consulate system would then facilitate the effectiveness of the office and improve its fund-raising capacity.[49]

The consul general, along with his colleague in Singapore, would partially fall under the jurisdiction of the Liangguang governor-general. The logic behind this suggestion was that both Manila and Singapore were closer to Guangzhou than to Madrid or London, and communication would be faster if the consuls turned to the governor-general for guidance rather than to remote ambassadors. In addition, Zhang argued that since Chinese overseas were a vital link in the Chinese trade flowing from the ports of Guangdong, the governor-general of Liangguang should play an active role in their protection.[50] Proximity and convenience aside, the placement of the consuls general under Zhang's command was also a deft political move. Zhang had relied heavily on foreign loans and donations from local elites and Chinese overseas to capitalize his modernization projects in Liangguang. Having the consulate under his purview, rather than that of the Zongli Yamen or the ambassador, would give Zhang the opportunity to dispense overseas collections as he saw fit.

Other aspects of the consulate general's structure, however, bore the mark of Zhang Zhidong's unique personal style. Attached to the Manila office was to be an experimental academy. With a library of classics, in part donated by Zhang himself, and a staff of local "gentry" to instruct youths in Confucianism, the academy would form the ideological counterpart to the political institution of the consulate general.[51] The academy, never realized, can be viewed as an early attempt to foment a prodynastic stance among the overseas Chinese.[52] Besides coopting the local Chinese elite into the imperial government through service to the consulate and the sale of titles, the academy would promote a sense of identification with the imperial orthodoxy.

The Zongli Yamen's reaction to Zhang's sweeping proposal was restrained and cautious. In its response, the yamen made it clear that the Manila consulate general was only a test and not a guarantee of further openings. Beijing felt that rapid expansion would antagonize the Western powers and strain the dynasty's finances, and expressed reservations about using local funds to cover consular expenses. The Singapore consulate, despite an initially enthusiastic response, had failed to become self-sufficient and still relied heavily on imperial support. In light of the financial condition of the dynasty, Zhang Zhidong's aggressive strategy had to be moderated. Recruiting local Chinese to fill consular posts might also result in the use of the offices for personal gain and exploitation, which would discredit the venture and hurt China's prestige. With these restrictions laid down by the Beijing authorities, the success or failure of the Manila consulate lay with the Chinese ambassador to the United States, Spain, and Peru, Zhang Yinhuan.[53]

## The Negotiations with Spain

In August 1886, Zhang Yinhuan was ordered to begin negotiations with the Spanish foreign ministry. The ambassador, however, was reluctant to act on those orders. Zhang Yinhuan's meetings with Zhang Zhidong had convinced him that the best way to establish the consulate in Manila was to have the governor-general simply choose an appropriate candidate for consul and then use his vice-regal authority to request a visa from the Spanish governor-general in Manila. In this way the political wrangling and vacillation that the Spanish home government had displayed in the initial negotiations for the consulate could be avoided. In the late summer, much against his inclinations, Zhang Yinhuan was ultimately required to take responsibility for the negotiations himself, though he had not received the investigative mission's full report.[54]

At this point, Zhang Yinhuan began to voice his own reservations about the project. The ambassador felt trapped between the divergent strategies advocated by Zhang Zhidong and the Zongli Yamen, and he was being criticized by Beijing for his lack of progress, which in turn damaged his bargaining position with the Spanish. In addition, the ambassador had concluded that the consulate's proposed financial arrangements might actually prevent its realization. Considering the growing hostility of *mestizos* and *indios* toward the Chinese and the unique social and economic role played by the Chinese in the Spanish colonial enterprise, Zhang Yinhuan warned that collecting consular funds locally might further antagonize the *indios* by setting the Chinese farther apart from the native population and might also raise doubts about the colonial government's ability to control the Chinese enclave. Moreover, the fact that the empire had to collect money from the very group it hoped to protect with the establishment of the consulate might even tarnish the dynasty's prestige.[55]

As Zhang Yinhuan had anticipated, the negotiations became bogged down among the different ministries in Madrid. On one side, the foreign ministry supported the consulate proposal as a means to assuage the Chinese government and to avoid a crisis that might accelerate the decline of Spain's colonial fortunes. On the other, the colonial office and the Philippine governor-general opposed the consulate for fear that it would hinder their ability to govern and collect taxes from the wealthy Chinese minority. Most disturbing to the Spanish and Philippine governments, however, was the possibility that concessions on this point would prompt China to use its growing naval power in the South China Sea to intimidate the Spanish and make further demands.[56]

As the Spanish government vacillated, Zhang Yinhuan resorted to a variety of new tactics, from invoking international law to reminding the Spanish of their former treaty agreements. Ambassador Zhang, however, was also hindered by the same factors that had hampered Chen Lanbin's negotiations with the Spanish to establish a consulate in Manila five years earlier. Zhang could hardly spend all his time and energies in Madrid when he had to deal with the rising tide of anti-Chinese activism in the United States. At the same time Zhang Yinhuan and his subordinates were negotiating with the Spanish over the Manila consulate general, the ambassador was also finalizing the difficult Bayard-Zhang Treaty and settling reparations claims for Chinese laborers murdered in the United States.[57] In 1889 the decision on the Manila consulate question was left to the Spanish colonial office, which succeeded in shelving the debate for the next few years. At this point Zhang Yinhuan's role in the negotiations came to an end.[58]

Soon after the end of the negotiations with Spain and his return to the United States, Zhang Yinhuan was recalled to China amid charges that he had bowed to American interests in the Bayard-Zhang treaty and had overstepped the bounds of ambassadorial decorum by engaging in extravagant conduct while overseas.[59] The year 1889 also saw the transfer of Zhang Zhidong from Liangguang to the governor-generalship of Hunan and Hubei. Zhang's move to Wuchang left behind scores of half-realized schemes and projects that were now doomed to failure. The movement for the Philippines consulate was one such program that soon faded from view. The reservations expressed by the Zongli Yamen, the resistance of the Spanish government, the disgrace of Zhang Yinhuan, and his own transfer inland combined to bring Zhang Zhidong's role as promoter of consular expansion to an abrupt end.

## Conclusion

The reorientation of China's foreign policy agenda to include the Chinese overseas was an integral part of the Qing dynasty's revolutionary eleventh-hour reforms. Chinese overseas, like those in the Philippines, played a major role in China's foreign relations revolution, both as actors and as the focus of many new policy initiatives. Far from these official machinations, the Manila-Chinese community, a growing enclave of elite merchants, craftsmen, coolies, and *tenderos,* continued to shape the Manila trade and the emerging agricultural export economy. The dynamics of the community were, in turn, shaped by this trade and by events in China, events in the Philippines, and increasingly by events on the world stage. When imperial China's attention returned to the Philippines in the closing days of the nineteenth century, its gaze would be drawn there not solely by its own interests, but by the actions of the Manila Chinese themselves. These early attempts to found a consulate in Manila provided the essential groundwork for later campaigns and demonstrated that local Chinese were very much aware of the value of consular representation. Moreover, they displayed a remarkable degree of sophistication by making their claims for representation based on precedent, not only the precedent of Qing consulates in other Spanish colonies but also the consular representation enjoyed by the French, Americans, and British residing in Manila. Even as early as the 1880s, Manila's Chinese merchant elite were developing knowledge of and linkages to external sources of authority. These linkages were not just local, that is, restricted to Manila or southern Fujian, but actually enabled a local elite to participate in the diplomatic relations between great powers.

This brief digression into the world of Qing foreign relations and specifically into the career of Zhang Zhidong is relevant for several reasons. The decentralized and ad hoc approach that the Qing took in this case underscores the difficulties that the dynasty faced in developing a coherent policy toward Chinese overseas and in uniting the two spheres of Sino-foreign interaction—the imperial and the local. Moreover, the fact that Zhang Zhidong's advocacy of the consulate ended as soon as he was transferred inland shows that the convergence of ambitions and identity that characterized the Chinese merchants in Manila was shared by some Qing officials, who identified with Chinese overseas as long as it suited their professional ambitions. Finally, the concerns raised by Zhang Yinhuan and the Zongli Yamen about the ability of local Chinese to fund the consulate and the danger that they might manipulate the office for their personal gain raise an interesting paradox that haunted much of the late Qing reform program: the problem of drawing distinctions between "public" (gong) and "private" (si) in the absence of concrete legal distinctions between these two realms.[60] Although it is difficult to inscribe the Western concepts of public and private directly onto gong and si, it is nonetheless possible to conclude that gong (often synonymous with "guan," meaning official) was conceived as a positive, public good, and si, the antithesis of gong, was traditionally a pejorative term describing personal selfish interests. The Qing state and its local officials thus had difficulty in reconciling their moral duties to the public good with their growing collaboration with self-interested merchants. Moreover, given the moral extremism of late Qing policy critique, exemplified by qingyi, it was possible to subvert an unpopular program or change how and by whom it was to be implemented solely by exploiting the unresolved, and artificial, contradiction between gong and si. The consulate was conceived as a public good to protect the Chinese community in the Philippines but also to further the interests of the Chinese state. And while Zhang Zhidong apparently saw no contradiction between his own personal ambitions and pursuing the public good, the motivations of the Chinese merchant elite were still suspect. Hence the good characteristics of a "Chinese," public, and self-consciously Confucian consulate were in danger of being highjacked by their perceived antitheses—local, private, and commercial ambitions. If that happened, not only would the consulate not serve the public good, but it might even make matters worse for the Chinese community in Manila. A successful consulate should, by necessity, have been a venue for negotiating between these complementary and conflicting interests, but when a Manila consulate was finally founded, the first consuls would be haunted by accusations that they served exclusively private and local ambitions. Ironically, these same accusations became a convenient way to satisfy such ambitions by criticizing and removing rivals from positions of community leadership.

Compounding the confusion between "public" and "private" was the blurring of "local" and "imperial" that was an outgrowth of the Qing's early approach to consular postings. Beijing had established conflicting precedents by both choosing local elites as consuls and dispatching imperial bureaucrats. While this was a very practical approach, it created fierce disagreements over who was best suited to represent the Manila Chinese. Manila was like Singapore in that it had a prosperous, motivated Chinese elite, but in other ways the increasingly volatile local environment looked more like Cuba. This volatility seemed to demand an imperial rather than a local consul. Ultimately, the burden for pushing the consulate project fell on those who had consistently been its most vocal supporters, the Chinese merchant elite and their leader, Don Carlos Palanca Chen Qianshan, who (by dint of his liminal virtuosity) very nearly managed to harmonize all of these interests and achieved consular representation in the closing days of Spanish rule.

# 4

# Carlos Palanca Chen Qianshan

Elite Activism in the Manila-Chinese
Community, 1896–1901

AT CENTURY'S END, Manila's Chinese community faced myriad crises and opportunities. In one sense, the world they knew as Chinese and as migrants was coming to an end. Within a few years the associations that had defined their community and had negotiated their relations with the "outside world" would be replaced by new institutions. Within the enclave, greater regional diversity threatened to loosen the bonds that held the *chinos* together, while the external environment grew increasingly chaotic. Over the course of a single decade, the Philippines suffered plague, pestilence, depression, two revolutions, a foreign invasion, and a change in colonial government. Simultaneously, the migrants' homeland was being transformed. The effort to save the failing Qing dynasty had forced China's rulers to reassess the importance of the Chinese overseas and to seek out closer relations with them as well as with merchant elites in China. The Chinese in Southeast Asia responded enthusiastically to the possibility of strengthening their links to China.

The drive for consular expansion, like so many nation-building and self-strengthening projects in the late Qing dynasty, was as much the product of local elite activism as it was a result of initiatives from Beijing and China's provincial governors. From the 1870s to the early 1900s, the overseas elite were increasingly aware that consular representation was an effective strategy to protect their interests and enhance their status in the often hostile world outside China. The first attempts at founding a Qing consulate in Manila were initiated not by Qing officials but by the local Chinese *cabecillas* who petitioned for protection. In Manila as elsewhere, the motives for overseas elite activism were both environmentally specific and conditioned by personal ambition and self-interest.

The appeal of a Qing consulate in Manila lay in the fact that a consul would have the official sanction of both Beijing and Madrid. Presumably, this dual recognition would give the consul an added measure of influence, legitimacy, and linkage to China that existing institutions, such as the Gobernadorcillo, were lacking. The consular movement was also an elite campaign designed to promote community solidarity. This solidarity, however, was not based on consensus or cultural affinity but was a unity conceived and controlled by the community's elite and exercised through institutions and migration networks. Although the position was new in the sense that the consul would be the official representative of one sovereign nation to another, his value for the Chinese elite lay primarily in the fact that the consul could further personal, local, and community interests. This role in turn raised the possibility that *cabecilla* influence over the consulate could be construed as private ambitions cloaked as public service.

Although attempts to establish a Chinese consular presence in the 1880s had failed, in 1898 the *cabecilla* petitioners were finally successful. It should come as little surprise, therefore, that local perceptions of the role of the consulate general and the early history of the office would be profoundly influenced by the dynamics of elite leadership within the Chinese community and especially by the actions of the dominant *cabecilla*, Don Carlos Palanca Chen Qianshan, and his vocal and well-connected adversaries. Chen Qianshan was the preeminent member of the community in the late nineteenth century, and he was the central figure in the campaigns to establish a Qing consulate in Manila. From the beginning, elite participation in the drive to establish a consulate hinged on their desire to maintain the community's institutional cohesion, which in turn would perpetuate their elite status and enhance their rapport with external sources of authority. This pattern of elite dynamics was a proven strategy for asserting and maintaining elite status in the Spanish Philippines.

Chen Qianshan was a skilled practitioner of the full range of *cabecilla* strategies, which gave him status within the Chinese community and an extensive network of external allies. His motives for taking an active role in this campaign and the methods he employed had a profound impact on the early history of China's first consulate in the

FIGURE 2. Don Carlos
Palanca Chen Qian-
shan. Huang Xiao-
cang, ed. *Feilübin
Minlila Zhonghua
shanghui sanshi zhou-
nian jinian kan.*
Manila: Zhonghua
Shanghui Chubanbu,
1936.

Philippines. Chen opportunistically coopted the consular campaign
to defend and enhance his position as the dominant *cabecilla* of his day
and to further the interests of the Hokkien majority. His actions were
dictated by his personal experience as a migrant and his rise to
*cabecilla* status, and thus by his understanding of the importance of official connections in migration to and success in the colonial Philippines. In part, the appeal to Beijing represented Chen's desire to emphasize his importance within the community by advertising his
linkages to external sources of authority in the face of intracommunity rivals. But what was perhaps most important about a Chinese consulate and what explains the consistent *cabecilla* activism was not protection or prestige, but paper. Virtually all the Chinese in the
late-nineteenth-century Philippines had been required to gain appropriate documentation from the Spanish consulate in Xiamen. In fact,
many in the consular corps at Xiamen were themselves in the business

of recruiting and exporting Hokkien labor.[1] The *cabecilla* elite would therefore have been intimately familiar with the foreign consular presence in Xiamen and in Manila, and eminently aware of the value of consuls in facilitating migration. A Chinese consul in Manila would have jurisdiction over Chinese migration to and from China, and would issue and validate those pieces of paper—visas and passports— that were critical to the success of migration networks, which in turn were the cornerstone of *cabecilla* wealth and power.

## A Nineteenth-Century Chinese *Cabecilla*

Chen Qianshan was the archetype of a late-nineteenth-century Chinese *cabecilla*.[2] He was also one of an elite group of Southeast Asian Chinese who walked the fine line between his Chinese identity and his service to colonial governments. He is one of the few local Chinese elite, such as Tan Kah Kee, Yap Ah Loy, Hoo Ah Kay, Lin Kunhe, and Jan Con, who played such a critical role in both the colonial enterprise and Chinese history that they filled nodal roles at points of convergence between local, national, and regional histories. For the historian, they are rich subjects, because their transnational prominence leaves enough of an archival record to provide for a nuanced portrayal of their interests and inclinations.[3]

Born on June 6, 1844, in Tongan County near the border of Zhangzhou and Quanzhou prefectures in Fujian, Chen claimed to have grown up poor and illiterate but to have taught himself to read and write. Given what John Omohundro has described as a Chinese propensity to "exaggerate and romanticize the randomness of their own biographies," one may want to question some of the Algeresque details of Chen's life.[4] When he was twelve, a bit younger than the average Chinese migrant, he embarked for Manila. Through Hokkien migration networks, Chen was hired on as an apprentice in a relative's draper business.[5] According to Omohundro's analysis of Chinese migration systems, the fact that Chen migrated at such a young age indicates that the migration network he traversed was well established in Manila and could therefore explain his very rapid rise to wealth and prominence.[6] Within a few years of his arrival, through hard work, frugal living, mastery of Spanish, and the assistance of friends from his home county, Chen had established his own business.[7] By the 1870s, while still in his twenties, Chen had prospered and secured a place within the ranks of the *cabecillas*. Chen's ascension to *cabecilla* status came at the same time that the *chinos* were expanding into retail and agricultural exports.

Chen Qianshan was initially successful in textiles but soon diversified. He was involved in agricultural brokerage, moneylending, running the cockfighting and opium monopolies, operating retail and import-export operations, and he invested widely in Chinese businesses throughout the Manila area while expanding his agent network and investments into the provinces. Chen was also a major coolie broker and a tax collector for the Spanish, two positions that gave him access to coercive force.[8] All of Chen's business ventures were in industries that relied heavily on *invernado* manpower, and thus he would have needed to control or have access to numerous migration networks to supply talent. Although no accurate figures exist for Chen's net worth at any specific time, he was considered by many to be the wealthiest of the *cabecillas* and was reputed to have paid 68,000 pesos per year for the license to operate the largest of the great cockfighting arenas *(galleras)* in Manila.[9] Based on court records relating to some of his peers, who left estates of 600,000 and 700,000 pesos, it is reasonable to imagine that Don Carlos was worth well in excess of one million pesos, or half a million U.S. dollars.[10] Moreover, given the transnational nature of Hokkien migration networks, Chen's wealth and power in the Philippines translated to influence in southern Fujian, to which he sent his sons to be educated and from which he cultivated protégés. In essence he and the other *cabecillas* were both a transnational and a translocal elite, playing critical roles in two localities within the territories of two empires.[11] Chen's prominence in Manila made him prominent in the sending villages of Zhangzhou and Quanzhou as the facilitator of out-migration, and his wealth and success in Manila were inseparable from his ties to those sending villages.

In the Chinese community, however, wealth and business connections alone were insufficient to justify social position. Consequently, Chen engaged in conspicuous acts of charity, presumably to enhance his elite status. He helped to found and took a leadership position in the main Chinese charitable organization, the Comunidad de Chinos (Shanju Gongsuo), raised funds for the Chinese hospital, and donated land for a Chinese cemetery.[12] Chen gained further renown for his skills as a mediator, resolving disputes within the Chinese community and filing lawsuits on behalf of his fellow expatriates, and serving as advocate *(abogado)* for Chinese appearing before Spanish courts.[13] Chen even supported the founding of a Chinese newspaper in Manila.[14] In the cultural realm, despite his own lack of formal education, Chen sent his son Chen Ziyan, who is commonly referred to as Chen Gang, to be educated in China and aided him in the purchase of an official rank.[15] The son later served as the first Chinese consul general in Manila and was able to secure the honorary title of Grand Master for Splendid Happiness (guanglu dafu) for his father.[16]

As did many of his peers, Chen Qianshan enhanced his influence with the Spanish by converting to Catholicism in the 1860s under the auspices of a powerful padrino, Colonel Carlos Palanca y Gutierrez, whose name he adopted.[17] Sponsored conversion gave Chen access to a network of vertical and horizontal connections that in time allowed him to expand his trade and social contacts, and made him eligible to become a naturalized Spanish subject. Chen became a subject of the Crown and received honors from both Madrid and Malacañang in recognition of his years of meritorious service to the Spanish colonial enterprise.[18]

By the 1870s, Chen Qianshan was poised to become one of the most powerful and influential Chinese in the Philippines. In 1875, at the age of thirty-one, he converted his business and religious connections into political capital when he was elected Gobernadorcillo de los Sangleyes. Wang Gungwu has suggested that Chen's native place, Tongan Xian, on the border between Zhangzhou and Quanzhou prefectures, made him an ideal compromise candidate for Chinese headman.[19] Chen's family connections and networks probably extended across the Zhang-Quan boundary and could have been leveraged to mediate disputes between rival Hokkiens. In sharp contrast to the subethnic feuds between Zhangzhou and Quanzhou natives on Taiwan, it was not until after Chen Qianshan's death that there were any significant intra-Hokkien feuds in the Philippines, and even those were short-lived. Apparently, Hokkien identities in Manila were not as finely stratified as on Taiwan, and the economic environment in Manila encouraged cohabitation and cooperation between the various Hokkien native places, whereas competition and residence patterns sharpened distinctions between Zhang and Quan on Taiwan.[20] Don Carlos consistently identified his constituency as either Min (pronounced "Bam" in Hokkien, meaning from the Min River region), or Zhang-Quan, referring to the two dominant sending prefectures in the Xiamen district. The organizations that he and his elite peers controlled were in turn dominated by these groups. To be one of the Chinese merchant elite in colonial Manila, therefore, meant that one was obliged to protect and further the interests of this group.

Just before Chen's election, the Gobernadorcillo's responsibilities had expanded and his power had increased. The headman's growing authority was largely due to the skill and drive of the men who occupied the post. Chen Qianshan continued this forceful leadership. As Gobernadorcillo, Chen was the officially recognized tax collector, chief executive, and chief jurist for the entire Chinese community and was the spokesman for the Chinese in all relations with the Spanish government: a role enhanced by his personal connections to the Spanish. He was also in charge of the Gremio de Chinos, the Tribunal de los Sangleyes, and the Shanju Gongsuo.[21]

Over the next quarter century Chen formally held the post of Gobernadorcillo three times (1875–1877, 1885, and 1894) and served as interim headman on two other occasions. Even when not in office, he was widely believed to maintain significant influence over the Gobernadorcillo and in the Tribunal de los Sangleyes and was a favorite choice as *abogado*.[22] The Spanish authorities were aware of the growing power of the Gobernadorcillo and the Gremio and initially sought to control them by appointing Chinese lieutenants, who would oversee the Chinese communities in the islands and be responsible to the Spanish and not the Gremio. This campaign, however, could not shake the entrenched and closely guarded power of the Gremio de Chinos or the elite that controlled it.[23] Although the Gobernadorcillo/Gremio system had been imposed on them, the *cabecillas* had made it their own.

Understandably, Chen Qianshan was a controversial figure in the Philippines. His wealth, social and political connections, and prominence were respected by many but feared and criticized by others. Chen's critics attacked his political and economic influence in many forms. In the novel *El Filibusterismo*, written by José Rizal in 1891, the character of Quiroga the Chinaman, based on Chen, is a tacky and duplicitous opportunist. In the words of Benedict Anderson, Rizal (a European-educated *mestizo sangley*) was the first to "imagine" Filipino identity in literary form.[24] In his brilliant novels *Noli Me Tangere* and *El Fili*, the progenitor of Philippine nationalism railed against the oppression of the Spanish and their collaborators, and in the process sought to invent or define a Filipino identity in opposition to *chinos, peninsulares,* and *frailes* (friars). The extensive excerpt below is illustrative of a popular impression of the Chinese headman and a vivid description, albeit baroque, of Manila high society.

That night Quiroga the Chinaman, who was hoping to open a consulate of his country in Manila, was giving a dinner at his residence. His party was very well attended and had drawn friars, bureaucrats, officers, merchants, all his customers, partners and patrons; for his shop supplied the parishes and convents with all they needed, allowed all government employees to open accounts. The friars themselves were not above spending hours in his shop, sometimes in full view of the public, and at other times in inner chambers in agreeable company. . . .

Dressed as a mandarin with a blue-tasseled cap Quiroga strolled from one room to another, erect and grave, although not without alert glances here and there as if to make sure that nobody pocketed anything. In spite of this instinctive distrust he exchanged hand-clasps with all and sundry, greeted some with a courteous and deferential smile, others with a protective air, and still others with a certain contempt that seemed to say:

"I know, you come not for me but for my dinner."

And Quiroga had every reason to think so. The stout gentleman who now sang the praises of his host and spoke of the advisability of opening a Chinese consulate in Manila, suggesting at the same time that the post could not be filled by anyone other than Quiroga, was the same Mr. Gonzalez who under the pen-name of Pitili attacked Chinese immigration in the press. Another, frowning over unkempt moustaches, was a government official who was considered to be the worthiest of office because he had courage to criticize the deals in lottery tickets between Quiroga and a lady in the highest social circles. Indeed one-half, if not two-thirds, of the lottery tickets were finding their way to China and the few that were available in Manila could not be bought without a premium. This worthy bureaucrat was sure that he would some day win the first prize and was infuriated by the thought of being frustrated by such dodges.

The dinner was coming to an end. Snatches of toasts, bellows of laughter, interruptions, guffaws reached the reception room from the dining-room; the name of Quiroga was heard again and again coupled with the words "consul," "equality," "rights."[25]

When Quiroga is unable to repay a substantial debt to one of his guests (the subversive Simoun), the guest offers the "future consul" a way out of this predicament.

> "Well, look here," Simoun continued in a whisper. "I want you to get through Customs some crates full of guns which have arrived tonight and I want you to keep them in your warehouse; I cannot keep them all in my house."
>
> Quiroga took alarm.
>
> "Don't worry. You are not running any risks. These guns are to be planted in certain houses from time to time; then there will be searches, many will be thrown in gaol, and you and I can make a lot of money to get them out again. Understand?"
>
> Quiroga hesitated. . . .
>
> "If you can't do it I shall go to someone else, but then I shall be needing my nine thousand pesos to grease palms and keep eyes shut."
>
> "All right, all right," Quiroga finally agreed. "But you get many peoples in gaol, you make searches soon, eh?"[26]

Despite these nefarious activities, or perhaps as a direct result of them, Quiroga is recognized as one of the most powerful men in the Philippines and one whose personal connections transcended ethnic divisions in local society. He was a force with which to be reckoned.[27] It would be tempting to conclude from this novel of the early 1890s that Rizal was conveying a general *indio* and *mestizo* antipathy toward the Chinese. In fact, despite the foreshadowing of later nationalistic sentiments, Rizal's portrayal of Quiroga was designed to incite an awareness of *chino* as alien "other" among a population that had not yet drawn such stark dichotomies between national identities.

Nonetheless, many of Rizal's criticisms of Chen/Quiroga were echoed by others in Manila. The justice dispensed by the Tribunal de los Sangleyes, in which Chen played a major role, was defined by one American broker as "rotten to the core."[28] But many of Chen Qianshan's most powerful enemies were fellow Chinese, in particular Cantonese *cabecillas* who accused him of misappropriating charity funds, buying favors from Spanish officials, bullying migrants, and blackmailing Chinese prisoners.[29] Enemies and critics notwithstanding, Chen Qianshan was the most prominent *chino* of his time; and his wealth and social standing made him the paramount *cabecilla*.

It was in his role as recognized leader of the Chinese community that Chen worked to convince Beijing to establish a consulate in the Philippines. As early as the 1880s, Chen and his fellow *cabecillas* petitioned Beijing and approached Liangguang governor-general Zhang Zhidong and Ambassador Zhang Yinhuan in the hope of securing their support. In these petitions, Chen and the other *cabecillas* argued for the establishment of a consulate to protect them from dangers to their economic and physical well-being and presumably to gain standing through links to the "homeland." The first consular campaign, in the 1880s, coincided with the appearance of potent anti-Chinese sentiment in local newspapers and literature that criticized the Chinese domination of the economy and sought to restrict Chinese in-migration. At the same time, the Spanish were also increasing taxes for the wealthiest segment of the Chinese community.[30] These anti-Chinese campaigns were short-lived and rarely posed a physical threat to the Chinese. Danger to life and property, however, increased dramatically in the context of the crises that occurred from the 1880s onward. In an environment of disease, banditry, rebellion, urban crime, and a declining export sector, redundant access to authority seemed essential. These forces posed the greatest danger to the Chinese community, because they were beyond the control of its leadership and, more important, because they were apparently beyond the control of their Spanish allies. The Chinese elite responded by turning to another government for protection.[31]

Chen Qianshan played a complicated role in these campaigns and authored petitions sent during all the phases of the consular movement. As a community leader, Chen was required to participate if the movement was to succeed. However, suspicions about Chen's motives for participating in the campaign and about the Hokkien elite in general would have a profound effect on the early history of the consulate and delay its recognition by the United States.

## The Founding of the Chinese Consulate General

Although the attempts at founding a consulate in the 1880s had failed because of Spanish resistance and lack of consistent support from the Qing government, the Chinese elite continued to explore the option and to petition the Qing government. Petitions were particularly numerous when Spanish policy seemed to be turning against the Chinese. For example, in the fall of 1889 and the summer

of 1890, Don Carlos petitioned the Zongli Yamen, requesting a review of Spanish taxation and residence policies and the recent rein-
stitution of a ban on Chinese practicing medicine in the Philippines.
Chen criticized these policies as cruel, petty, and harmful to the economic well-being of the Chinese and asked that the yamen try to convince the Spanish government to overturn them and allow the establishment of a Chinese consulate. The Zongli Yamen responded by
forwarding the petitions to its minister to the United States, Spain,
and Peru, Cui Guoyin, and to Vice-Minister Peng Guangyu, presumably to discuss the matter with the Spanish court; however, nothing
came of this request.[32] Over the succeeding years, the evanescence of
anti-Chinese polemics in the Philippine press and a brief recovery
from the economic slump of the late 1880s seemed to calm the fears
of local Chinese, and their ardor for a consulate abated. In any case,
the number of correspondences declined significantly between 1890
and 1896.[33]

When in 1896 a revolt against Spanish rule was imminent and
foreign trade was in sharp decline, the *cabecillas* tried again to take
advantage of Governor-General Li Hongzhang's visit to Europe
(once again demonstrating their awareness of political issues) by be-
seeching the powerful viceroy to pressure the equivocating Spanish
to allow the transfer of the Chinese consul in Cuba to Manila in order to protect the Chinese from violence and the inequities of Spanish rule.[34] In response to this memorial, the vice-minister to Spain,
Ying Zuyang, devised a creative plan to force the Spanish to allow a
Chinese consulate in the Philippines. Ying pointed out that the Spanish had only allowed China to establish one consulate in their empire, that being in Cuba, while China had granted them permission
to set up seven in its territory. The vice-minister went on to suggest
that, if the Spanish did not assent to an additional office in the
Philippines, the Chinese government should then shame them by
only recognizing one Spanish consulate in their empire.[35] As in the
1880s, the focus of this debate continued to revolve around protecting the economic well-being of the local Chinese. This situation,
however, changed dramatically in late 1896.

From 1896 to 1899, *cabecillas* were in regular correspondence
with Beijing, the governors and governors-general of Liangguang
and Fu-Zhe, as well as with Chinese ministers overseas. For much of
this period, the elite were concerned as much with their physical
safety as with their economic condition.[36] This renewed interest was

precipitated by the chaotic events that characterized the last years of Spanish rule in the Philippines, specifically the economic crisis, the Katipunan revolt in 1896, and the Spanish-American War. As with the other forces beyond their immediate control, the Chinese *cabecillas* responded to this challenge by seeking assistance and protection from Beijing. For the Chinese merchant elite, the attraction of the consulate lay in the added sanction granted by the emperor; but it did not mean that they were willing to sacrifice their dominant position in the local community. Instead, they sought to enhance their status through representation by an imperial official. After all, it was the *cabecillas'* activism that would ultimately found the consulate, and it was they who had the most to gain by the installation of a consul who was sympathetic to their needs and who would employ them as consular staff.

## The Katipunan Revolt

Two forces converged in the late Spanish Philippines: agrarian unrest and nascent nationalism. While the rebellion of 1896 was essentially a peasant revolt led by petty agrarian elites, it had the veneer of a war of national liberation under the nominal leadership of the nationalist Katipunan Society. For years, a narrow segment of wealthy and foreign-educated *indios* and *mestizos (ilustrados)* had been advocating reform of the Spanish administration and the end of the provincial friarocracy. Meanwhile, the Spanish and the friars had become increasingly paranoid about rebellion and, drawing lessons from the suppression of the Cuban uprising, brutally repressed whatever *ilustrado* activism they could find. This pacification campaign was typified by the public execution of the prominent reform activist and author José Rizal, the wanton slaughter of those suspected of sedition, and the arrest and exile of four hundred suspected *katipuneros.* In response, *ilustrados* and provincial elites seized on peasant unrest in the Manila hinterland in a vain attempt to wrest independence from Spain. War was declared in August of 1896. When reinforcements arrived from Spain and Cuba, the Spanish response was violent and destructive but in the long term generally successful in putting down the insurrection.[37]

In the near term, however, there was a significant twofold threat to the lives and property of local Chinese. Lacking even the rudiments of logistics, finance, and supply, insurgents periodically seized

Chinese stores and merchandise. Chinese *tenderos* in the Manila hinterland were directly in the path of the chaos, a cause of great concern for their *cabecilla* patrons. The *insurectos* pressed Chinese merchants for donations and impressed Chinese laborers into service in
rebel armies. In some cases the Filipinos went so far as to murder
Chinese merchants if they were not forthcoming with their support.[38] It should be added, however, that with rebellion came general
chaos in the provinces. Much of the violence against Chinese *tenderos*
was therefore random and not part of a coordinated rebel strategy.
To credit the insurrection with a coherent policy of anti-Sinicism
would be entirely too generous to the *insurectos* by averring that they
were themselves a coherent movement or that they possessed a fully
articulated sense of national identity. Such a portrayal would be ahistorical, especially considering the importance of Chinese money and
labor to sustaining the insurgents. A second threat was posed by the
panicked Spanish, who, seeking to crush the rebellion, demanded
the services of the Chinese but apparently did not offer them ade-
quate protection. The relations that the Chinese *cabecillas* had so
carefully cultivated with the Spanish authorities failed to protect
them in the crisis. Rather than promoting economic development,
the Spanish were now more concerned with suppressing the revolt
and controlling the insurgents, but apparently they lacked the resources and organization to do either. Faced with these dangers, the
Chinese elite exercised their other option and sent numerous petitions to the Qing government.

In November 1896, the Guangdong *huiguan,* the apical Cantonese association, appealed to the governor-general of Guangdong
and Guangxi provinces, Tan Zhonglin. The Cantonese were concerned that Spanish military resources were inadequate to protect
them from the rebels. Tan forwarded the Cantonese petitions to the
Zongli Yamen. As a temporary solution to the problem of providing
the Chinese with diplomatic representation without running up
against Madrid's apparent aversion to a Chinese consulate in Manila,
Tan suggested that the consul of a friendly government be asked to
take responsibility for protecting the Chinese.[39] Apparently unbe-
knownst to the governor-general, this option was already being ex-
amined in Beijing.

On November 21, 1896, the Zongli Yamen received two petitions
from Chen Qianshan representing the Chinese *cabecillas*. The first
petition claimed that the insurgents had become increasingly lawless

and were intending to massacre the Chinese. Chen explained that this dire state of affairs had come about because he had been approached by the Spanish, who wanted to hire coolies to transport military supplies. Chen felt trapped. Without an official with authority wider than the Gremio to represent them, it would be difficult to decline the Spanish requisition without angering the authorities. If they assented, however, the anger of the rebels would turn on the *chinos* for aiding their enemies. Chen also related that Chinese in the provinces had been forced to scatter and that rebels were looting their *tiendas*.[40] Clearly, Chen's hesitation to cooperate with the Spanish, although he was a Spanish subject, indicates that he felt that the Spanish were not capable of putting down the rebellion or adequately protecting the Chinese.

The second petition stated that Chen had been in communication with the Chinese ambassador to the United States, Spain, and Peru, Yang Ru, and had beseeched him to explore the possibility of seeking representation from the consul of a friendly government. This petition argued that, since they had no official to protect them, the merchants would suffer harm at the hands of unruly rebel bands. Minister Yang thereupon instructed Chen to approach the British consul and ask that he take temporary responsibility for the Chinese. This strategy also had the support of the Liangguang governor-general and eventually the Zongli Yamen, which agreed with Minister Yang's plan and ordered the news transmitted to the Chinese elite.[41] The Spanish foreign ministry responded that this plan was unnecessary, because the forces they had recently dispatched to the islands were sufficient to guarantee the physical safety of the Chinese, a task the Spanish saw as their responsibility.[42] The Zongli Yamen apparently ignored Spain's protests, and, for the time being, the Chinese in the Philippines had a protector in the person of the British consul, a result that gave the Zongli Yamen reason to be grateful to Great Britain.[43]

Chen Qianshan's petition had succeeded in getting a measure of protection for his countrymen, but he was not to serve as the intermediary between the Chinese community and the British consul. Instead that role was filled by another prominent *cabecilla*, the Cantonese Yang Shude. Chen apparently was not a good choice, because his close relations with the Spanish would have precluded his objectivity. Yang Shude was, moreover, far from an ally of Chen Qianshan and criticized him harshly in his memorials to the Zongli Yamen.

Among the accusations leveled at Chen was that he was extorting money from Chinese who had been caught in a gambling raid to secure their freedom.[44] This was in spite of the fact that the British consul had already negotiated their release. According to Yang Shude, Chen Qianshan was unhappy about British representation and had only attached his name to the petition because he was pressured by the other *cabecillas*. Yang further claimed that Chen was opposed to having the British consul speak for the Chinese, because it would be an infringement on his personal power. This power, he wrote, had been secured by toadying to the Spanish governor-general and by using Chinese community funds to bribe Spanish officials. Yang portrayed Chen Qianshan as caring little for the safety of the local Chinese and claimed that he was only interested in manipulating and extorting them to his own personal ends.[45] The conflict between Chen and Yang was symptomatic of a growing rift between the Cantonese and Hokkien *cabecillas*. In fact, the Cantonese *cabecillas* and the Guangdong *huiguan* frequently petitioned separately through the Liangguang governor-general, while the Hokkiens, led by Chen Qianshan, sent their correspondence directly to the Zongli Yamen, to China's ambassadors, or to officials in Fujian Province. The *cabecillas* were competing to speak for the community, because, in their experience, those who spoke for the community controlled the community. Provincial factionalism became one of the dominant characteristics of the consular campaign. Hokkien-Cantonese competition also went deeper than local and localist rivalries. Migration networks are routed through "bottlenecks," where privileged access to authority is the critical commodity in facilitating one's own network. Consuls, with their ability to issue and validate the paperwork of migration, were therefore invaluable allies. Good relations with the British consul, which the Cantonese clearly had, could in turn translate, through the consul's own network, into ease of migration through the British Crown colony at Hong Kong, the "bottleneck" of Cantonese migration.[46] In addition to challenging Chen himself, Yang Shude might have been trying to crack the labor system that was the foundation of Hokkien dominance.

The Zongli Yamen seems to have ignored this conflict within the community and, instead, concentrated on exploiting the opportunity presented by the Katipunan Revolt to renegotiate its treaty with Spain. Specifically, Qing officials were looking to take advantage of Spain's preoccupation with the uprisings in Cuba and the Philippines to gain concessions. The Sino-Spanish treaty was up for renewal in May 1897, and the yamen ordered Minister Yang to pursue a renegotiation that would eliminate many of the inequities in the existing treaty. In particular, the yamen insisted that the Qing government's right to establish a consulate in the Philippines be clearly spelled out in the new treaty. In the opinion of the yamen, such an office was necessary to do away with the onerous Spanish taxation of the Chinese. The Spanish, however, continued to resist Beijing's proposals.[47] The Spanish resistance probably had its origin in the fear that, if they handed over control of the community to a Qing official, they would lose whatever influence they still had in the wealthy *chino* enclave, which was so critical to the colonial enterprise.

## The Spanish-American War

The final push for the formal establishment of a Chinese consulate in Manila coincided with the outbreak of the Spanish-American War in 1898. Even before the American Fleet under Admiral Dewey sailed into Manila Bay on May 1, 1898, the Chinese were already concerned with their safety. On April 24, 1898, Liangguang governor-general Tan again raised the suggestion that, in the approaching hostilities between the United States and Spain, since there were no Chinese officials or troops to protect the *chinos,* the government should again ask the British consul to step in.[48] The Zongli Yamen agreed and on April 26 sent a request to Her Britannic Majesty's minister in Beijing, who quickly agreed.[49] The Zongli Yamen then ordered Governor-General Tan to relay that information to the Chinese *cabecillas* via a "charitable organization," presumably the Communidad de Chinos.[50] Chen Qianshan was specifically ordered to discuss this matter with the British consul and to collect funds from among the *cabecillas* to supplement the police budget.[51] In the midst of this correspondence, the yamen was informed on April 27 by the American minister plenipotentiary that a state of war existed between Spain and the United States.[52]

British consular representation was not, however, sufficient for Chen and the Hokkien *cabecillas*. In July, the Zongli Yamen received another petition from Don Carlos in which he asked why, if the Chinese were supposed to be accorded most-favored-nation treatment by the Spanish, and the other much less numerous foreigners living in the islands had consular representation, the Chinese were excluded and hence open to mistreatment by the Spanish troops sent

to fight in the islands. Moreover, he asked why so many Chinese officials had been involved in attempting to establish a Manila consulate
over so many years without success. Chen beseeched the yamen to try
to convince the Spanish, yet again, and offered to cover the set-up
costs for a consulate, an offer the *cabecillas* had also made in prior petitions.[53] Actually, the yamen was already pursuing this possibility and
had ordered Wu Tingfang, the new minister to the United States,
Spain, and Peru, to broach the subject with the Spanish court.[54]

Despite some initial hesitation, the Spanish government finally
relented and in July gave Beijing permission to establish a consulate
temporarily in Manila. Ironically, Manila, although nominally in
Spanish hands, was under siege from the sea by Dewey's fleet and on
land by Filipino troops under Emilio Aguinaldo, who had declared
Philippine independence in early June.[55] Perhaps by this time the
Spanish court was so disheartened by the humiliating series of defeats it had suffered that it hardly cared about the Chinese request.
Regardless, after several decades and hundreds of correspondences,
the Chinese in the Philippines would finally have Chinese consular
representation.

On July 28, 1898, the Zongli Yamen advised the Spanish minister
in Beijing and the Spanish governor-general of the Philippines that
they had selected Chen Gang, a middle-level secretary in the Grand
Secretariat, to serve as China's first consul general in the Philippines.
Chen, twenty-nine years old at the time, seemed an excellent choice
for consul. He was a Hokkien who had lived in the Philippines, where
he went by the name Engracio Palanca, son of Don Carlos Palanca
Chen Qianshan.[56] Chen Gang was notified of his posting on the same
day and was ordered to proceed to Manila, whereupon he was to un-
dertake the protection of the Chinese, engage in negotiations with
local officials, and report back to the yamen.[57]

Chen Gang's arrival in the Philippines, however, was delayed.
First, although the Spanish foreign ministry had given its approval,
the Spanish governor-general withheld permission, probably because
he had other issues to deal with at the time or perhaps because Ad-
miral Dewey had severed the telegraph cable between Manila and
Hong Kong. Second, Chen had to wait for the American blockade of
Manila to be lifted. As a result, Chen's departure was delayed until
September of 1898, and in the interim his father was appointed act-
ing consul.[58] By September, Manila had already fallen to the United
States, and Major General Elwell Otis had taken up duties as military

governor-general.[59] Therefore, the yamen now had to negotiate with the American departments of War and State, although as a courtesy it continued to keep the Spanish minister in Beijing informed of developments.[60] On September 10, 1898, the yamen learned that Minister Wu had the approval of the State Department for the dispatch of Chen Gang as consul.[61]

Armed with this knowledge, in September 1898, the Zongli Yamen memorialized to the throne its proposal for establishing a consulate in Manila with Chen Gang, now an upper-level secretary of the Board of Punishments, as consul general.[62] The memorial included information on the conditions affecting the Chinese in the archipelago, the dangers they were facing during the current hostilities, and the role of Chen Qianshan and the *cabecillas* in petitioning for the establishment of a consulate. On September 14, only days before he was to be forced out of power by the empress dowager in the coup that ended the Hundred Days Reform, the Guangxu emperor gave his approval to the plan, and the Manila consulate general became an official reality.[63] It is surprising that, in the midst of the tumult of 1898, both the Zongli Yamen and the court were paying as much attention to the Philippines and to the Chinese overseas as they were. Moreover, in contrast to common portrayals of the Hundred Days as a total failure, some small but substantive progress was made.[64] The Manila consulate general may not have been a major diplomatic achievement, but it did create an institutional link through which all subsequent governments of China would communicate with the Chinese in the Philippines.

As of late 1898, Chen Gang had not yet arrived at his post, although he had been sent his official seals and again been instructed that it was the responsibility of his office to protect the Chinese.[65] Chen was also informed by Beijing that his first duty upon arriving in Manila was to prevent General Otis from extending the American exclusion laws to the Philippines, thereby complicating Chinese entry and reentry.[66] Otis felt that, because "the Chinaman can outwit the Filipino" and because of an "active race enmity" between Chinese and Filipinos, the importation of Chinese labor was detrimental to what would later be known as the "Philippines for Filipinos" policy.[67] This was a critical issue and one of which Beijing was apparently aware. Thousands of Chinese had fled the chaos and returned to Xiamen and the *qiaoxiang* of southern Fujian to await a resolution to the crisis. Some regularized system of allowing the migrants to return and to facilitate the influx of new arrivals had to be arranged instead of the blanket ban that the Americans were contemplating. Such a ban was certainly not in the interest of the *cabecillas,* and it would have been detrimental to the Chinese coastal economy as well. Capital and provincial officials were demonstrating a growing awareness of the importance of the Manila trade, especially the continued influx of silver from Manila. Because of the depth of *qiaoxiang* linkages between southern Fujian and Manila, and the importance of Xiamen as a regional node, the prosperity of the coastal economy was important to Qing officialdom.[68] Any disruption in either trade or migration would have ripple effects that demanded the attention of imperial officials, who were increasingly looking to merchants and commerce.

Meanwhile in Manila, Chen Qianshan was still temporarily in charge of the consulate that had been set up in the offices of the Gobernadorcillo and the Tribunal de los Sangleyes. While in office, the elder Chen established a fee schedule for the issuance of the all-important Chinese passports and collected funds for the Chinese hospital operated by the Communidad de Chinos.[69] A hospital was essential given that there were simultaneous outbreaks of bubonic plague and cholera in Tondo and Binondo, and the death rate among coolies and craftsmen also required an expansion of the Chinese cemetery. Chen, however, was apparently not happy with his position and on October 10 submitted a general petition describing the conditions of the Chinese, expressing gratitude to the Qing government for its benevolent attitude toward its overseas subjects but also voicing reservations about his suitability to act as consul. In a fit of self-deprecation, he claimed that being a merchant for many years meant that he was familiar with trade but was unsuited to filling the office of consul more than temporarily. He beseeched the yamen to speed the arrival of the new consul.[70]

After leaving Beijing in late August and being waylaid in Shanghai and Xiamen by a bout of fever, Chen Gang finally arrived in Manila in January 1899, whereupon he immediately took up his duties as consul general.[71] Chen's term as China's first Philippine consul would, however, be far from routine.[72] Two days after his arrival in Manila, Chen's mother died. This sad event raised the possibility that Chen would be required to leave office to observe the requisite period of mourning. The Chen family was also informed that Washington would not recognize Chen Gang as Chinese consul general.[73] Apparently, General Otis had sent a dispatch to the State Department in which he presented complaints raised against Chen Qianshan by Cantonese, English, and German merchants in the Philippines. It was the opinion of these merchants that Chen Gang was an inappropriate choice for Chinese consul because of the activities and reputation of his father. The English complained that the elder Chen was a Spanish subject who had been employed by the colonial government to collect taxes from the Chinese and had thereby enriched himself. Moreover, he had colluded with other *cabecillas* to form monopolies and to embezzle funds from the Chinese community. Such a man would undoubtedly try to use his connections to circumvent the American ban on the importation of Chinese coolies to corner the labor market. If Chen's son were to serve as consul, they wrote, the father would control the office and continue his nefarious practices. The Cantonese, in turn, echoing the charges made by Yang Shude three years earlier, complained that Chen Qianshan had used the excuse of funding the Chinese hospital to wring money out of them without giving an accurate accounting, had collected a head tax, had arrogated to himself the power and authority of headman, and had otherwise abused the Chinese.[74] In other words, Don Carlos had used his public *(gong)* roles for private *(si)* gain.

The Chen family was not without its supporters. The Zongli Yamen and the United States government received counterpetitions requesting that Chen Gang be ordered to remain in his post, because he was needed to protect the Chinese from economic and physical harm in the approaching hostilities between the Americans and the resurgent rebels, and stating that the dispatch of a new and inexperienced consul would only complicate matters.[75] A fellow Hokkien *cabecilla* composed a lengthy defense of the Chens. Cai Zishen explained that the elder Chen's prominence in the community and his efforts over the last thirty years to protect the Chinese had shown him to be a good man. He further informed the Zongli Yamen that these false accusations were all part of a conspiracy that was cooked up by the military governor; the acting British consul, H. A. Ramsden; and some Cantonese merchants.[76] Cai claimed that, although General Otis initially had no quarrel with Chen Qianshan, Don Carlos' firm resistance to the billeting of American troops in the headquarters of the Quanzhou and Zhangzhou *huiguan* had aroused the ire of the American governor. General Otis, having a good relationship with the British consul, conspired with him to have some Cantonese present a false accusation against the Chen family. Furthermore, Cai explained that the Cantonese were involved because they had heard that Chen Gang's proposed replacement was a fellow Cantonese by the name of Li Rongyao (Li Yung Yew), who was currently serving as consul general in Cuba.[77] This accusation was later corroborated by the American consul, O. F. Williams, who determined that Li was also a personal friend of the British consul.[78] Cai Zishen warned the yamen against setting a poor precedent by removing Chen based on this personal attack. Cai was concerned some Hokkiens would use this as an excuse to make counteraccusations against the Cantonese consul at a later date, and the consul would then become more concerned with trying to protect himself than with protecting the Chinese.[79] Given the sophistication that the *cabecillas* consistently demonstrated, it seems likely that Cai was trying to play on the yamen's fears that the public good of a consulate would be undone by petty private squabbles. The yamen was clearly struggling with procedure and was caught in a conundrum. In contravention of the "rule of avoidance," Beijing had tried to coopt Chinese overseas by assigning fellow provincials as consuls. If they withdrew Chen Gang as a candidate, they were in danger of alienating the majority in Manila, but if they backed Chen, they would anger the Americans, all the while running the risk of having the consulate highjacked by private interests.

General Otis received a similar letter, which informed him that the Hokkien majority would be better served by a Hokkien consul. The petition, signed by dozens of local Chinese and three former Gobernadorcillos, reported that Hokkiens outnumbered Cantonese ten to one in the islands and that the recent charges against Chen Gang "simply served the ends of the enemies of the father."[80]

Despite this support, Chen Gang petitioned in March of 1899 to be relieved of his post so that he could observe a period of mourning for his late mother.[81] Chen remained in office through the spring of 1899 awaiting his replacement, Li Rongyao. During his brief tenure, Chen Gang witnessed the outbreak of hostilities between the Americans and the Filipinos. Caught in the cross fire, many Chinese shops, homes, and community buildings were destroyed. It fell to Chen to seek redress for the wrongs committed against the Chinese, give comfort to refugees, and raise funds to rebuild the Chinese hospital. On the more mundane side, Chen set up the physical and organizational structure for the consulate and arranged for the finances of that office to be collected through passport fees. He also assisted the Communidad de Chinos in founding the Anglo-Chinese school, offering foreign language, math, and science courses as well as instruction in the Confucian classics.[82] Yet, in spite of these notable accomplishments, the tenure of China's first consul in the Philippines came to an inglorious end with the arrival of his replacement in the spring of 1899.[83] After he resigned as Manila consul general, Chen Gang was reposted to Havana to fill the vacancy left by Li Rongyao.[84]

Even after his son's replacement, Chen Qianshan did not willingly relinquish his right to a voice in community affairs. Not one to be pushed aside easily, especially by a new consul with close ties to the Cantonese *cabecillas* and their ally the British consul, Chen fought back. Soon after Li Rongyao arrived at his post, he and Chen were involved in yet another controversy. The former Gobernadorcillo claimed that he had the right and the imperial sanction to issue passports to Chinese subjects residing in the islands. In a transnational migrant community—especially one to which American exclusion laws had just been applied—few things were more important than a valid passport.[85] To support his position, Chen blanketed Manila with wall posters that quoted his official appointment.

His excellency Hsu, minister of the Tsung-li Yamen, and Governor-General of the provinces of Fokien and Chekiang, being thoroughly acquainted with the condition of his subjects, petitioned H. M. the emperor to issue instructions to appoint a Chief of Department for protection of merchants, established at Amoy, and to authorize heads of committees at various points to establish branches of such departments for identification and protection.

I have therefore received proclamations and regulations for the purpose of enabling these people to return to their home-land in safety, and I have established a department and 24 committeemen, furnishing them with seals and forms of documents to be filled in, for the said purpose. . . .

All the natives of the prefectures of Chang and Chuan must not be fooled by him (Consul-General Li), and must beware. If you do what you should, you will not lose your baggage in going to China, but will receive protection at home. I, head of the committee, greatly hope this will be obeyed.

[Signed] Chen Chien-shien
Head of Department for Protection of Merchants in the Philippines[86]

Although Chen Gang had been ousted as consul general, Don Carlos nonetheless lobbied for the authority to issue critical travel documents for the Hokkien majority. Raising the possibility of losing baggage and of not receiving protection on their return to Zhangzhou and Quanzhou implied as well that the ability to move money back to the *qiaoxiang* would be compromised and that subsequent returns to Manila from Xiamen might be thwarted by inadequate documentation. Moreover, given that the number of committeemen mentioned was twenty-four, the same as the board of directors of the Communidad de Chinos, it would appear that Chen's bid to be "high muck-a-muck" as the *Manila Times* styled him, was backed by the Hokkien elite, who would have been equally concerned with the issuance of appropriate travel documents for themselves and their protégés.[87]

This publicity campaign provoked a response from Li Rongyao. The consul posted notices of his own that averred: "He [Chen], in having thus established a "Department" by false pretenses to extort money and cause public excitement, has regarded the law with supercilious and arrogant contempt, disregarding the authority of the law and doing just whatever he thinks it, without the slightest apprehension or scruple."[88]

In addition to the poster campaign and telegrams to both the Fu-Zhe governor-general and the Zongli Yamen, Li also approached his colleagues in the consular corps, who petitioned the American authorities on his behalf in hopes of forcing Chen to recant his claims. In the interests of protocol, the Americans assented, and Li's sole authority to represent the local Chinese was recognized.[89] Ultimately, however, a subsequent yamen investigation of the controversy early in 1900 decided the affair in favor of Chen.[90] Chen's repeated petitions against Consul General Li were answered by the dispatch of an investigative commission. According to the *Manila Times,* Chen Gang had used his influence with the Zongli Yamen to get the commissioner, Tan Lit Kang (Chen Ligang), sent to the Philippines under the pretext of investigating the activities of Kang Youwei's supporters in Manila; in actuality it was to build a case for the removal of Li. Li was reassigned to Madrid to serve as chargé d'affaires and Chen Gang was reinstated as interim consul general until the arrival of a permanent replacement, a fellow Hokkien, Cheng Ye-chiong (Zheng Yeqiong). Thus, even without official portfolio Don Carlos continued to play an active and prominent role in the community and through Chen Gang maintained a certain amount of influence with Chinese officialdom. Moreover, despite repeated protests that the Chen family's private interests had highjacked the consulate, Beijing ultimately recognized that the power of the consul was limited by his ability to compromise imperial aspirations with the interests of local elites. As such, subsequent consuls were generally conciliatory to majority elite interests, which were concerned primarily with local prosperity and the facilitation of migration networks, for which the consul's seal was invaluable.

The type of elite activism that Chen practiced so skillfully was all the more essential in the early American Philippines. There were numerous social, economic, and health crises in Manila. Overcrowding in Manila, as a result of the insurrection, had led to outbreaks of both bubonic plague and cholera in the city, especially in Binondo, which put great stress on the Chinese hospital and the cemetery.[91] In the face of epidemics, campaigns were launched by the military administration to crack down on the unsanitary Chinese shops of Binondo and Tondo and the unhygienic habits of local Chinese. These campaigns landed large numbers of Chinese in front of American judges for such infractions as well as for violations of the curfew and both the opium and gambling bans that came with martial law. Other new legislation, such as the ending of the revenue farms, displaced hundreds of Chinese workers, while at the same time the pressure on Chinese laborers was heightened by the logistical needs of the U.S. military, which relied heavily on coolies for the off-loading of cargoes at Manila and for the dangerous work of supplying troops in the field.[92] As a result there were numerous Chinese work stoppages in 1899 and 1900 that required elite mediation.[93] To complicate matters, critical changes in the immigration laws put even greater pressure on the managers of migration networks. There were also the political crises in China—coups, rumors that the Guangxu emperor had been either dethroned or murdered, and finally the Boxer Rebellion and foreign expedition—that concerned both the Chinese and the Americans. These pressures notwithstanding, the Chinese elite also raised over U.S.$3,000 for the Transvaal Widows and Orphans' Fund in gratitude for the British consul's protection during the Spanish-American War.[94]

For his part, Don Carlos continued to be locally active. He represented fellow Chinese in legal cases, thus continuing the role of *abogado* that he had played in the Tribunal de los Sangleyes, and he served briefly as vice-consul.[95] With his death in September 1901, community leadership passed to other *cabecillas,* many of whom, especially Don Carlos Palanca Tan Guing-lay (one of the most successful Chinese businessmen of the American period), had been protégés of the former Gobernadorcillo. Streets were named in Chen's honor, and his statue still graces the entrance to the Chinese cemetery he founded during the late-century epidemics. His daughter, Alejandra Palanca, married Emiliano Boncan, scion of another powerful Hokkien merchant family, who in turn intermarried with leading *mestizo* families, including the Limjaps, thus guaranteeing that a change in colonial regime did not mean a dramatic change in the elite. As for his son, after a brief reposting, Don Engracio Palanca Chen Gang returned to Manila in 1900 to serve as interim consul and continued to be prominent in the community. Like his father he served as advocate for fellow Chinese and as executor of Chinese estates. He was also given a subsequent post as collector of funds for famine relief in China.[96] In 1904–1905 Chen Gang and another *chino,* Zhang Zhongwei, led the Xiamen boycott of American goods to protest the U.S. Chinese exclusion policy. The boycott campaign in Xiamen was neither as large as those in Shanghai and Guangdong, nor was it closely coordinated with the main movement. Rather, it was a sympathetic but largely autonomous protest that brought together students and merchants—essentially the elite—in the port city. Nonetheless, the fact that Chen Gang was a leader of the Xiamen protest is a clear indication that he enjoyed elite status in both Manila and southern Fujian. Moreover, unlike the protesters in Shanghai and Guangdong, who opposed the American exclusion laws in their entirety and called for unregulated immigration, the Hokkiens specifically protested U.S. efforts to limit the regulated immigration of students, merchants, and craftsmen. Given the role of the Hokkien elite in managing exactly that type of migration to the American Philippines, such a difference in the tenor of the protests is not surprising.[97] As an apology to injured American pride, the Zhejiang-Fujian governor-general, Chongsan, suppressed the boycott and ordered Chen Gang cashiered and sent into exile, at which point it appears that he returned to Manila.[98]

## Conclusion

Elite status in the Manila-Chinese community during the late Spanish regime was as volatile as in mainland China, if not more so. The increasing rate of Chinese immigration (in particular the influx of Cantonese), economic opportunities and dangers, the rise of Filipino nationalism (economic and political), and Spanish colonial policy created instability in the community. In this critical time, the strategies the Chinese *cabecillas* employed to maintain their dominance within the community, while similar to those used by Chinese merchant elite in the major trading cities on the continent, were also the product of late Spanish colonial rule. Chen Qianshan, the supreme *cabecilla,* was the most skilled practitioner of these strategies. As such, in the life of Don Carlos one can see several points where Chinese, Spanish, Hokkien, and Manileño identities and strategies converged.

In many ways, Chen's life was a classic success story of the late Qing merchant elite. A poor migrant comes to a city ripe with economic opportunity and through hard work, connections, and savvy makes himself a fortune in trade. This wealth is converted into symbolic capital through charity, conspicuous consumption, and the affectation of an elite lifestyle, and into personal power through leadership positions in community associations and the forging of links to external authorities. Chen and his fellow Chinese *cabecillas* had an extensive and flexible repertoire of strategies for attaining and justifying their elite status. These strategies were well suited to life in the waning days of the Spanish colonial regime, when the limited Spanish ability to intrude in local society and the economy coupled with the Spanish government's hunger for revenue and an expansion in international trade opened tremendous opportunities for the Chinese.

Growing anti-Chinese sentiment, revolution, plague, pestilence, and the Spanish-American War, however, proved too much for existing Chinese community organizations to handle. Under these circumstances the elite hoped that an officially recognized Chinese consulate, similar to those available to other Manila expatriates, would carry enough prestige to protect the Chinese community from forces beyond its network or organizational control. A consulate would protect the interests of the community but would not eclipse the established elite. Instead, the consul general replaced the Gobernadorcillo, replicating the functions of that post as spokesman for and protector of the Chinese and as collector of passport fees and other surcharges. This impression was reinforced by the residence of the consul in the headman's offices. The consul, however, had something the Gobernadorcillo never had: official standing as the representative of a sovereign nation in the territory of another. In other words, the consul would have been the apical transnational. The *cabecillas* were not willing to sacrifice their dominant position in the community; rather, they were trying to enhance their status and facilitate the movement of wealth and talent through imperial representation. After all, it was the *cabecillas'* activism that had founded the consulate, and they stood to benefit by the installation of a consul who was sympathetic to their needs and who would employ them as secretaries and clerks. Throughout Southeast Asia, especially from the 1870s onward, the purchase of Qing titles and nominal official rank became a central element in factional competition among local Chinese. When the opportunity for substantive official rank and influence appeared with consular expansion, this competition intensified. In the Philippines, the consular movement arose at a time when competition between Hokkiens and Cantonese was on the rise. Evidently, this was an arena in which the Qing government's prestige could play a significant role.[99]

With the extension of American exclusion laws, another critical consideration came into play. Chinese migrants in colonial Manila (as well as elsewhere) were obsessed with any piece of paper that could facilitate the movement of money and talent across boundaries. The initial American attempt to register resident Chinese in Manila resulted in over twenty thousand claims of residence. When the American authorities tried to regulate opium use by issuing certificates to Chinese opium addicts in 1906–1907, nearly thirteen thousand Chinese applied for the certificates not because a third of the Chinese population were addicts, but because such a certificate proved that they were residents of the Philippines and could thus gain reentry.[100] Under the Spanish the primary certificate had been a *cedula personal,* a rudimentary identification card indicating race and tax bracket that was relatively easy to acquire or transfer. In the American Philippines, given the stricter enforcement of immigration laws, the desire for redundant forms of identification is entirely understandable, as too was the power held by those who could issue and validate those documents. Therefore, those who occupied or enjoyed privileged access to the offices that issued these immensely valuable pieces of paper—the American consul at Xiamen, the colonial administration in Manila, and the Chinese consul (preferably all three)—were, to borrow a contemporary phrase, "made men."[101]

The competition for the control of the consulate must be viewed from this perspective.

Some argued that Don Carlos was vocal in his support for a Chinese consulate because he desired that position for himself. This conclusion is reasonable when one considers the ambiguous nature of consular representation in the nineteenth century and the fact that many consuls, both Chinese and Western, were also locally prominent merchants. I disagree with this conclusion. Chen knew that if he were to serve as consul, it might negate the added prestige of that office, and he specifically pointed out his own unsuitability for the post. I would surmise that Chen was happier to dominate the consul, and having his own son assigned to the post was a perfect solution. Don Engracio was intimately linked to the Chinese government structure, had imperial certification, but was also familiar with the role of migration networks and privileged access for local elite success. He was perfect except that Chen had overestimated his ability to influence the new rulers of the Philippines. Perhaps, if the Spanish had retained the islands, the early history of the Chinese consulate would have been less controversial. The United States, however, was vitally concerned with the dangers posed by Chinese immigration and was also highly critical of Spain's colonial regime; therefore, the enemies of Chen Qianshan and Chen Gang found a sympathetic ear with General Otis and the State Department. The Hokkien *cabecillas*' success in gaining access to the Qing was temporarily undone by the Cantonese faction's short-lived influence with the Americans.

Nevertheless, Chen's story was that of an archetypal Chinese *cabecilla:* a man who buttressed his prestige within a transnational Chinese community with official recognition from the colonial authorities and the Qing government. Ironically, the nefarious deeds of which Chen was accused, namely, conversion to Catholicism; Spanish citizenship; bribery; service as a tax collector, coolie broker, Chinese headman, and mediator with the Spanish were the same strategies that he and the other *cabecillas* had employed to gain wealth and power in the Chinese community: the same wealth and power that qualified them to take a leadership role in campaigning for the Chinese consulate. Furthermore, these strategies were part and parcel of their status as transnational elites.

The *cabecillas* supported the consular campaign as a way to strengthen community solidarity in unstable times. The strategic importance of integrative institutions had been ingrained in them by their experiences both as migrants and as elites. The *cabecillas* had to protect their interests and defend against new rivals. This point is borne out by the conflict between the Hokkiens and the Cantonese over the choice of consul and the use of two distinct avenues of communication with the authorities in Beijing. Moreover, the factional rivalry that marked the early history of the consulate only increased in the early decades of the twentieth century, as did the *cabecillas'* ability and willingness to go to extreme lengths to eliminate rivals and to cultivate relations with the Chinese and colonial governments. In the end the *cabecillas,* led at first by Chen Qianshan, would discover that American annexation would demand changes in the nature of the community and in certain elite strategies but would not diminish the centrality of integrative institutions and migration networks or the importance of privileged access to the authorities.

Chen's story illustrates the dynamics of elite leadership among a group of Chinese migrants in a colonial environment and their system of self-identification. The Chinese elite, despite having left China and in many cases having adopted Catholicism and Spanish citizenship, still saw the need to legitimate their elite position in the community by acquiring Qing degrees, titles, and official positions. What might seem like a irreconcilable conflict of identities and loyalties from a nationcentric perspective was for this group a natural and eminently practicable response to their role as a transnational local elite. To be a *cabecilla* meant that one was not merely prominent in Manila but also commanded authority and exercised influence in the sending villages of Zhangzhou and Quanzhou. That the elite seemed incapable of conceiving of their own status and interests in the absence of state sanction, demonstrated by their desire for a consulate as an organ of local control rather than international diplomacy, proves that such sanction, whether granted by colonial authorities, Beijing, or the Fu-Zhe governor-general, was what facilitated the movement of talent and wealth across boundaries and guaranteed their prominence in two localities.

The above discussion helps answer the question of how the Chinese overseas negotiated imperial sovereignty and nationhood at a time when both of these concepts were being redefined. In the Spanish Philippines, the Chinese elite were never forced to choose between Beijing and Madrid, nor were they forced to think of these states as more than cultural entities. They were not bound to these nations as rigid territorial and legal institutions with total authority over them and to which they, as subjects, had binding obligations. The Chinese who became Spanish subjects in the nineteenth century also saw themselves as subjects of a Chinese empire that was territorially boundless, mainly culturally determined, and derived its fundamental authority from its mission to transform the world morally. But perhaps most important, they saw themselves as subjects of a Chinese state that needed their wealth, talent, and ostensible loyalty and that could provide them with validation and documentation that affirmed their elite status and facilitated their transnational networks. Chinese *cabecillas* saw no inherent contradiction in the idea that they could serve both the Qing and the Spanish empires and could appeal to each on a situational basis. This is evident in the fact that many of the *cabecillas* that appealed to Beijing were also Catholic Spanish subjects. The socioeconomic environment and Spanish policy encouraged them to conceive of themselves as a distinct cultural minority, and both governments offered the institutions to reinforce that identity without preventing them from seeking alliances with both sets of political power holders or developing extracommunity linkages. There was nothing remarkable about being a transnational local elite in an age before nation-spaces became more reified and politicized; it was simply how things were done. What is remarkable was the extent to which this elite could coopt institutions to further their ambitions.

As the segment of the Chinese population that dealt most directly with the Spanish authorities and with the Qing, *cabecillas* negotiated the fluid boundaries between imperial China and colonial Southeast Asia. For the Chinese elite, the 1890s was just the beginning of a prolonged period of instability. In the volatile environment of the American Philippines, the Chinese merchant elite would coopt new institutional forms to promote community cohesion, and they would seek broader linkages to the colonial authorities and the Chinese government to secure their elite status. In that environment, they would go to even greater lengths to protect their interests and cultivate transnational ties.

# 5

# Institutional Change in the Manila-Chinese Community, 1899–1916

THE TRANSFER OF the Philippines from Spanish to American rule altered the balance of power in East Asia, sparked a major political conflict in the United States, and created both dangers and opportunities for the residents of the archipelago, be they native or expatriate.[1] Crisis, opportunity, a new colonial administration, and the evolving nature of the Chinese community prompted the development of new institutions and the deployment of new strategies and identities by the Chinese merchant elite to deal with these conditions. Elsewhere in Southeast Asia, local Chinese faced similar challenges. Throughout the 1890s and the early 1900s, political and economic change was sweeping the region. The laissez-faire economies and free-wheeling commerce of the late nineteenth century gave way to a more systematic exploitation of European colonies to supply resources for the last stage of the Industrial Revolution and to fuel the growing arms races in Europe, the Americas, and Northeast Asia. In Singapore, increasing economic rationalization and the expanding reach of the British colonial government signaled an end to opium and tax farms and other brokerage roles that Chinese had filled. This, in turn, realigned the bases of Chinese elite power and forced merchant elites to reorient their socioeconomic activity.[2] In Java, "the demise of the farms meant not only that the Chinese were kept from the legal opium trade and its vast profits but also . . . lost their organizations as a force in the countryside and, as a result, their controlled access to Java's rural markets."[3] Furthermore, the influx of Hakka and Cantonese engendered competition between Peranakans and these new *totok* (unassimilated Chinese) arrivals. Each group jockeyed for economic advantage and tried to outdo the other in asserting their Chinese identity.[4] In the Philippines, the advent of an aggressive American colonial administration also brought an end to the revenue farms that had been a mainstay of *cabecilla* prosperity and a market for *invernado* manpower. The established *cabecilla* elite, however, managed to weather the storm better than other Southeast Asian Chinese, perhaps because opium and other revenue farms did not enjoy the singular importance in the Philippines that they did in the Straits Settlement or Java, but also because Manila's Chinese merchant elite had already begun a transition to agricultural export as a supplement to monopoly contracts. Simultaneous with these changes within the Philippines, the Japanese annexation of Taiwan had deflected Hokkien mercantile energy, especially in the sugar trade, away from Taiwan—which was forcibly decoupled from the Chinese economy—toward Southeast Asia and especially toward Manila.[5]

Given these overlapping local, regional, and global trends, change within the Chinese community during this period occurred along three interconnected fronts: socioeconomic, political, and institutional. This chapter focuses on institutional changes, since they are the best documented and reveal the evolving nature of a Southeast Asian Chinese community in the heyday of Western colonialism. The most important institutional development at the turn of this century was the abolition of the Chinese headman system and the transition to consular representation and Chinese chambers of commerce. In Manila, the last Gobernadorcillo de los Sangleyes, Juan Pina Tan Chuaco, who had authority over the Manila-Chinese community as a legally autonomous ethnic enclave, stepped down in 1898, but community leadership was immediately transferred to the interim consul and former Gobernadorcillo, Don Carlos Palanca Chen Qianshan.[6] This transfer would seem to indicate a continued pattern of a single dominant *cabecilla* governing the community. But this is an illusion derived from the tendency of both the Spanish and Chinese governments to work through a single figure of authority.[7] While he was certainly the most prominent *cabecilla*, Don Carlos had consistently spoken for a corporate group of *cabecillas,* frequently mentioned by name, that were the heads of the occupational and trade *gremios* and the board members of the various charitable and community institutions who had rotated through the apical office. Nonetheless, new institutional forms that emerged in the American period were more transparent and revealed a diverse group of merchants, professionals, and businessmen.

This diversity was not exclusively a product of American rule. While occupational diversification naturally increased with the maturation and recovery of the Philippine economy in the first two decades of American rule, it was built on the patterns of Chinese economic activity in the late Spanish period. This dynamic favored institutions that were designed to coordinate the activism of a diversified Chinese elite but also to cohere this corporate elite and give them a venue for collective action. The institution that was offered, and that they skillfully coopted, was the Chinese chamber of commerce. Chambers of commerce, which had recently gained the sanction and support of the Qing government, were part of a campaign to appropriate Western institutional forms in order to obtain a more rational means of coopting merchant interests into state service, but they also were well suited to local cooptation.

As with the late Spanish period, the dominant Chinese institutions in the American Philippines were dominated by a narrow stratum of the wealthiest and most prominent elites seeking to further personal and localist agendas, especially to facilitate migration networks. This trend continued under the American colonial administration, and, although some of the personnel had changed, the pursuit of personal and interest group agendas alternately enhanced and limited the effectiveness of these community institutions. Under the Spanish, these interest groups were primarily defined by regional origin, specifically Hokkien or Cantonese, but under American colonial rule the availability of a broad range of institutional forms meant that competition among the Hokkien majority could be played out openly. In the American Philippines "traditional" Chinese associations increased but so too did new types. Older associations were renamed and reorganized based on "modern" institutional models, and entirely new political, social, and economic institutions appeared. Consuls, corporations, and chambers of commerce supplemented or replaced headmen, *huiguan, hang,* and secret societies. Institutional leadership still defined the elite, but the overlapping social and economic crises as well as new institutional forms meant that the patterns and forms of elite dominance were not as clearly constituted as they had been in the late nineteenth century. In this fluid environment new groups and new types of elites could vie for prominence and for privileged access to authority. New models could not totally eclipse previous institutions, nor could the acquisition of new elite strategies eliminate older patterns. Traditional and modern strategies coexisted and were adapted to suit elite ambitions. This simultaneity shaped Chinese identity in the American Philippines.

## The Nature of American Colonial Rule

Without delving too deeply into historiographical debates about the extent to which American progressive values informed our rule of the Philippines or the ways in which racism and repression colored our treatment of the Filipinos, it is nonetheless necessary to draw some general conclusions about the social, legislative, and economic terrain of the American Philippines.[8] Once the decision for annexation had been made by the McKinley administration in December 1898, the objectives of the United States were threefold: extend civilian and military control over the islands outward from Manila, suppress those forces in opposition to American rule (both *insurectos* and various indigenous tribes), and ultimately replace military rule with a rationalized, egalitarian government of law to facilitate the "benevolent assimilation" of the entire population of the archipelago.

In the first two years of American military rule, the requirements of fighting and defeating the insurrection took priority. Martial law was imposed in Manila, and U.S. troops were employed to maintain order in the city, but the presence of so many troops and refugees also invited chaos. Fear of the Chinese using the islands as an entrée into the United States convinced military governor Elwell Otis to ban the entry of Chinese who could prove neither exempt status nor prior residence in September 1898, and the military rulers instituted bans on gambling, which had long been tolerated if not actively encouraged by the Spanish. Opium was commodified, which opened the market to more merchants, and all manner of controls were placed on the importation of contraband. These acts disrupted a good deal of the Chinese economy. But given that General Otis had a war to fight, he was unlikely to care about the implications of these policies for the Chinese. Large amounts of men and materiel were required to support a military effort that included at one time more than seventy thousand U.S. troops, the largest overseas deployment the U.S. military had ever attempted, which in turn required requisitions or impressments. The campaigns against the insurrection, while bloody, protracted, and carrying yet another cholera epidemic in their wake, were generally successful in defeating or coopting those who had taken up arms against the Americans. Campaigns against the Moros in the south were equally hard fought and even more protracted but managed to extend Manila's control even further than had been possible under the Spanish.[9]

Although the incorporation of the Philippine Islands into an American empire was a fait accompli by the early years of the twentieth century, it remained to the military and civilian governments to decide how potentially disruptive alien groups might be dealt with in America's Pacific possessions. One of the central tasks assigned to the first Philippine Commission was to formulate an answer to the "Chinese Question." How was the colonial administration supposed to deal with a population of alien Chinese who were viewed as essential to the continued health of the Philippine economy but who could also be a corrupting racial influence, a drain on the economy (especially in terms of the amount of Mexican silver dollars flowing to China), and a convenient scapegoat for Filipino agitation?

In March 1899 a group of three distinguished Americans arrived in the Philippines charged by President McKinley with the mission "to facilitate the most humane, pacific and effective extension of authority throughout these islands and to secure, with the least possible delay, the benefits of a wise and generous protection of life and liberty to the inhabitants."[10]

The Philippine Commission brought to the islands a microcosm of the debates over the colonial mission of the United States and the feasibility of incorporating alien races into the American polity. The original commission included Jacob Gould Schurman, philosophy professor and president of Cornell University; Dean Worcester, a zoologist who had spent many years conducting research in the Philippines and hence was considered an expert on the archipelago; and Charles Denby, a conservative Democrat who had served as the United States envoy to China.[11]

The main concern of the commission, in terms of the "Chinese Question," was to determine whether the various exclusion acts then in force in the United States should be extended to the Philippines. The Gresham-Yang treaty of 1894 had "stipulated that Chinese laborers be prohibited from coming to the United States for a period of ten years."[12] In addition, there were strict registration policies for Chinese residing in the United States and various provisions that gave the government significant leeway "to adopt harsh measures against both labor and nonlabor classes of Chinese."[13] These various exclusion and prohibitive statutes were the product of anti-Chinese labor agitation in the western United States. Anti-Chinese sentiment was manifested not only in state and federal legislation, but also in the violence against the Chinese in California, Washington, Colorado, Oregon, Wyoming, and Massachusetts.

Colonial administrators in the Philippines had to create a Chinese immigration policy in this often confusing context. For their part, the Bureau of Insular Affairs and many Manila residents accepted the need for a Chinese community in Manila given the *chinos'* generally positive effect on the economy. Some local merchants even claimed that the Manila economy would grind to a halt without the Chinese.

> In my opinion, I don't think the native is good enough; I don't think he is as good a skilled laborer as the Chinaman. You want Chinese here for carpenters; you must have them here for boiler makers and riveters. . . . You must have Chinese labor for working in coal and other mines. . . . The native has a great antipathy to the Chinaman, but the native is too indolent to be a merchant, and the Chinaman is a great merchant, a great peddler, and if you keep the Chinaman out of the country I don't see who is going to do the peddling over the country . . . the whole system of business all over the Islands is all dependent on the Chinese peddlers. . . . I don't see how the country is going to get on without them.[14]

Having recorded and considered the opinions of numerous respondents and reviewed two memoranda sent to them, the commissioners submitted their final report to the president and Congress in January of 1900, less than a year after their dispatch to the islands. The Philippine Commission's concluding remarks on the "Chinese Question" is a masterpiece of politic ambiguity:

> In the regions inhabited by the civilized natives sentiment toward the Chinese varies considerably in different provinces and islands. Where it is strongly hostile the Commission feels that we are bound to take it into serious consideration. And we further believe that the inhabitants of all parts of the Archipelago should be saved from the necessity of being forced to compete with Chinese labor under con-

ditions such that they can not hope to compete with success, always provided that the legitimate economic development of the country is not thereby retarded.

On the other hand, we feel that Chinese labor might be very advantageously used in those portions of the Archipelago where, from the character of the inhabitants and their indisposition to engage in manual toil, or from the absence of inhabitants, and the well-known disinclination of the civilized native to leave his home and settle in a new region, it would not come into competition with the labor of the country.

We therefore commend to your careful consideration the question as to how, where, and for what purpose the Chinese should be allowed to enter the Archipelago.[15]

In other words, the commissioners left the decision up to the Congress, which decided to extend the American exclusion laws to the Philippine Islands in toto, perhaps feeling that by doing so the United States could more quickly pacify the Filipinos and indicate to their new subjects that the United States was a different kind of colonial power. The Qing government had raised objections to the extension of the exclusion law as did local Chinese, but there was little either Beijing or the *cabecilla* elite could do about the law except to develop ways to circumvent it. Thus, at the same time American troops were in the process of pacifying the Philippine countryside, American politicians were crafting policies that would largely determine the evolution of the late colonial Philippines and the role of local elites in the colonial enterprise.

Even before the various rebellions had been suppressed, the Americans began the transition to civilian rule. The Second Philippine Commission, headed by William Howard Taft, took over control of the pacified areas in July 1901 and began rapidly to establish the basic infrastructure of civilian rule. They enacted the Philippine Organic Act of 1902, which was designed to both routinize colonial rule and gradually bring Filipinos into the government, thus building toward democratic tutelage of the native population. Perhaps the most significant result of the act and the founding of a Philippine legislature was the drawing together in Manila of what had previously been a dispersed provincial elite of *indio* and *mestizo* landholders. This group became the core of the emerging Filipino national elite. As for foreigners residing in the islands, censuses were undertaken to count the various indigenous minorities, Europeans, Americans, and the "Yellow Race." While some Chinese could become Philippine citizens because they had previously been Spanish subjects, the majority were classed as aliens and were therefore required to maintain "section six" certificates, especially after the formalization of the exclusion policy in 1902. This in turn meant that local Chinese continued to be viewed, at least legally, as a group apart from Philippine society, defined by their foreign origin and increasingly by their occupations. Moreover, although they were subject to more direct colonial rule, the Chinese were effectively the responsibility of the Chinese consul and the Chinese elite.

The fact that the Americans were at first consumed with the insurrection and then with the program of benevolent assimilation meant that significant portions of the Spanish era social structure endured, especially among the Chinese. Moreover, key legal innovations would actually reinforce the utility of migration networks and the importance of Chinese institutions, in much the same way that the Organic Law buttressed the power of provincial elites through the Philippine legislature. Nor were the Americans able to solve the various social, economic, and health crises that had plagued the islands since the 1880s. It was only with the extension of a coherent health policy that cholera, plague, and rinderpest were brought under control, and it was not until the passage of the Payne-Aldrich Tariff Act, which lifted the standing tariff on Philippine exports to the United States, that the moribund economy at last began to shown signs of life.[16] Finally, despite claims to be significantly different (and better) from the Spaniards who had preceded them, the Americans were forced to maintain key aspects of Spanish economic and legal policy. The taxation system was not reformed until 1904, and Spanish legal precedents continued to dictate both criminal and civil judgments.[17] Thus, while U.S. annexation of the Philippines had a dramatic effect on the islands, that effect was not completely revolutionary, nor were the effects immediately apparent.

In the main, however, American rule was a mixed blessing for the Chinese.[18] The application of Chinese exclusion laws did not lead to the exclusion of Chinese from the Philippines but required adaptation. The laws reinforced familial migration patterns and the importance of elite management of migration networks. In the economic realm, after a rough start in the 1900s, the economy recovered dramatically within the umbrella of U.S. tariff exemption. This recovery opened numerous opportunities for the Chinese, who rapidly came to dominate key export sectors and built on the existing marketing systems established in the late Spanish era to control most of the retail trade on Luzon. Other legal innovations had less salutary effects for the Chinese. In particular the Organic Law of 1902, while necessary for the transition to Philippine self-rule, was constructed in such a way as to encourage the rise of provincial elite dynasties *(caciques)*, made even more powerful by the acquisition of former friar haciendas. The *caciques* exercised dominance in their native places, because single families could hold office for generations, and also began to travel to Manila to serve in the legislature and thus become a national elite.[19] These policies sharpened trends emerging in the late Spanish period that shaped the formation of Filipino identity, an identity, like that of the Chinese, largely defined by the elite. As Filipino national consciousness evolved, it became increasingly exclusive, and that exclusiveness was increasingly directed against the Chinese. Thus an often hostile sociopolitical landscape was encouraged by an immigration system that kept the majority of Chinese a legally (and occupationally) distinct alien enclave. In a paradoxical spin on assimilation theory, which has so clouded the study of human migrations, the Chinese had both become Filipinos, in that the modern category of Filipino is inconceivable without Chinese *mestizos*, but the Chinese also became the antithesis of the Filipino, an ungrounded, transnational, and alien "other." Those trends were, however, several decades from fruition when the Americans first arrived and would be shaped by choices made by the Americans, *caciques*, and the Chinese elite.

## Socioeconomic Developments

In the late nineteenth century, the socioeconomic composition of the Chinese community had been clearly structured. At the apex was the small elite group of wealthy *cabecillas*, primarily Hokkiens from Zhangzhou and Quanzhou prefectures, who shaped the institutional superstructure of the community. Below this elite stratum were several layers of subordinate agents employed by or tied to the *cabecillas* as wholesalers, retailers, and clerks in Manila and as *tenderos* in the provinces.[20] Craftsmen and tradesmen made up a middle stratum, which was filled out at the lowest level by a large *invernado* population of Chinese laborers, who were employed as stevedores and coolies. The relative stability of this hierarchy was enhanced by the structure of the economy and by the bonds of loyalty and obligation among the Hokkien migrants. As the heads of merchant houses and the holders of labor brokerage monopolies, *cabecillas* exercised critical controls (although not hegemonic control) over the community, most of whom relied on the elite to facilitate their migration and guarantee their prosperity. Most new in-migrants were recruited, housed, offered credit, and employed through the agency of native-place associations, *cabecilla* labor recruiters, or the *cabecilla*-agent system. As a result, nearly all of the Chinese in the islands were bound in some way by *qiaoxiang* ties, employment, or debt to the Chinese *cabecillas* who controlled these institutions. Nonetheless, under the Spanish there had still been significant opportunities for individual migrants to traverse various migration networks and to cultivate personal and business ties outside the superstructure of the *chino* community.

Under the Americans, numerous changes occurred in the socioeconomic makeup of the Chinese community, but perhaps most important, the advent of American rule strengthened the hand of the Chinese elite and narrowed the recruiting base to southern Fujian. The application of the exclusion laws, under which only merchants and their families could enter Manila, and entrants had to prove at least U.S.$200 in assets, prior residence in the islands, or kinship to a legally resident Chinese, meant that the overwhelming majority of new arrivals had to be managed through established migration networks that could provide the funds and documentation necessary to satisfy or circumvent these strictures. The application of the law also made a document called a "section six certificate," issued by American consuls in China, immensely valuable, as American policy had succeeded in further commodifying privileged access to document-issuing authority. In fact, the American consul in Xiamen, Anson Burlingame Johnson, who served in the late 1890s and early 1900s, was accused of official malfeasance for selling these certificates to migrants bound for Manila. Johnson had long been dealing with the Chinese elite in Xiamen, many of whom were simultaneously the Manila merchant elite. Besides defusing crises, Johnson had also helped found a modern Chinese school, the Tongwen Institute, in partnership with some of the most prominent local Chinese.[21] Not surprisingly, after Johnson stepped down from his post in Xiamen, he moved to Manila, where he made a fortune in the lumber business, which was a primarily Hokkien market sector.[22] Cultivating ties with consuls was critical at both ends of the migration network.

The increased need for managed migration meant that Hokkiens in general and Zhangzhou and Quanzhou migrants specifically, managed as they were through robust migration networks, comprised 90 percent of the Chinese population in the American Philippines. Even so, there was significant occupational diversification among this group. The exclusion laws did effectively stop the inflow of unskilled Chinese labor, and in subsequent decades the Chinese were almost completely supplanted in manual labor by Filipinos; but rather than excluding Chinese, the exclusion laws succeeded in facilitating their domination of key service and commercial sectors.[23] Recovery and maturation of the Philippine economy opened new market niches. While the merchant elite remained at the apex of the hierarchy, they were accompanied by an ever larger group of middle-level and up-and-coming merchants and manufacturers. Likewise, the trades, crafts, and professional occupations, including criminal entrepreneurs, enjoyed considerable expansion. Chinese merchants and professionals, trained in China's treaty ports, were also growing more sophisticated in Western enterprises and professions, and found willing employers in Manila's European firms. Although enrollments were quite limited, the Anglo-Chinese School, founded in 1899, could produce literate, bilingual, and professionally oriented locally born Chinese and *mestizos* to supplement those traveling over from Fujian. As a result, a Chinese middle class made an earlier appearance in Manila than in San Francisco, New York, or Chicago.[24] Chinese also worked as cooks, waiters, and busboys at the finer hotels, the Hotel Oriente and the Manila Hotel. They managed and served in gambling parlors, dealt fan-tan, and ran numbers rackets along Calles San Jacinto and David.[25] Such diversification was not simply a product of the Manila labor market but reflected the ability of Hokkien sending communities to adapt to new economic opportunities. The constant two-way communication through migration networks facilitated both ends of the exchange of wealth and talent between South China and the colonial Philippines.

Because American law inhibited the importation of Chinese coolies, only Chinese merchants and professionals were allowed into the islands. Within a restructuring economy, there were opportunities to pursue trades without the need to rely on a *cabecilla*. During the American period, while commuter migrations continued, more Hokkiens began to settle in the islands. The increase in Chinese female migration to the Philippines, encouraged by the exclusion laws, which allowed them to enter as kin, is partly responsible for this demographic shift. Since more Chinese were taking a long-term approach to residence, they could pursue extramural linkages and occupational strategies that did not rely on the merchant elite for credit or employment, or the need to reach back to the *qiaoxiang* to recruit young men.[26]

The increasing socioeconomic diversity of the Manila Chinese community that resulted seems then to parallel what Bryna Goodman has referred to in her case study of Shanghai as the "subdivision of the native-place community."[27] In the case of the Philippines, the Hokkien community began to subdivide along occupational, class, educational, and political lines. But to conclude that such a subdivision was inherently divisive or meant an end to the importance of the elite and the migration networks they managed would be erroneous. While migrations within China were quite arduous and in some cases required elite facilitation, it was still significantly easier to move from one province to another in search of work. Hence Goodman's "subdivision" of native-place groups in Shanghai is to be expected given the growth in the size of Shanghai and its rapid industrialization in the late nineteenth and early twentieth centuries. The lower Yangzi economy could therefore consume the labor funneled into it through numerous channels. To migrate to the Philippines, in contrast, required that one travel through two "bottlenecks," Xiamen and Manila, where influence, documentation, and significant capital (U.S.$200 per migrant) was needed. Unless a migrant had independent means, it was unlikely that he would gain access to Manila. Moreover, even though more Chinese brought Chinese brides to Manila and fathered sons in the islands, ties to the *qiaoxiang* were still deep and critical. Even locally born children returned to southern Fujian, often attending the missionary-run Anglo-Chinese colleges in Xiamen and Fuzhou.[28] Alfonso Sycip (Xue Fenshi), was born in Manila to the *cabecilla* José Zarate Sycip but spent fourteen years in Fujian before returning to Manila. Other merchant elites, despite decades of residence in Manila, retired to the *qiaoxiang* after handing over their enterprises to kin. In addition, given the scale of Chinese enterprises in the late Spanish and American Philippines, locally born sons were an insufficient pool to supply all of the layers of subordinates. New arrivals were still critical. Dee C. Chuan's lumber empire relied on generations of young Dees (Lis) from Jinjiang County to staff its numerous mills and subsidiaries.[29]

Dee's elite status was clearly transnational. As early as 1900, his father, Calixto Dyyco, raised more than 200,000 *yuan* (Chinese dollars) among his fellow *cabecillas* for the Tongwen Institute in Xiamen— where the younger Dee was enrolled—which educated the children of the elite in both Western and Chinese subjects. After taking over his father's business and prospering greatly, Dee invested vast sums in construction projects and charities in Xiamen, while at the same time serving repeatedly as chairman of Manila's Chinese Chamber of Commerce and contributing to local educational and charitable causes.[30] Moreover, in addition to homes in the Philippines, Dee C. Chuan built a lavish mansion on the exclusive Gulangyu Island in Xiamen harbor, thus cementing his role as a conspicuous local elite in two localities.[31] Thus I must disagree with James Blaker's contention that "Dee and Sycip had relatively little in common with previous" Gobernadorcillos and *cabecillas*.[32] If anything, their strategies were refinements of the transnational tactics of their predecessors. Nor were Dee's transnational philanthropy and investment a rare occurrence. Other *cabecillas,* such as F. M. Lim Tuico (Lin Xuedi) and his son Lim Chu Cong (Lin Zhuguang), sponsored educational and athletic programs in both Manila and Xiamen, while still others diversified their Philippine investments by funding manufacturing, banking, and infrastructure projects in Xiamen and the *qiaoxiang.* Infrastructure especially not only contributed to the maturation of the Hokkien economy, but also facilitated the movement of talent and wealth through migration networks.[33] Even more significant than elite philanthropy and investment were the tens of millions of yuan that all classes of migrants pumped into the towns and villages of southern Fujian in the form of remittances *(qiaopi),* making the region one of the most prosperous and modern in all of China and skewing the regional economy toward labor/talent export.[34] This was not a new development; it built on linkages formed during the great burst of migration in the nineteenth century. In many ways native-place and transnational ties became even more important and cohesive in early-twentieth-century Manila, but rather than Antonio Tan's contention that "the path to leadership in the 20th century was to be found in working for the realization of Chinese national aspirations and objectives," the primary path for the American era leadership remained the maintenance and extension of transnational links for the realization of translocal aspirations and objectives.[35]

This pattern of Chinese socioeconomic development should come as no surprise to those familiar with the history of the Chinese community in the United States and elsewhere. While Chinese exclusion laws succeeded in reshaping some migration systems and resulted in social and economic stagnation in some communities, the larger reality was that Chinese migrants adapted to or circumvented the exclusion laws. The laws did not exclude the Chinese; in some ways they facilitated their control of key trade and occupational sectors, because migration networks were reengineered to fill specific market niches. This in turn enhanced the power and prestige of those elites who could facilitate cross border migrations. Even in the American west, where there was pronounced anti-Chinese sentiment (especially among white labor), as well as segregation and ghettoization, prosperity was still possible. For the Chinese in the Philippines, migration from coastal China may have been cheaper and quicker, but that did not diminish the value of elite-run migration networks. Yet the lack of an extensive white elite stratum in colonial Manila left gaps in the colonial system that *chinos* competed to fill, and they were able to gain much greater wealth, power, and influence than Chinese in America.[36]

Although the *cabecillas* continued to dominate Philippine retail trade and the import-export market, the other classes of the Chinese community began to diversify into the small-scale manufacturing and service industries, which grew and contracted in response to the boom-and-bust cycles of the Philippine economy.[37] New occupational patterns also promoted the growth of occupational organizations, which, in an increasingly competitive market, served as alternative foci of individual economic loyalty. Occupational associations and social groupings increased and diversified the Chinese community. This diversity complicated intracommunity dynamics and often precipitated internal conflict, usually in periods of economic contraction.

New occupational associations were not above using violence and intimidation to enforce their agendas. In 1908 the Wing Wo Tong, a cabinetmakers guild, attempted to establish a monopoly over Chinese furniture manufacturing. All Chinese cabinetmakers were expected to join the *tong* for a fee. When Tam Chee, an independent carpenter, refused to join, *tong* members threatened him and then

assaulted him in his shop.[38] Strong-arm tactics were just another facet
of entrepreneurial strategy. David Ownby's work on Chinese secret
societies like the Wing Wo Tong has demonstrated the fundamental
importance of occupational monopolies in the survival of these associations, especially when a particular market was threatened by competition or decline in demand. Occupational associations did not begin as inherently criminal but were forced into acts of violence in the
interests of economic survival.[39] Although the assault on Tam Chee
was a minor case, it is indicative of a degree of violence that was present in Manila in the early years of this century. A perusal of the
*Manila Times*' daily police blotter shows frequent arrests of Chinese
for all manner of legal infractions. Initially under martial law and
then in the transition to a civilian police force, Chinese ran afoul of
American law enforcement on a daily basis for violations of the curfew, gambling prohibitions, opium controls, public morals, public
decency, and hygiene laws—critical given the plague and pestilence
ravaging wartime Manila. Smuggling was also epidemic, given the
high tariffs and bans on all variety of contraband. These strictures actually invited smuggling by Chinese.[40] But the appearance of Chinese
"crime" must also be seen as a result of American laws that expanded
the definition of criminal to a wide range of activities that had been
either tolerated or encouraged in Spanish Manila. As the institutions
of the corporate elite gained influence, however, they were increasingly able to coopt or eliminate disruptive elements. Responding
deftly to new definitions of criminality, the Chinese elite began to police themselves and to cultivate an improved image of themselves, as
the Americans phrased it, as the "better class of Chinamen." Moreover, given their fixation with law and order the Americans were desperate to know who comprised this "better class" and the leaders of
the Chinese community were more than happy to draw the distinctions for them.

Before American annexation, intracommunity conflict tended to
revolve around contests for institutional leadership and rivalry between migrants from different native places. This conflict was handled by elite institutions that maintained a monopoly on coercive
force within the community. By the early twentieth century, conflict
appeared among the Hokkiens, as did rivalry between different socioeconomic groups. The most obvious breakdown in community
solidarity occurred as the increasingly bold secret societies split from
the *cabecillas* in the first years of American rule. The *cabecillas* lost

some of their influence with the demise of the coolie trade and the abolition of the various monopolies, such as opium and gambling rings, that had required close cooperation between the elite and the secret societies. Consequently, the *cabecillas* vigorously opposed the ban on coolie importation and made periodic pleas to lift the exclusion laws.[41]

By abolishing the opium and gambling monopolies, the Americans were also opening the door for small-scale Chinese entrepreneurs. With these lucrative industries out of the hands of the Chinese elite, there were now opportunities for freelance opium dealers and casino operators to move into a deregulated market. Despite the switch from the opium monopoly to a commodity system, opium was actually more expensive in Manila than in China, and small amounts of opium could be purchased in Fujian and sold in the Philippines for substantial profit. Xiamen, the point of departure for the vast majority of Chinese in the Philippines, was also one of the major opium trade centers on the China coast and had a large talent pool that was preadapted to both smuggling and the opium trade. As they had done with nearly every change in the Manila economy, the Hokkiens rapidly filled an emerging market niche.[42] Under the Spanish, only the elite could afford to be dealers; the Americans opened the market. Moreover, the rise in opium prices mirrored the two- to fivefold increase in the prices of other staples.[43] Periodic depressions increased the criminal population and forced occupational associations like the Wing Wo Tong to resort to violence to protect guild interests. As the next chapter will show, these developments were a matter of great concern for American administrators. But after an initial surge in crime during the war, partly due to the broader strictures of martial law, criminal activity among the Chinese rapidly diminished. Civilian law enforcement had a better handle on the local scene, and Chinese learned the laws and how to bend the laws in collusion with law enforcement. Moreover, while the Americans had initially approached legal reform in the Philippines with optimistic zeal, they rapidly discovered that the extent to which they could actually change Manila was limited by finite resources, limited manpower, and lack of familiarity as well as by the socioeconomic landscape of the city itself. In other words, after a brief period of chaos, Manila settled back into subtly altered rhythms of a colonial city.

Nonetheless, criminal activity was an important indicator of a volatile and dynamic society and of increased diversity and competition in the economic realm. Chinese criminality in the American Philippines was a direct consequence of American colonial policy, which attempted to implement stricter definitions of criminal activity than had the Spanish. Yet crime was also a logical response to the continuing economic depression and the increasing lawlessness that plagued the Philippines from the 1880s to the 1900s, issues that would not be sufficiently resolved until the second decade of American rule. Ultimately, however, crime was just one characteristic of a dynamic and competitive Chinese community.

## Political Developments

Diversification of the Chinese enclave was echoed in the political realm. When Sun Yat-sen visited the Philippines in the 1890s, he was disappointed by the low level of political—read revolutionary—consciousness among the Chinese expatriates. This seemed to change in the aftermath of American annexation. Yet the Chinese elite had consistently demonstrated a high level of political consciousness, although it tended to be directed toward established authority. Coincident with American annexation, however, new venues for political activism and orientation that questioned authority began to appear in the Philippines.

Throughout Asia, America's capture of the Philippines and the suppression of the Philippine Insurrection sparked interest in the islands and heightened awareness of the ideological and geopolitical significance of these events. Even as Chinese politics was consumed by the empress dowager's coup of 1898, the Qing government remained interested in the impact on the local Chinese of events in the Philippines. Beijing responded to the conflict with a renewed campaign for establishing a Chinese consular presence in the islands.

Beyond the immediate impact on Chinese merchants, the geostrategic significance of the Spanish-American War and other recent developments in Southeast Asia were not lost on Chinese officialdom. When taken in the context of a growing formal American empire and virulent anti-Chinese sentiment in the United States, the changes in the Philippines were a matter of concern among some high mandarins. Li Hongzhang, one of China's leading statesmen, was alarmed at the United States' aggressive posture in the Pacific and the persecution of Chinese in America.[44] America, it seemed, was following in the footsteps of European and Japanese imperialism.[45]

Dewey's victory in Manila Bay was big news in China. China's emerging news media—both Chinese-owned and foreign—followed the story closely. Many in the Chinese media viewed the events with mixed emotions. Some accounts, based on translations from British and American newspapers, hailed the American conquest and pointed to the past injustices visited upon the local Chinese by the Spaniards. It seemed that American annexation would be a definite improvement over Spanish dominion.[46] The generally favorable impression of the United States shared by many of China's intellectuals made the glowing American accounts much more palatable. In spite of various Chinese exclusion laws, many in China viewed the United States as decidedly more beneficent and enlightened than the imperial powers of Europe and Japan, who were bound to move into the islands if the Americans did not. America's assumption of Spain's regional holdings may have seemed the least distasteful alternative.[47] Other reports, however, cast doubts on the high ideals of American "liberation." The *Shenbao,* printed in Shanghai, questioned President McKinley's decision to dismiss Washingtonian principles of isolation and anticolonialism.[48] The editors at another Shanghai paper, *Chixing bao,* saw the expansion of American naval power as the United States' instrument for the economic and political penetration of Asia.[49]

Chinese throughout Asia viewed the Spanish-American War and the Philippine Insurrection with similarly mixed emotions. In Japan, nationalistic Philippine *ilustrados* and Chinese students mingled with exiled political figures. Liang Qichao, who fled to Japan after the failure of the Hundred Days Reform, voiced concerns similar to those of Li Hongzhang. In an extension of Li's geopolitical vision, however, Liang argued that if the Americans were to defeat the Filipinos, not only would they be masters of the Pacific from California to the South China Sea and control a key entry for an invasion of southeast China, they would also have dealt a crushing blow to nascent Asian nationalism. Liang viewed the American annexation of Hawai'i and the attempted suppression of Aguinaldo's rebels as a sign of America's quest for formal colonies. This quest was driven by America's desire to compete with the other imperialists.[50] Liang had a favorable impression of the Filipino nationalists. Ethnically and culturally tied to the Chinese, Aguinaldo and his followers represented the new tide of anti-imperialism.[51] Liang believed that Filipino success meant new hope for the cause of self-determination in Asia, while defeat meant an accelerated partition of the entire region.[52]

Other Chinese exiles also established relations with the Filipino rebels. When Sun Yat-sen was in medical school in Hong Kong, one of his professors, Dr. Lorenzo P. Marquez, was a close friend of the author José Rizal.[53] Later, between 1898 and 1900, Sun helped Mariano Ponce, one of Aguinaldo's aides, purchase weapons and ammunition in Japan.[54] Sun supported Filipino nationalism and wanted to form a pact of reciprocal aid and revolutionary solidarity between his party and Aguinaldo's. An issue of Sun's revolutionary journal *Minbao* bemoaned the lack of truly independent states in East Asia and featured photographs of Aguinaldo and one of his generals, the Hokkien José Ignacio Paua. However, neither of the two weapons shipments from Japan reached the Philippines. The first was lost at sea, and the second was seized by Japanese officials who wanted to avoid antagonizing their new American neighbors.[55] Ironically, the second shipment ended up in Japanese-held Taiwan and was eventually used by Sun's anti-Qing forces in the 1911 revolution.[56] In this early interaction can be seen the beginnings of the Chinese nationalist movement's awareness of the Philippines and its symbolic importance to the cause of Chinese nationalism.

## Local Chinese Views of American Annexation

For Chinese in the Philippines, the beginning of the twentieth century was a time of crisis: The siege of Manila by both American and Filipino forces, the insurrection, and the economic depression, exacerbated by war and rebellion, severely affected their safety and prosperity. By the 1890s, the Chinese population had reached one hundred thousand, half of whom lived in Manila, but many *chinos* had temporarily returned to China to escape the chaos. Others, however, were able to take advantage of the unstable situation to improve their social or economic standing. The *cabecilla* elite who remained generally viewed the coming of American rule favorably and foresaw increased economic benefit. The large American military force, far in excess of any the Spanish had ever garrisoned in Manila, required housing, supplies, and support services. The Chinese, as the main provisioners of Manila, met these demands, although not always without conflict. Chen Qianshan had initially approached the Americans with offers of support and aid: "I do a lot of work for the United States. . . . Get the coolie laborers out to the lines, building barracks. . . . When the Americans came here I furnished the carabaos and transportation. . . . I used to give alot of information to the American Government, and assisted in getting houses in the commencement for the troops, furnishing my own godowns out at San Miguel for the quartering of troops, too."[57] When Chen provided these same services for the Spanish in their struggle against the Filipinos, he was awarded a Medal of Civil Merit and the Grand Cross of Isabel the Catholic, but the Americans were not as grateful.[58] Chen quickly ran afoul of General Elwell S. Otis, commander of American ground forces, by refusing to let the army billet troops in the Zhangzhou and Quanzhou *huiguan*.[59]

The Filipinos also needed provisioning, first in their conflict with the Spanish and then later against the United States, and they turned to Chinese for supplies and labor. The thirty thousand Filipino troops who besieged the Spanish in Manila in the summer of 1898 were armed with weapons and ammunition purchased from Chinese smugglers.[60] The war in fact expanded the role of the Chinese in the Philippine economy, as other foreigners fled to Hong Kong and Singapore.[61] Chen Qianshan even offered Aguinaldo's revolutionary government material assistance in exchange for rights to the opium monopoly.[62] Seeing the Chinese benefit from their misfortunes, however, turned some Filipinos against them.[63] Mariano Limjap (Lin He), son of a *chino* father and a *mestiza* mother, was also a critical financier of Aguinaldo's rebellion. While technically a *mestizo,* the fluidity of ethnic identities in the colonial Philippines allowed Limjap to deploy numerous identities. While he was born locally, many of his business dealings were with *chinos* and thus much of his support for the cause of Philippine independence was probably drawn from the Chinese economy.[64]

For other Chinese, American annexation would be a welcome change, because they believed that they would enjoy greater legal protection under American law. In the Spanish Philippines, the Chinese had suffered periodic persecutions and legal discrimination. The Chinese also had grave reservations about Filipino self-rule. The Katipunan Revolt in 1896 had been marked by acts of violence against Chinese.[65] And yet, while many Chinese took a wait-and-see approach to American annexation, more were concerned with the immediate crisis and dangers to themselves than they were with the broader implications of American annexation and the Philippine revolt.

Some migrants went so far as to participate in the rebellion. One such Chinese was José Ignacio Paua, born Hou Bao in Fujian in 1856. Paua arrived in Manila at the age of sixteen—perhaps indicating that he had not entered the islands through a well-established migration network—and within a few years he had become a master blacksmith and trader. According to some sources, he was a respected community leader, although he did not appear among the ranks of the senior *cabecillas*. In Manila, Paua continued his association with the Tiandihui, which he had joined before his departure from Xiamen and which may have been the migration network through which he had traveled to Manila. By the late 1880s, he had become the leader of the Manila chapter.[66] In the 1890s, Paua was active in anti-Spanish activities and made acquaintance with several prominent Filipino nationalists; he even courted Emilio Aguinaldo's cousin Antonia Jamir.[67] When the revolution began, Paua joined Aguinaldo's army and distinguished himself through loyal and enthusiastic service. Paua gained fame as a soldier and by operating the rebels' first munitions factory. He also recruited three thousand Chinese troops from among the Tiandihui membership. Paua's ability to recruit Chinese mercenaries is also indicative of economic trends in the late 1890s. With most of Luzon embroiled in a civil war, the Chinese economy suffered. Disruptions in revenue farms and labor contracting left many unemployed at the same time the rebels were looking for soldiers. The Tiandihui's protomilitarized membership was well suited to this task.

Paua was steadily promoted and by 1897 had become a colonel. He had proven his worth to Aguinaldo by helping the general eliminate two of his main rivals in the movement, Andres and Procopio Bonifacio, leaders of the 1896 uprising, whom Paua helped to arrest in April 1897. The brothers were judiciously executed the following month.[68] Even with the elimination of the Bonifacio brothers, the revolt continued to be plagued by internecine fighting. Facing the prospect of Spanish reinforcements, Aguinaldo surrendered. In December 1897, the general signed the Treaty of Biacnabato, in which he accepted an indemnity of 800,000 pesos and exile in Hong

Kong.[69] While in the British colony, Paua served as Aguinaldo's interpreter and was instrumental in enlisting the support of Chinese revolutionary groups for the Filipino cause.[70]

The exiles returned to Luzon in the spring of 1898 under the protection of the Americans, and Paua embarked on a fundraising campaign among the Chinese. He ultimately collected 386,000 pesos for the new Philippine government. By February 1899, however, relations between the United States and the Filipinos were disintegrating, and Aguinaldo launched another insurgency. Paua was promoted to brigadier general and returned to the field in September 1899. Active in Albay Province in the Bikol region of southeastern Luzon, Paua's forces initially proved a difficult foe for the Americans, but they were ultimately driven out of the critical ports of Albay and forced to fight a running battle against the United States.[71] Military defeats, aggravated by continued in-fighting within the movement, convinced Paua that he was fighting for a lost cause. Disillusioned, disheartened, and pining for his new wife, Carolina Imperial (a wealthy *india*), Paua resigned his commission in the rebel army and he and his father-in-law, Lieutenant Colonel Paciano Imperial, surrendered at Legazpi in March 1900. After the Amnesty of 1900, he returned to his new family and pursued a career as a businessman and politician until his death in 1922.[72]

Although Paua was not unique among *chinos* in his support for the insurrection, his case is informative. His ability to provide as many as three thousand troops and the significant amounts of cash and materiel he was able to collect from among his countrymen demonstrates that elements of the Chinese community did support the Filipino cause. Those Tiandihui members who participated in the fighting were directly supporting the cause, but most of them would have had prior experience with high levels of illicit violence and banditry in South China, and many were probably experienced mercenaries.[73] As such, they can be seen as yet another Hokkien labor export filling market demand in the Philippines. One advantage that a sworn brotherhood organization like the Tiandihui had over native-place associations and more narrowly defined migration networks was that, because of its fictive brotherhood, the Tiandihui could recruit labor from a wider pool than those other networks that were tied to a handful of sending villages or lineages.[74] Hence Paua could use the Tiandihui to meet Aguinaldo's labor needs rapidly. Perhaps more significant were the funds that Paua collected. While some may have been coerced from his fellow *chinos,* it was not immediately clear that the Filipinos would fail, and hence support for the cause might be in the interests of the Chinese merchant elite. Paua's initial support for and ultimate abandonment of the revolt can also be viewed as a calculated socioeconomic strategy. Paua himself emerged from the revolt with wealth and connections, and his recruiting efforts among the Chinese secret societies promised employment in an otherwise stagnant economy. His American enemies went so far as to accuse Paua of using the revolution as a pretense to extort wealth from Albay, in other words, of taking an entrepreneurial approach to the insurrection. As the movement rapidly unraveled, support waned not just among the Chinese, but also among *indios* and especially *ilustrados,* who, although sympathetic to the cause of independence, were troubled by Aguinaldo's policies and practices and eventually gave their support to the American regime.[75] Paua's success in meeting the labor needs of the insurrection had one other unexpected consequence. Demobilized Chinese mercenaries and unemployed labor, whom Paua had been able to recruit, were a potentially dangerous element, especially as many of them were drawn back to Manila. They may partly explain the spike in urban crime that followed American annexation.

Finally, Paua's case is indicative of the fluidity of identity categories in the colonial Philippines. While the rebellion had been marked by violence against Chinese, it would be wrong to contend that the *insurectos* were instinctively anti-Chinese or that there were rigid identity categories that required someone like Paua to make a defining choice as to whether he was Chinese or Filipino. Paua's intimate acquaintance with Aguinaldo and his later marriage into the Imperial clan show that individual *chinos* could develop robust extra-community connections, but this did not mean that he had left his "Chineseness" behind and become assimilated into *indio* society. Although Paua eventually settled permanently in the islands, his initial value to Aguinaldo arose from the fact that he was Chinese. His connections within the local Chinese community provided the money, and his links back, through the Tiandihui, to the labor supply of coastal China supplied the bodies. His prominence in the short-lived war for Philippine national liberation was attributable to the fact that he was a transnational elite.

The open participation of people like Paua and Mariano Limjap in the cause of Philippine independence demonstrates yet again the remarkable degree of political sophistication among the Chinese. As transnationals, *chinos,* and even *mestizos,* were exceedingly sensitive to the political landscapes of both the colonial Philippines and late imperial China. As such they positioned themselves for maximum advantage in their relationship with political authority. As the political environment became more complex in the first years of the twentieth century, local Chinese would adapt themselves to it.

## Political Diversification in the Chinese Community

In the Philippines, the Katipunan Revolt, the Spanish-American War, annexation, the insurrection, and American political reforms served as catalysts for the development of a more complex and articulated political arena. These changes were quite obvious among the Chinese, who were also influenced by the new political currents emerging in China. Under the Spanish, the Chinese *cabecillas,* as the group with financial resources and official connections, were the only politically active element of the Chinese community. Their orientation was generally proestablishment, and they constructed networks with the Spanish authorities by converting to Catholicism, seeking out Spanish patrons, and becoming Spanish subjects. The *cabecillas* simultaneously communicated with the Qing government, purchased official rank, educated sons for the imperial exams, and affected Qing bureaucratic form in their correspondence. At the time, affiliation with radical anti-establishment political movements was rare and was antithetical to the interests of the Chinese elite. There is some indication of sympathies within the elite for Kang Youwei's reformist agenda, but even these do not seem to have been disruptive.

Although it appeared that during the American period the lower strata of the community were primarily concerned with the mundane matters of migration and employment, the expansion of the middle and upper classes provided for a rapid diversification of the political arena. While this diversification may have been fostered by American attitudes that were more tolerant toward political activism than the Spanish had been, they were more a result of the fact that these types of affiliations appeared only in the late nineteenth century. From that time on, the privileged classes of Chinese began to affiliate not only with proestablishment Qing institutions, but also with the reformist Baohuanghui (Protect the Emperor Society) and the revolutionary Tongmenghui (Revolutionary Alliance). The decade before the Qing dynasty's fall witnessed a slow but steady diversification of political affiliations among the Chinese. The first political group to gain a foothold in the islands was Kang Youwei's Baohuanghui. Kang, a Confucian-trained philosopher and former Qing official, was a leading figure in the Hundred Days Reform of 1898. Kang and his protégé Liang Qichao were forced to leave China after the empress dowager quashed the reforms and imprisoned the Guangxu emperor. In exile, Kang focused his efforts on mobilizing expatriate Chinese in hopes of restoring the emperor and initiating constitutional reforms. A Baohuanghui branch was founded in Cavite in 1899 but soon shifted it headquarters to Manila. Early reformists also launched two newspapers to support the cause, but they had very limited appeal at the time and soon folded.[76] After the founding of the Baohuanghui, more radical political groups began to appear.

By the first decade of this century, revolutionary tracts published by Sun Yat-sen's Tongmenghui in Tokyo and other organizations in Hong Kong were circulating in the Philippines.[77] The Tongmenghui was a loose alliance of various anti-Qing factions under the nominal leadership of Dr. Sun. They advocated the overthrow of the Qing and the establishment of a republican government. In Manila, the pro-Sun group was led by Zheng Hanqi, known in the Philippines as Dr. Tee Han Kee. Dr. Tee, a Hokkien from Xiamen, was educated at the Methodist-run Anglo-Chinese College in Fuzhou, where the sons of many *cabecillas* received their secondary education. After graduation he moved to Hong Kong to pursue a medical career.[78] While in Hong Kong in the 1890s, Tee met classmate Sun Yat-sen at the Hong Kong Medical College. In 1902, Tee moved to the Philippines, where he was hired by the colonial Bureau of Health to work as the medical inspector for the Chinese community. [79] Dr. Tee's education, facility with English, and respected position made him an important figure in the Chinese community, and he was elected to the board of directors of the Chinese Commercial Council in 1904.[80] Membership in such an ostensibly conservative merchant institution did not, however, dampen his enthusiasm for Sun's cause. In May 1906, Tee and another Chinese, Huang Haishan, cut off their queues (the hairstyle mandated by the Qing) as a sign of their revolutionary commitment.[81] Much of the revolutionary movement has been seen as a primarily Cantonese enterprise because of Sun's Canton roots and the fact that his overseas fundraising successes were generally limited to Cantonese enclaves. In this light Dr. Tee seemed to be a bridge between Cantonese and Hokkiens. The rapidity with which he moved into the elite was likely facilitated by his place of birth and shows as well that, despite a generally conservative bent among the Chinese merchant elite, even radical sympathies did not disqualify one from elite standing.

Other young revolutionaries were also active in the Philippines. Yang Haolü, the son of a prominent local merchant and newspaper editor, took the lead in organizing demonstrations among the Cantonese. Although his family was originally from Fujian, Yang was born and raised in Guangdong. The young man had become an active revolutionary while studying at Waseda University in Japan but was forced to return to the Philippines in 1905, when the Japanese government began a campaign to suppress radical Chinese student organizations. One notable event of Yang's revolutionary career in the Philippines was his verbal assault on Xu Qin, a Baohuanghui delegate, while the latter was giving a speech on the need for constitutional reform to the Cantonese *huiguan* in 1905.[82] Yang led his young colleagues to the *huiguan*, where they hurled insults at Xu.[83] A riot ensued and several people were injured.

The 1905 anti-American boycott was another galvanizing event for Chinese progressives in the Philippines. When the United States strengthened the Chinese exclusion laws in 1905, many in China and overseas responded with outrage. The nationwide boycott of Ameri-

FIGURE 3. Dr. Tee Han Kee. Huang Xiaocang, ed. *Feilübin Minlila Zhonghua shanghui sanshi zhounian jinian kan.* Manila: Zhonghua Shanghui Chubanbu, 1936.

can products, which began in Shanghai and spread to Southeast Asia, is viewed by many as a watershed in the history of Chinese nationalism.[84] In the Philippines, Yang Haolü supported the boycott and collected donations for Cantonese strikers.[85] Even the *cabecillas* joined in calling for a relaxation of the exclusion laws, and the former consul, Chen Gang, organized a sympathetic boycott in Xiamen.[86] But in the main, the local Chinese merchant elite demonstrated less enthusiasm for the boycott than their peers in Shanghai and Guangzhou. At that moment they were more occupied with implementing a range of institutional innovations in Manila.

Although active in the Philippine Islands, revolutionary groups were atomized and attracted few adherents among the commercially oriented Chinese community. They were also hampered by the tendency to be organized by native-place orientation. However, since they were wealthy and well educated, like Dr. Tee, and often were the sons of local elite, like Yang Haolü, the revolutionaries were not completely ostracized from the Chinese merchants. For example, various guilds and *huiguan* allowed them to conduct meetings at their halls. At the Hok Lien Ho Po Siong Hui (Fulian Hebu Shanghui), a textile merchants guild, young radicals held a rally to criticize Manchu rule and promote political discussion.[87]

This diverse group of revolutionaries began to coalesce in 1908 with the posting of Yang Shijun as consul general in Manila. The new consul was harshly criticized by the local activists and was lambasted for his shabby etiquette. Yang Shijun's elder brother, Yang Shiqi, was vice-minister of the Qing's Ministry of Agriculture, Industry, and Commerce (Nonggong Shangbu) and, in 1907, had commanded an official mission to root out anti-Qing agitators among the Southeast Asian Chinese.[88] The public critique of the younger brother indicates that the radical youth in the Philippines assumed that Yang Shijun had been given the same task. In the absence of a local Chinese paper through which to voice their critique, the activists sent a letter to the *China Daily (Zhongguo ribao)* in Hong Kong, which printed their attack on Yang Shijun.[89] The following year, a revolutionary reading society (Puzhi Yue Shubaoshe) was founded to disseminate literature and newspapers, and to sponsor speeches. Soon after its founding, the society was visited by three Tongmenghui delegates, Wu Zongming, Chen Jinfang, and Huang Jiasheng (see fig. 4). In the spring of 1911, Li Qi, a Tongmenghui organizer, was dispatched from Hong Kong to Manila. In Manila, Li helped Dr. Tee Han Kee set up a chapter of the Tongmenghui, which was soon reorganized into a Guomindang cell. And again in 1911 there was a second visit by delegates Wu Zongming, Chen Jinfang, and Huang Jiasheng (see fig. 5). The founding of a party branch and the first unfurling of the party flag in the Philippines was cause for celebration among the young activists (see fig. 1). That summer the group began publishing its own newspaper, the *Kong Li Po (Gongli ribao)*, which remained the leading Chinese paper and the main Guomindang mouthpiece in the American Philippines until it was forced to cease publication by the occupying Japanese in 1942. The new party not only attracted young foreign-educated Chinese, but also gained adherents among the older and more established members of the community.[90]

Consequently, by the time of the Chinese revolution in 1911–1912, an active and diverse political discourse was already taking place among a small group of Chinese in the Philippines. In part, this diversification was an outgrowth of the more lenient attitude the new colonial authorities took toward political activity: Chinese political parties were not suppressed in the United States or its possessions as they were elsewhere. The diversification of political orientation among the Chinese was also a function of the existence of various political alternatives that had not existed during the Spanish period. However, this did not mean that Manila's Chinese community was riven with political conflict or, as Blaker has argued, that there was a dichotomy between "nationalists" and "traditionalists."[91] The divisions between the various reformist, revolutionary, and conservative groups in Manila were not as starkly drawn as they were in other overseas communities, and there was significant room for overlap. By contrast, the divisions between various Chinese political groups in Singapore were much clearer. In the British colony, the deaths of the empress dowager and Guangxu emperor in 1908 were a joyous occasion for Tongmenghui activists, who were primarily Cantonese. Their refusal to close their shops to observe a day of mourning sponsored by the Hokkien-controlled and Baohuanghui-oriented Chamber of Commerce that still idolized Guangxu nearly resulted in riot. This mutual animosity was heightened in the pages of rival newspapers.[92] The Chinese community in the Philippines was significantly less polarized, most likely as a result of native-place ties that overcame political differences and the integrative strength of the main Chinese institutions, especially the Manila Chinese Chamber of Commerce, which was rapidly able to gain a dominant role in the community and to either stifle or coopt divisive elements.

FIGURE 4. Founders of the *Puzhi Yue Shubaoshe* with visiting Tongmenghui delegates, 1909. Delegates are Chen Jinfang, far right in front row; Wu Zongming, second from left in front row; and Huang Jiasheng, third from left in third row. Dr. Tee Han Kee is third from right in front row. Courtesy of Guomindang Party Archives, Jinshan, Taiwan.

FIGURE 5. The second visit of Wu Zongming, Chen Jinfang, and Huang Jiasheng (seated right to left) to Manila, 1911. Courtesy of Guomindang Party Archives, Jinshan, Taiwan.

## Institutional Developments

The first decade of the twentieth century witnessed the appearance of many new "traditional" Chinese associations, such as *huiguan, hang, gongsi,* and a proliferation of secret societies like the Gee Hock Tong. The Gee Hock was a brotherhood of Cantonese from the Chaozhou (Teochow) region of northern Guangdong. They had been particularly active in the secret society riots in Singapore in the 1840s and 1850s. Their appearance in Manila, possibly indicative of an attempt at infiltrating other regional economies, created alarm among American law enforcement.[93] This era also witnessed the founding of several new "modern" institutions such as the Chinese Consul General, the Manila Chinese Chamber of Commerce, and Western-style Chinese corporations, which tended to eclipse other institutional forms. Under the Spanish, Chinese community institutions were what are commonly considered "traditional" Chinese forms: *huiguan,* surname groups, sworn brotherhoods, temples, and charitable associations. The number of these associational structures, although increasing in the late nineteenth century, was still relatively small. These "traditional" Chinese associations were supplemented by Spanish institutions that allowed the Chinese community to function as a self-governing entity. The Gremio de Chinos and the Gobernadorcillo de los Sangleyes were controlled by a corporate elite of the wealthiest Chinese *cabecillas* and represented the primary means of communication between the Chinese state, Spanish authorities, and the local Chinese, although during the consular campaign the Guangdong *huiguan* had tried to capitalize on its own external linkages.

The most significant institutional change within the community in the early years of this century was the abolition of the Gobernadorcillo system and with it the Gremio de Chinos and the Tribunal de los Sangleyes. The post of Gobernadorcillo was officially abolished in 1898, with the establishment of a Chinese consulate general in Manila. In the increasingly complex environment of the American Philippines, however, the consul general could not fully replace the Gobernadorcillo, in part because the consul was appointed from outside, nor could the consul hope to exert central power without access to broad-based community institutions.[94]

The transition from Gobernadorcillo to consul was eased, at first, by the appointment of the leading *cabecilla,* Chen Qianshan, as

interim consul and eventually by the posting of Don Engracio
Palanca Chen Gang. As the preceding chapter has shown, however,
this transition was far from smooth and created conflicts within the
community that forced the resignation of Chen Gang. During his
brief tenure as consul, Chen did oversee the first phase of Chinese
institutional change. With the abolition of the headman system,
some Chinese community institutions, like the Tribunal de los Sangleyes (the Chinese small claims court and legal aid service), had to
be dismantled, while others, like the Communidad de Chinos (the
main charitable institution), were reorganized. In 1899, Chen Gang
placed the Communidad's management in the hands of his father.
At the time, that organization was active in establishing the Anglo-
Chinese School as well as overseeing the management and fund-raising for the Chinese General Hospital and the Chinese cemetery.
The Communidad also provided financial and medical aid to Chinese who had been dislocated or injured during the fighting, or who
were suffering from plague and cholera. Chen Qianshan had had a
long involvement with the hospital and the cemetery, and had personally provided the capital for founding the Chinese General Hospital. His rivals, however, accused him of misusing funds collected
for the hospital's operation.[95]

With the arrival of Chen Gang's replacement, Li Rongyao, in
April 1899, control of the Communidad de Chinos was taken away
from Don Carlos, and the whole institution was reorganized under
the name of the Philippine Chinese Charitable Association (although the Chinese name remained the same). As before, the
Charitable Association supervised the funding and operations of
the Chinese hospital and cemetery, but, rather than being officially
controlled by a single individual, the association was placed under a
board of twenty-four directors nominally selected by the consul
general from "among prominent overseas Chinese business leaders," which in turn meant that it was dominated by the Hokkien majority.[96] Historian Liu Chi-Tien has argued—mistakenly in my view:
"Although in name and in organization the association remained
an independent body, it was in actuality a sub-agency of the consul-
general. The directives of the consul-general were faithfully carried
out."[97] It is unlikely that the consul could have dominated a local institution or the local elite so easily. The example of Don Carlos'
confronting Consul Li with broad elite backing demonstrates the
limits of the consul's power to dictate to the local elite. In fact, the

directives of the consul general were rarely issued without the approval of the *cabecillas*. The Charitable Association was less a creature of the consul than an early structural link between the Chinese government and the local elite. Thereafter, the Charitable Association was nominally controlled by the consul general, who selected the directors, but it was unlikely that the consul could do more than approve a slate of elites. The directors were designated by the title *"shangdong,"* the same term the Chinese merchant elite had been using for decades to translate the term *"cabecilla."*[98] Over the next few years the association's directors were the core membership around which new Chinese community institutions were formed, thus allowing for a relatively smooth transition from Spanish to American rule, and from Gobernadorcillo to consul general and chamber of commerce with minimal disruption.

The Qing empire, unlike many countries at the time, took great care in selecting its consular officers in Manila.[99] Among those to serve were several prominent and well-connected young officials. Zhong Wenyao, who served in Manila from 1904 to 1905,[100] had been a member of the first educational mission to the United States headed by Yung Wing. Later he attended Yale, where he was a coxswain for the men's crew team. After leaving Yale, Zhong filled various foreign posts, including chargé d' affaires in Madrid and consul in Barcelona, before being transferred to Manila. He visited Manila again in 1907 aboard the warship *Haiqi* with Nonggong Shangbu vice-minister Yang Shiqi, served as director of the Shanghai-Nanjing Railroad, and was ultimately posted to the Chinese embassy in Washington in 1909.[101] Another Manila consul, Yang Shijun, was the younger brother of the vice-president of the Nonggong Shangbu, which was the blanket organization for all Chinese chambers of commerce. And the nephew of Wu Tingfang, Qing ambassador to Washington, served briefly as military attaché at the Manila consulate.[102] The Qing government clearly placed some emphasis on the Manila post. In the declining years of the Qing, however, Beijing was hard-pressed to exert any substantive influence through its consuls.[103] In Manila, the consul's duties were limited to issuing and validating travel documents, fund-raising, and presiding over community rituals, such as the emperor's birthday celebrations. It is not surprising that the talented and ambitious Zhong Wenyao requested, and was granted, a transfer after less than a year in Manila.

In addition to these communitywide institutions, the American

第五任中國總領事梁詢先生暨廿四商董

FIGURE 6. Twenty-four *cabecillas* (probably directors of the Philippine Chinese Charitable Association) with the fifth Qing consul general, Liang Xun. Huang Xiaocang, ed. *Feilübin Minlila Zhonghua shanghui sanshi zhounian jinian kan.* Manila: Zhonghua Shanghui Chubanbu, 1936.

period also witnessed the reorganization and founding of dozens of specialized associations. Institutional diversification was a result of greater socioeconomic articulation, the maturation of the economy, and the availability of new institutional models. While the Spanish had begun to alter the social and organizational landscape, the number and variety of associations increased significantly after 1898. The Americans brought chambers of commerce, professional associations, newspapers, labor unions, country clubs, and social clubs all of which employed Chinese. The *Fookien Times* and *Kong Li Po* newspapers, the Chinese Labor Union, the Oriental and Cosmos social clubs, and a variety of sports clubs became cornerstones of the Chinese community. New institutions were quickly adopted and adapted by the Chinese to reinforce status distinctions, promote class and occupational interests, and provide the institutional means to influence the authorities. The Chinese elite, in particular, were able to draw on new institutional models and strategies to assert and maintain their position, but the most important institutions continued to be those with the closest links to China, those that defined community identity, and those that had the best relations with the colonial administration.

New institutional forms perpetuated *cabecilla* control, on the one hand, since the Chinese merchant elite was the major force behind their founding and therefore allowed for the continued viability of certain "traditional" elite strategies. On the other hand, these merchants were forced by their reorganization into "modern" institutions and by the circumstances of the early American period to reorient themselves and adopt new strategies, which sometimes replaced and sometimes complemented earlier tactics. Moreover, generational change, which began to affect the leadership of key community institutions and Chinese firms in the 1910s; changes in the economy, which pushed Chinese into new markets; and the passage of the Payne-Aldrich Act combined to reshape the role of the Chinese in the Philippine economy and the superstructure of the community.[104]

## The Manila Chinese General Chamber of Commerce

The founding of the Manila Chinese General Chamber of Commerce is an excellent case study for examining the continuity of elite strategies. Recent scholarship on chambers of commerce in China describes a few independently founded local merchant associations based on foreign models, for example, in Shanghai and Hong Kong, whose form was coopted and standardized by the Qing government. The Qing assimilated these models to promote more modern and rational merchant organizations, expand the dynasty's fiscal base, and spur economic growth.[105]

In the Philippines there was a similar phenomenon. In 1904, partly on the advice of Governor-General William Howard Taft, the Chinese merchant elite founded the Manila Chinese Commercial Council (Zhonghua Shanghui), which was a direct linear successor to the Hock Kain (Hokkien) Club.[106] The twenty-four founders of the Commercial Council were, moreover, drawn from the same circle as the twenty-four *cabecillas* who directed the Chinese Charitable Association. Taking the lead in initiating the council were four younger *cabecillas*, Xu Xiaowu, Ye Qizhen, Xie Qing'an, and Sun Gaosheng. Presumably to give the council legitimacy, these young *cabecillas* enlisted the support of several older elite. The founding membership was predominately Hokkien, a reflection of their numerical and commercial dominance, and throughout its history the chamber was controlled by Hokkiens. Overseas chambers of commerce tended to reflect the relative numerical superiority of different native places. In both Singapore and Manila, Hokkiens had the numerical and financial advantage and thus controlled the chamber. Chamber leadership also coincided with control of the major native place and dialect associations and migration networks. The chamber president in both places was usually the former or acting head of the Hokkien association.[107]

Preliminary discussions for the Manila chamber were held in 1903, and, in August 1904, the council held its first meeting in the rooms on the ground floor of the building that had once served as the Gobernadorcillo's office. The twenty-four founders and Consul General Zhong Wenyao were photographed in mandarin robes.[108] That same month Guillermo Cu Unjieng (Qiu Yunheng) was elected president of the council, and the Chinese Commercial Council was invited to join the Manila International Merchants Union the fol-

FIGURE 7. Directors of the Chinese Commercial Council, 1904. The Commercial Council was later renamed the Manila Chinese General Chamber of Commerce. Huang Xiaocang, ed. *Feilübin Minlila Zhonghua shanghui sanshi zhounian jinian kan.* Manila: Zhonghua Shanghui Chubanbu, 1936.

lowing November.[109] Cu, a Hokkien from Jinjiang County, was a prominent dry-goods merchant who had been a protégé and business partner of Mariano Limjap, financier of the insurrection. Between 1904 and 1920, Cu was president of the chamber on five separate occasions.[110]

In 1906, the council was rechartered and reorganized based on regulations set down by the Nonggong Shangbu in Beijing and was renamed the Manila Chinese General Chamber of Commerce. In addition to the reorganization, the Chinese consul general was made an honorary member of the chamber and thus institutionalized the link between the Qing government and the *cabecillas*. Like a county magistrate in China, the Chinese consul general in Manila was inclined to develop close ties to the most influential members of the local elite. This affiliation would make the consul's job a great deal easier and, likely, more financially remunerative during his limited tenure. Through the agency of the consul, the Chamber of Commerce had more influence vis-à-vis the Americans and had an official link to Beijing. The links between the consul and the chamber were further strengthened by the consul's nominal authority over the Philippine Chinese Charitable Association. Consulate-chamber cooperation was not unique to the Philippines. The Chinese "city hall"

FIGURE 8. Guillermo Cu Unjieng, drygoods merchant, banker, and first president of the Chinese Chamber of Commerce. Huang Xiaocang, ed. *Feilübin Minlila Zhonghua shanghui sanshi zhounian jinian kan.* Manila: Zhonghua Shanghui Chubanbu, 1936.

in New York appealed to the New York consul and the Chinese ambassador in Washington for help in recruiting literati from China to serve as chairmen. Historian Wu Jianxiong has explained this cooperation as a result of the general lack of sophistication among New York's petty Chinese merchants and their need for an educated outsider to overcome factional problems within Chinatown.[111] Given the sophistication demonstrated by the Chinese elite in Manila and elsewhere, I think it unlikely that this was the case. To prosper in New York or anywhere, Chinese elites needed to buttress their intracommunity authority through external validation. While I would not dispute the importance of the conflict mediation role, I would not be surprised to learn that the New York merchant elite coopted and even manipulated their nominal superior. The *cabecillas* in Manila had little trouble in selecting chamber presidents from among their ranks or, when necessary, using their social and economic power to guide those above them. Nonetheless, both cases demonstrate the importance of merchant-official interaction in the organization of local institutions.

Cooptation by Qing officialdom did not mean that control of the Chinese Chamber of Commerce devolved to Beijing. All of those in the service of national projects, from consuls to Guomindang representatives, would encounter what James Blaker has described as a "tenacity" of commitment to local interests.[112] Instead of serving primarily national agendas, the Chinese elite were able to manipulate the status and influence of the chamber and its institutional ties to the Chinese consul in the pursuit of local and personal interests. This represented an opportunistic, mutual cooptation of these institutions by the Qing government—for coordination and fund-raising—and by the merchant elite to assert their localist interests. The status and influence of the Chinese Chamber of Commerce and its elite membership was further enhanced by the American reliance on Chinese talent and capital to promote the development of the Philippine economy and by the administration's deference to the chamber on matters affecting the Chinese community.

Although some aspects of colonial rule had changed dramatically, the Americans shared the Spanish desire for a stable, law-abiding, and economically viable Chinese enclave. To promote stability and economic growth, the new colonial administration favored the elite, be they the cultured Filipino *ilustrados* or wealthy *chinos*. Early administrations began a policy, clear in the Organic Law, of cultivat-

ing a local elite to serve in the Philippine legislature and as middlemen and administrators. The Americans were also beholden to the
wealthy Chinese and *mestizo* merchants whose money was needed to
develop the lumber, sugar, and tobacco industries that would make
the Philippines a profitable possession. The leadership of the Chinese Chamber of Commerce, who controlled many of these key industries, could therefore readily influence the administration.[113]

> This powerful organization performed two broad functions: busi-
> ness and civic. Under the first heading the Chamber collected and
> disseminated information about trade conditions; recommended
> or introduced Chinese business with proper credentials; provided
> for the exhibition of goods produced in China; conducted research
> in business problems and methods; and in any crises or troubled pe-
> riod in business it afforded a forum for discussion and machinery
> for action. On the civic side the Chamber was an instrument for the
> collection of funds for Philippine public causes, such as Red Cross,
> Anti-Tuberculosis, hospital and charitable organizations, and
> calamity relief.[114]

Economic coordination and charity had always been the central
functions of the dominant Chinese associations, and the chamber's
founding shows no significant break with the merchant-elite strategies of the Spanish period. The photograph of the founders of the
chamber was a vivid indicator. In the front row sit upper elite
founders, dressed in mandarin robes indicating various purchased
and honorary ranks; behind them the younger *cabecillas* stand
solemnly. There was significant continuity in membership between
this group and Spanish period elite institutions, notably the Gremio
de Chinos. Leading Spanish era cabecillas, such as Lin Anbang and
Mariano Fernando Yu Chingco, were prominent chamber members.
Yu Chingco had been a close ally of Chen Qianshan, had served as
Gobernadorcillo in the 1870s, but also played a highly visible role in
the establishment of the chamber and served on its board of directors until his death in 1913.[115] The ease of this transition may have
been a direct result of the abolition of the headman system. In Semarang, the Dutch headman system (Kongkoan) existed simultaneously with the Chinese Chamber of Commerce (Tiong Hwa Sianghwee) from 1907 to 1931. As a result, competition for community
leadership was contested by these two associations. The Kongkoan

had better connections with the colonial authorities (which brought criticism of their collaborationist role), and the Sianghwee was much more closely tied to the Chinese government.[116] Manila's Chinese managed to avoid this kind of institutional bifurcation.

The chamber was also flexible enough to offer a venue for new types of elite to make their influence felt over the community. The leading revolutionary in the islands, Dr. Tee Han Kee, was also a director of the chamber in the early 1900s, as were other founding members of the Manila branch of the Tongmenghui. Rather than representing the emergence of a completely new type of community leadership, as some historians have argued, the founding of the Chamber of Commerce was a step along a continuum that represented an intermingling of approaches to elite status and self-identification that were under constant revision.[117]

This revision of strategies derived partly from institutional inertia. Although the Manila Chinese General Chamber of Commerce continued to replicate some of the functions of a traditional *huiguan*, it was also based on Western models. The charter called for a broad membership of Chinese, a board of directors, and a president, each with clearly defined roles and responsibilities. The chamber also had as broad a membership base as previous overarching elite organizations in that it nominally accommodated all strata of the commercial community and all native places. It could also encompass new types of elite, such as Western-educated professionals. Perhaps because of the elite's prior institutional experience with the Gremio de Chinos and the Communidad de Chinos, bringing all these interests together in the Chamber of Commerce was surprisingly unproblematic.

In addition to its activities in the Philippines, the chamber responded to civic crises in China. As early as 1905, the members collected donations for flood relief in Quanzhou prefecture in Fujian and also raised funds for neighboring Jiangxi Province, as well as relief collections for other areas in China. During the Chinese civil war of 1911 and 1912, the chamber funneled aid through the Shanghai Red Cross. The chamber also organized local political and cultural events, such as the emperor's and empress dowager's birthdays, New Year's celebrations, and receptions for visiting dignitaries. When Yang Shiqi, vice-minister of the chamber's imperial sponsor, the Nonggong Shangbu, visited the islands in November 1907, the chamber provided a lavish reception at the mansion of local millionaire Mariano Limjap at a cost of U.S.$6,000.[118] Interestingly, Limjap was technically a *mestizo,* but the fact that he hosted this and other receptions and was a partner of the chamber's former president is, as Richard Chu has shown, a clear indication of the flexibility of identity in colonial Manila.[119] True to its founding charter, the chamber also reported to the Nonggong Shangbu on economic conditions in the islands and the size of the Chinese population. For its services the chamber was granted a Qing official seal and was selected to choose a local delegate to the Qing Constitutional Assembly.[120]

When the Chinese revolution began in the fall of 1911, there was a brief surge in local activism in support of the anti-Manchu struggle. Various campaigns managed to raise 300,000 pesos for the cause, and Dr. Tee spoke out against Yuan Shikai, who at that point was in charge of the Qing suppression campaign.[121] After the last Qing emperor abdicated in January 1912, the chamber continued its mediating role between China and the Chinese in the Philippines. Early in 1912, the chamber sent its congratulations to provisional president Sun Yat-sen and president-elect Yuan Shikai. Mr. Li, a government representative, perhaps the same Li Qi who had helped organize the local Tongmenghui, visited the islands soon after and was reported to have collected over U.S.$600,000 in donations.[122] Many local Chinese were enthused by the founding of a new Chinese government, and in May 1912, the Manila Chinese General Chamber of Commerce formally recognized the Chinese Republic and the government of Yuan Shikai. President Yuan sent a letter of greeting to the chamber and dispatched a new consul general.[123] In October 1912, Benito Siy Congbieng (Shi Guangming), the man who had served as chamber president for the last five years, was named the Manila community's representative at a Nonggong Shangbu conference in Beijing and was later elected to the new National Assembly. Siy, however, resigned his seat on the assembly in favor of his fellow *cabecilla* Shi Zhihua and returned to Manila, where he again took up his post as chamber president. Connections between the Chamber of Commerce and Beijing were supplemented by offers from the new Fujian provincial government for local Chinese, in recognition of the value of the transnational ties between Fujian and Manila, to join the provincial legislature, thus institutionalizing their elite status in two locales.[124] In the short term, the transition from imperial to republican China proved relatively painless for Manila's Chinese elite. Nonetheless, after Sun Yat-sen stepped down as provisional president, there continued to be a faction, primarily composed of Cantonese but including some prominent Hokkiens, who remained loyal to Sun and who grew increasingly vocal after the failed Second Revolution and as it became apparent that Yuan Shikai was not willing to share power. Despite frequent editorials and fund-raising campaigns, as well as periodic visits by prominent Sun supporters, there is little to suggest that the majority of the community was fired by national issues. Local interests were best served by maintaining cordial relations with the new government, but it was still the ties to the native place and in Manila that mattered most. Thus the shift in loyalty from dynasty to republic was achieved with negligible change in elite personnel or in the prominence of the Chamber of Commerce.

The 1911 Revolution had a very different effect on the Singapore Chinese Chamber of Commerce. In fact, the fall of the Qing resulted in a major power struggle among the Singapore-Chinese elite. The unwillingness of the Hokkien-dominated, pro-Qing and pro-Baohuanghui chamber to organize a celebration of the 1911 Revolution prompted local Tongmenghui members to found a rival chamber of commerce. In April 1912, the Chinese Merchants General Chamber of Commerce, representing primarily Cantonese and Tongmenghui (now Guomindang) interests, was founded and recognized by Beijing. The rival chambers competed in fund-raising for the new Chinese government, and the older chamber founded its own political party, the Kong Ho-tang (Gonghedang), to counter Guomindang activities. The final split occurred in 1913, when the increasingly autocratic Yuan Shikai suppressed the Guomindang and contracted an unpopular foreign loan. In China, this precipitated the abortive "Second Revolution." For the Singapore Chinese, the Guomindang's failure to stop Yuan Shikai spelled the end of the Chinese Merchants General Chamber of Commerce. With the dissolution of the local Guomindang branch (under pressure from both Beijing and the British government, which backed the majority Hokkiens), the new chamber was doomed and finally ceased operations in August 1914.[125] A Chinese chamber of commerce could not hope to contest for power unless it was on good terms with the Chinese government. The Manila chamber avoided the fate of Singapore's Chinese Merchants General Chamber of Commerce by remaining loyal to Beijing and by distancing itself from political intrigue.[126] As the subsequent chapter will demonstrate, the fact that no major rivals appeared in Manila may also be attributable to the chamber's remarkable ability to manipulate colonial officials to eliminate its competition.

As long as the Yuan Shikai government remained viable, and with it the centralized authority of a Chinese state and Beijing's ability to confer authority on its consuls, it made good sense for the elite to maintain at least cordial relations with Beijing and with the consul general. There were certainly incidents of controversy and disagreement, but until the Yuan government collapsed in 1916, the consul had some measure of influence. The relative authority of the consul general was significantly enhanced when there was a strong government in China, as were the advantages for the local elite of identifying with the Chinese state. Between 1916 and 1928, when central authority collapsed in China, the consul general probably had little value outside his ability to validate migration documents. During this interregnum, it was the Chinese Chamber of Commerce in its fundamentally local guise that was the dominant institution.[127] I would surmise, although it is beyond the scope of the present study, that between 1916 and 1928 it was links to officials in the provincial government of Fujian and the American consul at Xiamen that were the most critical to Manila's Chinese merchant elite.[128] Beijing's "man in Manila" was just one point of contact. In fact, during the warlord period Manila's Chinese merchant elite threw their wealth and energies into local rather than national projects, expanding their various market shares in the Philippines and remaking the urban landscape of Xiamen to facilitate its role as a critical node in the global economy.[129]

Beyond its institutional ties to the Chinese government, the chamber was able to use its prominence and power to affect American colonial policy. The main instrument of influence was the petition. Throughout its history, the Manila Chinese General Chamber of Commerce used petitions as a means of collective action to criticize immigration restrictions, duties on Chinese imports, and laws that demanded that Chinese *tenderos* keep their business accounts in either English, Spanish, or Tagalog. In these petitions the chamber most often took the lead, but it was often joined by other business organizations that added their seals.[130] Using petitions to assert socioeconomic interests also became a common tactic by which other Chinese groups circumvented the chamber and appealed directly to the colonial authorities.

In the first decade of American rule, the Chinese were particularly avid petitioners. Petitions came from major community organizations like the Chinese Charitable Association or the Chamber of

Commerce but also included numerous suits brought by individual Chinese against the United States government and the Bureau of Insular Affairs (the branch of the Department of War responsible for governing the Philippines). Outside the proposed bookkeeping law and the dispensation of Chinese estates, the primary focus of these cases involved facilitating access to the Philippines for entertainment troupes, skilled workers (such as staff for a newspaper), or the kin of current and even deceased residents.[131] This was a significant development, since the Spanish had largely limited access to the colonial government to the Gobernadorcillo. While late Spanish legal reforms and the growing number of lawyers in Manila had allowed individual *chinos* access to Spanish justice, American reforms greatly accelerated this trend.

Under the Americans, the elite and even those outside the elite—trying to break in—employed new tactics and cultivated new extra-community alliances to improve their standing within the Chinese community and vis-à-vis the American and Chinese governments. Chen Qianshan's Cantonese rivals could petition the Qing government and with the help of the British consul could attempt to influence the Spanish. When the Americans arrived, the Cantonese circumvented the established channels and effectively influenced colonial policy. This pattern proliferated in the 1900s and demonstrates the competition for recognition and influence among the Chinese. In 1908, for example, the Chinese Labor Union of Manila ignored the chamber and directly petitioned Washington, Beijing, and the Chinese ambassador to the United States to complain about the mistreatment of local Chinese laborers.[132]

The increased access to Western legal counsel, that is, employing lawyers to both challenge and defend the legality and actions of the colonial government and new Chinese institutions, became a popular and effective supplement to existing connections and traditional tactics of suasion.[133] The colonial legal system offered the Chinese a way to interact with the authorities as individuals or groups outside of the community's main institutions. Some Chinese could skirt the authority of Chinese community institutions, while others established themselves as rivals to the chamber and the Chinese consul general. In other cases, individuals and small groups of Chinese tested Chinese exclusion laws: these included two attempts to bring in editors and typesetters to work for a Chinese-language newspaper and a long campaign on the part of three merchants to bring a troupe of Chi-

nese actors to the islands for the entertainment of the residents of
Manila. In the latter case, the three merchants employed an American lawyer, J. B. Early. Through the creative use of legal precedents,
Early successfully pleaded the case to Secretary of War Taft, who ordered that the actors be admitted. This ruling overturned the decisions of both the Manila collector of customs and the secretary of finance and justice.[134] Taft was ultimately forced to reverse himself
when it was revealed that coolie brokers in Manila were importing laborers and prostitutes disguised as actors.[135] Clearly, the Chinese
showed remarkable creativity in circumventing the exclusion laws.

Litigation and the diffusion of influence added to the competition among the Chinese and increased the number of challenges
faced by the merchant elite. Uncertainty, innovation, and the continuing socioeconomic crisis meant that the Chamber of Commerce
was hard-pressed to maintain sufficient community cohesion to further their interests.[136] Fortunately for the elite, the exclusion laws and
the American tendency to rely on the chamber perpetuated elite
dominance. The elite, however, also showed a remarkable ability to
manipulate colonial aspirations, respond to market demand, and
maintain robust transnational ties that allowed them to exploit a permissive environment to protect the community in a time of crisis but
also to lay the groundwork for greater prosperity in the coming
decades.

## Conclusion

As they had under the Spanish, the Chinese elite in the American
Philippines employed a wide array of strategies and deployed a wide
range of identities to attain and assert status in a volatile environment. Associations and occupations, both "traditional" and "modern," proliferated: the Chinese community in the early American period was more occupationally diverse and less static than ever before,
yet at the same time key integrative systems, especially migration networks, had been enhanced. Continuing *cabecilla* dominance was negotiated among this variety of newly emerging socioeconomic and
political groups. As a result, the merchant elite were forced to rework
their strategies, adopt new identities, and recreate their institutions.
The Chinese community was an arena in which numerous established and emergent groups contested and challenged, and yet institutional and strategic diversification was not always antagonistic.

There was significant overlap between associations representing diverse interests. In the early 1900s, revolutionary affiliations
did not prevent Dr. Tee Han Kee from joining the ostensibly pro-
Qing and occasionally pro-Baohuanghui Chamber of Commerce.
The most important criteria for membership was prominence, not
political affiliation. In a changing world, the chamber admitted not
only established *cabecillas*, but also new types of elite with new political and economic strategies. On the chamber's board of directors
sat men in mandarin robes, like former Gobernadorcillo Mariano
Fernando Yu Chingco, side by side with the Western-educated Dr.
Tee. Yang Huixi, also known as Yang Weihong, was a *cabecilla*, a protégé of Chen Qianshan, and a founding member of the chamber
who not only fathered a revolutionary son, Yang Haolü, but himself
became a founding member of the Manila Tongmenghui. This kind
of adaptability allowed the chamber to give its support to the Republic of China once the Qing had ceased to matter and once the
Chinese consul general represented a republican rather than an
imperial government. Continuity in elite personnel also underscores local elite flexibility and the Chinese government's accom-
modating attitude and demonstrates that the political makeup of
the Chinese community was quite amorphous in this early period.
In many cases, employing labels such as pro-Qing, Republican,
monarchist, or revolutionary to distinguish groups of Chinese overseas is inappropriate and serves only to obscure the extensive and
flexible repertoire of strategies and affiliations from which local
Chinese could draw.[137]

The reasons for the chamber's enduring success in this contentious and often hostile environment lay in this adaptability and
its access to external sources of authority (the Chinese and American governments). Although it was dominated by and served elite interests, the chamber's power was enhanced by its institutional link
with the Chinese government and its favored position under American rule. Thus, although it represented primarily a Zhangzhou and
Quanzhou elite, the chamber could nonetheless claim to speak for
the "Chinese" in Manila. This strategy, in turn, limited the ability for
narrower native-place affiliations, occupational associations, or political parties to have the same type of privileged access to authority
that the chamber enjoyed. The real challenges to the chamber's
authority would not come from radical revolutionaries but from rising elite groups that sought to usurp the chamber's position as

spokesman for and protector of the Chinese. Experience had shown that these two tasks could not be surrendered, and when the chamber was challenged in the American period, its leaders would pursue new avenues, develop new identities, and employ new tactics to eliminate rivals.

# 6
# Benevolent Merchants or Malevolent Highbinders?
The Deportation of Agapito Uy
Tongco et al., August 1909

ON THE AFTERNOON of Friday, August 20, 1909, officers of
the Manila police department and the United States Secret Service,
acting under orders from their respective chiefs, took into custody
twelve reputed members of two Chinese societies, the Ban Siong
Tong (Minshangtang) and the Gee Hock Tong (Yifutang). The
twelve Chinese were taken to the Legaspi landing on Manila Bay,
where their identification papers and migration documents (section
six certificates) were confiscated, effectively denying all twelve legal
reentry into the American colony.[1] The twelve were then placed on
the steam launch *Bohol* and, under the watchful eyes of secret service
agents, conveyed to the steamer *Yuensang*. Having secured their prisoners on board the steamer, the secret service agents returned to the
pier, and the *Yuensang* sailed for China. Within the span of an afternoon, the American authorities had summarily deported twelve subjects of the Qing empire without trial.

By Saturday morning, the events of the previous afternoon had
become a citywide sensation. The major dailies in Manila carried
bold headlines alternately praising and condemning the colonial authorities. For the rest of the year, the deportation was a popular topic
of conversation and editorial not only for what it revealed about the
Chinese community, but also for what it said about the nature of
American administration in the Philippines. This chapter examines
this deportation and the reasons why Agapito Uy Tongco (Huang
Youdang), a rising member of Manila's Chinese elite, was not only
among the deportees but had been the major target of the sweep. Uy
Tongco's removal was engineered by a group of his social and eco-

nomic rivals within the Manila Chinese General Chamber of Commerce, who portrayed him as a gang leader, a drug dealer, and an extortionist. Colonial officials, for their part, overreacted to this specter of Chinese gang (tong) violence, and their obsession with law, order, and good government left them open to manipulation by the established Chinese elite. Uy Tongco may have been a criminal, but he was more of a danger to the Chinese Chamber of Commerce because of his charitable works and community activism. Therefore, more than the legal validity of the deportation, the case of Agapito Uy Tongco is illustrative of the extent to which the Chinese elite had mastered the new colonial environment and could manipulate the fears and aspirations of their rulers.

Under American rule, the social and economic order in the Philippines had diversified and matured. For the Chinese, new economic opportunities and the application of the exclusion laws had altered the occupational landscape and reinforced the value of those elites who could facilitate transnational flows of talent and wealth. At the same time, American colonial rule, especially after the passage of the Payne-Aldrich Act, followed the Spanish example by promoting an economic environment that was conducive to Chinese entrepreneurial spirit. Despite the radical nature of many efforts at "social engineering," the Americans were unable completely to displace social, political, juridical, and economic conditions that carried over from the Spanish period.[2] The rulers of the Philippines were thus beholden to local elites—*chino, mestizo,* and *indio*—to maintain order and, most important, to fill key middleman roles in the colonial enterprise. This laid the groundwork for Chinese dominance of key sectors of the Philippine economy and for the emerging dynasties of Filipino elites. Local power as the merchant and landholding elite, in turn, translated into influence with and privileged access to the American authorities.

One factor that demonstrated increasing economic dynamism was a rise in the crime rate. Chinese organized crime, which included smuggling, gambling, prostitution, unlicensed opium dealing, and extortion were all on the rise in the early American period, especially in wartime Manila. A career of choice for some and a last resort for others, crime was a product of an unstable economy that was plagued by a protracted crisis. Criminal entrepreneurship was also the result of the application of American law to the islands. American opium policy, in particular, ended *cabecilla* monopolies, opened the market to petty entrepreneurs, and encouraged smuggling. The same was true for gambling and prostitution. Crime was also indicative of greater complexity in the Philippine economy and the markets of opportunity in Manila, where vice grew in proportion to the swell of refugees and American troops. Among the local Chinese, real criminal activity as well as accusations of wrongdoing (leveled at economic and social rivals) were already part of a tested repertoire of social and economic strategies. But more important than actual crime, which judging by the *Manila Times* police blotter had in fact declined, was the fear that the colonial enterprise might have been undone by Chinese organized crime. Paradoxically, not only had the American attitudes toward criminality that differed significantly from their Spanish predecessors, created crime in colonial Manila, but the American obsession with law and order offered a new means by which the local elite could manipulate the Americans. The colonial enterprise had unintended consequences for both colonizers and colonized.

## America's Pacific? Possessions

After a decade of ruling the Philippines, the U.S. government and the Bureau of Insular Affairs were still experimenting with administration and legislation. In general, the soldiers and civil administrators assigned to the islands were not well versed in the law, nor did they enjoy a deep familiarity with colonial Southeast Asia. The experienced military officers sent to the islands were either Civil War veterans or had fought in the Indian Wars. Bureaucrats and law enforcement personnel, though well-meaning, knew little about the islands before arriving, having cut their professional teeth in America's cities, not in the trading meccas of China, Japan, or Southeast Asia. To complicate matters, while the American rule of the Philippines was more enthusiastic and better funded than Spanish efforts, the actual reach of the state was nonetheless quite limited, necessitating a reliance on local elites. Furthermore, the United States was in the process of reassessing its global role in the aftermath of the imperial vogue of the late 1890s, and the War Department (charged with ruling the islands) was undergoing a profound restructuring of its domestic and overseas posture. In such an environment, it was difficult for the Americans to create a rational strategy for ruling the Philippines. As the previous chapter has shown, among the persistently vexing issues for colonial officials was the problem of Chinese in-migration to the islands. Policy was complicated by the frequent legal and procedural blunders committed by the governor-general and the overseas consular staff and by their contradictory views of the Chinese population. Moreover, successful application of the law was complicated by the ability of the local elite skillfully to circumvent and manipulate colonial rule. Hokkien migration networks, in particular, proved particularly resilient in this context.

At the same time that local authorities were concerned with Chinese in-migration in general, they were deeply concerned about the threat of Chinese crime in particular. Echoing their peers in the United States, colonial officials saw Chinese migrants as a threat to law, order, and good government, in terms of both unfair Chinese economic competition with the *indios*—the fact that the vast Chinese labor market could easily swamp the *indios* in the short term—and the threat to order posed by Chinese "secret societies." During the course of the late nineteenth and early twentieth centuries, the United States had continually strengthened the Chinese exclusion laws. Labor activists in the western United States, particularly California's Workingman's Party, had pressured state and federal governments to exclude Chinese labor completely by the beginning of this century. In their campaigns against the "yellow peril," anti-Chinese activists pointed to the inscrutability, debased character, and secretive associations of these seemingly unassimilable aliens. This view of the Chinese as a dangerous element gained credence when intra-Chinese gang violence erupted during the depression years of the 1880s.[3]

Although very few Chinese associations in the United States consistently employed violence and criminal activities, by the late nineteenth century the word "tong" (*tang,* literally a hall or meeting place) had become synonymous with a criminal gang or triad that "lived off the opium smugglers, gamblers, and prostitutes."[4] Chinese secret societies and sworn brotherhoods, commonly mislabeled "tongs," were often formed as mutual aid societies in the absence of kinship and native-place associations.[5] In hostile and alien environments, sworn brotherhoods were an effective way to unite poor immigrants and compete with larger, wealthier native-place and kinship groups. Secret societies were also entrepreneurial and could double as migration networks. They pooled resources, coordinated collective action, protected and promoted member interests, and pursued occupational monopolies. In Malaya, *kongsi (gongsi)* were closely bound societies of Chinese immigrant laborers who worked collectively to exploit agricultural and mining opportunities. In the United States, Chinese labor gangs were the organizational foci for railway workers and miners. These same structures were also suited to urban environments. Chinese occupational and craft associations routinely employed some form of sworn allegiance ritual for new members.[6] Others, like Chicago's On Leong Tong, while maintaining a criminal side, nonetheless evolved into a respectable blanket organization for Chicago's Chinese.[7]

Because organized violence was both endemic and effective in late imperial China, many Chinese migrants and potential migrants were preconditioned to the use of violence as an economic and social strategy. As a result, rivalries between Chinese secret societies overseas frequently escalated into violent feuds *(xiedou)*.[8] In New York and San Francisco, where competition for social and economic resources was most intense, there were a rash of "tong wars" in the 1880s and 1890s. One particularly violent conflict in San Francisco in 1886 resulted in the heavy loss of lives and property.[9] Chinese gang warfare was fodder for the popular media, which sensationalized the lurid details of individual conflicts and fueled anti-Chinese activism in the United States. For many Americans, a penchant for violence and crime defined Chinese identity.

To control these "tong wars," Chinese consuls worked in concert with American law enforcement to deport suspected tong members. Some consuls even threatened to arrest the families of "tong men" back in China, thus threatening both ends of the migration network, an action supported by the Chinese ambassador.[10] Although violence in America's Chinatowns declined after the turn of this century, there were still sufficient spikes in gang violence, in Boston in 1903, for example, to keep the issue in the minds of many Americans, especially those sent to the alien environment of the Philippines to administer America's new possession. The *chinos'* visibility and vigor caused many Americans to compare Manila to the major centers of Chinese residence in the United States and to assume that the same dangers to social order lurked in the streets of Tondo and Binondo. Insular officials were very conscious of the tong wars and the Chinese "highbinders" back home and constantly made reference to them. Even the threat of Chinese criminal activity in the islands evoked explicit comparisons to San Francisco, Chicago, and New York. Even worse, such a threat would mean that the Americans had failed to bring law and order to the archipelago, a mission that they considered central to the colonial enterprise. The express purpose of America's colonial endeavor was to bring "happiness, peace, and prosperity" to the Philippines so as to facilitate the "Philippines for Filipinos" policy.[11] The American sense of mission and exceptionalism made it imperative that the Philippines become a model of just and enlightened rule and a sharp contrast to colonial administrations elsewhere. The U.S. government was so self-conscious about setting the Philippines apart that it "expunged the word *colonial* from its official vocabulary."[12] One had only to travel to Saigon, Batavia, or Macao or to recall the Spanish Philippines—places where opium use, gambling, and prostitution were endemic—to see the insidious and demoralizing effects of "typical" European colonialism. This experiment in the self-replication of American society, however, was more often than not an exercise in self-deception and was occasionally counterproductive.[13]

In part, this self-deception was based on a distorted impression of the Spanish era Philippines. Opium, gambling, and other regulated vices had been used by the Spanish to fund their colonial enterprise and to keep various groups quiescent, and they had been central to the maintenance of social order. Likewise coolie brokerage and the ties between the *cabecillas* and the "secret societies" had allowed the Chinese elite to manage their own community. The Spanish had significantly less trouble with organized crime than the Americans were to have, partly because they directed the local Chinese into these lucrative industries and offered them the autonomy to maintain order within the Chinese community. In fact, for the Spanish, it was the *indios* who were seen as the dominant criminal element, whereas the Chinese were seen as a largely law-abiding enclave, albeit often judged by different legal standards. In the American Philippines the *chinos* were now the subversive element and the *indios* were to be praised.[14] The growth of crime and violence in the last years of Spanish rule was more a result of the general chaos that followed in the wake of rebellion and war as well as the change in attitudes toward criminality than it was indicative of flaws in Spanish policy.

The impetus to make the Philippines a model was balanced by decidedly racist attitudes of turn-of-the-century Americans and the distinctly pro-British and high-handed inclinations of many Bureau of Insular Affairs administrators. This attitude hindered America's ability to truly "export itself," to the colonial Philippines.[15] Likewise the American desire to bring order and prosperity to its new possessions often required bending or reinventing the law, ignoring the principles of "free trade" and the "open door," and courting entrenched interests to the detriment of true social reform. A symptom of this flawed approach to governance was the colonial government's new opium policy and its response to the perceived threat of Chinese gang violence.

Malacañang's decision to deport the "tong men" was an outgrowth of the administration's concern with law and order and a direct result of campaigns against opium use but not in the manner the colonial authorities may have hoped. The Americans were so obsessed with social order that the governor-general's staff was willing to bend the law to eliminate an alleged threat and then to appeal to the American legal system to sanction their actions ex post facto. Furthermore, in their enthusiasm to do away with the threat posed by Chinese "tongs," the Americans became involved in the internal conflicts and rivalries of the Chinese community by siding with the Chinese Chamber of Commerce against its rivals. The established Chinese elite were thus able to manipulate the representatives of a distant government in the pursuit of local interests. To understand why the twelve Chinese men were deported requires a look first at developments in the local Chinese community and then at the assumptions that informed American colonial policy.

## Prelude to a Deportation

If the case of Agapito Uy Tongco is taken to be indicative of general trends, then by the summer of 1909 the Chinese community in Manila was less unified and more openly fraught with internal conflict than it had been under the Spanish. This state of affairs would contradict Antonio Tan's argument that "the fact that the spirit of national solidarity spread quickly among the Chinese in the Philippines [during the American period] may be explained by the combined effects of two major stimuli: dissatisfaction with the restrictions placed upon them by the exclusion law, and the sudden influx of nationalist influences from China itself."[16] In other words, Tan argues that the advent of American rule, especially the application of the exclusion laws, and political trends in China had cohered the Chinese community in colonial Manila. The reality is somewhere in between that of a fractious community and a nationalistic enclave. While there was some vocal opposition to the exclusion laws and a small cadre of local Chinese were discussing Chinese political issues and nationalism at the time, the majority of the *chinos* were primarily concerned with more immediate problems: income, health, and family. Furthermore, in contrast to the situation in the continental United States, American rule in the Philippines, especially the application of the exclusion laws, actually facilitated Chinese control of key sectors of the colonial economy and reinforced the importance of localistic kin or native-place migration networks. Thus, it was not victimization or growing political consciousness but economic rationales that were drawing Chinese migrants together. Moreover, the community was not nearly as riven with conflict as the case of Agapito Uy Tongco might suggest. Certainly the occupational makeup of the community had diversified, thus complicating some of the internal dynamics and potentially exacerbating internal rifts, but this was not a pathologically contentious community. In actuality, the contest between Agapito Uy Tongco and the Chinese Chamber of Commerce was a contest among elites, a contest encouraged by the fact that the flux of the first decade of American rule left open the possibility that rival elite organizations could limit the power of the established Chinese elite or even wrest influence away from the Chinese Chamber of Commerce.

Disorder in the final days of Spanish rule opened the door for intracommunity conflict between the Cantonese and Hokkiens in Manila. In addition, the abolition of the Gobernadorcillo/Gremio system and the application of American law to the islands eliminated the need for a single man to act as the head of the Chinese community. Instead, community leadership became more diffuse and hotly contested by rival groups. The founding of the Chinese Chamber of Commerce and the reorganization of the Communidad de Chinos into the Chinese Charitable Association had been attempts to reverse this trend, restore order, and place authority in the hands of a clearly identified group of prominent businessmen with privileged access to the Chinese consul general and the colonial government. The Chinese elite in San Francisco had partly overcome intracommunity conflict through the agency of the famous Chinese Six Companies (Chinese Consolidated Benevolent Association), which coordinated community action, offered mediation services, promoted education, and served as community representative. To some observers, however, the Six Companies was an alliance of Chinese oligarchs who oppressed the rest of the Chinese in the name of community.[17] Thus, while resolving some intracommunity tensions, the consolidation of the six companies created new conflicts that made San Francisco consistently notorious for Chinese gang violence. New York City's Chinese "city hall" tried to mediate conflicts between the fractious Chinese associations that vied for social and economic opportunities.[18] In Manila, similar appeals to ethnic solidarity and community cohesion were an elite strategy to maintain influence in times of disorder. In a volatile environment, especially in the midst of institutional change, these efforts were constantly being challenged by the appearance of rival institutions.

Despite the general cohesiveness of the Chinese community, conflicts existed between Chinese from different native places but also within these groups. Factions of elite merchants competed against each other as well as with more radical groups of revolutionaries and with a growing Chinese labor movement. Improvements in steam navigation and the expansion of Chinese, Japanese, American, and British steamship services lowered the costs of travel to the Philippines. At the same time, economic growth was attracting new Chinese entrepreneurs and professionals who no longer needed to rely as heavily on the good offices of the established Chinese *cabecillas*. As I have shown, the end of Spanish rule had eliminated some of the economic factors that promoted Chinese community cohesion. Even that cohesion was not absolute, nor was *cabecilla* authority hegemonic. But by eliminating the coolie trade and the government monopolies that the Spanish had employed, the Americans had eliminated two of the means by which elite merchants maintained social control. Furthermore, by promoting economic growth (albeit slow in coming), and pumping cash and consumers into Manila, especially during the insurrection, the American colonial government created an economic environment that allowed for increased occupational diversity and the accumulation of wealth by a broader section of the Chinese community. Chinese residents, in Manila especially, began to band together in associations based on class, occupational group, native place, and criminal activity to exploit these opportunities. Although craft guilds, surname and native-place associations, and secret societies had existed in the Spanish Philippines, they proliferated under American rule. These associations, in turn, competed with each other and with the Chinese

Chamber of Commerce. Even among the majority Hokkiens, new organizations, such as the Fooking (Fujian) Merchants Benevolent Association (Minshang Huiguan), rose to challenge the entrenched power of the Zhangzhou and Quanzhou *huiguan* and even to contend for control of the chamber.

Ironically, American policies had created the exact problems the Bureau of Insular Affairs officials were trying to avoid. As the exclusion laws, steam travel, and economic growth encouraged socioeconomic diversity among the local Chinese, the application of a new system of criminal law encouraged criminal entrepreneurialism. To generate revenue, the Spanish had legalized, taxed, and placed in the capable hands of the Chinese *cabecillas* (and their secret society allies) opium sales, gambling, and Chinese labor importation. The end of tax farming, monopoly contracts, and the coolie trade—which had encouraged the development of cooperative and mutually remunerative relations between sworn brotherhoods and Chinese *cabecillas*—temporarily undermined the authority of the Chinese elite and promoted intracommunity strife. While many prominent Chinese merchants, including the leadership of the Chinese Chamber of Commerce, maintained their ties to secret societies, they did not have the same measure of control they had enjoyed under the Spanish. In their drive to bring law and order to the islands, the Americans made once-legitimate professions illegal and created criminal activity that, in turn, promoted competition and violence. There was a marked increase in the number of violent crimes reported in Manila newspapers in the 1900s. In addition to cases of petty theft, gambling, assault, and murder, there were also stories about organized criminal activity, including the smuggling of opium, silver coin, and Chinese labor, as well as prostitution and extortion.[19] Given the long history of smuggling and the opium trade in Xiamen, such a development should not have surprised the Americans.

The American approach to the opium trade is a telling example of the changing attitudes toward criminality. The Spanish had allowed the importation and cultivation of opium in the islands but had limited its legal use to the Chinese minority. In this way, the Spanish could profit from the trade by farming out sales contracts to Chinese *cabecillas*, while insulating the native population from the debilitating effects of the drug. The United States was one of the first Western powers to take a legal and moral stand against the drug in its colonial possessions. Soon after annexation, Dean Worcester, a mem-

ber of the Philippine Commission, counted almost two hundred
opium dens in Manila, which, he estimated—overestimated in my
opinion—served twenty thousand addicts, or almost one-half of the
resident Chinese population. As with alcohol, recreational use of
opium was far more common than addiction. While there were certainly Chinese opium addicts in Manila, given that most migrants
were recruited to be productive laborers in a competitive labor market, I doubt that so many "addicts" made it to Manila. With almost
missionary zeal, however, the new colonial government shut down
the opium farm. This was a bold move, especially because opium revenue had contributed approximately U.S.$500,000 a year to the
Spanish colonial budget, but ending the Philippine monopoly did
not end opium consumption. In fact, addiction rates appear to have
risen in the immediate aftermath—but, in actuality, the more than
ten thousand Chinese who registered for opium licenses were more
concerned with the documentation value of the opium license for
migration than with access to drugs. The Dutch had pursued a similar policy in Java. In 1902, the Batavian government brought an official end to the opium farm and began selling government-produced
opium through its own retail operations. The new Opium Regie
spelled the end for Chinese opium farmers, as the state collected
more revenue through the Regie than it had ever realized through
the contracting system.[20] The Americans, however, had more in mind
than mere regulation of opium sales, and the colonial administration
implemented a gradual ban on opium sales and poppy cultivation,
which culminated in a total ban on all opium use in March 1908, a
year before opium was declared illegal in the United States.[21] This
process offered medical treatment to addicts at state expense and
even included licenses for Chinese addicts to acquire small amounts
of opium legally.[22] Leading up to the total ban, prices for opium licenses were gradually increased, and by November 1907, the American authorities were reporting a dramatic decline in the number of
users.[23] Whether this represented a successful campaign against drug
use or a decline in the value of the certificates relative to their rising
cost is unclear, but the latter seems more likely. After the total ban
had taken effect, the Manila Police and the Secret Service launched a
campaign to eradicate opium use in Manila completely. Convicted
dealers faced fines, imprisonment, and, in some cases, deportation,
which had been used to remove foreign criminals from Manila in the
past.[24]

The anti-opium campaign put pressure on opium dealers to evade capture and in many cases encouraged them to help the authorities crack down on their rivals while taking the heat off themselves. Naturally, this sparked open conflict between various opium dealers and criminal gangs, which often decayed into violence.[25] The end of the monopoly and opium's rising price also attracted entrepreneurs. Small amounts of opium could be purchased overseas and sold in the Philippines for substantial profit. Whereas under the Spanish only the elite could afford to be dealers, the Americans opened the market to everyone. During the first decade of the twentieth century, therefore, rivalries within the Chinese community—both between "legitimate" associations and between "secret societies"—were encouraged by colonial policy and, as I will show, were often marked by the unwitting participation of American administrators. Bureau of Insular Affairs officials could have learned a lesson from the Dutch experience in Java. Although the Opium Regie brought in substantial revenue, the high price of Regie opium encouraged smuggling, which could only be controlled with significant increases in police and naval forces.[26] Dutch colonial officials gradually lost interest in controlling black market opium sales and focused instead on Regie profits.[27] The suppression of smuggling was even more difficult for an American government new to the region and generally ignorant of its newly acquired territory and subjects. Given that the Americans had brought many of these problems on themselves and could never hope to insulate Manila from criminal forces, they eventually managed to restore a semblance of order to Manila, through either enforcement or compromise. But the spike in Chinese "crime" in the first years of American rule as well as the memories of Chinese "tong wars" in America's cities continued to color American views of the Chinese community even after conditions in Manila had stabilized.

## The "Better Class of Chinamen"

By 1909, the Manila Chinese General Chamber of Commerce, with its visibility, the wealth of its membership, and its rapport with the Chinese consul general, was the single most powerful institution in the Chinese community.[28] The Chinese Chamber of Commerce also benefited from the good offices of the Americans. As noted earlier, the chamber had originally formed at the prompting of Governor-General Taft, and, since it represented the established Chinese mer-

chant elite and even Western-educated professionals like Dr. Tee
Han Kee, the chamber was looked on as a respectable force for stability and thus enjoyed the support of and privileged access to the
colonial authorities and the Chinese government.[29] The policy of fa-
voring the elite, however, created tensions between the entrenched
elite and those without similar access to external sources of authority.
The Chinese *cabecillas* were some of the most prominent figures in
this colonial oligarchy. Early in the twentieth century, the prominence and power of the Chinese Chamber of Commerce engendered
antipathy among those who lacked such influence.

Generally subordinate but occasionally standing in opposition
to the Chinese Chamber of Commerce were various smaller Chinese associations, including labor unions, trade guilds, native-place
associations, and local chambers of commerce, which cooperated
and competed with each other and with the Manila chamber for resources and influence. Chinese associations adapted older strategies or adopted new ones to meet the challenges of life in colonial
Manila. Several became prominent by petitioning the United States
on various issues, usually relating to immigration policy. Some of
these associations also had occasion to petition Beijing, while others developed ties with various expatriate political groups, such as
the Baohuanghui and the Tongmenghui. With the proliferation of
associational forms came a proliferation of points of contact that
institutions, both new and old, could work. Various groups vied for
influence through networking with colonial administrators, with
the consular corps both in Manila and in Xiamen, and with the Chinese state. They also engaged in conspicuous charitable acts, again
in both Manila and Fujian, and cooperated in public campaigns,
such as the opium eradication effort, public health, and urban renewal.[30] As had been the case under the Spanish, elite status and activism in the American Philippines were fundamentally transnational. Chinese associations also sought to improve their own
positions at the expense of other organizations through collective
labor action, boycotts, violence, sabotage, and most visibly through
litigation. In fact, by the end of the first decade of this century, the
Chinese community had become extremely litigious both internally
and externally, and it was not uncommon for a Chinese businessman to have one if not several American attorneys on retainer. One
Hokkien, Don Albino Sycip (Xue Minlao), studied law in the
United States and became the first Chinese admitted to the Philip-

pine Bar. He served as house counsel for the Chinese Chamber of Commerce and later as president of the chamber and director of the China Banking Corporation.[31]

Agapito Uy Tongco (Huang Youdang) was a well-connected and ambitious member of this dynamic Chinese community. Uy, a Hokkien Chinese, arrived in Manila sometime in the early 1900s and prospered in trade. By 1907, he had become president of the Fooking Merchants Benevolent Association and was a prominent businessman. The Fooking Merchants Benevolent Association engaged in acts of charity within the community and, in November 1907, had petitioned Secretary of War Taft on matters relating to Chinese immigration. The merchants asked Taft to use his influence to extend home-stay visas for Chinese migrations and eliminate the time-consuming and painful trachoma tests required of all Chinese migrants.[32] Given that both of these policies complicated the movement of talent and wealth between the *qiaoxiang* of Fujian and Manila, they had been the main targets of Chinese community activism in the early American period. But rather than representing a commonality of interests and a joint effort to overturn these unpopular laws, the established elite viewed Uy Tongco's activism, in taking a prominent stand and communicating directly with the American authorities, as poaching in their realm. By taking a leading role in this kind of protest, the Fooking Merchants Benevolent Association was challenging the Hokkien-controlled Chamber of Commerce for community leadership.

As a prosperous merchant, Agapito Uy Tongco required sound legal service. He engaged the services of the firm of O'Brien and DeWitt. Coincidentally, Frederick O'Brien was also the editor of one of the leading English-language newspapers in Manila, the *Cablenews-American,* which published stories about Uy's community-minded activities. The *Cablenews* was also the leading advocate for relaxing Chinese exclusion laws and, in contrast to the other major paper, the *Manila Times,* a strident critic of American colonial policy.[33] Thus, in addition to having intracommunity status, Uy reached out to establish linkages to the American elite. In 1908, Uy, thoroughly in keeping with his position as head of a prominent Hokkien association, made a bid for the presidency of the Manila Chinese Chamber of Commerce.[34] Uy was defeated by incumbent president Benito Siy Cong Bieng, and, after the election, relations between the Fooking Merchants Benevolent Association and the Chamber of Commerce

FIGURE 9. Benito Siy Cong Bieng, Chamber president at the time of Uy Tongco's deportation. Huang Xiaocang, ed. *Feilübin Minlila Zhonghua shanghui sanshi zhounian jinian kan.* Manila: Zhonghua Shanghui Chubanbu, 1936.

worsened. In the impending conflict between the two associations, the chamber's superior connections enabled their victory over Uy Tongco and led directly to his deporatioün.

In the spring of 1909, the Chinese Chamber of Commerce leadership—Benito Siy Cong Bieng, Mariano Fernando Yu Chingco, Miguel Salva, and Mariano B. Zarate—communicated to local authorities that two Chinese secret societies were threatening "respectable" local Chinese: the Ban Siong Tong and the Gee Hock Tong. The Gee Hock Tong, as described in the preceding chapter, was a brotherhood of Chaozhou immigrants that was active throughout Southeast Asia, especially in Singapore. The appearance of such a notorious transnational criminal organization was guaranteed to concern the Americans. The Ban Siong Tong, in contrast, was a little-known local phenomenon and was none other than Uy Tongco's Fooking Merchants Benevolent Association. But rather than referring to it by its proper Hokkienese title, Ban Siong Hoikoan, the chamber's directors had cunningly morphed an association of benevolent merchants into a malevolent den of "tong men."

In May, the chamber's directors contacted Acting Governor-General W. Cameron Forbes to inform him "that numerous assaults have been committed upon some of the most respectable citizens of this city by certain members of Chinese secret societies, while others have been blackmailed into paying for their exemption."[35] Enclosed in the petition were affidavits from Chinese merchant and chamber director Mariano B. Zarate as well as Zarate's staff, which identified Agapito Uy Tongco, the head of the so-called Ban Siong Tong, and seven of his cronies as the gang who had threatened the life of Señor Zarate. Tong members allegedly forced their way into Zarate's house armed with knives and clubs. Apparently the men were enraged by the results of a suit between the Ban Siong Tong and a certain Eusebio Zarate Sy Sipco that had been decided in the Chinese Chamber of Commerce in favor of Zarate Sy Sipco by his relative Mariano Zarate.[36] Accusations of intimidation and protection rackets would immediately have resonated with any one familiar with Chinese crime in the continental United States and would have impelled those responsible for law and order to react forcefully: W. Cameron Forbes was no exception.

In response to the Chamber of Commerce complaints, the acting governor-general's executive secretary referred the case to Chinese Consul General S. C. Yang (Yang Shijun), who had arrived in the islands only a month earlier. Forbes' office requested that Consul Yang suggest a course of action. In response, the consul investigated the matter and, despite his recent arrival, submitted a full report to the executive office in August. Yang, the younger brother of Yang Shiqi, a vice-president of the Nonggong Shangbu (the blanket organization for all Chinese chambers of commerce), determined that the only effective way to deal with the "dangerous evils" posed by these "Tong leaders" was to deport them immediately. The consul thereupon requested "the kind assistance of the Insular Government that the Police be ordered . . . to effect the immediate arrest of Agapito Uy Tongco, Fua Can O, Uy Kiu, and several others and put them on board of a direct steamer to Amoy." Consul Yang attached a detailed list of forty-one Ban Siong and Gee Hock members.[37] Yang claimed that both gangs had engaged in opium smuggling, prostitution, and gambling.[38]

This request for deportation was well within the consul's sphere of responsibilities. The consul was acting in accord with precedent and apparently with the support of the Chinese government, which had sanctioned such action in the 1880s.[39] Yang also had the support of local precedent. The Gobernadorcillo and later the consul general were responsible for deporting undesirable, insolvent, and unregistered Chinese, but in even these minor cases, potential deportees were granted a local trial and a chance to submit a writ of habeas corpus.[40]

On August 19, the tong list was relayed from the governor-general's office to Manila's police chief, John E. Harding.[41] On the afternoon of the August 20, the police, acting in concert with the United States Secret Service (under Chief Charles Trowbridge), sought out the men listed by the consul but were only able to find twelve of them. Having secured passage for the deportees aboard the steamer *Yuensang,* the Secret Service placed them aboard the ship at approximately 8:00 P.M. that evening, and the *Yuensang* departed immediately for Xiamen (Amoy). On Saturday morning, Chief Harding reported the successful deportation of the twelve men to the Chinese consul and turned over the deportees' section six certificates.[42] The deportation, however, was just the beginning of a citywide news sensation that would cover the pages of the leading daily newspapers in Manila for weeks to come. In addition, the legal ramifications of the Americans' actions continued to pester the colonial authorities until the case was finally resolved by the United States Supreme Court in 1913.

### "A Free Ride to Amoy"

While news of the deportation was spreading through Manila, the *Yuensang* was making its way toward the China coast.[43] The *Yuensang* was originally scheduled to dock first in Hong Kong, but at the insistence of Consul Yang, the ship was diverted to Fujian. According to the consul's critics, Yang had diverted the ship to prevent the presentation of a writ of habeas corpus at Hong Kong, which could have resulted in the deportees' immediate return.[44] In fact, Louis Sane Esq., an attorney for "some of the deported Chinamen," did ask for such a writ from the judge of the Manila Court of First Instance, Amasa S. Crossfield, but was rejected because the named parties were already far beyond his jurisdiction. In later cablegrams to relatives in Manila, the deportees reported that they were well treated on the voyage to Xiamen, and on their arrival at the port, they were not turned over to Chinese officials but were instead immediately released.[45]

Once freed, the twelve immediately called on the American consul at Xiamen to determine the cause of their deportation. The consul pleaded ignorance of their case, indicated to them that no charges had been filed with his office, and assured them that they were free to return to Manila. Taking leave of the consul, the twelve then had an audience with the Xiamen *daotai* ("circuit intendant," the ranking Qing official in the city). The *daotai* echoed the opinions of the American consul.[46] Neither official had any knowledge of the case; in fact, Consul General Yang Shijun never informed his superiors in Beijing that he had taken any action against local Chinese, nor had Malacañang telegraphed the American consul. Within six months of their summary deportation, six of the twelve were on their way back to Manila.[47] Moreover, the fact that these alleged "tong men" could so easily gain audiences with two of the most prominent officials in Xiamen seems to indicate that at least some of the deportees were of relatively high social standing or had prior contact with the *daotai* and the consul.

## Debating Deportation

Considering Uy Tongco's earlier association with Attorney Frederick O'Brien and his newspaper, it is not surprising that his deportation was headline news. On the morning of August 21, the *Cablenews* carried the bold, albeit inaccurate, headline: "Twenty Chinese Deported Untried." The morning issue included a scathing editorial that criticized the actions taken by the Manila police and the Secret Service as "an outrage of law by the law's guardians."[48] The *Manila Times,* in contrast, lauded the government's actions. The *Times* characterized the deportees as "highbinders" (a direct reference to the associations of Chinese brothel owners in San Francisco) and as "blackmailers, hoodlums and secret societies whose malignant influence makes of justice a farce and brings discredit upon the integrity of the Chinese colony."[49] *Times* reporters interviewed "Benito Sy Cong Beng,"[50] a member of the Chamber of Commerce—identified as the "wealthiest Chinese merchant in the city"—whose views were assumed to be typical of Chinese businessmen. Sy, while sorry to see his countrymen deported, nonetheless identified the dozen tong members as a "vicious type" and contrasted the secretive and suspect activities of the Ban Siong Tong to the open and legitimate functions of the Chamber of Commerce.[51]

Newton W. Gilbert, a member of the Philippine Commission and second in command to Forbes, who was currently away from his post, was the man directly responsible for the deportation. Gilbert opined in a *Times* interview that, although he had no knowledge of the deportation until the following morning, he felt that "the manner of arresting and deporting twenty Chinamen yesterday may be contrary to our ideas of justice and the right of the individual, but I hope we may never see the day that Manila is at the mercy of Chinese secret societies, as is San Francisco today."[52] This would be just one of several occasions on which colonial administrators would explicitly raise the specter of Chinese gang violence in the United States to justify the deportation of suspected tong members.

Gilbert defended the action by stating that, since the request for deportation had come from the imperial Chinese consul general and since all the deportees had been Chinese subjects, there was no reason why he should refuse. Furthermore, Gilbert applauded the actions of the Chinese community in identifying these malefactors and announced that their actions showed "a laudable intention to preserve the good name of the Chinese colony here."[53] Gilbert made this statement on the assumption that the deportees were in fact criminals. His opinions, however, were based entirely on hearsay, because the governor's office did not receive the deportees' police records for another ten days.

Even at this early date, Commissioner Gilbert had clearly established the American colonial government's position. Over the following months, Governor-General W. Cameron Forbes would take full responsibility for and staunchly defend the actions of his underlings to both the Philippine press and his superiors at the War Department. To the papers, Forbes stated that "the act was committed with his full knowledge and consent,"[54] although he admitted to his superiors that he had actually known nothing about the matter.[55] According to the governor-general, his staff had merely followed custom and courtesy in acceding to the consul's request for aid in capturing these men. In the past, the governor-general had delivered to the Japanese consul "vagrants" and "certain degraded characters of evil reputation," and therefore he had both precedent and the implied authority to hand over Chinese subjects, no matter how long they had lived in the islands or how wealthy or influential they were.[56]

On September 4, 1909, Forbes received the police records of the twelve deportees, which he conveyed to his superiors at the Bureau of Insular Affairs, albeit with the proviso that the charges seem to have been "prepared more as a defense for action already taken than as an impartial statement made without any axe to grind."[57] For example, Chief Harding's men had arrested Agapito Uy Tongco on two previ-

ous occasions, but he had never been convicted. At the time of his deportation, he had been under charges for assaulting Zarate's employees, but these charges were later dropped by Manila's prosecuting attorney. A few of the other deportees, notably the alleged Gee Hock
members, had extensive police records, including arrests for gambling, suspicion of opium smuggling, corruption of minors, assault,
and vagrancy. However, half of the deportees—all from the Ban
Siong Tong—were suspected only of having close ties to Agapito Uy
Tongco and of accompanying him on "several of his raids through
Chinatown."[58] As with Major General Otis' decision to decline recognition to Consul General Chen Gang in 1899 because of the reputation of his father, the civil authorities in Manila had deported six Chinese subjects primarily because of their association with a prominent
man with vocal enemies.

Forbes publicly assumed responsibility for the deportation but
refused to discuss the merits of his staff's actions with the local
press.[59] A week later, however, Forbes reported to the secretary of
war that the results of the actions had been positive and that he had
been congratulated by "practically the whole foreign community."
Although Forbes sympathized with those who were outraged by the
deportation, he nonetheless felt that much of the scathing critique of
his office carried on the pages of the *Cablenews*—which labeled the
deportation an "official kidnaping"—arose from the fact that
O'Brien's law firm represented one of the deportees.[60] Malacañang
further claimed that they had had no choice but to deport the men if
they wanted to rid the islands of the Chinese secret societies. They
could not resort to the courts, because "we could not find them guilty
or bring home to them their evil doings, nor could we very well suppress them."[61] Forbes argued that it was nearly impossible to pursue a
case against tong members, because they invariably bribed or intimidated potential witnesses.[62] Apparently, the governor did not know
that six Gee Hock members had been successfully tried and convicted of attempted murder in July 1908.[63]

Governor-General Forbes was one of the interesting and contradictory figures who staffed the Bureau of Insular Affairs. Forbes de-
liberately modeled himself on the archetypes of the British colonial
civil servant and was a workaholic who obsessed over the task of remaking the Philippines and the Filipinos "in the manner that I felt
best for them, regardless of whether they liked it or not."[64] Nonetheless, he also found the time to found the prestigious Manila Polo

Club to satisfy his passion for the sport.[65] Forbes liked to think of himself as a man of action who bridled under the restraints placed on him by his superiors in Washington.[66] The deportation of these "undesirables" was an act he likely wished he had taken but could not, and, in his words, their removal from the islands was "a curious dispensation of providence."[67] In his first report to Secretary of War Dickinson, Forbes sustained the actions of his underlings and opined that they had "probably ended an extremely difficult situation." In conclusion, Forbes cited a story by the poet laureate of British colonialism, Rudyard Kipling, "in which the head master of a school, in delivering a caning to a boy who has made mischief while technically innocent of wrongdoing, remarks: 'This will be useful to you in [the] after life.' When you find an abnormal situation meet it in an abnormal manner."[68]

Frederick O'Brien at the *Cablenews*, however, was not nearly so sanguine. O'Brien did not consider the deportation to be providential and continued to print articles, throughout the late summer and fall, that were critical of the colonial government's actions and motives. Not only did O'Brien's writers rail against the illegality of the deportation and its disregard for judicial procedure, but they also accused the government of becoming a "tool of one faction of the Chinese community, the adherents of one tong, to wreak vengeance on the members of another tong" and reported that rumors were already circulating that the police and the Secret Service had been paid off by one tong to eliminate its rivals.[69] This accusation was reminiscent of the highly publicized kickbacks that police in the continental United States were paid to overlook Chinese criminal activity.[70]

Polemical though they may have been, there was a ring of truth in the *Cablenews* editorials. O'Brien's paper revealed the real origin of the deportation. The chamber's motives and the consul general's complicity were not part of a noble campaign. Instead they betrayed a fierce rivalry between the tongs and the chamber. Although some of the deportees may have been criminals and unsavory characters, the same could be said of many of the members of the Chinese Chamber of Commerce. "The better class of Chinese" that the chamber claimed to represent had made their fortunes through gun running during the insurrection as well as opium, prostitution, and gambling, in addition to more legitimate professions. Many in the chamber had also been Spanish era *cabecillas* who buttressed their power through alliances with secret societies. The Chamber of Commerce was the most powerful tong.

None of the groups involved were acting out of purely selfless intentions. Earlier in the year, the Ban Siong and the Gee Hock helped the Manila police break up several opium operations with ties to members of the Chamber of Commerce. These events precipitated the legal battle between the Ban Siong and Eusebio Zarate Sy Sipco that was the immediate catalyst for Uy Tongco's deportation.[71] Furthermore, the attack on Zarate's house, if it really occurred (there is some reason to believe the incident was a fabrication), was only a symptom of the larger conflict between the Chamber of Commerce and the Ban Siong. By petitioning the secretary of war, practicing conspicuous charitable acts, and assisting in the anti-opium campaign, Uy Tongco and the Ban Siong were competing with the chamber for community leadership and trying to undermine the chamber's image.

Even after the deportation, the factions continued to wrangle. In a petition to the Qing Ministry of Foreign Affairs (Waiwubu), members of the Fooking Merchants Benevolent Association, again exercising their external linkages, accused chamber president Siy Cong Bieng of bribing the consul, forging documents, and deceiving the ministry while at the same time oppressing the local Chinese.[72] By petitioning the Waiwubu, Yang Shijun's direct superiors, the Fujian merchants, were circumventing their opponents' connections at the Nonggong Shangbu. Not surprisingly, however, the foreign ministry made no response to the petition. The ministers may have felt that they had little time for petty squabbles and that local issues were best handled locally. Furthermore, neither ministry had the resources or the inclination to punish the Chamber of Commerce. After all, the failing dynasty relied on local chambers to funnel donations and investment into China. The conflict between Uy Tongco and the chamber was an outgrowth of the chamber's monopoly on community power, which was based partly on its link to the Qing government. The chamber had influence, wealth, and connections. The Chinese consul general, for example, tended to side with the established elite, because they were best suited to help him perform his job. This monopoly on power forced weaker associations to pursue more drastic measures, such as violence and extortion, which caused them to be identified as the more insidious element. In this case, once all avenues for peaceful mediation had been exhausted, that is, when the

Ban Siong lost their case in the chamber, they resorted to more direct means.

The Chinese consul general and the Chamber of Commerce, by enlisting the aid of the Americans, had also effectively preyed on the fear and aspirations of the colonialists. By changing the appellation of the merchant association from a *"huiguan"* to a "tong" (words that can have almost identical meanings in Chinese) and by associating Uy's organization with a well-known criminal society (the Gee Hock Tong), the chamber preyed on colonial fears. The mere mention of words like "tong" and "secret societies," evoked images of the "tong wars" in the United States. In response to the threat of Chinese gang warfare, the administrators were willing to compromise law for order. Likewise, the snap decision made by the American administrators to side with the consul and the chamber against the Ban Siong Tong and the Gee Hock Tong was typical of the American pattern of courting the wealthy and influential to promote growth and stability. How better to bring order to Chinatown than to eliminate those Chinese whom "the better class of Chinamen" had identified as malefactors? What better way to eliminate a prominent rival than to accuse him of associating with criminal tongs? American colonial officials, from Otis to Forbes, were more than willing to listen to slander, and the local Chinese repeatedly demonstrated the efficacy of accusation. In the short term, the Americans had perhaps brought a greater degree of order to its new colonial possession, but they had also helped to buttress the power of the Manila Chinese General Chamber of Commerce against its rivals.

The case of the deportation of Agapito Uy Tongco et al. did not, however, end there. After the deportees returned to Manila, three of them brought suit against the officials responsible for their removal. The ensuing legal case would question the authority and methods of the American executive branch in the Philippines as well as test the rights of Chinese residing in America's insular possessions.

### An Atypical Migration

On March 29, 1910, six of the deportees returned to Manila. Three of the men had obtained section six registration papers and were therefore admitted to the islands without incident.[73] The other three, Chuoco Tiaco, Gan Tico, and Sy Chang (all members of the Ban Siong Tong), did not have the appropriate documentation and were denied entry. At the urging of the Chinese consul general, Governor Forbes began proceedings to redeport all six of the men, but before he could take action, Judge Crossfield released the three detainees on bail in habeas corpus proceedings and enjoined Forbes, Trowbridge, and Harding from redeporting the entire group.[74] On April 1, Forbes received word from Washington that his superiors at the bureau, while hesitant to "disapprove action already taken and closed," could not sanction redeportation and ordered that "all effort in that direction should be abandoned."[75] This decision was based on a report composed by the bureau's law officer, who could find no legal precedent for the deportation and recommended that a judicial resolution be sought.[76] Meanwhile, Forbes was preparing to take action against Judge Crossfield (whom he regarded as too liberal in cases regarding Chinese) for lack of jurisdiction in the injunction. It was Forbes' plan to move the case to a more amenable venue that would support his intention to deport the six Chinese again.[77]

In the interim, the three men released on bond by Judge Crossfield filed lawsuits against the governor, Chief Harding, and Chief Trowbridge for "conspiracy and illegal deportation" and were seeking damages in the amount of U.S.$10,000 each.[78] On April 19, however, the defendants' case received a major boost when the Philippine Legislature officially declared that "the action of the Governor-General in deporting . . . twelve persons of the Chinese race . . . is hereby approved, ratified, and in all respects declared legal, and not subject to question or review."[79] In its second full year of existence, the Philippine Legislature, a body made up almost entirely of wealthy *ilustrados,* had evolved into a moderate institution under the skilled leadership of Sergio Osmeña.[80] Since the insidious classes of Chinese were emerging as a favorite scapegoat for Filipino politicians, it was no surprise that the legislature supported the governor-general's decision. It should be noted, however, that Forbes would likely have vetoed any resolution condemning him. Rather than second-guessing the governor-general and risking angering the islands' chief executive or exposing themselves to charges of being soft on Chinese crime, the legislature supported the removal of those individuals whose presence "might . . . constitute a serious danger to the public tranquility and welfare."[81] Despite some vocal criticism, the passage of this legislation worked to the advantage of Osmeña and the government by arraying the leading elements of both Filipino political parties, the Nacionalistas and the Progresistas, in support of the deportation.[82] The passage of this legislation would later prove to be a key element in the case.

Undeterred by the legislature's proclamation, Frederick O'Brien continued to press the case for the deportees and directly contacted the secretary of war to charge Forbes and his underlings with conspiracy and kidnaping. O'Brien went on to challenge the secretary's support for Forbes and asked, in an apparent fit of hyperbole, if the secretary would act to see justice done or "officially white-wash one of the greatest stains on American history."[83] The editor's wrath also fell on the Filipino legislators, whom he lampooned in the *Cablenews*.

> He did not doubt he had the right
> To ship the Chinos out by night
> Or that Osmeñas little bunch
> If given but the proper hunch
> Would undertake to legislate[84]

In the face of continuing charges of misconduct and overstepping the bounds of his executive authority, Forbes sought and received additional support from the Philippine legal establishment. In early June, the Attorney-General of the Philippine Islands, Ignacio Villamar, rendered an opinion favorable to the governor-general's right to summarily deport suspect Chinese in the interest of the public good. This decision greatly bolstered Forbes' confidence that the redeportation would proceed.[85] On July 30, the Supreme Court of the Islands also supported the initial deportation on the grounds that the secret societies to which the deportees belonged had acted in a manner similar to societies in San Francisco and had thereby "placed reputable Chinese merchants under a system of blackmail and practically a state of terror." Furthermore, since the courts were unable to convict the perpetrators, because of their ability to intimidate complainants and provide perjured witnesses, the governor-general had no recourse but to assist the Chinese consul general in expelling the men; the executive had the power to "use such methods as his judgment and conscience dictate." The court also upheld Forbes' complaint that Judge Crossfield lacked the jurisdiction to enjoin him from redeportation. Ironically, Judge Crossfield's failure to enjoin the redeportation earned him the dubious honor of being named the fourth defendant in the suit filed by the three deportees.[86]

In spite of this legal sanction, the Bureau of Insular Affairs was still skeptical of Forbes' implied authority in this case and the Philippine Legislature's right to grant sanction to an act that appeared to be in direct contradiction to an earlier act of the United States Congress. As predicted by the bureau's law officer, the case of *Chuoco Tiaco, Gan Tico, and Sy Chang v. W. Cameron Forbes, J. E. Harding, C. R. Trowbridge, and A. S. Crossfield* became a test case that would "finally reach the Supreme Court of the United States."[87]

## Justice Is Served

In March 1911, the case of the three deportees was filed with the Supreme Court. Over the next two years, lawyers for both sides would submit innumerable motions before the case was finally decided. While the case was proceeding, Forbes was petitioned in February 1913 by the new Chinese consul general in Manila, Yang Shouwen. According to Yang, a group of Chinese had organized a boycott against Chinese merchants dealing in Japanese goods. These facts were supported by Forbes' subsequent investigation. According to the governor-general, the leaders of the boycott had "resorted to threats, intimidation, and murder" and had offered a U.S.$5,000 reward for the murder of the Chinese consul general. Concerned by the threat to order, Forbes had again begun proceedings for the deportation of the suspect Chinese.[88] Forbes' superiors immediately warned him against deportation, because the last case was still pending in the Supreme Court, and urged him to prosecute the Chinese for criminal offenses instead.[89] Forbes disagreed with his superiors and argued that the courts would be useless in this case but was again told not to "exercise power of deportation until confirmed [by the Supreme] Court."[90] Forbes finally relented, but in May the actions of his underlings three summers earlier were finally and completely vindicated.

On May 5, 1913, Justice Oliver Wendell Holmes delivered the opinion of the Supreme Court of the United States in the matter of *Chuoco Tiaco, Gan Tico, and Sy Chang v. W. Cameron Forbes, J. E. Harding, C. R. Trowbridge, and A. S. Crossfield*. The justices had determined that the Philippine Legislature had passed an act authorizing the deportation that had not been annulled by the United States Congress and was therefore legal. Thus, even though the authorization had occurred more than six months ex post facto, the governor-general had been legally justified, and the deportation of the Chinese did not represent the deprivation of liberty without due process of law.[91] Responding from Manila, Forbes informed his superiors that news of the decision had been met by a "great rejoicing among the faithful."[92]

## Conclusion

In the history of the American Philippines, the deportation of Agapito Uy Tongco et al., although a media sensation in the summer of 1909, was only a minor incident. After the right of the governor-general to deport undesirable Chinese had been affirmed, there were actually very few occasions on which Forbes or his successors had need to exercise this authority. Even with the support of the Supreme Court, Forbes did not take any further action against the Ban Siong Tong. This case is important, however, because of what it reveals about the internal dynamics of the Chinese community during the first decade of American rule, how American policy shaped those dynamics, and how American administrators became involved in conflicts between Chinese. The deportation seemed an immediate cure to the problem of disorder and associational rivalry within the Chinese community, which in turn was a symptom of the greater problem of growing conflict and violence among the Chinese. The great irony, one that was almost surely lost on the Americans, was that it was their policies regarding immigration, criminality, and the economy, and their fears of a "tong war" in Manila that had precipitated conflict. The colonial government had created a situation in which the established Chinese elite could manipulate their fears and aspirations to exercise a substantial measure of control over the Chinese community. The deportation was not about chaos but about control.

The attempt to replicate American values, society, and justice in the Philippines was constrained by circumstances, the inclinations of colonial administrators, and flaws in the American system itself. The result was a confused colonial mission that employed a series of expedient measures that were later ratified as standard procedures. Like General Otis' emergency application of the exclusion laws and his refusal to recognize Chen Gang, the summary deportation of twelve Chinese was not based on any clear policy. Instead, the colonial response (and later justification) was a knee-jerk reaction to the implied threat of "tong" activity in Manila. Furthermore, it was difficult, if not impossible, for the Americans to reverse a decision once taken because of either bureaucratic inertia or the fear of appearing "soft" on the "Chinese Question." The result was an administration that was frequently inconsistent and vulnerable to manipulation.

I doubt that Agapito Uy Tongco was much of a criminal or that he represented a profound threat to social order in Manila. If he was a criminal, he was probably no worse than many of the "better class" he was compared to. Agapito Uy Tongco and his Ban Siong companions were deported because they were making trouble for the Chamber of Commerce and because the chamber was able to exploit the ignorance and fears of the colonial authorities. Ignorance was born out of the profound belief in American cultural and moral superiority, and the sense of mission to rescue the Philippines from its sordid past. Fear arose from the anxiety that the machinations of Chinese criminal entrepreneurs could undo the American colonial mission as easily as they had bedeviled American law enforcement in San Francisco, New York, and Chicago. Furthermore, the policy of siding with the established elite meant that the Chinese Chamber of Commerce had an inordinate amount of influence with the Philippine government and could use that influence to eliminate rivals. By labeling enemies as members of "tongs" and "secret societies," the Chinese Chamber of Commerce and the Chinese consul general evoked images of the "tong wars" that had been sensationalized by the American press. Virtually all of the government's comments on this case make some reference to the malignant influence of Chinese secret societies in San Francisco or New York. These references were freely made even though Manila was very different from San Francisco and New York. The Chinese in the United States (especially in San Francisco) were primarily Cantonese, while those in Manila were mostly Fujianese. Furthermore, whereas the American Chinese population comprised mainly manual laborers and petty entrepreneurs, the Chinese in the Philippines were wealthier and included more professionals. The "blue-collar" nature of Chinese criminality in the United States led colonial officials to the misguided assumptions that crime was class-specific and that they could distinguish between the "better class of Chinamen," who were important to the health of the Philippine economy, and the undesirable low-class "highbinders." Ignorant of local conditions, the Americans' blanket assessment was that Chinese "secret societies" could also evade normal legal practice. Therefore, men like Governor-General Forbes felt that they, like the colonial administrators of the British Empire, should possess the discretionary power to meet the challenge of an "abnormal situation" in an "abnormal manner." Pressed to bring law and order to the islands, the authorities had no idea that they were involved in an intraelite conflict and were willing to bend the law in the service of order.

Despite all the claims to American exceptionalism in the colonial enterprise, the policy of siding with the Chinese elite was in no way an innovation. This practice was completely in line with the colonial tradition. The British, French, Dutch, and Spanish had all identified rich and powerful Chinese collaborators to aid in the colonial enterprise and to control the Chinese enclave. The Americans were, however, unique in their willingness to delegate authority to the Chinese consul general and the Chinese Chamber of Commerce. Unlike their fellow colonialists, the Bureau of Insular Affairs did not engage in a battle for the political allegiance of the local Chinese. The Chinese consul in Singapore, in particular, was constantly coming up against colonial resistance to his "political activities." The Straits government was uneasy about the collection of donations, the sale of Qing titles, and the issuing of Chinese passports by the consul. The British preferred to think of the Chinese consul as little more than a commercial agent, and in the 1890s, Huang Zunxian's campaign to issue passports to the Straits Chinese became a major conflict between Huang and the colonial government. In contrast, the American colonial officials showed little concern for Chinese "political activities," and when they intervened in the rivalry between Chen Qianshan and Li Rongyao, it was to uphold the latter's sole right to grant official documentation to the Chinese. The Bureau of Insular Affairs was never desirous of winning the loyalty of the local Chinese or even willing to grant more than a few of them citizenship. This may be the primary reason why the Americans had no qualms about the strengthening ties between the local Chinese elite and the Chinese government. The British and the Dutch were much more inclined to take responsibility for the Chinese and maintained separate institutions (the Chinese Protectorate in the Straits, and the headman system in Java) for just that purpose.[93] The Bureau of Insular Affairs, it would seem, was content to hand over responsibility for Chinese affairs to the consul general and the Chamber of Commerce and, as the deportation of Uy Tongco demonstrates, was willing to step in to fulfill the wishes of these two allies.

The preceding discussion offers some important insights into the evolving nature of the host environment in the American Philippines (information that is central to the study of any migrant community), which on the surface seemed to be becoming more violent and contentious. This is a result of documentary evidence that places the American response to Chinese criminality at the center of this story. Yet, the deportation of Agapito Uy Tongco can reveal much more about the structure of power within the Chinese community than about Chinese crime. With the exception of the colonial officials themselves, the elite leadership of the Manila Chinese General Chamber of Commerce was the single most powerful group in the early American Philippines. They had obvious wealth and connections, but, more important, they were able to translate socioeconomic power into political influence. They had done the same with the Spanish and with Chinese officials and foreign consuls in Xiamen. The Americans were beholden to the Chinese elite to keep order within the community and to keep the economy working. This left the colonial government open to chamber manipulation. In time, the Filipino elite would also learn to manipulate the fear and ignorance of the Americans. The Chinese, however, had another connection which the *ilustrados* lacked.

The Chinese consul in Manila, while the formal representative of one sovereign nation in the territory of another, was nonetheless a critical component of local elite dominance. In the declining years of the Qing dynasty and throughout China's warlord era (1916–1928), that is, in the absence of a strong central government, the local Chinese consul could do little to dictate to his charges, and his duties were mainly confined to issuing travel documents. It was not until China was nominally reunified in the late 1920s that the consulate could effectively assert central directives. In the 1930s, the Guomindang was able to use the consul general and the Manila Chinese General Chamber of Commerce to organize a local party branch, a Sanminzhuyi Youth Corps, several anti-Japanese boycotts, and a very successful fund-raising campaign. But even then, the success of these endeavors was largely due to the party's sensitivity to local realities, its willingness to help the Manila Chinese Chamber of Commerce rein in its local rivals, and the fact that donations to patriotic causes, funneled through the chamber, were rewarded with prestige both in Manila and in the *qiaoxiang* of southern Fujian. Throughout its early history, therefore, the Chinese consulate general was little more than a pawn of the local elite, and yet the consul was still the official representative of a sovereign nation who enjoyed specific rights and privileges. The Chamber of Commerce, as is evident in this case, could use the consul's authority in the service of its local interests.

For Agapito Uy Tongco, there was a simple formula for socioeconomic success in the Philippines and for joining the Chinese elite. That formula included conspicuous charity and institutional leadership, and Uy aspired to both. Attaining and maintaining status also depended on external allies. The leadership of the Chamber of Commerce, however, jealously guarded their authority from upstarts like Uy. After he failed in his bid to become president of the chamber, it is not surprising that he pursued alternative avenues to community leadership. In that pursuit, he ran afoul of the chamber, and it was inevitable that men like Benito Siy Cong Bieng and Mariano Zarate sought to silence him. As with Chen Qianshan's difficulties with the Cantonese and the crisis over the post of consul, factional competition determined who best represented the interests of the community, which, in turn, defined who sat at the apex of the community. Slander played a central role in this type of community rivalry, and access to external authorities was frequently the deciding factor. It made sense for the chamber to slander Uy Tongco and his associates and for the Fooking Merchants Benevolent Association to respond with accusations of its own. How better to show that one's rivals lacked the moral fiber to speak for the "better class of Chinese"? It also made sense for Uy Tongco to hire Frederick O'Brien to speak for him as both attorney and editor. American annexation had added complexity to the environment, especially with the proliferation of lawyers and newspapers, but the bottom line was still the same. Uy Tongco and the Ban Siong Tong had ammunition and a hired gun, but the Chamber of Commerce's arsenal was much larger.

Once the chamber's leaders had identified the Ban Siong Tong as a threat and communicated this to colonial officials, Uy Tongco's deportation was a foregone conclusion. By targeting the Ban Siong's president and his close acquaintances, the Chamber of Commerce effectively decapitated a rival institution. Moreover, the Fooking Merchants Benevolent Association had facilitated its own defeat, because it was too narrow and too anachronistic to compete openly with the chamber in this context. In the Philippines, it was "modern" chambers of commerce and consuls that the Americans recognized as speaking for all local Chinese. It was the chamber, not the more narrow and "traditional" *huiguan* (even if they were Hokkien associations), that would dominate the Chinese community. The same was not necessarily true in other Chinese communities, where other institutional forms, both traditional and modern, held the dominant position, but in Manila the Chinese Chamber of Commerce possessed sufficient means and influence to assert and defend its position, not the least of which was its alliances with the Chinese and Bureau of Insular Affairs governments.[94] The amount of influence the chamber was able to leverage at this early point shows, in contrast to James Blaker's contention that 1919 was the critical turning point in the local power of the chamber, that the institution was the dominant Chinese organization nearly from its inception.[95] Even so, its predominance was not inevitable, nor was its power absolute: Uy Tongco *was* deported, but he managed to return to Manila and to use his own external linkages to prevent another deportation. Nonetheless, he no longer had sufficient connections or institutional backing to ascend to the top of the Chinese community. Thus, in spite of, and perhaps owing to, the continuing crises and the institutional innovations that marked the early American era, because it represented the majority of the elite and had the most diverse repertoire of local and transnational connections, the new Chinese Chamber of Commerce was rapidly able to assert its dominant position as community spokesman, and in many ways the elite that controlled the chamber continued to define what it meant to be Chinese in the colonial Philippines.

# Conclusion

THE PURPOSE OF this book has been to offer a nuanced understanding of the Chinese in colonial Manila that is free from the biases of nationcentric historiography, be it Philippine or Chinese, and to see the Chinese merchant elite in colonial Manila as masters of a liminal place, a place whose history cannot be confined within a single national or local narrative. Because they lived on the boundaries between China and Southeast Asia, the story of the Nanyang Chinese is embedded in the nationalist scholarship of this region's new nations. At the same time, *huaqiao* are celebrated as progenitors of the Chinese republic whose gaze is inevitably drawn to the Chinese motherland.[1] The literature on the Chinese overseas has thus generally fallen into two camps: that attacking the Chinese and that praising them for their notable contributions to the cultures and economies of either modern China or Southeast Asia (but rarely both).

Contemporary Philippine Chinese have often found themselves blamed for the economic underdevelopment of the Philippines, attacked for their parasitism, and accused of collaborating with colonial oppressors and corrupt regimes. A similar fate has befallen other Chinese enclaves throughout Southeast Asia. Contemporary conditions of the Philippine economy are an outgrowth of late Spanish era economic policy and the unique nature of American rule, specifically, bringing the Philippines under the umbrella of American tariffs. This created a dependency economy and favored labor-intensive over capital-intensive industry. The Chinese did not create this state of affairs, but they were present in the Philippines with the resources, strategies, and ambition to exploit these opportunities.

A common pitfall, therefore, when researching and writing the history of the Chinese in Southeast Asia is that one will encourage negative stereotypes of the ethnic Chinese or become trapped within nationcentric narratives. An emphasis on opportunistic and manipulative activities, in particular, can too easily be appropriated by those who would portray the Chinese as colonial collaborators and economic parasites. Without a doubt, the Chinese elite discussed in this work were ambitious and opportunistic, and were willing to exploit their relations with external sources of authority to satisfy personal and group interests: this portrait is borne out by the available evidence. Moreover, one might be tempted to conclude from the preceding chapters that the Chinese community in colonial Manila was perpetually riven by conflicts between Chinese. Intracommunity conflict is better documented and easier to analyze historically than the more common patterns of cooperation, because it divides the subjects into recognizable camps. The contest over the consulate and Uy Tongco's deportation were both well-documented intracommunity conflicts that poured over into government and public spheres, and both demonstrated the efficacy of slander. The frequent recourse to slander, in turn, conditioned the contemporary portrayal of the local Chinese as litigious schemers and obscured many of these men's true qualities.

Periodic conflicts can also artificially polarize groups within a community and temporarily draw stark boundaries between Manichean categories that would otherwise be too simplistic. Unlike conflict, which is the historian's bread and butter, cooperation tends to be more nebulous and generally less interesting. The result is an emphasis on the contentious qualities of our subjects. Yet in these conflicts we can glimpse community dynamics in their sharpest relief so that we might draw conclusions about patterns of behavior, especially cooperation, in more mundane and less contentious times. What becomes most clear from these cases is that competition for privileged access to colonial and consular authority maintained the relative cohesion and prosperity of the Chinese community.

The great irony is that the intramural conflicts discussed in this book were an outgrowth of cooperative strategies. The matrices of trust—native-place associations, surname groups, gremios, sworn brotherhoods, migration networks, and chambers of commerce— which were the sinews of the community and had given the Chinese a commercial advantage in the colonial economy, required points of contact with the colonial government and with Chinese officialdom. The Spanish had provided numerous points of contact between the state and the Chinese community that satisfied the social and economic ambitions of the Chinese elite. When the possibility for new points of contact appeared, such as with the consulate general, competition for this point of contact was understandably fierce. Likewise, when the systematized links between the state and the Chinese community were reduced, for example, when the Americans abolished revenue farms and delegated near-total authority to the consul and the Chamber of Commerce, the social and economic ambitions of many in the community were thwarted. The result of this frustration was the kind of crisis-mode activity displayed in the conflict between Agapito Uy Tongco and the Chamber of Commerce. But such open conflict was relatively rare among the Chinese in Manila, especially compared to San Francisco, New York, Singapore, and Chicago.

Another potential methodological pitfall, the overwhelming focus on the Chinese elite in this history, is also a result of the evidence. The narrow stratum of elite were much better documented as individuals than the tens of thousands of clerks and coolies who made the pilgrimage to Manila. The elite's semi-official standing and frequent interaction with colonial and Chinese governments provide a wealth of information from which to construct character studies and track elite strategies. The *cabecillas* enjoyed greater access to political power holders who recorded their activities and thus left a greater archival imprint. When newspapers and litigation appeared in the later years of the nineteenth century, the potential points of contact and the potential documentary sources multiplied. While Manila's ubiquitous Chinese coolies and clerks certainly registered with colonial officials and foreign observers, those who were managed by the elite were far more generic than the elite themselves. Mary Somers Heidhues has appropriately challenged the elite studies bias in the historiography of the Chinese overseas, and the history of the average Chinese migrant to the Philippines should be written, but we still need to understand the aspirations and inclinations of the elite who made these migrations possible. Analyzing elite strategies and identities is thus indispensable to analyzing the entire community.[2] Moreover, outside the records for in- and out-migration, the majority of the material on the lower classes of Chinese in Manila must, by necessity, be drawn from the criminal courts, and therefore would be limited to an analysis of the crimes perpetrated by and against Chinese. Such an approach might encourage even more negative stereotypes.

Rather than praising or condemning the subjects, we must try to see the Chinese merchant elite as products of and, in some cases, masters of multiple overlapping trends. Events of great historical moment converged at colonial Manila, as did more personal histories. Empires contended for the great entrepôt at the same time that the history of a poor family in a Hokkien *qiaoxiang* was changed forever when their breadwinner succumbed to cholera. Colonial Manila was a liminal space; a place where all of these personal, local, provincial, national, regional, and global stories converged, where the ragged edges of these narratives overlapped. It was a place that both invited and demanded elites and average migrants to move across what later would be stark national boundaries. Even within this local context, "Chinese" elites were transnational, for example, Mariano Limjap and José Ignacio Paua, who moved easily, for the time being at least, across the range of identities at play. Colonial Manila's Chinese merchant elite were thus liminal virtuosos who were able to negotiate numerous boundaries: physical (between southeast China and colonial Southeast Asia), cultural (between the Chinese, Hokkien, Hispanic, Filipino, and American popular and political cultures), and historical (between late imperial and republican China and between early modern and modern colonialism). A vivid example of this liminal virtuosity is provided by José Rizal in his portrayal of the Chinese *cabecilla* Quiroga.

> The main reception room had an air all its own that night. It was full of friars and bureaucrats, seated on cane-bottomed chairs or marble-topped stools of dark wood from Canton, playing three-handed *ombre* at small square tables in front of them, or making conversation in the bright light cast by gilt lamps or the more subdued one from Chinese lanterns ornately decorated with long silken tassels. The walls were covered with a lamentable confusion of delicate blue landscapes painted in Canton and Hong Kong, loud chromos of odalisques and half-naked women, and lithographs of effeminate Christs and the deaths of the Just Man and the Sinner produced by Jewish publishing houses in Germany for sale in Catholic countries. Nor were there lacking Chinese prints on red paper depicting a seated man of venerable aspect, smiling serenely, and behind him an ugly attendant, fearsome, diabolical, menacing,

armed with a broad-bladed spear; some of the natives knew him as Mahomet, others as St. James, for no known reason; nor could the Chinese themselves give any clear explanation of this popular dual personality. The popping of champagne corks, the clink of glasses, laughter, cigar smoke, and a certain smell peculiar to Chinese houses—a mixture of exotic perfume, opium and preserved fruit—completed the ensemble.

Dressed as a mandarin with a blue-tasseled cap Quiroga strolled from one room to another, erect and grave, although not without alert glances here and there as if to make sure that nobody pocketed anything. In spite of this instinctive distrust he exchanged hand-clasps with all and sundry, greeted some with a courteous and deferential smile, others with a protective air, and still others with a certain contempt that seemed to say:

"I know, you come not for me, but for my dinner."[3]

If one views *El Filibusterismo* from a nationcentric perspective, Rizal's distaste for the Chinaman is obvious, but in this hatred for an agent of Spanish oppression, there is a clarity of representation.[4] Quiroga's serpentine passage through the rooms of his mansion and the "lamentable confusion" of styles that fill these rooms attest to his position on the border between European, Southeast Asian, and Chinese cultures and political systems. Furthermore, Quiroga's mandarin affectations, those attributes that formally tied him to the Chinese state, did not prevent him from cultivating relations with Spanish bureaucrats and clergy or Manila's *mestizo* and *criollo* elites. The success of Don Carlos Palanca Chen Qianshan, on whom Quiroga was based, and the rest of the Chinese *cabecillas* rested on this same facility simultaneously to deploy a range of identities and employ a vast repertoire of social and economic strategies. The boundaries they negotiated were fraught with dangers, both economic and physical, but were also full of opportunity. Danger and opportunity required vigilance, flexibility, and a willingness to act aggressively to protect personal ambitions and community interests.

However numerous and diverse its cultural models may have been, Manila's Chinese merchant elite never lost sight of what their fundamental interests were: managing the flows of talent, wealth, and capital between Luzon and coastal Fujian. Moreover, this elite assumed that it had a duty to take the lead in defending those interests and to provide the social services that states either would not or could not provide. Long before the "gospel of wealth" gained currency in the United States, Manila's Chinese elite provided a social safety net in an unstable environment and used their influence not merely for their own profit but for the interests of their fellow migrants. Charity and community activism, as much as education and official position, were the criteria of elite status in late imperial China and in the colonial Philippines. This fact allowed a fundamentally transnational elite to bridge the physical and political divide between southern Fujian and Manila, and by their actions to knit together the ragged edges of empire. Since it was through these migration networks that nearly all Hokkien migrants came to the islands, elite interests were thus inseparable from the community's interests. To be sure, some of the elite abused their authority and oppressed clerks and coolies, but the protracted crisis in the Philippines underscored the importance of community cohesion and strong leadership. These lessons were hard-learned and conditioned the way the Chinese responded to internal and external threats.

Migration networks and patron-client relations were the bases for cohesion, and community institutions were the agency for elite activism. The most successful, and often the most problematic, integrative institutions in Chinese history have been those that were able to offer a venue for negotiation and compromise between state and local interests. The same was true for Chinese institutions in colonial Manila. In the late Spanish era, the nexus of state-local interaction was the Gobernadorcillo de los Sangleyes, but after 1898 the Chinese were offered new institutional forms that held out the possibility of even stronger links to the Chinese government and a new venue for relations with colonial authorities. Although they arrived too late to overcome the fissiparous forces plaguing the late Qing, Chinese consuls and local chambers of commerce could sometimes integrate local merchant interests with the state's agenda, and they would reemerge as critical institutional nodes in the late 1920s. The works of Joseph Fewsmith, Bryna Goodman, and Parks Coble on Shanghai's merchant elite have gone a long way toward examining the complexities and antagonisms of this interaction. In the Philippines, the relations between the Chinese Chamber of Commerce and the Chinese government were significantly less antagonistic than in other merchant communities, and the chamber rapidly became the nexus of interaction between the local elite and external authority. The nature of the colonial environment meant that the Chinese Chamber of Commerce, which was a local elite project, was the key point of contact with the American authorities and with the Chinese state. As they had throughout the Spanish period, American colonial policy allowed the recognized Chinese elite to mediate between the Chinese government, the colonialists, and the Chinese community.

Perhaps more than any other colonial power in the region, the Americans were willing to delegate responsibility for the Chinese community to the Chinese consul general and the Manila Chinese General Chamber of Commerce. This was an outgrowth of the American political environment, in which belief in the "yellow peril" had precluded any possibility of the Chinese being systematically incorporated into the American polity. Like the Spanish, the Bureau of Insular Affairs needed a prosperous and cooperative Chinese elite, but it was even more willing to keep the Chinese at arm's length as both a national category distinct from "Filipino" and as a corporate entity. As a result, the Chinese community's relative autonomy and the Chinese elite's influence increased. Therefore, even in a contentious and dangerous environment (and even with the introduction of the handmaidens of civil society, lawyers and newspapers), the established Chinese elite were able to survive the transition from imperial to republican China and from Spanish to American rule with a significant, if not greater, measure of local authority intact. In collaboration with both the colonial enterprise and China's late imperial state-building, the *cabecillas* had a hand in creating and shaping these institutions that in turn largely defined the Chinese as an alien enclave. With the emergence of a Filipino national elite, a process that was also shaped by the intersection of American policy and local elite ambition, coupled with the advent of the totalizing narratives of national identity in the twentieth century, there appeared a much starker divide between Chinese and Filipino identities than had been the case in this earlier time. Ironically, the flexibility and virtuosity of the Chinese merchant elite, those attributes that had allowed them to manipulate colonial officials and Chinese mandarins, would be lost as the institutions and identities that their ambitions had created bounded and constrained the Philippine Chinese as an ethnic enclave within an increasingly nationalistic Philippines.

The ambitions of the elite will by now be abundantly obvious, but the question of identity remains. How and why did these migrants come to see themselves as "Chinese" and to identify with China? Furthermore, how was it that the Chinese elite largely defined what it meant to be Chinese in colonial Manila? Prasenjit Duara and Wang Gungwu have already delved into the birth of overseas Chinese nationalism and Chinese ethnic identity and shown that this process was much more complicated than previously thought.[5] The emergence of national consciousness is not a spontaneous apprehension of a country's or a community's transcendent identity. Instead, national identity is a variable construct that is a product of and a reaction to conditions in a specific environment.[6] Chinese *cabecillas* opportunistically chose to promote Chinese identity and to strengthen their ties to China in response to conditions in the Philippines in the late years of Spanish rule: relative insularity and management of migration networks had proven their economic value, and maintaining cohesion was the primary function of Chinese community institutions. With increased competition, social mobility, and status volatility, the Chinese elite sought new strategies to establish and protect their social status and economic interests in an unstable environment. External "othering," through the application of national labels and autonomous institutions favored by colonial rulers, reinforced these distinctions. But what of the rest of Manila's Chinese for whom these issues were remote?

While not an absolute definition, it is possible, because of the strategies and ambitions of the elite, to draw a composite sketch of the average Chinese migrant in colonial Manila. Migration networks, patron-client relations, kinship, native-place ties, and sworn brotherhoods were the endogenous relational patterns that defined the Chinese in Manila as a distinct and cohesive ethnic enclave. Moreover, the dress, language, hairstyles, and vices of the Chinese further defined them as a group apart. To be Chinese in Manila meant most likely that one was from one of the sending villages of Zhangzhou and Quanzhou prefectures arrayed around the southern Fujian port of Xiamen. Migration had been managed either directly by a Chinese elite (whose status was defined by this role) or by a Chinese labor network tied to the elite. Whether he worked as a clerk, coolie, *tendero de sari-sari*, or craftsman, the new migrant was likely tied by kin, native place, debt, or duty to a *cabecilla*, who had made his migration and employment possible and also facilitated the remittance of his earnings back to the *qiaoxiang*. In their few leisure hours, Chinese migrants would play cards; drink tea, wine, or liquor, and snack in the food stalls and wine shops of Tondo and Binondo; some would visit their *india* or *mestiza* girlfriends. If he had some extra cash, a *chino* might visit a prostitute, smoke a bit of opium or tobacco, play cards, shoot dice, or bet on a cockfight or the lottery, that is, partake in the vices of a predominantly bachelor community. While most of these leisure activities, if taken in isolation, would not have distinguished a *chino* from an *indio* or a *mestizo,* the whole range of signifiers—dress, language, hairstyle, occupation, vice, and migrant status—combined to define, in broadest strokes, "Chineseness" in colonial Manila, and all of these were bound up with the elite who managed transnational migration systems and profited from *invernado* labor. Ambition and identity went hand in hand.

At the root, to be Chinese in the Philippines, that is, one nationality residing in the space of another, was to be transnational. The movement of talent, wealth, and information across national boundaries dictated both the internal structure and the external perception of the community. Thus, to be Chinese in Manila was, by definition, different from what it meant to be Chinese elsewhere. And to return to China from overseas was to be something familiar to but nonetheless distinct from one's neighbors who had not made the journey. But "transnational" is perhaps a misleading term without significant qualification. These transnational linkages were for the most part confined to a shallow ninety-mile band of the southern Fujian coast at one end and central Luzon at the other. Therefore, to call these networks transnational, without remaining aware of the inherent local character of migration, is to run the risk of imputing to discrete linkages a degree of historical import that these natural and mundane exchanges of talent, wealth, and information did not hold for their practitioners. During the period from the 1880s to the 1910s, and for many years after, the key ties were translocal more than transnational. The elite may have managed higher-level relations between nations and nationalities, but for a *tendero* in the provinces or a coolie in Manila, it was the structural link between his immediate environs and his *qiaoxiang* that mattered most. Each locality was inseparable from the other, and there were robust linkages between southern Fujian and central Luzon that were forged by the two-way movement of wealth and talent. Yet at the same time, to ignore the impact that these mundane exchanges of wealth, talent, and information had on larger historical trends, for example, in facilitating the commercialization of Philippine agricultural export economy and with it a socioeconomic revolution in the islands, would be equally myopic. These were essentially unremarkable border crossings that were remarkably important. The intentions of the average Chinese in the Philippines were mundane, yet the consequences of his migration and those of his peers could be tremendous. It was the Chinese merchant elite who had an awareness spanning the mundane to the cosmopolitan, and while they might not have been aware of all the consequences of their actions, they evinced a deep understanding of larger historical trends, changes in colonial and imperial policy, and the impact that developments from local to global had on the Chinese community that they dominated.

The defining characteristic of the Chinese elite that endured through these decades of dramatic change was the aggressive cooptation of imperial symbols and national institutions in the pursuit of local agendas and self-interest. This is not to say that the construction of a Chinese identity in the Philippines was purely opportunistic. The ties of family, native place, ethnicity, and shared hardship could be equally important for promoting a corporate identity, but these foundations of identity would be shaped by the localities and by the superstructure of the community in which an individual migrant moved. In spite of periodic anti-Chinese activism in the Philippines and discriminatory legislation, to be Chinese in Manila was still an asset. The Qing and republican governments encouraged the opportunistic manipulation of identity in the hopes of exploiting overseas talent and capital, as did the American and Spanish colonial governments. Local institutions with access to external authority helped to define that identity, and mutual institutional cooptation provided an arena in which central and local interests could be negotiated and balanced. In colonial Manila, the local elite used these institutions to coordinate collective action and influence colonial policy but most critically to facilitate the flow of talent, wealth, and information between Manila and Xiamen. The adaptability of Chinese community institutions, the strength of migration networks, and the skill of the elite explain the ability of the Chinese in colonial Manila not only to endure a protracted crisis but ultimately to prosper to such an extent as to fundamentally change both the Philippines and southern Fujian.

# Notes

## Introduction

1. Given political overtones of the term *"huaqiao,"* commonly translated as "overseas Chinese," I prefer to apply the terms "Chinese overseas" or "Chinese migrants" to describe ethnic Chinese who settle or sojourn outside the Chinese nation-space.

2. Sing-wu Wang, *The Organization of Chinese Emigration, 1848–1888*, 17–33; Wu Jianxiong, "Cong haiqin dao huaqiao," in his *Haiwai yimin yu huaren shehui*, 2–11.

3. Michael R. Godley, *The Mandarin Capitalists from Nanyang*, 92–93.

4. Wang Gungwu, "A Note on the Origins of *Hua-ch'iao*," in Wang Gungwu, *Community and Nation: Essays on Southeast Asia and the Chinese*, 118–127.

5. Foreign media and host governments were very interested in the loyalties of the local Chinese and their responses to major events in China. One

can often get a better idea of how Chinese overseas felt about specific issues than of an analogous merchant community in a Chinese city, whose opinions were less frequently polled.

6. Duara claims that the republican vision of the revolution subsequently buried the alternative strands of Chinese modernity offered by the Qing and by the reformist movement. Prasenjit Duara, "Nationalists among Transnationals," 53–58.

7. These enterprises were initially designed to defray the costs of the movement. One notable and scandalous business venture was the King Joy Lo Restaurant in Chicago, which began as a joint effort between the Chin family and Kang Youwei. It was partly conceived as a way for the Chins to displace the Moy family at the apex of Chicago's Chinatown, but it ultimately failed as both a business venture and a Chin power play as the Moys parlayed rival connections with Beijing into local political clout. Adam McKeown, *Chinese Migrant Networks and Cultural Change*, 205–206.

8. Duara, "Nationalists among Transnationals." In this essay, Duara returns to themes he raised in his *Rescuing History from the Nation*. See also Wang Gungwu, "The Limits of Nanyang Chinese Nationalism, 1912–1937," in Wang, *Community and Nation: Essays on Southeast Asia and the Chinese*, 142–158.

9. G. William Skinner, "Creolized Chinese Societies in Southeast Asia," 51.

10. See also Christine Dobbin, *Asian Entrepreneurial Minorities*, and Skinner, "Creolized."

11. Notably Lea Williams and Kwee Tek Hoay.

12. Claudine Salmon examines attempts by the Peranakans in Java to reassert their Chinese identity through institutional and educational reform in "Ancestral Halls, Funeral Associations, and Attempts at Resinicization in Nineteenth Century Netherlands India."

13. As the number of potential allies—including various Chinese governments and political movements, agencies of the colonial government, and new social groups in Philippine society—and institutional models—consulates, chambers of commerce, political parties—increased in the late nineteenth and early twentieth centuries, so too did the complexity and sophistication of the Chinese elite's alliance-forming strategies.

14. See John Omohundro, *Chinese Merchant Families in Iloilo*, and Modesto P. Sa-onoy, *The Chinese in Negros*.

15. Alfonso Felix, Jr., ed., *The Chinese in the Philippines, 1770–1898;* Emma H. Blair and James. A. Robertson, eds., *The Philippine Islands, 1493–1898* (hereafter BR); Khin Khin Myint Jensen, "The Chinese in the Philippines during the American Regime."

16. Edgar Wickberg, *The Chinese in Philippine Life, 1850–1898*, vii.

17. For the late Qing dynasty, see Henry Shih-shan Tsai, *China and the*

*Overseas Chinese in the United States, 1868–1911;* Yen Ching-hwang, "Overseas Chinese Nationalism in Singapore and Malaya, 1877–1912"; Yen Ching-hwang, "Ch'ing Sale of Honours and the Chinese Leadership in Singapore and Malaya, 1877–1912"; Yen Ching-hwang, *Coolies and Mandarins;* and Michael R. Godley, *The Mandarin-Capitalists from Nanyang.* Two notable exceptions to this tendency are Lea F. Williams, *Overseas Chinese Nationalism,* and Zheng Liren, "Overseas Chinese Nationalism in British Malaya, 1894–1941."

18. A history of China-Philippine Chinese relations between the fall of the Yuan government and the reconstitution of "central" authority under the Guomindang in 1927–1928 based on Chinese, American, and Philippine sources is beyond the scope of the present study but is a good subject for a future monograph. Nonetheless, the relative authority of the consul general was significantly enhanced when there was a strong government in China, as were the advantages of identifying with China. The Chinese governments between 1916 and 1928 do not meet even the liberal criteria of strength and unity I apply here. This formula was not, however, absolute. For example, when a strong China was an expansionist or Communist China, it was dangerous for local Chinese to identify with the motherland.

19. This work is therefore analogous to attempts by Philippine studies experts who seek to "rescue" the histories of local and indigenous peoples in the Philippines from the nation-based discourse. See Thomas M. McKenna, *Muslim Rulers and Rebels,* and the following works by William Henry Scott: *Looking for the Prehispanic Filipino; Cracks in the Parchment Curtain;* and *The Discovery of the Igorots.*

20. The Kaisa, a nonprofit Chinese community organization in Manila, not only sponsors community programs and advocates Chinese community interests, but also maintains the library collection of the late Dr. Chinben See and promotes scholarly projects on the Chinese in the Philippines.

21. I use the abbreviation BIA when referring to the Bureau of Insular Affairs Archives, National Archives II.

22. Unlike the study of Chinese communities in Thailand, Singapore, Indonesia, and (in recent years) the United States, the field of Philippine-Chinese studies has been relatively dormant. This is not to say that it has been entirely neglected. There are several sociological and anthropological studies of the Philippine Chinese, generally produced in the Philippines, that shed light on the complexity of community dynamics.

23. Skinner's "Creolized Chinese Societies in Southeast Asia" and Christine Dobbin's *Asian Entrepreneurial Minorities* demonstrate Wickberg's enduring relevance and have provided corroboration for many of my own conclusions.

24. Wickberg continues to set the tone for the field. In one of the best works on the subject produced in the last decade, Wickberg locates the ori-

gins of Filipino anti-Sinicism in the evangelical mission of the Spanish and the tutorial colonialism of the United States. Edgar Wickberg, "Anti-Sinicism and Chinese Identity Options in the Philippines."

25. Antonio Tan, *The Chinese in the Philippines, 1898–1935: A Study of Their National Awakening,* 6–9.

26. Ibid., 2.

27. Ibid., 73–213.

28. Ibid., 210–213.

29. Wong Kwok-chu, *The Chinese in the Philippine Economy, 1898–1941.*

30. Tan, *National Awakening,* 74, 84–87.

31. Tan also mischaracterizes Chinese migrants to Manila as "poor, illiterate peasants and coolies." While many were in this category, there were also a significant number of literate and commercially sophisticated merchants who frequently moved in elite circles in their native places. When they made the voyage from Xiamen to Manila, their kit bag consisted not simply of Chinese "cultural baggage" but also included a complex array of socioeconomic strategies drawn from the sophisticated commercial history of southern Fujian.

32. Tan, *National Awakening,* 88; Eufronio M. Alip, *Ten Centuries of Philippine-Chinese Relations,* 64.

33. Teresita Ang See and Go Bon Juan, *The Ethnic Chinese in the Philippine Revolution;* Teresita Ang See, "The Ethnic Chinese As Filipinos (Part II)."

34. Chinben See, "Chinese Clanship in the Philippine Setting"; "Chinese Education and Ethnic Identity"; "Chinese Organizations and Ethnic Identity in the Philippines."

35. The most pressing need for contemporary Chinese community leaders, who are also its most prolific chroniclers, is to sell the Chinese community as being "of" the Philippines. Only rare attempts are made to address the sojourner dynamic employed by the Manila Chinese other than to show that remittances and travel to the homeland echo the close bonds that Filipinos also feel for their native place. This elision of sojourning is echoed in a significant amount of Asian American scholarship, which is often constrained to defend Asian Americans from charges of parasitism. See McKeown's discussion of nation-based research in McKeown, *Chinese Migrant Networks,* 3; see also Leo Douw, "The Chinese Sojourner Discourse."

36. The propensity of Philippine-Chinese historians to inscribe the history of the Chinese in the Philippines within the larger narrative of the Philippine nation-state (see, for example Teresita Ang See, ed., *Ethnic Chinese as Filipinos*) is echoed in other major works on the Chinese in Southeast Asia that are mainly concerned with portraying the Chinese as being "of" Southeast Asia. For example, see Leo Suryadinata, ed., *Ethnic Chinese as Southeast Asians.*

37. Jacques Amyot's *The Manila Chinese* employs this familial bonds

trope, as do Antonio Tan's works on national identity and John Omohundro's *Chinese Merchant Families in Iloilo* and "Trading Patterns of Philippine Chinese."

38. Richard Chu, "Rethinking the Chinese Mestizos of the Philippines"; "The 'Chinese' and 'Mestizos' of the Philippines"; "The 'Chinese' Entrepreneurs of Manila from 1875 to 1905"; "Catholic, *Sangley*, Mestizo, Spaniard, Filipino."

39. Gregory Bankoff, *Crime, Society, and the State in the Nineteenth-Century Philippines.*

40. Wang Gungwu, "Sojourning"; Anthony Reid, "Flows and Seepages in the Long-Term Chinese Interaction with Southeast Asia"; Skinner, "Creolized"; Leonard Blussé, "The Vicissitudes of Maritime Trade"; Mary Somers Heidhues, "Chinese Settlements in Rural Southeast Asia." See also Anthony Reid, *Southeast Asia in the Age of Commerce, 1450–1680,* vols. 1 and 2; and Anthony Reid, ed., *Southeast Asia in the Early Modern Era.*

41. Another provocative, yet also potentially problematic, trend in recent scholarship is the comparison of entrepreneurial minorities across Asia to middlemen communities elsewhere. Anthony Reid and Daniel Chirot's *Essential Outsiders* compares the Chinese and Jewish experiences as entrepreneurial minorities and seeks out the origins of anti-Semitism in Europe and anti-Sinicism in Southeast Asia. A central irony of this volume is that the Jewish experience in Central Europe is important for understanding contemporary anti-Sinicism, but the analogy is not welcomed among the Chinese in Southeast Asia because of the endurance of anti-Semitism in Muslim Southeast Asia and the negative stereotypes attached to Jewish identity in the region. The antiliberal origins of anti-Semitism in Europe gave rise to a belief in an international Jewish conspiracy that was manifested in all Jews, be they orthodox, assimilated, or atheist. In Southeast Asia, the same demonization was applied to the Chinese, who could simultaneously be heathen cultural pollutants, parasitic capitalists, as well as the agents of international communism and China's plans for regional hegemony. See, in particular, Daniel Chirot, "Conflicting Identities and the Dangers of Communalism," 3–31; and Anthony Reid, "Entrepreneurial Minorities, Nationalism and the State," 33–73.

42. In the case of the Philippines, as opposed to the Dutch East Indies, where the conjoint community of Peranakans became more "Chinese" in the late nineteenth century, social and economic conditions encouraged Chinese *mestizos* to identify themselves as "of" the Philippines—gradually developing a Filipino identity—rather than as Chinese, whose transnational linkages were suspect in the eyes of Philippine nationalists. This focus on "middleman minorities" in the development of the world economy has its origin in Dobbin's earlier works on India and Indonesia and her engagement with the various classical sociological formulations of the origins and mani-

festations of capitalism: Georg Simmel, Max Weber, Joseph Schumpeter, and André Gunder Frank. See Dobbin, *Asian Entrepreneurial Minorities.*

43. Skinner, "Creolized," 51; Claudine Salmon, "Ancestral Halls."

44. See in particular Leo Douw, ed., *Unsettled Frontiers and Transnational Linkages.*

45. It is particularly among those that Winston Hsieh describes as the "Orthodox School" of 1911 historiography that the critical role of overseas communities as a training and fund-raising ground for the first (or Southern/Pearl River) stage of the Chinese national revolution is strongly emphasized. Winston Hsieh, *Chinese Historiography on the Revolution of 1911,* 29. For Hsieh, the writings of Feng Ziyu are exemplary of the strengths and weaknesses of this particular school. See Feng Ziyou, *Huaqiao geming kaiguo shi,* and *Huaqiao geming zuzhi shihua.* Other examples include Yen Ching-hwang and Lee Enhan, eds., *Xing, Ma huaren yu Xinhai geming;* Chinese Academy of Social Sciences, *Huaqiao yu Xinhai geming;* and Li Yinghui, *Huaqiao zhengce yu haiwai minzu zhuyi, 1912–1949.*

46. Another issue that is often ignored is the role that Chinese overseas, especially in the Philippines, played in the short-lived Fujian secessionist movement in the early 1930s, an attempt to wrest the province from Guomindang control that was bankrolled by Philippine-Chinese lumber king Dee C. Chuan (Li Qingquan). James Alexander Cook, "Bridges to Modernity," 421–434. Despite some notable progress in challenging the orthodox view of *huaqiao,* the historiographical bias endures. See, for example, the mainland journal *Huaqiao huaren lishi yanjiu,* published by the China Society for Overseas Chinese History; Zhou Nanjing, *Feilübin yu huaren;* Huang Zisheng and He Sibing, *Feilübin huaqiao shi;* and Chen Yande, *Xiandaizhong de chuantong.* For an excellent discussion of the relevant scholarship and the limitations of nation-based claims to the histories of Chinese overseas, see Adam McKeown's "Conceptualizing Chinese Diasporas, 1842 to 1949," and Wang Gungwu's earlier *China and the Chinese Overseas.* See also Liu Zhitian, *Zhongfei guanxi shi,* 557–558; and James Blaker's critique of Liu: James R. Blaker, "The Chinese in the Philippines."

47. In particular Prasenjit Duara, *Culture, Power, and the State;* Prasenjit Duara, "Elites and the Structures of Authority in the Villages of North China, 1900–1949"; Lenore Barkan, "Patterns of Power"; and Madeline Zelin, "The Rise and Fall of the Fu-Rong Salt-Yard Elite." See also William T. Rowe, *Hankow: Commerce and Society in a Chinese City,* and *Hankow: Conflict and Community in a Chinese City;* Joseph Fewsmith, *Party, State and Local Elites in Republican China;* Bryna Goodman, *Native Place, City, and Nation;* and Zhang Xin, *Social Transformation in Modern China.*

48. Historiographically, this has been a circular process. The Chinese communities in Southeast Asia, studied in the 1950s and 1960s (a time when field research in China was prohibited for all but a few), informed the un-

derstanding of mainland Chinese society and shaped the scholarship on local society in China that followed. See in particular Maurice Freedman,
"Colonial Law and Chinese Society"; *Lineage Organization in Southeastern
China; Chinese Lineage and Society;* as well as G. William Skinner, *Chinese Society
in Thailand;* and *Leadership and Power in the Chinese Community of Thailand.*

### Chapter 1: Origins and Evolution of the Manila-Chinese Community

1. Ng Chin-keong, *Trade and Society;* Wang Gungwu "Merchants without
Empire," 400–421.

2 Hokkien is the pronunciation of "Fujian" in the Minnan dialect.

3. Dobbin, *Asian Entrepreneurial Minorities,* 63–68. Dobbin draws on Ng's
work on the Amoy network to argue that the Chinese who migrated to the
Philippines were preadapted to commerce.

4. Within the limited scope of this chapter I cannot offer a systematic
breakdown of the Qing empire's fiscal and administrative structure. Nor do I
claim that the two empires were identical; rather, I contend that the similarities arose from fundamental approaches to taxation, social control, and administrative and cultural practices shared by both governments.

5. Chinese cities were themselves too diverse to allow for easy general-
ization. Every Chinese community, be it in China or abroad, is deserving of
systematic historical analysis to determine which social characteristics and
economic strategies can be said to be inherently Chinese and which are conditioned by the local context.

6. Charles Tilly, "Reflections on the History of European State-Making,"
35.

7. Only when silver flow stopped in the 1800s did the Spanish government pursue substantive policy reform. As seen in recent scholarship on the
late imperial economy, China was equally addicted to silver.

8. John H. Coatsworth, "The Limits of Colonial Absolutism, 27–28.

9. Murdo J. Macleod, "The Primitive Nation State, Delegations of Functions, and Results," 53.

10. Ibid., 57.

11. Although the Chinese had developed a systematized law code in the
Tang dynasty (618–907) and had continued to add new precedents and
statutes to this code, the state had very little day-to-day control of local adju-
dications and only became involved in major cases such as murder, rebellion, and official malfeasance. From the Ming dynasty onward, the imperial
government recognized its limited reach and delegated responsibility for local mediation and law enforcement to the local elite. When local mediation
failed and official intervention was requested, an elite plaintiff or defendant
often had the upper hand in litigation because of his superior connections
with local officials. See Edward L. Farmer, "Social Order in Early Ming
China," 17–22.

12. The increasing localist orientation of the late imperial elite was partly a result of the demographic crunch that left millions of members of the elite with aspirations for government service frustrated by a government recruitment system that could absorb only a few hundred new officials every three years. Fortunately for the state, Neo-Confucianism, which appeared in the eleventh and twelfth centuries, and became official orthodoxy in the fourteenth century, emphasized the morally transformative value of socially responsible local activism and provided the blueprints and institutional models for elite activism. See in particular Patricia Buckley Ebrey, *Family and Property in Sung China*; and Patricia Buckley Ebrey, *Chu Hsi's Family Rituals*.

13. Gabriel Ardant, *Théorie sociologique de l'impôt*. Ardant's theories have been applied to the study of the Spanish colonial empire in Murdo J. Macleod, "The Sociological Theory of Taxation and the Peasant." See also MacLeod, "Primitive Nation State," 53–68; Ardant, *Théorie* 1:32 is cited on p. 65.

14. Coatsworth, "Limits," 27–28.

15. Wickberg, "Chinese Mestizo," 62–100; Wickberg, *Chinese in Philippine Life*, 9–10; Skinner, "Creolized," 67.

16. F. De Haan, *Oud Batavia* (Bandoeng, 1935), 1:67, cited in Leonard Blussé, *Strange Company*, 58.

17. Macleod, "Primitive Nation State," 57. For a discussion of a similar process in China, see Duara, *Culture, Power, and the State*.

18. Edilberto C. de Jesus, *The Tobacco Monopoly in the Philippines*; Felix M. Keesing, *The Ethnohistory of Northern Luzon*.

19. Wickberg, *Chinese in Philippine Life*, 113.

20. Chinese cities were crucial to Asian maritime trade. Denys Lombard distinguishes between the "hydraulic" city, connected to an agricultural space, and merchant cities, which depended, in fact, on the maritime nexus and its links with foreign lands. On the history of Hokkien "merchant" cities, see Chen Dasheng and Denys Lombard, "Foreign Merchants in Maritime Trade in 'Quanzhou' ('Zaitun')," 114. For the *yanghang* system, see Zeng Shaocong, *Dong yanghang lüyimin*, 275–284; Blussé, "Vicissitudes"; Susan Mann, *Local Merchants and the Chinese Bureaucracy, 1750–1950*; Duara, *Culture, Power, and the State*; Freedman, *Lineage Organization in Southeastern China*, 73–76; Dobbin, *Asian Entrepreneurial Minorities*; and Ng, *Trade and Society*, 174–175.

21. For scholarship on the dynamics of this local negotiation of the integrative cultural consensus in China, see James L. Watson, "Standardizing the Gods," and Prasenjit Duara, "Superscribing Symbols."

22. J. L. Phelan, *Hispanization of the Philippines*, 13–14; Dobbin, *Asian Entrepreneurial Minorities*, 25.

23. Mazu, sometimes referred to as Tianhou or Tianfei, was also a mem-

ber of the late imperial pantheon of local deities. Skinner, "Creolized," 64; Wickberg, *Chinese in Philippine Life*, 193.

24. Macleod, "Primitive Nation State," 54.

25. Gregory Bankoff, *Crime, Society, and the State*, 93–100.

26. For marginalized young men, secret societies also offered spiritual satisfaction through ritual observances. See in particular David Ownby, "Chinese Hui and the Early Modern Social Order; and David Ownby, "The Heaven and Earth Society as Popular Religion," 1035.

27. Attaching the diminutive *"cillo"* or *"cilla"* to a title such as *"gobernador"* (governor) or *"cabeza"* (head) indicated the leadership of an organization that was subordinate to the colonial government. *Gobernadorcillos* who possessed both judicial and executive powers were a common fixture throughout the colonial Philippines, not just in the major cities.

28. Coatsworth, "Limits," 37.

29. Mak Lau Fong, "Chinese Secret Societies in the Nineteenth Century Straits Settlements"; Carl A. Trocki, *Opium and Empire*; Carl A. Trocki, "Rise and Fall of the Ngee Heng Kongsi"; Skinner, "Creolized," 82.

30. McKeown, *Chinese Migrant Networks*, 214.

31. Bankoff, *Crime, Society, and the State*, 41–56.

32. Susan Naquin and Evelyn S. Rawski, *Chinese Society in the Eighteenth Century*; David Ownby, *Brotherhoods and Secret Societies in Early and Mid-Qing China*; Ownby, "Chinese Hui"; Dian H. Murray, "Migration, Protection, and Racketeering"; Philip A. Kuhn, *Rebellion and Its Enemies in Late Imperial China*; John Robert Shepherd, *Statecraft and Political Economy on the Taiwan Frontier, 1600–1800*.

33. Murray, "Migration"; Ownby, "Heaven and Earth," 1035.

34. Spanish reconnaissance ships fired on Chinese junks during the first Spanish trip to Luzon in 1570. Twenty Chinese were killed in the skirmish, and the Spanish seized their cargo. The attack on the Chinese dismayed the commanders of the expedition, Juan de Salcedo and Martin de Goiti, both of whom were under orders to attract the Chinese rather than expel them by force. Gregorio F. Zaide, ed., *Documentary Sources of Philippine History* (hereafter *DSPH*), vol. 2, 61–63, 82–83.

35. BR, 44:271 and William Lytle Schurz, *The Manila Galleon*, 81.

36. Schurz, *Manila Galleon*, 63–64, 71–72; Wickberg, *Chinese in Philippine Life*, 4.

37. Maria Lourdes Diaz-Trechuelo, "The Role of the Chinese in the Philippine Domestic Economy (1570–1770)," 209–210; Schurz, *Manila Galleon*, 195.

38. Zheng He's treasure ships, built at Nanjing in the early fifteenth century, dwarfed even the largest of the Manila galleons. See Louise Levathes, *When China Ruled the Seas*.

39. Schurz, *Manila Galleon*, 195–196.

40. Diaz-Trechuelo, "The Role of the Chinese," 179–180; Milagros Guerrero, "The Chinese in the Philippines, 1570–1770"; Rafael Bernal, "The Chinese Colony in Manila, 1570–1770." See also Bon Juan Go and Teresita Ang See, *Heritage*, 70–77.

41. Bendict Anderson, "Cacique Democracy in the Philippines," 5–8.

42. Dobbin, *Asian Entrepreneurial Minorities*, 47–49.

43. Ibid., 49; Blussé, *Strange Company*, 94–95; Skinner, "Creolized," 54.

44. Wickberg, *Chinese in Philippine Life*, 8–15.

45. Ibid., 7–8.

46. Bankoff, *Crime, Society, and the State*, 99–100, 121–123.

47. Blussé, *Strange Company*, 60–68.

48. Wickberg, *Chinese in Philippine Life*, 9–11.

49. Spanish governors had a technical monopoly on all interprovincial trade.

50. Most notably in the sixteenth and seventeenth centuries. See Eufronio M. Alip, *Chinese in Manila*, 11, 17; and Liu Chi-Tien, "Comments by a Chinese Scholar," 252–285.

51. *DSPH* 3, no. 98, pp. 169–178; BR, 7:212–238.

52. The different *mestizo* communities were initially sponsored by rival Catholic orders. Wickberg, *Chinese in Philippine Life*, 18–20; Dobbin, *Asian Entrepreneurial Minorities*, 25–26.

53. *DSPH* 3, no. 98, pp. 169–180; Tan, "National Awakening," 52; Wickberg, *Chinese in Philippine Life*, 23. See also BR, 7:212–238.

54. Wickberg, *Chinese in Philippine Life*, 15.

55. Victor Purcell, *The Chinese in Southeast Asia*, 515.

56. *DSPH* 3, no. 98, pp. 169–180; BR, 7:212–238. These are translations of Bishop Domingo de Salazar's 1590 letter to King Philip II in which he describes the Chinese enclave in Manila.

57. Wickberg, "Chinese Mestizo," 88; Skinner, "Creolized," 77–78.

58. Schurz, *Manila Galleon*, 80.

59. Before the establishment of banks in the nineteenth century, credit was almost entirely managed by charitable foundations. Chinese could not have access to these funds unless they were baptized and had patronage ties to the locals who managed the *obras pias*. Wickberg, *Chinese in Philippine Life*, 69–70; Dobbin, *Asian Entrepreneurial Minorities*, 32.

60. Skinner, "Creolized," 77–78; Wickberg, "Chinese Mestizo," 88–95.

61. Schurz, *Manila Galleon*, 80, 94–95.

62. J. M. Zuniga, *Status of the Philippines in 1800*, 233–234, 268; Dobbin, *Asian Entrepreneurial Minorities*, 28–29, 36–37; Shepherd, *Statecraft*, 137–176; Ng, *Trade and Society*, 20–22, 25–32, 36–37; Blussé, *Strange Company*, 104, cited in Dobbin, *Asian Entrepreneurial Minorities*, 63–68.

63. Skinner, *Chinese Society*.

64. Skinner, "Creolized," 73.

65. Phelan, *Hispanization*, 18–20; Dobbin, *Asian Entrepreneurial Minorities*, 25.

66. *DSPH* 3, no. 120, pp. 301–303; no. 131, pp. 383–387; BR, 11:56–58, 8:271–276.

67. Yen Ching-hwang, *A Social History of the Chinese in Singapore and Malaya, 1800–1911*, 84–87.

68. In 1662, Zheng Chenggong, commonly known as Koxinga, demanded the submission of the Spanish colony to his rule. The Spanish rejected the ultimatum and Zheng died soon afterwards. His successors turned instead to the consolidation of their rule on Taiwan. Domingo Abella, "Koxinga Nearly Ended Spanish Rule in the Philippines in 1662"; Charles J. McCarthy, "On the Koxinga Threat of 1662."

69. Anthony Reid, "The Seventeenth-Century Crisis in Southeast Asia," 647.

70. William S. Atwell, "A Seventeenth-Century 'General Crisis' in East Asia?" 681.

71. Purcell, *Chinese in Southeast Asia*, 516–517, 526.

72. Wickberg, "Chinese Mestizo."

73. Reid, "Flows and Seepages," 15–50.

74. Diaz-Trechuelo, "The Role of the Chinese," 192–193.

75. Wickberg, "Chinese Mestizo"; Skinner, "Creolized," 55.

76. Purcell, *Chinese in Southeast Asia*, 512.

77. John Larkin, *Sugar and the Origins of Modern Philippine Society;* Dobbin, *Asian Entrepreneurial Minorities*, 65.

78. Tomas de Comyn, *State of the Philippines in 1810* (Manila, 1969), 37, cited in Dobbin, *Asian Entrepreneurial Minorities*, 29.

79. Purcell, *Chinese in Southeast Asia*, 526–527.

80. Diaz-Trechuelo, "The Role of the Chinese," 207–210.

81. Wickberg, *Chinese in Philippine Life*, 53; Purcell, *Chinese in Southeast Asia*, 503.

82. W. E. Cheong, "The Decline of Manila as the Spanish Entrepôt in the Far East, 1765–1826."

83. Wickberg, *Chinese in Philippine Life*, 23–24.

84. *Invernado* were initially segregated from the *radicado* and the natives. Ibid., 155.

85. Guerrero, "Chinese in the Philippines," 15–19; Wickberg, *Chinese in Philippine Life*, 53.

86. J. T. Omohundro, "Trading Patterns."

87. See also Bruce L. Fenner, *Cebu under the Spanish Flag (1521–1896)*, esp. chap. 3.

88. Wickberg, *Chinese in Philippine Life*, 49.

89. Gregorio F. Zaide, "The Economic Development of the Philippines and the Contributions of Foreigners," 13–15.

90. M. Cullinane, "The Changing Nature of the Cebu Urban Elite in the 19th Century"; Alfred McCoy, "Introduction."

91. Skinner, *Leadership and Power;* Robert Irick, *Ch'ing Policy toward the Coolie Trade;* Wang Gungwu, *China and the Chinese Overseas.*

92. Douglas S. Massey, Rafael Alarcon, Jorge Durand, and Humberto Gonzalez, eds., *Return to Aztlan.*

93. Maria Lourdes Diaz-Trechuelo, "The Economic Background," 18–44.

94. Wickberg, *Chinese in Philippine Life,* 47; Guerrero, 4–6.

95. Guerrero, "Chinese in the Philippines," 7.

96. Stanley Karnow, *In Our Image,* 60–61; Diaz-Trechuelo, "Economic Background," 39. Although not as scholarly as some other works on the American Philippines, such as Glenn Anthony May, *Social Engineering in the Philippines,* and Peter Stanley, *A Nation in the Making,* Karnow's work is nonetheless valuable for its evocative portrayals of the personalities involved in the colonial enterprise.

97. Manuel Sarkisyanz, *Rizal and Republican Spain and Other Rizalist Essays.*

98. Rather than being fully assimilated, a distinct *mestizo* identity was an important component of the new Filipino elite identity.

99. It has been argued that the roots of the Philippine economy's present dependent underdevelopment are found in the nineteenth-century reforms. By focusing on quick-fix revenue-generating enterprises like agricultural exports and labor-intensive tobacco and sugarcane processing, instead of capital intensive industries, the Philippines became locked into a cycle of dependence that was exacerbated by the extension of the American economic umbrella. See Daniel F. Doeppers, *Manila, 1900–1941;* and Larkin, *Sugar.*

100. Fenner, *Cebu,* 78–80.

101. Marshall S. McLennan, "Changing Human Ecology on the Central Luzon Plain, Nueva Ecija, 1705–1939," 57. A major contribution of this essay and the others in McCoy and de Jesus' volume is that, rather than portraying the Chinese as a "group apart" in the Philippines, these authors demonstrate their integral role in shaping social and economic trends. See Alfred W. McCoy and Edilberto C. de Jesus, *Philippine Social History.*

102. Wickberg, *Chinese in Philippine Life,* 46.

103. Denise Helly, ed., *The Cuba Commission Report;* Wu Jianxiong, "Shijiu shiji qianwang guba de huagong, 1847–1874," in Wu Jianxiong, *Haiwai yimin yu huaren shehui,* 50–107.

104. Wickberg, *Chinese in Philippine Life,* 58–59.

105. With the notable exception of the Maguindanao/Mindanao.

106. Wickberg, *Chinese in Philippine Life,* 59.

107. Omohundro, "Trading Patterns," 125–129.

108. Edilberto C. de Jesus, "Control and Compromise in the Cagayan Valley," 31–32.

109. The Chinese role in moneylending and foreclosure did not always endear them to *indio* farmers. *Los Chinos en Filipinas,* 77–79, 104, 120; Guerrero, "Chinese in the Philippines," 7–8. For a commodity by commodity discussion of the role of the Chinese in the agricultural economy, see Wickberg, *Chinese in Philippine Life,* 94–106.

110. Foreigners were allowed to bid on monopoly contracts beginning in 1857. Wickberg, *Chinese in Philippine Life,* 59, 113–115.

111. The British pursued a similar policy in Singapore and Malaya. Various local Chinese were awarded special titles, and some were even granted knighthood. In the 1910s and 1920s, the Dutch in Java tried to encourage local Chinese to identify with the Dutch government by granting them Dutch citizenship. These efforts have been seen as attempts to counteract the increasing China-orientation of the Chinese overseas in the late nineteenth and twentieth centuries. See Lee Lai To, "Chinese Consular Representatives and the Straits Government in the Nineteenth Century," in Lee Lai To, ed., *Early Chinese Immigrant Societies,* 91–92.

112. Wickberg, *Chinese in Philippine Life,* 61.

113. Diaz-Trechuelo, "Economic Background," 35.

114. Skinner, "Creolized"; Wickberg, "Chinese Mestizo"; Dobbin, *Asian Entrepreneurial Minorities;* Margaret Wyant Horsley, "Sangley."

115. *Nipa* is an indigenous Philippine palm that is widely used for constructing residences, and its extract is used in making alcohol.

116. Brian Fegan, "The Social History of a Central Luzon Barrio," 99–100; Dennis Morrow Roth, "Church Lands in the Agrarian History of the Tagalog Region," 144–145. During the period from 1883 to 1903, commonly known as the "years of mourning," the Philippine mortality rate was among the highest in the world. Ken De Bevoise, *Agents of Apocalypse,* 6–15, 164–183.

117. Doeppers, *Manila,* 8; Karnow, *In Our Image,* 59–60.

118. Benito Legarda Jr., *After the Galleons,* 211.

119. Ibid., 335–338.

120. Bankoff, *Crime, Society, and the State,* 34–58.

121. Wickberg, *Chinese in Philippine Life,* 111–113.

122. Diaz-Trechuelo, "Economic Background," 38–39; Jade Joy R. Lim, "Carlos Palanca Tan Quien-sien, a Case Study of a Chinese in the Nineteenth Century Philippines."

123. *El Comercio,* 8/22/86, quoted in Bankoff, *Crime, Society, and the State,* 21.

## Chapter 2: Patterns of Chinese Elite Dominance in Spanish Manila

1. Mary Backus Rankin and Joseph W. Esherick, "Concluding Remarks," 306–307.

2. L. Eve Armentrout Ma, *Revolutionaries, Monarchists, and Chinatowns,* 14–29; L. Eve Armentrout Ma, "The Social Organization of Chinatowns in North America and Hawaii in the 1890s."

3. Jacques Amyot, *Manila Chinese; Zhongmei guanxi shiliao* (hereafter *ZMGXSL*), 3723.

4. Omohundro, "Trading Patterns," 119–125; Wickberg, *Chinese in Philippine Life,* 179–181.

5. Wickberg, *Chinese in Philippine Life,* 179.

6. Amyot, *Manila Chinese,* 13; Wickberg, *Chinese in Philippine Life,* 39.

7. Gerald A. McBeath, *Political Integration of the Philippine Chinese,* 45–47; Wickberg, *Chinese in Philippine Life,* 179.

8. Philip E. Ginsberg, "The Chinese in the Philippine Revolution"; Wickberg, *Chinese in Philippine Life,* 201–203.

9. Trocki, *Opium and Empire,* 39–40.

10. Bidding for opium farm contracts was hotly contested. Furthermore, the efforts of one secret society to control the smuggling activities of another secret society (which may have previously held the contract or had brokerage ambitions) were the frequent catalysts for riots and "tong wars" in colonial Singapore. Ibid., 129–130; see also Yen, *Social History,* 116–128; and James R. Rush, *Opium to Java,* 148–158.

11. "*Cabecilla*-agent system" as it is used in this work refers to the structure of patron-client relations within the *chino* community and to the patterns of Chinese migration to and employment in the Spanish Philippines. See Wickberg, *Chinese in Philippine Life,* 37–38.

12. Rankin and Esherick, "Concluding Remarks," 321–322.

13. Helly, *Cuba Commission.*

14. Lim "Carlos Palanca"; Omohundro, "Trading Patterns," 124–129.

15. "*Towkay*" (chief merchant), taken from Chinese, and "*cabang ata*" (lit. "highest branch"), from the local dialect, are often used interchangeably. Leonard Blussé, "Testament to a Towkay: Jan Con, Batavia and the Dutch China Trade," in Blussé, *Strange Company,* 49–72; Blussé, "Vicissitudes," 148–163; Rush, *Opium,* 83–107.

16. McKeown, *Chinese Migrant Networks,* 25

17. There were also Spanish, *mestizo,* and *indio cabecillas.* Lim, "Carlos Palanca," 2, 7–12.

18. Norbert Dannhaeuser, "Evolution and Devolution of Downward Channel Integration in the Philippines"; Guerrero, "Chinese in the Philippines," 7–9; Lim, "Carlos Palanca," 2.

19. Omohundro, "Trading Patterns," 125.

20. Robert E. Entenmann, "Migration and Settlement in Sichuan,

1644–1796"; Richard Von Glahn, *The Country of Streams and Grottoes;* Johanna Menzel Meskill, *A Chinese Pioneer Family;* Rowe, *Hankow: Commerce and Society* and *Hankow: Conflict and Community;* Shepherd, *Statecraft.*

21. Fe Caces and Douglas T. Gurak, "Migration Networks and the Shaping of Migration Systems."

22. The issue of the extent, nature, and purpose of *qiaoxiang* ties is something of a cottage industry in Chinese overseas history, spawning numerous conferences and volumes. See Leo Douw, Cen Huang, and Michael R. Godley, eds., *Qiaoxiang Ties;* and Zhuang Guotu, Zhao Wenliu, Tanaka Kyoko, and Cen Huang, eds., *Zhongguo qiaoxiang yanjiu.*

23. Huang Jianchun, *Wanqing xinma huaqiao dui guojia rentong zhi yanjiu.*

24. McKeown, "Chinese Diasporas," 321.

25. Here I agree with Madeline Hsu's description of migration "as a fluid process of mobility and diversification rather than as an invasion or uprooting." Madeline Yuan-yin Hsu, *Dreaming of Gold, Dreaming of Home,* 11.

26. McKeown, "Chinese Diasporas," 321.

27. Guerrero, "Chinese in the Philippines," 8; N. A. Simoniya, "Overseas Chinese in Southeast Asia," 44.

28. Dobbin, *Asian Entrepreneurial Minorities,* 160–168; Skinner, "Creolized," 84.

29. Lim, "Carlos Palanca," 15.

30. Amyot, *Manila Chinese,* 40–42; Dobbin, *Asian Entrepreneurial Minorities,* 167–168.

31. Dannhaeuser, "Evolution and Devolution," 577–595. See also S. Gordon Redding, *The Spirit of Chinese Capitalism,* 28.

32. Wickberg, *Chinese in Philippine Life,* 67–80, 94–108; Wickberg, "Chinese Mestizo," 90–93; Skinner, "Creolized," 84; Dobbin, *Asian Entrepreneurial Minorities,* 167–168.

33. Lim, "Carlos Palanca," 3.

34. The cities of Cebu and Iloilo had relatively large Chinese populations (numbering several thousand) and had their own *cabecillas,* but 45 to 50 percent of Philippine Chinese and nearly all the important *cabecillas* lived in Manila. Omohundro, "Trading Patterns," 113–136.

35. Lim, "Carlos Palanca," 7; Simoniya, "Overseas Chinese," 44.

36. Thomas Knox, "John Comprador," *Harper's New Monthly Magazine* 57 (1878): 427–437, cited in Hao Yen-p'ing, *The Comprador in Nineteenth-Century China,* 55. Hao's work can be used to understand some of the functions of the Chinese *cabecilla,* but there are certain notable dissimilarities. In particular, Hao contends that compradors departed from tradition in the way they educated their children and in the lifestyles they affected. This is not the case for the Manila *cabecillas,* who constructed self-conscious linkages to Chinese tradition.

37. Wickberg, *Chinese in Philippine Life,* 147; Lim, "Carlos Palanca," 5.

38. Wickberg, *Chinese in Philippine Life,* 111–113; Diaz-Trechuelo, "Economic Background," 37–39.

39. Skinner, "Creolized," 84–85, 89.

40. This phenomenon is best demonstrated by the ever-growing number of petitions presented by *cabecillas* to the Spanish government.

41. The Spanish tended to view their relations with the Chinese as highly lucrative, which may in part explain their resistance to allowing the Qing to set up an office that would get in the way of this relationship. "Testimony of Neil Macleod" and "Memorandum on the Chinese in the Philippines," *Report of the Philippine Commission to the President of the United States* (1900) (hereafter *ROPC* 1900), 27–50, 432–455; Lim, 4, 9–10; Wickberg, *Chinese in Philippine Life,* 113. The Straits government was equally fearful of losing the loyalty of local Chinese and responded with their own rewards. See C. F. Yong, *Chinese Leadership and Power in Colonial Singapore;* and Lai To Lee, "Chinese Consular Representatives and the Straits Government in the Nineteenth Century," 95.

42. Lim, "Carlos Palanca," 6–9; Omohundro, "Trading Patterns," 124–129.

43. Charles Tilly and C. H. Brown, "On Uprooting, Kinship and the Auspices of Migration."

44. Redding, *Spirit of Chinese Capitalism,* 28, 36, 57–58, 205–240. Francis Fukuyama has also offered some interesting observations on trust and the insularity of Chinese family businesses. See Francis Fukuyama, *Trust,* 69–95.

45. Each of the Chinese communities in Java responded to changes in the nineteenth century in different ways. The main comparative community is the one in the Dutch East Indies capital of Batavia, which most closely corresponds to Manila. See Donald E. Willmott, *The Chinese of Semarang.*

46. Skinner, "Creolized," 90.

47. J. A. C. Mackie and Charles A. Coppel, "A Preliminary Survey," in J. A. C. Mackie, ed., *The Chinese in Indonesia,* 5. See also Cornelius Fasseur, *The Politics of Colonial Exploitation.*

48. Dobbin argues that the Guandi cult, which emphasizes loyalty and obligation, was particularly conducive to creating bonds between Peranakans and the recent migrants. Dobbin, *Asian Entrepreneurial Minorities,* 67–68.

49. Dobbin, *Asian Entrepreneurial Minorities,* 63. See also Rush, *Opium,* 97.

50. It is not surprising that the Peranakans' relative economic decline can be traced to the end of the opium monopoly. Subsequent chapters will show that the end of certain Spanish colonial practices in the Philippines also destabilized the Chinese community. Skinner, "Creolized," 88.

51. Richard Chu, "Rethinking the Chinese Mestizos of the Philippines";

Richard Chu, "The 'Chinese' and 'Mestizos' of the Philippines"; Richard Chu, "Catholic, *Sangley*, Mestizo, Spaniard, Filipino."

52. This seems to imply that native-place rivalries and resistance to assimilation are as much a product of inherent or historic antipathy between specific groups of Chinese as they are a reflection of the competition for scarce resources.

53. Omohundro, *Chinese Merchant Families*, 84; Dobbin, *Asian Entrepreneurial Minorities*, 171.

54. Alip, *The Chinese in Manila*, 64.

55. Bankoff, *Crime, Society, and the State*, 43–44.

56. I use the term "bachelor" as a general signifier. It is not exclusive to unwed men, but rather includes both the unwed and those who, because of distance, are not cohabitating with their spouses. McKeown, "Chinese Diasporas," 318.

57. Spanish Manila, reel 7, 1841, quoted in Bankoff, *Crime, Society, and the State*, 51.

58. Some of these cases went as far as the Philippine and United States Supreme Courts. See http://laws.lp.findlaw.com/getcase/US/228/335.html and http://www.chanrobles.com/cralaw19122.html. For a cogent analysis of other cases see Chu, " 'Chinese' and 'Mestizos.' "

59. It is important also to keep in mind that many of these unions were arranged marriages, and thus nuclear cohabitation could be undesirable or not economically optimal.

60. Skinner, "Creolized," 79.

61. Lim, "Carlos Palanca," 15; Wickberg, *Chinese in Philippine Life*, 191–193.

62. Richard Chu, "The 'Chinese' Entrepreneurs of Manila from 1875 to 1905."

63. Bankoff, *Crime, Society, and the State*, 94, 117–118.

64. Gift-giving to local officials has a long history in China but was equally encouraged by the prebendal nature of Spanish colonial rule. Chinese merchants in Batavia offered equally impressive gifts to the Dutch governors. In Semarang, where the Chinese *kapitan* was appointed by the Dutch administrators, bribery was used to guarantee appointment. Ong Tai Hae, *The Chinaman Abroad; or, A Desultory Account of the Malayan Archipelago, Particularly of Java* (Shanghai, 1849), 4, cited in Willmott, *Semarang*, 148–149. See also Blussé, "Vicissitudes," 151–152; and Wickberg, *Chinese in Philippine Life*, 165–166.

65. Go and See, *Heritage*, 44.

66. Blussé, *Strange Company*; C. F. Yong, *Leadership and Power*; Yen Ching-hwang, *Social History*.

67. Peng Naiyang and Li Maozhou, "Xiaoshi," 103.

68. *Feilübin huaqiao Shanju gongsuo ban Zhonghua chongren yiyuan yu luo-jian jinian kan;* Wickberg, *Chinese in Philippine Life,* 185.

69. Hokkiens were preadapted to blanket organization that coopted subordinate organizations. James Cook has concluded, "Xiamen's merchant organizations were, therefore, limited to simplex-type associations that combined either a common trade or integrated members of diverse trades who did business in one geographic territory." The largest possible constituency of Chinese in Manila brought under a single organization was therefore both familiar and economically sound. "Bridges," 83.

70. Williams, *Overseas Chinese Nationalism;* Skinner, "Creolized," 87.

71. Skinner argues that the pan-Chinese cultural movement, of which Chinese schools were a major part, "never had a chance in the Philippines," because the *mestizos* were already too far removed from the *chinos.* Skinner, "Creolized," 89.

72. Peng Naiyang and Li Maozhou, "Xiaoshi," 103; Yi Jingxian, "Wushi nianlai huaqiao guoyu yundong," in Chen Zhiping, ed., *Xiaolusong huaqiao Zhongxi xuexiao,* 287. See also Wickberg, *Chinese in Philippine Life,* 188; and Skinner, "Creolized," 89.

73. In fact much of the governance of the islands was handled through Dominican friars who were both feared and hated by the Filipinos. O. D. Corpuz, *The Bureaucracy in the Philippines,* 26–27; Karnow, *In Our Image,* 69–71; Lim, "Carlos Palanca," 9.

74. Bankoff, *Crime, Society, and the State,* 122.

75. *"Sangleyes"* or *"sangley"* was a commonly used term for the Chinese derived from *shangye,* "trader," or *shanglai,* "he who comes to trade."

76. Wickberg, *Chinese in Philippine Life,* 180.

77. Willmott, *Semarang,* 135–137, 147–152.

78. Chinos Manila, Project 102, Institute of Asian Studies, University of the Philippines, reels 1–13.

79. Lim, "Carlos Palanca," 15–16; Amyot, *Manila Chinese,* 13–14; Wickberg, *Chinese in Philippine Life,* 194–199.

80. Wickberg, *Chinese in Philippine Life,* 37–38.

81. Ibid., 181.

82. Chinos Manila, reels 16–30. These microfilms contain extensive records of the Gobernadorcillo's daily activities. Unfortunately, because of damage they are difficult to decipher, and access is currently restricted.

83. *ZMGXSL,* 3279 and 3760.

84. Duara, "Structures of Authority," 280.

85. Wickberg, *Chinese in Philippine Life,* 182–183.

86. Lim, "Carlos Palanca," 17.

87. Chinos Manila, reels 1–19.

88. "Testimony of William A. Daland," United States Philippine Com-

mission, *Report of the Philippine Commission to the President, 1900* (hereafter, *ROPC 1900*), vol. 2, 164.

89. Esherick and Rankin, *Chinese Local Elites,* 323.

90. Wickberg, *Chinese in Philippine Life,* 184.

## Chapter 3: China and the Philippines

1. James Peter Geiss, "Peking under the Ming," 157–158; Li Jinming, *Mingdai haiwai maoyi shi;* William S. Atwell, "Notes on Silver, Foreign Trade, and the Late Ming Economy" and "International Bullion Flows and the Chinese Economy"; Pierre Chaunu, *Les Philippines et le Pacifique des Ibériques,* 92, 260; Pierre Chaunu, "Manile et Macao, face à la conjoncture des XVI de XVII siècles." See also Charles Kindleberger, *Spenders and Hoarders;* and John J. TePaske, "New World Silver, Castile and the Philippines, 1590–1800."

2. At that time China also had the largest economy in the world. Kindleberger, *Spenders,* 67–71.

3. See Atwell, "Notes," and "International Bullion Flows."

4 . Ng, *Trade and Society;* Wang Gungwu, "Merchants without Empire"; Jennifer Wayne Cushman, *Fields from the Sea.*

5. Wu Jianxiong, "Haiqin," in *Haiwai yimin,* 2–9; Ng, *Trade and Society.*

6. Wang Gungwu, "Early Ming Relations with Southeast Asia," in Wang Gungwu, *Community and Nation: Essays,* 30.

7. Cook, "Bridges," 23

8. After the initial trading bans, Qing maritime policy, in particular inflated tariffs on European ships, actually encouraged Chinese trade. Anthony Reid, "Economic and Social Change, c. 1400–1800," 494–495.

9. For an excellent treatment of the Qing era junk trade, see Cushman, *Fields from the Sea.*

10. Despite their small numbers, the Nanyang Chinese were central to the regional economy. See Cushman, *Fields from the Sea;* Reid, *Age of Commerce,* vols. 1 and 2; and Dobbin, *Asian Entrepreneurial Minorities.* See also Yen, *Coolies and Mandarins,* 72.

11. Ho Ping-ti, *Studies in the Population of China, 1386–1953;* A. B. C. Whipple, *The Challenge,* 228.

12. The ban remained on the books until 1893, although the Beijing Convention of 1860 recognized the right of Chinese to emigrate freely and thus made the statute moot.

13. Robert L. Irick, *Ch'ing Policy toward the Coolie Trade;* Yen, *Coolies and Mandarins,* 74–114.

14. According to Yen Ching-hwang, this event represented a watershed in the Qing's new "sympathetic attitude towards overseas Chinese." Yen, *Coolies and Mandarins,* 122.

15. Yen argues that the inclusion of a French and an English member gave the commission the appearance of impartiality, while in fact it was

staffed with individuals certain to be sympathetic to China's cause. Ibid., 123–124.

16. The final resolution of the treaty was delayed by the Margary Affair and by Spain's insistence on reparations for the *Sovrana* incident. The *Sovrana* was a Spanish ship attacked by Fujianese pirates off the coast of Taiwan in 1864. In retaliation, the Spanish threatened to launch an invasion of Taiwan from the Philippines, to which the Fujian governor, Ding Richang, responded with calls to shore up China's coastal defenses. No attack ever materialized, but twelve years later the Spanish minister still used the issue of reparations to delay the new treaty negotiations. Wang Liang, ed., *Qingji waijiao shiliao* (hereafter *Q JWJSL*), 8:35a–38b, 9:20a–26a, 12:8a–10a; Yen, *Coolies and Mandarins*, 126–127.

17. W. F. Mayers, ed., *Treaties between the Empire of China and Foreign Powers*, 204–208; Yen, *Coolies and Mandarins*, 127.

18. Irick, *Ch'ing Policy;* Yen, *Coolies and Mandarins*, 74–114, 135–140; Immanuel C. Y. Hsü, *China's Entrance in the Family of Nations*, 163–184.

19. Li Hongzhang, *Li wenzhong gong quanji* (hereafter *LWZGQ J*), 31:30a–30b; *Chouban yiwu shimo*, 55:17a–26a; Yen, *Coolies and Mandarins*, 139.

20. Zhang Zhidong, *Zhang wenxiang gong quanji* (hereafter *ZWXGQ J*), 1:333–334, 15:10a.

21. J. D. Frodsham, *The First Chinese Embassy to the West*, xxix–xxx; Yen, *Coolies and Mandarins*, 140–144; David Hamilton, "Kuo Sung-t'ao," 1–29; Hsü, *China's Entrance*, 180–181; *Q JWJSL* 11:13b–15a.

22. Wickberg, *Chinese in Philippine Life*, 214–215. According to Michael Godley, as of 1880 the Qing had begun raising much-needed funds by selling official ranks to the overseas Chinese. Godley, "The Late Ch'ing Courtship of the Chinese in Southeast Asia," 365.

23. Yen, *Coolies and Mandarins*, 140–153.

24. The self-financing scheme for the Singapore consulate, which was to serve as a model, proved woefully inadequate. Liu Jinzao, ed., *Qingchao shu wenxian tongkao* (hereafter *QCSWXTK*), 338, *waijiao* 2:796–797; Yen, *Coolies and Mandarins*, 153.

25. Wickberg, *Chinese in Philippine Life*, 209–210.

26. *LWZGQ J* 19:21a.

27. *Q JWJSL* 15:38a, 84:1b.

28. Wickberg, *Chinese in Philippine Life*, 215.

29. Biographical information on the life and career of Zhang Zhidong is based on Meribeth E. Cameron, "The Public Career of Chang Chihtung: 1837–1909"; "Chang Chih-tung," in Arthur W. Hummel, ed., *Eminent Chinese of the Ch'ing Period*, 27–32; Daniel H. Bays, *China Enters the Twentieth Century*, 7–11; and William Ayers, *Chang Chih-tung and Educational Reform in China*.

30. Lloyd E. Eastman, "Ch'ing-I and Chinese Policy Formation during the Nineteenth Century," 596; Lloyd E. Eastman, *Throne and Mandarins.*

31. Although Eastman accepts that there was no unanimous motivation or political agenda among the *qingyi* practitioners, "the tone or spirit of their opinions was alike." Eastman, "Ch'ing-I," 596; see also Hao Yen-p'ing, "A Study of the Ch'ing-liu Tang."

32. *ZWXGQ J* 34:15a–15b; Yen, *Coolies and Mandarins,* 156.

33. *ZWXGQ J* 13:12–13b, 15:7b–14a.

34. Eastman, "Ch'ing-I," 605.

35. *ZWXGQ J* 15:10b. Wickberg, *Chinese in Philippine Life,* 216.

36. *ZWXGQ J* 15:7b–14a. The Singapore office had since been upgraded to a consulate general. Yen, *Coolies and Mandarins,* 156–157.

37. *ZWXGQ J* 15:12b.

38. *ZWXGQ J* 15:12b; Wickberg, *Chinese in Philippine Life,* 218.

39. *ZWXGQ J* 15:7b–8b.

40. Yen, *Coolies and Mandarins,* 158–159.

41. *ZWXGQ J* 1:333–334, 15:10a.

42. Yen, *Coolies and Mandarins,* 150.

43. *ZWXGQ J* 15:9b–10a; *Q JWJSL* 68:5a–7a.

44. Li's rejection of the gunboat idea is ironic, considering that he had proposed a similar plan for backing up the Chinese consuls in Japan. *Q JWJSL* 68:5a–7a.

45. Zhang Zhidong, *Zhang wenxiang gong sigao* (hereafter *ZWXGSG*), 16:6b–7a; *ZWXGQ J* 23:9a–9b; *Q JWJSL* 74:23a–28a.

46. Zhang Yinhuan, *Sanzhou riji* (hereafter *SZRJ*), 2:76b–77a.

47. *ZWXGQ J* 23:12b.

48. This was the same strategy as proposed in the petition that the two Zhangs had received in 1886. *ZWXGQ J* 15:7b–14a.

49. *ZWXGQ J* 23:9b–10a, 13a–14a.

50. *ZWXGQ J* 23:9b–10a, 13a–14a.

51. *ZWXGQ J* 23:14a–14b.

52. *Q JWJSL* 70:10–11; Godley, "Late Ch'ing," 366.

53. *QCSWXTK,* 338, *waijiao* 2:796–798; *Q JWJSL* 75:20b; *SZRJ* 2:76b–77a.

54. *SZRJ* 2:76b–77a, 5:83a–85a.

55. *SZRJ* 5:83a–85a.

56. Li Hongzhang had apparently been foresighted in rejecting Zhang Zhidong's proposal to send Wang Yonghe's commission on Chinese warships. *SZRJ* 2:76b–77a, 3:64a, 65a, 86a; Wickberg, *Chinese in Philippine Life,* 220–222.

57. Although Zhang succeeded in reducing American demands for a thirty-year suspension of Chinese immigration to twenty years (except in cases where the immigrant could prove either U.S.$1,000 in assets or immediate family in the United States), opposition to the treaty was fierce (espe-

cially in Guangdong). The treaty was never ratified, and Zhang Yinhuan was recalled in disgrace. The United States responded by passing the Scott Act. Henry Shih-shan Tsai, *China and the Overseas Chinese*, 81–93.

58. *Q JWJSL* 71:9a–21b.

59. Hummel, *Eminent Chinese*, 60–63. Zhang Zhidong participated in the criticism of the Bayard-Zhang treaty and Zhang Yinhuan's alleged failures as ambassador. *ZWXGQ J* 24:25b–26a.

60. Benjamin A. Elman, *Classicism, Politics and Kinship*, 279. For the definitions of public and private crime, see Ch'u T'ung-tsu, *Local Government in China under the Ch'ing*, 32–33; and John R. Watt, *The District Magistrate in Late Imperial China*, 170–71.

## Chapter 4: Carlos Palanca Chen Qianshan

1. James Tait, one of the largest coolie exporters of the mid–nineteenth century, served simultaneously as Spanish vice-consul at Xiamen, exporting Hokkien labor to the Philippines and Cuba, and later became Dutch vice-consul as well. John Connolly was French consul and exported coolies to Peru. Interestingly, both Tait and Connolly were British. Cook, "Bridges," 73, 91, 94.

2. Zheng Guanying, *Chen Qianshan*, 3. Chen is also frequently referred to by his hispanized names Tan Quien-sien, Tan Chuey-liong, and Tan Chueco, as well as his baptismal name Don Carlos Palanca. The biographical background I offer is a synthesis of the works of Zheng, Wickberg, and Lim; Chen's own testimony to the Philippine Commission; and the biographies of Chen Qianshan and his son Chen Gang in the *Nanyang nianjian*.

3. Carstens, "Chinese Culture and Polity"; Lee, "Consular Representatives," 64–94; C. F. Yong, *Leadership and Power*, and his *Tan Kah-kee*; Godley, "Late Ch'ing Courtship"; Yen, *Coolies and Mandarins*, and *Social History*; Blussé, "Vicissitudes" and "Testament to a Towkay."

4. Omohundro, *Chinese Merchant Families*, 21.

5. "Testimony of Carlos Palanca," *ROPC 1900*, 2:219–220.

6. Omohundro, *Chinese Merchant Families*, 22.

7. My assumption is that this assistance refers to start-up capital from the native-place association *(tongxianghui)* to which Chen belonged. Zheng, *Chen Qianshan*, 5–6.

8. "Testimony of Carlos Palanca," *ROPC 1900*, 2:220; Lim, "Carlos Palanca," 14–16; Wickberg, *Chinese in Philippine Life*, 199–201.

9. Somewhere between U.S.$30,000 and 35,000. Henry Norman, *The Peoples and Politics of the Far East*, 178; Lim, "Carlos Palanca," 17; Bankoff, *Crime, Society, and the State*, 52–54.

10. See the cases of the heirs of Sy Quia and Son Cui: http://laws.lp.findlaw.com/getcase/US/228/335.html and http://www.chanrobles.com/cralaw19122.html. Given the risk dispersion and creative bookkeeping

inherent to the *cabecilla*-agent system, a true accounting of his wealth is probably impossible.

11. Xin Liu, "Space, Mobility, and Flexibility."

12. A statue to the memory of Chen Qianshan was erected at the entrance to this cemetery. For a more complete list of Chen's charitable works, see Zheng, *Chen Qianshan*, 7–10, 20; and *ZMGXSL*, 3723.

13. For the structure and function of merchant mediation, see Sybille Van Der Sprenkel, "Urban Social Control." See also Zheng, *Chen Qianshan*, 7–10, 20; and *ZMGXSL*, 3723.

14. In his research on southeastern China and Taiwan, Stephan Feuchtwang has found that "merchants desirous of converting their wealth into status and moving into the literati class would contribute to the building of official temples." Conspicuous acts of "face-improving" also included the founding of schools and other acts of charity. Stephan Feuchtwang, "School Temple and City God," 584; Wickberg, *Chinese in Philippine Life*, 189.

15. Some sources claim that Chen Gang attained *jinshi* status. I have not been able to find mention of him in the *jinshi* rolls, and the posts he held are consistent with purchased rank. See Zheng, *Chen Qianshan*, 21–24; Wickberg, *Chinese in Philippine Life*, 188; and *Nanyang nianjian, zheng*, 251.

16. Honorary rank 1a; see Charles O. Hucker, *A Dictionary of Official Titles in Imperial China*, no. 3349; Zheng, *Chen Qianshan*, 19; and Wickberg, *Chinese in Philippine Life*, 188.

17. Lim, "Carlos Palanca," 15; Wickberg, *Chinese in Philippine Life*, 191.

18. Wickberg, *Chinese in Philippine Life*, 201; Amyot, *Manila Chinese*, 14.

19. Wang Gungwu, personal communication, March 8, 1997.

20. Shepherd, *Statecraft and Political Economy*, 322–335.

21. Lim, "Carlos Palanca," 15–16; Amyot, *Manila Chinese*, 13–14; Wickberg, *Chinese in Philippine Life*, 180, 194–199.

22. "Testimony of William A. Daland," *ROPC 1900*, 2:163–168.

23. Wickberg, *Chinese in Philippine Life*, 182–183.

24. Benedict Anderson, *Imagined Communities*, 26–29.

25. José Rizal, El Filibusterismo, trans. Leon Maria Guerrero, 122–123.

26. Ibid., 125.

27. Rizal's writing was often punctuated with anti-Chinese sentiments, but the critique of Quiroga/Chen is particularly scathing. See ibid., 122–123; see also pp. 160–161, 169–179, and 254; and Wickberg, *Chinese in Philippine Life*, 201. Anderson is critical of the distortions in the Guerrero translation. Having read *El Fili* in the original, I agree with Anderson's general characterization, but the passages extracted here are sufficiently accurate renderings of the original. Anderson, *Imagined Communities*, 237.

28. "Testimony of William A. Daland," *ROPC 1900*, 2:164.

29. *ZMGXSL*, 3279 and 3723.

30. Wickberg, *Chinese in Philippine Life*, 164–165.

31. *ZMGXSL*, 1847, 3196, 3247, and 3279.

32. *ZMGXSL*, 1847 and 1937.

33. The dearth of correspondence may also indicate that the Chinese elite were disheartened by the failure of the previous attempts, and only when the situation became dire did they pursue this avenue again.

34. *ZMGXSL*, 3052.

35. *ZMGXSL*, 3090.

36. For this period I have found over one hundred correspondences in the *Zhongmei guanxi shiliao* that refer specifically to the Chinese in the Philippines and to the establishment of a Chinese consulate in Manila.

37. Karnow, *In Our Image*, 72–77.

38. *ZMGXSL*, 3279. In February 1900, twenty Chinese merchants were murdered in Albay Province, and their heads were placed on poles. *Manila Times* (hereafter *MT*), 02/28/00.

39. *ZMGXSL*, 3207.

40. *ZMGXSL*, 3196.

41. *ZMGXSL*, 3223.

42. *ZMGXSL*, 3214 and 3232.

43. The formal expression of gratitude from the yamen to the British minister is contained in *ZMGXSL*, 3284.

44. This type of extortion bears similarities to the blackmail of those caught holding weapons planted by Quiroga and Simoun in *El Filibusterismo*. Rizal, *El Filibusterismo*, 125.

45. *ZMGXSL*, 3247 and 3279. See also Wickberg, *Chinese in Philippine Life*, 232.

46. McKeown, "Chinese Diasporas," 320–321.

47. *ZMGXSL*, 3090 and 3231.

48. *ZMGXSL*, 3454.

49. *ZMGXSL*, 3454 and 3459.

50. Tan may have been referring to another charitable association such as the Tung Wah Hospital in Hong Kong, which often served as a conduit in the relations between the Qing authorities and the overseas Chinese. See G. B. Endacott, *A History of Hong Kong*, 156–157, cited in Wickberg, *Chinese in Philippine Life*, 216–217; and *ZMGXSL*, 3460.

51. *ZMGXSL*, 3460 and 3466.

52. *ZMGXSL*, 3455 and 3456.

53. *ZMGXSL*, 3514. For the prior offers of financial support for the consulate from the *cabecillas*, see *ZMGXSL*, 3052.

54. *ZMGXSL*, 3515.

55. Karnow, *In Our Image*, 117–125.

56. *ZMGXSL*, 3534, 3535, and 3539.

57. *ZMGXSL*, 3536.

58. *ZMGXSL*, 3557, 3560, 3567, and 3568.

59. These facts were relayed to the Zongli Yamen by Wu Tingfang in early September. *ZMGXSL*, 3567 and 3568. For an interesting personality sketch of Otis, see Karnow, *In Our Image*, 132.

60. *ZMGXSL*, 3609.

61. *ZMGXSL*, 3573.

62. Chen Gang had apparently purchased the higher rank to better suit his status as consul general. *ZMGXSL*, 3576.

63. *ZMGXSL*, 3576.

64. For a more detailed reappraisal of other institutional and cultural achievements of the Hundred Days, see Rebecca E. Karl and Peter Zarrow, eds., *Rethinking the 1898 Reform Period*.

65. *ZMGXSL*, 3610.

66. *ZMGXSL*, 3589, 3591, 3592, 3622, and 3667. Otis later made allowances for Chinese laborers to serve as litter bearers during the insurrection.

67. *MT*, 05/11/00.

68. Cook, "Bridges."

69. *ZMGXSL*, 3760.

70. *ZMGXSL*, 3601.

71. *ZMGXSL*, 3718, 3734, and 3735.

72. The Zongli Yamen received notice of Chen's arrival at his post and the duties he was undertaking on January 31, 1899. *ZMGXSL*, 3718.

73. *ZMGXSL*, 3697 and 3729.

74. *ZMGXSL*, 3724. See attachment for specific charges, in particular *fu* no. 4.

75. *ZMGXSL*, 3696, 3717, and 3719. BIA, 29-22, 29-26, 29-27.

76. BIA, 29-11; *MT*, 12/04/99.

77. *ZMGXSL*, 3723. See also BIA, 29-13, 29-14, and 29-15.

78. "U.S. Consul, O. F. Williams to Assistant Secretary of State, Thomas W. Cridler, 01/31/99," BIA file "U.S. Consulate, Manila P.I." See also BIA, 29-12, 29-14, 29-22, and 370-37.

79. *ZMGXSL*, 3723.

80. BIA, 29-22. See also BIA, 29-26 and 29-27 for more petitions in support of Chen's retention.

81. *ZMGXSL*, 3729.

82. *ZMGXSL*, 3730, 3731, 3736, and 3743.

83. *MT*, 04/10/99.

84. BIA, 370-37.

85. After American annexation, Chinese returning from the mainland had to prove they had previously lived in the Philippines.

86. *MT*, 10/23/99.

87. *MT*, 10/17/99.

88. *MT*, 10/23/99.

89. BIA, 29.

90. *MT*, 04/26/00.

91. *MT*, 03/09/00, 03/21/00, 06/10/00.

92. The Americans also instituted new standards for weights and measures. The Chinese were hard-pressed or disinclined to meet these new standards, thus landing many of them in court. The matter was so serious that Consul Li intervened on their behalf. *MT*, 08/02/99.

93. *MT*, 05/04/00, 6/13/00; *El Comercio*, 04/22/00.

94. *MT*, 01/09/00.

95. *MT*, 02/03/00, 02/07/00, 06/02/00.

96. See http://206.142.245.159/judjuris/juri1905/dec1905/gr_l-2108_1905.html; *MT*, 02/07/00; and Blaker, "Chinese in the Philippines," 102.

97. Wang Guanhua, *In Search of Justice*, 160–177.

98. Telegram from Amoy, 6 August 1905, U.S. Department of State, CD, Amoy, NAM, M 100, roll 15, cited in Ts'ai, *China and the Overseas Chinese*, 114, 120.

99. I am indebted to Professor Philip A. Kuhn for this insight. See Yen Ching-hwang, "Ch'ing Sale of Honours."

100. Kwok-chu Wong, *Chinese in the Philippine Economy*, 30–31.

101. McKeown, "Chinese Diasporas," 320.

**Chapter 5: Institutional Change in the Manila-Chinese Community**

1. Richard E. Welch, Jr., *Response to Imperialism*; Akira Iriye, *Pacific Estrangement*.

2. Trocki, *Opium and Empire*, 233–234.

3. Rush, *Opium to Java*, 242.

4. Ibid., 242–255. See also G. William Skinner, "The Chinese of Java," 3; Williams, *Overseas Chinese Nationalism*, 126–128.

5. This was part of a larger trend that was shifting the mercantile focus of Xiamen away from Japan and East Asia and toward Southeast Asia. Cook, "Bridges," 101–104.

6. Go and See, *Heritage*, 43.

7. I disagree with Blaker as to the extent of fragmentation this caused in the community in the early American period. While the Gobernadorcillo had been the apical figure, the highest elite stratum had always been corporate. Blaker, "The Chinese in the Philippines," 262.

8. Stanley, *A Nation in the Making*, 64–67; May, *Social Engineering*, xvii.

9. McKenna, *Muslim Rulers*, 86–112.

10. *ROPC 1900*, 1:1–20.

11. The commission was also supposed to include both Major General Otis and Rear Admiral Dewey, but neither military man attended its meetings or hearings.

12. "The Chinese in the Philippines," *ROPC 1900*, 1:150–159.

13. Henry Shih-shan Tsai, *The Chinese Experience in America*, 76.

14. *ROPC 1900*, 2:209.

15. *ROPC 1900*, 1:158–159.

16. The tariff had been set at 75 percent of full American tariffs. Recovery was also slowed by a general worldwide depression in 1907. Wong, *Chinese in the Philippine Economy*, 26–27.

17. Wong, *Chinese in the Philippine Economy*, 34–35.

18. See Blaker's discussion of the historiographic debate on the impact of American Rule. "Chinese in the Philippines," 81–85.

19. Anderson, "Cacique Democracy," 11–12.

20. Wong, *Chinese in the Philippine Economy*, 153–159.

21. Cook, "Bridges," 181.

22. BIA, 370; http://archiver.rootsweb.com/th/read/CALOSANG/2002-01/1010108317.

23. Doeppers, *Manila*, 52–56.

24. See, in particular, Rodrigo C. Lim, *Who's Who in the Philippines* (Chinese Edition); *Feilübin huaqiao mingren shilüe*.

25. *MT*, 08/21/99.

26. Ginsburg, "Philippine Revolution," 157.

27. Goodman, *Native Place*, 236.

28. Cook, "Bridges," 179.

29. Wong, *Chinese in the Philippine Economy*, 77–78, 162–164.

30. Dee's transnational activism was rewarded with official posts in the new Guomindang government and privileged access to American officials. Wong, *Chinese in the Philippine Economy*, 186–192; Cook, "Bridges," 337–341.

31. In building such a large and impressive home, Dee was following the lead set by his fellow elite Uy Siuliong (Huang Xiulang), a Spanish era *cabecilla* and business partner of Mariano Limjap who built a smaller but, for its time, equally impressive home on Gulangyu. Cook, "Bridges," 139–141.

32. Blaker, "Chinese in the Philippines," 264.

33. Cook, "Bridges," 186, 240–272; Wong, *Chinese in the Philippine Economy*, 76.

34. Zhongguo yinhang Quanzhou fenhang hangshi weiyuanhui, eds., *Minnan qiaopi shi jimi* (Xiamen, 1996), cited in Cook, "Bridges," 226.

35. Tan, *National Awakening*, 213. For a cogent discussion of the role that formal associations played in facilitating these transnational linkages, see Liu Hong, "Bridges across the Sea."

36. For an analogous case, see McKeown's discussion of the Chinese in Peru and Hawai'i, where "clear-cut social stratification . . . created middleman occupations that produced many notable migrant success stories." McKeown, *Chinese Migrant Networks*, 25.

37. Doeppers, *Manila*, 52–56.

38. *Cablenews-American* (hereafter *CNA*), 05/14/08.

39. David Ownby, "Introduction," 18–19. See also David Ownby, *Brotherhoods and Secret Societies.*

40. *MT*, 08/09/99.

41. BIA, 370-69, 89, 124, 125, 127.

42. Cook, "Bridges," 74, 99.

43. *MT*, 06/05/00.

44. Alicia B. Little, *Li Hung-chang*, 310–311, cited in Michael H. Hunt, *The Making of a Special Relationship*, 199.

45. Hunt, *Special Relationship*, 199.

46. *Guangxu rishi sinian Zhongwai dashi huiji*, vol. 2, 914–915, 1076–1077.

47. Hunt, *Special Relationship*, 200–202.

48. *Shenbao*, 11/25/97.

49. *Chixing bao*, 04/19/98.

50. Liang Qichao, *Yinbingshi heji* 4, sec. 11.

51. Aguinaldo was himself a *mestizo sangley*. Antonio S. Tan, "Chinese Mestizos and the Formation of Filipino Nationality."

52. Liang, *Yinbingshi heji* 4, sec. 11.

53. Gideon C. T. Hsu, "Jose Rizal and Sun Yat Sen," 76.

54. Go and See, *Heritage*, 87.

55. Ginsburg, "Philippine Revolution," 174.

56. Feng Ziyou, *Geming yishi* (hereafter *GMYS*), 4, 80–82; Alip, *Ten Centuries*, 46–47.

57. "Testimony of Carlos Palanca," *ROPC 1900*, 2:219–220. Such aid was not without risk, especially to the coolies themselves, who were frequently set upon by insurgents. *MT*, 10/19/99.

58. Lim, "Carlos Palanca," 20.

59. *ZMGXSL*, 3723.

60. Karnow, *In Our Image*, 115.

61. Elwell S. Otis, *Annual Report of Major General E. S. Otis*, 35–36, 62–64, 69.

62. Wickberg, *Chinese in Philippine Life*, 201.

63. *MT*, 09/05/99.

64. Richard Chu, "Rethinking Chinese Mestizos."

65. *ZMGXSL*, 3196, 3279; Wickberg, *Chinese in Philippine Life*, 148, 160, 200.

66. Gideon C. T. Hsu, "The Life and Work of Jose Ignacio Paua."

67. Gregorio F. Zaide, "Chinese General in the Philippine Revolution," 123.

68. Ibid., 127.

69. Approximately U.S.$400,000. Karnow, *In Our Image*, 75–77.

70. Zaide, "Chinese General," 128.

71. *MT*, 04/04/00.

72. Zaide, "Chinese General," 131, 133–137; Gideon C. T. Hsu, "Jose Ignacio Paua," 44–50.

73. Harry Lamley, "Lineage Feuding in Southern Fujian and Eastern Guangdong under Qing Rule."

74. McKeown, *Chinese Migrant Networks*, 112.

75. Karnow, *In Our Image*, 176–177.

76. Yan Wenqu, "Sanshi nianlai feidao huaqiao baozhi shiye," 2; Chen Xiaoyu, ed., *Feilübin yu huaqiao shiji daguan* 2, *she* 3, 5, 21; Tan, *National Awakening*, 93–94.

77. *GMYS* 4, pp. 154, 180. See also Tan, *National Awakening*, 118–119.

78. Tee's biography identifies his native place as Siming County. Siming, which means "remembering the Ming (dynasty)" was an anti-Qing statement. It was the name given to Xiamen Island in the late seventeenth century, a moniker later suppressed by Beijing. Until 1910, Xiamen and Jinmen had been part of Tongan County, but they were reorganized into Siming County in 1912. Referring to oneself as being from Siming before 1912 was thus a revolutionary statement. Cook, "Bridges," 287–288, 357.

79. Huang Xiaozang, ed., *Feilübin Minlila Zhonghua shanghui sanshi zhounian jinian kan* (hereafter *FMZS*), *jia* 169.

80. *FMZS*, *jia* 26.

81. *MT*, 05/14/06.

82. *GMYS* 4:180–181.

83. *GMYS* 1:192.

84. Ma, *Revolutionaries*, 34–35.

85. Tan, *National Awakening*, 119–120; *GMYS* 1:192.

86. Tsai, *China and the Overseas Chinese*.

87. *FMZS*, *jia* 99.

88. *CNA*, 03/12/08. See also Tan, *National Awakening*, 120.

89. Tan, *National Awakening*, 121; *GMYS* 1:192.

90. *GMYS* 4:181.

91. Blaker, "Chinese in the Philippines," 132–135.

92. C. F. Yong, *Chinese Leadership*, 27–30.

93. Trocki, *Opium and Empire*, 128–129, 145–146, 157–158, 230–231.

94. In the absence of the Gobernadorcillo, there were at least twelve major guilds and associations that took a role in advocating community interests. See in particular BIA, 29-26.

95. *ZMGXSL*, 3724.

96. The number of directors was later reduced to fifteen. Tan Santo, "A History of Chinese in the Philippines," *Fookien Times*, December 13, 1939, cited in Liu Chi-Tien, "The Chinese Point of View," 214.

97. Liu, "Chinese Point of View," 213–214.

98. *FMZS*, *jia* 122–127.

99. In an interesting twist, the majority of Chinese consuls general between 1900 and 1933 were Cantonese (9) as opposed to Fujianese (5). There were also consuls from Zhejiang (2), Anhui (1), Zhili (1), and Jiangxi (1). To its credit, the Hokkien-controlled Chamber of Commerce managed to maintain relatively cordial relations with all of them. *FMZS, jia* 203.

100. BIA, 41.

101. *CNA,* 11/16/08, 12/06/08.

102. Wu's nephew, Wu Juwei, died suddenly at a consular reception at the Hotel Oriente at the age of thirty-two. *MT,* 02/19/00.

103. Lai To Lee has described a significant reduction in the bargaining power of the Singapore consul at the beginning of this century. Lee, "Consular Representatives," 93–94.

104. Wong, *Chinese in the Philippine Economy,* 74–75.

105. Yu Heping, *Shanghui yu Zhongguo zaoqi xiandaihua,* 84–86. See also Goodman, *Native Place,* 177.

106. There is some confusion as to the date on which the chamber was founded. I have discovered a petition dated November 18, 1902, from the "Chinese Chamber of Commerce of the City of Manila" to the United States Philippine Commission on the need for Chinese labor in the Philippines. Although this document predates the Commercial Council by nearly two years, my assumption is that the "chamber" described was an ad hoc organization or perhaps another incarnation of the Chinese Charitable Association. BIA, 370-89.

107. C. F. Yong, *Chinese Leadership,* 31, 63–64. See also Rodrigo C. Lim, *Who's Who;* and *FMZS.*

108. *FMZS, jia* 1–6.

109. *FMZS, jia* 7–19. See also Tan, *National Awakening,* 176–177; and Liu Zhitian, *Zhongfei guanxi shi.*

110. Wong, *Chinese in the Philippine Economy,* 39–42.

111. Wu Jianxiong, "Niuyue Zhonghua gongsuo yanjiu," in Wu, *Haiwai,* 298–311.

112. Blaker, "Chinese in the Philippines," 261.

113. Karnow, *In Our Image,* 198.

114. Tan, *National Awakening,* 178.

115. This fact clearly contradicts Antonio Tan's conclusion that "the beginning of the 20th century . . . also brought into being a new type of leadership." Ibid., 207. For Yu Chingco's biography, see *FMZS, jia* 182.

116. Willmott, *Semarang,* 135–136, 151; Rush, *Opium to Java,* 247–255.

117. Tan, *National Awakening;* Liu, *Zhongfei guanxi shi.*

118. *MT,* 11/06/07; *CNA,* 11/16/07, 11/17/07.

119. Chu, "Chinese and Mestizos," 351–360.

120. *FMZS, jia* 56–59.

121. Tan, *National Awakening*, 127–128.

122. Ibid., 216; *MT*, 03/19/12, 06/22/12; *CNA*, 03/28/12.

123. *MT*, 05/09/12, 05/19/12; *FMZS*, *jia*, 59; Tan, *National Awakening*, 215.

124. *FMZS*, *jia* 59.

125. C. F. Yong, *Chinese Leadership*, 24–43.

126. Considering Yuan Shikai's later suppression of the National Assembly, Siy Cong Bieng made a wise choice in stepping down from that body in 1912.

127. Blaker, "Chinese in the Philippines," 78–159.

128. This supposition is borne out by James Cook's study of Xiamen in the early twentieth century. In the 1910s and 1920s, hundreds of wealthy merchants returned to Xiamen from overseas. Their return and the construction program they sponsored radically altered the city's landscape. They also became the city's dominant Chinese elite, translating overseas prominence into local prominence. The chaos in the Hokkien countryside under the rule of General Zang Zhiping, however, prevented the merchant elite from returning to their native places outside the city. They had to content themselves with a leading role in a city protected by its treaty port status from many warlord predations. Nonetheless, "Zang was notorious for using the merchant community as his personal piggy bank." Cook, "Bridges," 132, n. 72. This forced the Chinese elite to work even more closely with foreigners to protect the city and limit Zang's rapacity.

129. Wong, *Chinese in the Philippine Economy*, and Cook, "Bridges," 276–342.

130. Some of these petitions were published for distribution in Manila in both English and Spanish. BIA, 370-127.

131. See in particular "Roa v. Insular Inspector of Customs" and "Lim Teco v. Insular Inspector of Customs," http://www.geocities.com/ussc 2010/.

132. BIA, 370-204, 307-206.

133. I have found dozens of legal suits filed by individual Chinese against the United States Government via the Court of First Instance for the City of Manila under Judge Amasa Crossfield. See Supreme Court of the United States, October Term 1911, case nos. 550, 551, 552, and October Term 1912, case nos. 254, 255, 256; and BIA 370-249½ , 250, 251, 258, 259, 260, 261, 262, 263, 267, 269, 271. See also United States, Philippine Commission, *Official Gazette*, December 14, 1910.

134. "Memorandum on the matter of Hoo Foy et al.," 10/13/05, approved by Taft 1/30/06. BIA, 370-134.

135. The Qing authorities were also concerned that this low element would emigrate to the United States and thus warned the American legation in Beijing of the threat posed by "actors." BIA, 370-134, 155, 156, 160, 163,

167. For more on the problems of determining who should and who should not be admitted to the Philippines, see BIA, file 12177, 370-1, 9.

136. During the first decades of American rule, local Chinese chambers of commerce and specialized professional associations became so numerous and contentious that in 1931 they had to be reined in by the Guomindang and put under the authority of the main Chamber of Commerce. Yoji Akashi, *The Nanyang Chinese National Salvation Movement*, 1; *Zhongguo Guomindang yu huaqiao xianqu bian, 1908–1945*, 5–17, document nos. 1–13; *Zhongguo Guomindang nianjian*, sec. 5, 1 and 10; Antonio S. Tan, *The Chinese in the Philippines during the Japanese Occupation, 1942–1945*, 4–5; *Nanyang huaqiao kangri jiuguo yundong shimo, 1937–1942*, 45–46.

137. For an extensive treatment of associational ambiguity in the American Chinese community, see Ma, *Revolutionaries*.

### Chapter 6: Benevolent Merchants or Malevolent Highbinders?

1. The 1880 Immigration Treaty between China and the United States stated that the exempt classes of Chinese—teachers, students, merchants, and government officials—"shall be allowed to go and come of their own free will and accord." Yet the actual implementation of the treaty set documentation requirements even on the exempted classes.

> At a time when immigrants from all other countries might enter without documents of any sort, Chinese belonging in these exempted classes were required under section 6 of the Act of May 6, 1882, as amended by the Act of July 5, 1884, to present a certificate vouching for their identity and for the fact that they were entitled to the exempt status they claimed. These certificates, according to section 6, were to be issued by the Government to which the Chinese person in question owed allegiance, to be in the English language, to bear the owner's photograph and personal description and to be duly visaed by the American diplomatic or consular officer in the foreign country in which the certificate was issued—this, incidentally, was the first responsibility connected with immigration placed on the American Consular Service." (http://www.ins.usdoj.gov/text/aboutins/History/mraug 43.htm)

2. May, *Social Engineering*.

3. Anti-Chinese activism was catalyzed by the competition for jobs between white Americans and the Chinese during the depression. The same depression contributed to negative stereotypes of the Chinese, who resorted to violence and intimidation in this hostile environment. K. Scott Wong, "Cultural Defenders and Brokers."

4. Tsai, *Chinese Experience*, 51.

5. See Ma, *Revolutionaries*; Trocki, *Opium and Empire*; and Rush, *Opium to Java*.

6. June Mei, "Socioeconomic Origins of Emigration, Guangdong to Cal-

ifornia, 1850–1882"; Eric Fong and William T. Markham, "Immigration, Ethnicity, and Conflict"; Alexander Saxton, *Indispensable Enemy*; Stanford M. Lyman, *Chinese Americans*; Peter K. Kwong, *Chinatown, New York*; Bernard Wong, *A Chinese American Community*.

7. McKeown, *Chinese Migrant Networks*, 214–218.

8. For an excellent treatment of *xiedou* in Southeast China, see Ownby, "Chinese Hui," and Ownby, *Brotherhoods*. See also Frederic Wakeman Jr., "The Secret Societies of Kwangtung, 1800–1856." For the activities of secret societies overseas, see Rush, *Opium to Java*; Trocki, *Opium and Empire*; Trocki, "Rise and Fall"; Yen, *Social History*; and Skinner, *Chinese Society in Thailand*.

9. Tsai, *Chinese Experience*, 54.

10. Zhang, *Sanzhou riji* 1:70–80; Tsai, *Chinese Experience*, 54.

11. *ROPC 1900*, vol. 1. See also May, *Social Engineering*.

12. Karnow, *In Our Image*, 197.

13. Stanley, *Nation in the Making*, 265–278.

14. Bankoff, *Crime, Society, and the State*.

15. Karnow, *In Our Image*, 196.

16. Tan, *National Awakening*, 108.

17. Tsai, *Chinese Experience*, 47–50.

18. Kwong, *Chinatown*, 41–43.

19. BIA, 370-155, 156, 158, 160, 163, 167. For one celebrated case of extortion see *CNA*, 05/08/08.

20. Rush, *Opium to Java*, 217–241.

21. Martin Booth, *Opium*, 180–181.

22. Ricardo M. Zarco, "The Philippine Chinese and Opium Addiction," 100–104.

23. *CNA*, 11/15/07.

24. *CNA*, 11/12/07.

25. *CNA*, spring 1909.

26. The Philippine Commission actually sent a team to Java to observe the Opium Regie in 1904. Bureau of Insular Affairs, *Report of the Committee Appointed by the Philippine Commission to Investigate the Use of Opium and the Traffic Therein* (Washington, 1905), 8–9, 39, 123–127, cited in Rush, *Opium to Java*, 231–232.

27. Holland did pursue diplomatic solutions to the smuggling issue and participated in several international opium conferences in the early years of this century. Rush, *Opium to Java*, 229–231.

28. The phrase "better class of Chinamen" appeared frequently in the press and in colonial correspondence. The Americans, such as acting governor W. Cameron Forbes, used it to distinguish the law-abiding Chinese elite from the criminal element.

29. The down side of this policy was that the Philippine economy and so-

ciety continued to be skewed in favor of a wealthy minority of *ilustrados, mestizos,* and Chinese merchants.

30. Cook, "Bridges."

31. Wong, *Chinese in the Philippine Economy,* 78.

32. *CNA,* 11/13/07.

33. O'Brien balanced his favorable impression of the Chinese with the view that the Filipinos were incapable of initiative and industry. See Karnow, *In Our Image,* 212.

34. Leadership of the Hokkien group was the prerequisite for chamber leadership.

35. BIA, 370-235.

36. Ibid., see attachments.

37. It seems unlikely that Consul Yang could have come up with so many names without the help of the Chamber of Commerce. It is clear that these two agencies were working closely together, as both were credited by the Americans for having identified the "malefactors." Ibid.

38. BIA, 370-235, 370-234.

39. Zhang Yinhuan, *Sanzhou riji* 1:70–80; Tsai, *Chinese Experience,* 54.

40. *CNA,* 09/13/08, 10/31/08, 11/03/08.

41. Commissioner Newton W. Gilbert, who was acting in place of Governor-General W. Cameron Forbes, and assistant executive secretary Thomas Cary Welch later denied any knowledge of this action.

42. BIA, 370-235.

43. The *Cablenews* referred to the deportation as a "free ride to Amoy" for the deportees. *CNA,* 04/01/10.

44. *MT,* 08/23/09.

45. *CNA,* 08/23/09, 08/25/09, 03/30/10.

46. *CNA,* 08/31/09.

47. *MT,* 09/03/09; *CNA,* 09/04/09.

48. *CNA,* 08/21/09.

49. *MT,* 08/21/09. For San Francisco's "highbinders" see Tsai, *Chinese Experience,* 41.

50. This was probably Benito Siy Cong Bieng.

51. *MT,* 08/21/09.

52. Ibid.

53. Ibid.

54. *CNA,* 09/05/09.

55. BIA, 370-227.

56. Ibid.

57. BIA, 370-232.

58. BIA, 370-234.

59. *CNA,* 09/05/09.

60. BIA, 370-232.

61. Ibid.

62. Ibid.

63. *CNA*, 08/01/08.

64. Stanley, *Nation in the Making*, 99–100.

65. Karnow, *In Our Image*, 213.

66. Ibid., 216.

67. BIA, 370-227.

68. Ibid.

69. *CNA*, 08/22/09.

70. Tsai, *Chinese Experience*, 39.

71. *CNA*, 04/10/09, 08/24/09; *MT*, 04/10/09, 04/11/09.

72. Zhongfei guanxi shi ziliao, *xuantong yi*, Waiwubu Archives, Institute of Modern History, Academia Sinica.

73. BIA, 370-242.

74. BIA, 370-240, 370-242.

75. BIA, 370-239.

76. BIA, 370-238.

77. BIA, 370-256.

78. BIA, 370-241.

79. Second Philippine Legislature, act no. 1986, April 19, 1910, BIA, 370-247.

80. Karnow, *In Our Image*, 239.

81. Second Philippine Legislature, act no. 1986, April 19, 1910, BIA, 370-247.

82. BIA, 370-256.

83. BIA, 370-250.

84. *CNA*, 04/21/10.

85. "Opinion of the Attorney-General of the Philippine Islands of June 8, 1910 on the power of the Governor-General to order the expulsion of Chinese persons under certain circumstances," in BIA 370-256.

86. "Decision of the Supreme Court, no. 6157, July 30, 1910," *Official Gazetteer*, vol. 8, Manila, December 14, 1910, 1778–1779, in BIA, 370-263; see also 370-251.

87. BIA, 370-249.

88. BIA, 370-282.

89. Ibid.

90. BIA, 370-283.

91. Supreme Court of the United States, October Term, 1912, case nos. 254, 255, 256.

92. BIA, 370-290.

93. Lee, "Consular Representation," 71, 75, 85, 90–91; Willmott, *Semarang*; C. F. Yong, *Chinese Leadership*; Rush, *Opium to Java*; and Trocki, *Opium and Empire*.

94. Chicago's On Leong Tong and San Francisco's Six Companies are examples of other institutional forms that played a role similar to that of the Manila chamber.

95. Blaker, "Chinese in the Philippines," 264.

**Conclusion**

1. Jonathan D. Spence, *The Gate of Heavenly Peace*; Duara, *Rescuing History*; Duara, "Nationalists."

2. Heidhues, "Chinese Settlements."

3. Rizal, *El Filibusterismo*, 122–123.

4. See Reid and Chirot, *Essential Outsiders.*

5. Wang Gungwu, "The Limits of Nanyang Chinese Nationalism, 1912–1937"; Duara, "Nationalists."

6. Lowell Dittmer and Samuel S. Kim, "In Search of a Theory of National Identity."

# Select Glossary of Chinese Terms and Names

Baohuanghui　保皇會
Cai Zishen　蔡資深
Changheshe　長和社
Chaozhou　潮州
Chen Gang (Engracio Palanca Tan Kang)　陳綱
Chen Jinfang　陳金方
Chen Lanbin　陳蘭彬
Chen Qianshan (Carlos Palanca Tan Quien-sien)　陳謙善
Chen Ziyan　陳紫衍
Chongren Yiyuan (Chinese Hospital)　崇仁醫院
Chongsan　崇善
Cui Guoyin　崔國因
daotai　道台
Donghua Yiyuan (Tung Hwa Hospital)　東華醫院
Fulian Hebu Shanghui (Hok Lien Ho Po Siong Hui)　福聯和布商會
Fuzhou　福州
gong　公
gongguan (Kongkoan)　公館
Gonghedang (Kong Ho Tang)　共和黨
*Gongli ribao (Kong Li Po)*　公理日報
gongsi (kongsi)　公司
guanglu dafu　光綠大夫
Guo Songtao　郭嵩燾
hang　行
Hou Bao (José Ignacio Paua)　候鮑

Hu Xuanze (Hoo Ah Kay/Whampoa)　胡旋澤
Huang Jiasheng　黃家聲
Huang Youdang (Agapito Uy Tongco)　黃友党
huaqiao　華僑
Huaqiao Shanju Gongsuo (Communidad de Chinos)　華僑善舉公所
Huarenqu Gonghui　華人區公會
huiguan　會館
jiabidan (kapitan)　甲必丹
Jinjiang　晉江
Langjunhui　郎君會
Li (Dee, Dy)　李
Li Qi　李其
Li Qingquan (Dee C. Chuan)　李清泉
Li Rongyao (Li Yung Yew)　黎榮耀
Liang Xun　梁詢
Lin Anbang　林安邦
Lin He (Mariano Limjap)　林合
Lin Xuedi (F. M. Lim Tuico)　林挺梯
Lin Zhuguang (Lim Chu Cong)　林珠光
*Minbao*　民報
Minnan　閩南
Minshang Huiguan (Fooking Merchants Benevolent Association)　閩商會館
Minshangtang (Ban Siong Tong)　閩商堂
Neige Zhongshu　內閣中書

265

Nonggong Shangbu 農工商部

Peng Guangyu 彭光譽

Puzhi Yue Shubaoshe
普智閱書報社

qiaoxiang 僑鄉

qiaopi 僑批

qingyi 清議

Qiu Yunheng (Guillermo Cu
Unjieng) 邱允衡

Quanzhou 泉州

shangdong 商董

shanglai 商來

shangtou 商頭

shangye 商業

*Shenbao* 申報

Shi Guangming (Benito Siy Cong
Bieng) 施光明

Shi Zhihua 施至華

si 私

Siming Xian 思明縣

Sun Gaosheng 孫高陞

Tan Zhonglin 譚鍾麟

tang (tong) 堂

Tiandihui 天地會

Tongan Xian 同安縣

tongxianghui 同鄉會

toujia (towkay) 頭家

touke (towkay) 頭客

Waiwubu 外務部

Wang Yonghe 王榮和

Wu Tingfang 伍廷芳

Wu Zongming 吳宗明

Xiamen (Amoy) 夏門

Xie Qing'an 械清垵

xiedou 械斗

xinyong 信用

xingbu langzhong 刑部郎中

Xu Qin 徐勤

Xu Xiaowu 許孝鳴

Xue Fenshi (Alfonso Zarate Sycip)
薛芬士

Xue Minlao (Albino Zarate Sycip)
薛敏老

yangchuan 洋船

yanghang 洋行

Yang Haolü 楊豪侶

Yang Huixi 楊匯溪

Yang Ru 楊儒

Yang Shijun 楊士鈞

Yang Shiqi 楊士琦

Yang Shude 楊樹得

Yang Weihong 楊維洪

Yang Zunqin (Mariano Fernando
Yu Chingco) 楊尊親

Ye Qizhen 葉其蓁

Yifutang (Gee Hock Tong)
義福堂

Ying Zuyang 應祖錫

Yu Qiong 余瓊

Zhang Bishi 張弼士

Zhang Yinhuan 張蔭桓

Zhang Zhidong 張之洞

Zhang Zhongwei 張仲維

Zhangzhou 漳州

Zheng Hanqi (Tee Han Kee)
鄭漢淇

Zhong Wenyao 鍾文耀

*Zhongguo ribao* 中國日報

Zhonghua Shanghui (Tiong Hwa
Sionghwee) 中華商會

Zhongxi Xuexiao 中西學校

Zongli Yamen 總理衙門

# Select Bibliography

**Newspapers and Periodicals**
*Chixing bao.* Shanghai. April 1898.
*Cablenews-American.* Manila. Aug. 8, 1902–Dec. 31, 1916.
*El Comercio.* Manila. Aug. 16, 1898–June 14, 1899; July 6, 1899–July 19, 1900; Aug. 20, 1903–Aug 19, 1905; June 18, 1906–Sept. 30, 1908.
*Manila Times.* Manila. Oct. 12, 1898–Dec. 31, 1916.
*Minbao.* Tokyo. Nov. 16, 1905–Feb. 1, 1910.
*Shenbao.* Shanghai. April 1, 1897–Dec. 31, 1897.


**Archival Materials**
Archives of the Ministry of Foreign Affairs (Waiwubu and Waijiaobu). 1901–1916. Foreign Relations Archives, Institute for Modern History (Jinshisuo), Academia Sinica. Taipei, Taiwan.
Archives of the Tsungli Yamen (Zongli geguo shiwu yamen). 1861–1901. Foreign Relations Archives, Academia Sinica.
Bureau of Insular Affairs Archives. United States National Archives II. College Park, Maryland.
Chinos Manila, Project 102, Institute of Asian Studies, University of the Philippines, in 69 Reels. Spanish Archives, Philippine National Archives, Records Management and Archives Office, University of the Philippines. Quezon City. Reels 1–69, 1862–1898.
Chinos Provincias, Project 103, Institute of Asian Studies, University of the Philippines, in 35 Reels. Spanish Archives, Philippine National Archives, Records Management and Archives Office, University of the Philippines. Quezon City. Reels 1–35, 1862–1898.
*Chouban yiwu shimou* Archives. National Palace Museum. Taipei, Taiwan.
*Files on the Chinese in the Philippines.* Records of the Bureau of Insular Affairs, United States National Archives II. College Park, Maryland.
Supreme Court of the United States. October Term 1911, case nos. 550, 551, 552; October Term 1912, case nos. 254, 255, 256, 258, 259, 260, 261, 262, 263, 267, 269, 271.
Zhongguo Guomindang Dangshihui. Jinshan, Taiwan.
Zhong-Mei guanxi shiliao (Historical Documents on Sino-U.S. Relations). 1873–1916. Foreign Relations Archives, Academia Sinica.

**Published Sources and Dissertations**

Abella, Domingo. "Koxinga Nearly Ended Spanish Rule in the Philippines in 1662." *Philippine Historical Review* 2:1 (1969), 295–334.

Academia Sinica, Institute for Modern History. *Collection of the Catalogue for Documents on Modern China's Foreign Affairs.* Taipei: Academia Sinica, 1991.

Adshead, S. A. M. "The Seventeenth Century General Crisis in China." *Asian Profiles* 1 (1973): 271–280.

Akashi, Yoji. *The Nanyang Chinese National Salvation Movement.* Lawrence, Kansas: Center for East Asian Studies, University of Kansas, 1970.

Alip, Eufronio M. *The Chinese in Manila.* Manila: National Historical Commission, 1974.

———. *Ten Centuries of Philippine-Chinese Relations.* Manila: Alip and Sons, 1959.

Amyot, Jacques. *The Manila Chinese: Familism in the Philippine Environment.* Quezon City: Institute of Philippine Culture, Ateneo de Manila University, 1973.

Andaya, Barbara Watson, and Leonard Y. Andaya. *A History of Malaysia.* 2d ed. Honolulu: University of Hawai'i Press, 2001.

Anderson, Benedict. "Cacique Democracy in the Philippines: Origins and Dreams." In Vicente L. Rafael, ed., *Discrepant Histories: Translocal Essays on Filipino Cultures,* 3–47. Philadelphia: Temple University Press, 1995.

———. *Imagined Communities: Reflections on the Origins and Spread of Nationalism.* Revised ed. London: Verso, 1991.

Ardant, Gabriel. *Théorie sociologique de l'impôt.* 2 vols. Paris: SEVPEN, 1965.

Atwell, William S. "International Bullion Flows and the Chinese Economy." *Past and Present* 95 (1982), 68–90.

———. "Notes on Silver, Foreign Trade, and the Late Ming Economy." *Ch'ing-shih wen-t'i* 8:3 (1977), 1–33.

———. "A Seventeenth-Century 'General Crisis' in East Asia?" *Modern Asian Studies* 24:1 (1990), 661–682.

———. "Some Observations on the 'Seventeenth-Century Crisis' in China and Japan." *Journal of Asian Studies* 45:2 (1986), 223–244.

Ayers, William. *Chang Chih-tung and Educational Reform in China.* Cambridge: Harvard University Press, 1971.

Bankoff, Gregory. *Crime, Society, and the State in the Nineteenth-Century Philippines.* Honolulu: University of Hawai'i Press, 1997.

Barkan, Lenore. "Patterns of Power: Forty Years of Elite Politics in a Chinese County." In Joseph W. Esherick and Mary Backus Rankin, eds., *Chinese Local Elites and Patterns of Dominance,* 191–215. Berkeley: University of California Press, 1990.

Bays, Daniel H. *China Enters the Twentieth Century: Chang Chih-tung and the Issues of a New Age, 1895–1909.* Ann Arbor: University of Michigan Press, 1971.

Bergère, Marie-Claire. *The Golden Age of the Chinese Bourgeoisie, 1911–1937.* Trans. Janet Lloyd. Cambridge: Cambridge University Press, 1989.

Bernal, Rafael. "The Chinese Colony in Manila, 1570–1770." In Alfonso Felix Jr., ed., *The Chinese in the Philippines, 1570–1770,* 40–66 Manila: Solidaridad Publishing House, 1966.

Berriz, Miguel Rodríguez. *Diccionario de la Administración de Filipinas, Annuario 1888.* Manila: M. Perez, 1888.

Beyer, H. Otley. *Early History of Philippine Relations with Foreign Countries, Especially China.* Manila: O. Beyer, 1948.

Blair, Emma H., and James. A. Robertson, eds. *The Philippine Islands, 1493–1898.* 55 vols. Cleveland, Ohio: The A. H. Clark Company, 1903–1909.

Blaker, James R. "The Chinese in the Philippines: A Study of Power and Change." Ph.D. dissertation, Ohio State University, 1970.

Blussé, Leonard. *Strange Company: Chinese Settlers, Mestizo Women and the Dutch in VOC Batavia.* Dordrecht and Riverton: Foris Publications, 1986.

———. "Testament to a Towkay: Jan Con, Batavia and the Dutch China Trade." In Leonard Blussé, *Strange Company: Chinese Settlers, Mestizo Women and the Dutch in VOC Batavia,* 49–72. Dordrecht and Riverton: Foris Publications, 1986.

———. "The Vicissitudes of Maritime Trade: Letters from the Ocean *Hang* Merchant, Li Kunhe, to the Dutch Authorities in Batavia (1803–09)." In Anthony Reid, ed., *Sojourners and Settlers: Histories of Southeast Asia and the Chinese: In Honour of Jennifer Cushman,* 148–163. St. Leonards, N.S.W.: Asian Studies Association of Australia in association with Allen and Unwin, 1996.

Blussé, Leonard, and Femme Gaastra, eds. *Companies and Trade: Essays on Overseas Trading Companies during the Ancien Regime.* Leiden: Leiden University Press, 1981.

Bonacich, Edna. "A Theory of Middleman Minorities." In Norman R. Yetman and C. Hoy Steele, eds., *Majority and Minority: The Dynamics of Racial and Ethnic Relations,* 77–89. 2d ed. Boston: Allyn and Bacon, 1975.

Bonacich, Edna, and J. Modell. *The Economic Basis of Ethnic Solidarity: Small Business in the Japanese American Community.* Berkeley and Los Angeles: University of California Press, 1980.

Boorman, Howard L., ed. *Biographical Dictionary of Republican China.* 2 vols. New York: Columbia University Press, 1967.

Booth, Martin. *Opium: A History.* New York: St. Martin's Press, 1996.

Caces, Fe, and Douglas T. Gurak. "Migration Networks and the Shaping of Migration Systems." In Mary M. Kritz, Lin Lean Lim, and Hania Zlotnik, eds., *International Migration Systems: A Global Approach,* 150–176. Oxford: Clarendon Press, 1992.

Cai Jianhua and Liang Shangyuan. *Feilübin huaqiao kangri youji zhidui.* Hong Kong: Hong Kong University Press, 1980.

Cameron, Meribeth E. "The Public Career of Chang Chih-tung, 1837–1909." *Pacific Historical Review* 7:3 (September 1938), 187–210.

Carino, Theresa, ed. *Chinese in the Philippines.* Manila: China Studies Program, De La Salle University, 1985.

Carroll, John. *The Filipino Manufacturing Entrepreneur: Agent and Product of Change.* Ithaca, N.Y.: Cornell University Press, 1965.

Carstens, Sharon. "Chinese Culture and Polity in Nineteenth-Century Malaya: The Case of Yap Ah Loy." In David Ownby and Mary Somers Heidhues, eds., *Secret Societies Reconsidered: Perspectives on the Social History of Modern South China and Southeast Asia,* 120–152. Armonk, N.Y.: M. E. Sharpe, 1993.

Chan, Albert. "Chinese-Philippine Relations in the Late Sixteenth Century and to 1603." *Philippine Studies* 26 (1978): 51–82.

Chang, Pin-tsun. "The First Chinese Diaspora in Southeast Asia in the Fifteenth Century." In Roderick Ptak and Dietmar Rothermund, eds., *Emporia, Commodities, and Entrepreneurs in Asian Maritime Trade, c. 1400–1750,* 13–28. Stuttgart: Steiner Verlag, 1991.

Chaunu, Pierre. "Manile et Macao, face à la conjoncture des XVI et XVII siècles." *Annales: économies, sociétés, civilisations* 1962, 568–671.

———. *Les Philippines et le Pacifique des Ibériques (xvi, xvii, xviii siècles): Introduction methodologique et indices d'activité.* Paris: SEVPEN, 1960.

Chen Dasheng and Denys Lombard. "Foreign Merchants in Maritime Trade in 'Quanzhou' ('Zaitun'): Thirteenth and Fourteenth Centuries." In Denys Lombard and Jean Aubin, eds., *Asian Merchants and Businessmen in the Indian Ocean and the China Sea,* 20–82. New Delhi: Oxford University Press, 2000.

Chen Jinghe. "Feilübin dashi zhi." *Dalu zazhi* 6 (1953): 137–154.

———. *Shiliu shiji zhi Feilübin huaqiao.* Hong Kong: Xinya Yanjiusuo Dongnan Yanjiu Shi, 1963.

Chen Liefu. *Dongnan Yazhou di huaqiao huaren yu huayi.* Taipei: Zhengzhong Shuju, 1979.

———. *Feilübin di ziyuan jingji yu feihua zhengce.* Taipei: Zhengzhong Shuju, 1969.

———. *Feilübin huaqiao jiaoyu.* Taipei: Zhengzhong Shuju, 1958.

———. *Feilübin yu Zhong-Fei guanxi.* Hong Kong: Nanyang Yanjiu Chubanshe, 1955.

Chen, Matthew. "The Ming Records of Luzon." In Alfonso Felix Jr., ed., *The Chinese in the Philippines, 1570–1770,* 246–251. Manila: Solidaridad Publishing House, 1966.

Chen Taimin. *Zhong-Fei guanxi yu Feilübin huaqiao.* Hong Kong: Chaoyang Chubanshe, 1985.

Chen Xiaoyu. *Feilübin yu huaqiao shiji daguan.* 2 vols. Manila: n.p., 1948.

Chen Yande. *Xiandaizhong de chuantong: Feilübin huaren shehui yanjiu.* Xiamen: Xiamen Daxue Chubanshe, 1998

Chen Zhiping, ed. *Xiaolusong huaqiao Zhongxi xuexiao wushi zhounian jinian kan.* Manila: Anglo-Chinese School, 1949.

Cheong, W. E. "Canton and Manila in the Eighteenth Century." In Jerome Ch'en and Nicholas Tarling, eds., *Studies in the Social History of China and Southeast Asia: Essays in Memory of Victor Purcell,* 227–246. Cambridge: Cambridge University Press, 1970.

————. "The Decline of Manila as the Spanish Entrepôt in the Far East, 1765–1826: Its Impact on the Pattern of Southeast Asian Trade." *Journal of Southeast Asian Studies* 2:2 (September 1971), 142–158.

Chesneaux, Jean, ed. *Popular Movements and Secret Societies in China, 1840–1950.* Stanford: Stanford University Press, 1972.

Chinese Academy of Social Sciences. *Huaqiao yu Xinhai geming.* Beijing: Zhongguo Shehui Kexue Chubanshe, 1984

*Los Chinos en Filipinas.* Manila: Tipolitografia de "La Oceania Espanola," 1886.

Chirot, Daniel. "Conflicting Identities and the Dangers of Communalism." In Anthony Reid and Daniel Chirot, eds., *Essential Outsiders: Chinese and Jews in the Modern Transformation of Southeast Asia and Central Europe,* 3–31. Seattle: University of Washington Press, 1997.

*Chouban yiwu shimo.* Vol. 611: *Tongzhi chao.* Taipei: Wenhai Chubanshe, 1972.

Chu, Richard. "Catholic, *Sangley,* Mestizo, Spaniard, Filipino: Negotiating 'Chinese' Identities at Turn-of-the-Twentieth-Century Manila." In Maruja Asis, ed., *The Philippines as Home: Sojourners and Settlers,* 41–87. Quezon City: Philippine Migration Research Network, 2001.

————. "The 'Chinese' and 'Mestizos' of the Philippines: Towards a New Interpretation." *Philippine Studies* 50:3 (2002), 327–369.

————. "The 'Chinese' Entrepreneurs of Manila from 1875 to 1905: Aliases, Powers-of-Attorney, and other Border-Crossing Practices." In *Proceedings of the Fourth International Chinese Overseas Conference,* vol. 3, 285–302. Taipei: Academia Sinica, 2002.

————. "Rethinking the Chinese Mestizos of the Philippines." In Shen Yuanfang and Penny Edwards, eds., *Beyond China: Migrating Identities,* 44–74. Canberra: Coombs Publishing, Australian National University, 2002.

Ch'u T'ung-tsu. *Local Government in China under the Ch'ing.* Cambridge: Harvard University Press, 1962.

Coatsworth, John H. "The Limits of Colonial Absolutism: The State in Eighteenth Century Mexico." In Karen Spalding, ed., *Essays in the Political, Economic and Social History of Colonial Latin America,* 25–51. Newark: University of Delaware Press, 1982.

Comenge y Dalmau, Rafael. *Cuestiones Filipinas: La Parte los Chinos.* Manila: Tipolitografia de Chofre y Companía, 1894.

Cook, James Alexander. "Bridges to Modernity: Xiamen, Overseas Chinese and Southeast Coastal Modernization, 1843–1937." Ph.D. dissertation, University of California, San Diego, 1998.

Corpuz, O. D. *The Bureaucracy in the Philippines.* Quezon City: University of the Philippines Press, 1957.

Cullinane, Michael. "The Changing Nature of the Cebu Urban Elite in the 19th Century." In Alfred W. McCoy and Edilberto C. de Jesus, eds., *Philippine Social History: Global Trade and Local Transformations,* 251–296. Quezon City: Ateneo de Manila University Press, 1982.

Cushman, Jennifer Wayne. *Family and State: The Formation of a Sino-Thai Tin-Mining Dynasty, 1797–1932.* Ed. Craig J. Reynolds. Singapore: Oxford University Press, 1991.

————. *Fields from the Sea: Chinese Junk Trade with Siam during the Late Eighteenth and Early Nineteenth Centuries.* Ithaca, N.Y.: Cornell University Press, 1993.

Cushman, Jennifer Wayne, and Wang Gungwu, eds. *Changing Identities of the Southeast Asian Chinese since World War II.* Hong Kong: Hong Kong University Press, 1988.

Dannhaeuser, Norbert. "Evolution and Devolution of Downward Channel Integration in the Philippines." *Economic Development and Cultural Change* 29, no. 3, 577–595.

De Bevoise, Ken. *Agents of Apocalypse: Epidemic Disease in the Colonial Philippines.* Princeton: Princeton University Press, 1995.

de Jesus, Edilberto C. "Control and Compromise in the Cagayan Valley." In Alfred W. McCoy and Edilberto C. de Jesus, eds., *Philippine Social History: Global Trade and Local Transformations,* 21–37. Quezon City: Ateneo de Manila University Press, 1982.

————. *The Tobacco Monopoly in the Philippines: Bureaucratic Enterprise and Social Change, 1766–1880.* Manila: Ateneo de Manila University Press, 1980.

Diaz-Trechuelo, Maria Lourdes. "The Role of the Chinese in the Philippine Domestic Economy (1570–1770)." In Alfonso Felix Jr., ed., *The Chinese in the Philippines, 1570–1770,* 209–210. Manila: Solidaridad Publishing House, 1966.

Dittmer, Lowell, and Samuel S. Kim. "In Search of a Theory of National Identity." In Lowell Dittmer and Samuel S. Kim, eds., *China's Quest for National Identity,* 1–31. Ithaca, N.Y.: Cornell University Press, 1993.

Dobbin, Christine. *Asian Entrepreneurial Minorities: Conjoint Communities in the Making of the World-Economy, 1570–1940.* Richmond, Surrey: Curzon Press, 1996.

Doeppers, Daniel F. "Destination, Selection and Turnover among Chinese

Migrants to Philippine Cities in the Nineteenth Century." *Journal of Historical Geography* 14:4 (1986), 381–401.

———. *Manila, 1900–1941: Social Change in a Late Colonial Metropolis.* Quezon City: Ateneo de Manila University Press, 1984.

Douw, Leo. "The Chinese Sojourner Discourse." In Leo Douw, Cen Huang, and Michael R. Godley, eds., *Qiaoxiang Ties: Interdisciplinary Approaches to "Cultural Capitalism" in South China*, 22–44. London and New York: Kegan Paul International in association with International Institute for Asian Studies, 1999.

———, ed. *Unsettled Frontiers and Transnational Linkages: New Tasks for the Historian of Modern Asia.* Amsterdam: V U University Press, 1997.

Douw, Leo, Cen Huang, and Michael R. Godley, eds. *Qiaoxiang Ties: Interdisciplinary Approaches to "Cultural Capitalism" in South China.* London and New York: Kegan Paul International in association with International Institute for Asian Studies, 1999.

Duara, Prasenjit. *Culture, Power, and the State: Rural North China, 1900–1942.* Stanford: Stanford University Press, 1986.

———. "Elites and the Structures of Authority in the Villages of North China, 1900–1949." In Joseph W. Esherick and Mary Backus Rankin, eds., *Chinese Local Elites and Patterns of Dominance*, 261–281. Berkeley: University of California Press, 1990.

———. "Nationalists among Transnationals: Overseas Chinese and the Idea of China, 1900–1911." In Aihwa Ong and Donald Nonini, eds., *Ungrounded Empires: The Cultural Politics of Modern Chinese Transnationalism*, 39–58. New York: Routledge, 1997.

———. *Rescuing History from the Nation: Questioning Narratives of Modern China.* Chicago: University of Chicago Press, 1995.

———. "Superscribing Symbols: The Myth of Guandi, Chinese God of War." *Journal of Asian Studies* 47:4 (1988), 778–794.

Eastman, Lloyd E. "Ch'ing-I and Chinese Policy Formation during the Nineteenth Century." *Journal of Asian Studies* 24:4 (August 1965), 596–620.

———. *Throne and Mandarins: China's Search for a Policy during the Sino-French Controversy, 1880–1885.* Cambridge: Harvard University Press, 1967.

Ebrey, Patricia Buckley. *Chu Hsi's Family Rituals: A Twelfth-Century Chinese Manual for the Performance of Cappings, Weddings, Funerals, and Ancestral Rites.* Princeton: Princeton University Press, 1991.

———. *Family and Property in Sung China: Yuan Ts'ai's Precepts for Social Life.* Princeton: Princeton University Press, 1984.

Ebrey, Patricia Buckley, and James L. Watson, eds. *Kinship Organization in late Imperial China, 1000–1940.* Berkeley: University of California Press, 1986.

Elman, Benjamin A. *Classicism, Politics and Kinship: The Ch'ang-chou School of New Text Confucianism in Late Imperial China.* Berkeley: University of California Press, 1990.

Entenmann, Robert Eric. "Migration and Settlement in Sichuan, 1644–1796." Ph.D. dissertation, Harvard University, 1982.

Esherick, Joseph, and Mary Backus Rankin, eds. *Chinese Local Elites and Patterns of Dominance*. Berkeley: University of California Press, 1990.

Fairbank, John King. *Trade and Diplomacy on the China Coast*. Cambridge: Harvard University Press, 1953.

———, ed. *The Chinese World Order: Traditional China's Foreign Relations*. Cambridge: Harvard University Press, 1968.

Fairbank, John King, and Ernest R. May, eds. *America's China Trade in Historical Perspective: The Chinese and American Performance*. Cambridge: Harvard University Press, 1986.

Fairbank, John King, and Ssu-yu Teng, eds. *Ch'ing Administration: Three Studies*. Cambridge: Harvard University Press, 1960.

Farmer, Edward L. "Social Order in Early Ming China: Some Norms Codified in the Hung-wu Period." In Brian McKnight, ed., *Law and the State in Traditional East Asia: Six Studies on the Sources of East Asian Law*, 1–36. Honolulu: University of Hawai'i Press, 1978.

Fasseur, Cornelius. *The Politics of Colonial Exploitation: Java, the Dutch, and the Cultivation System*. Trans. R. E. Elson and Ary Kraal; ed. R. E. Elson. Ithaca, N.Y.: Cornell University Press, 1992.

Fegan, Brian. "The Social History of a Central Luzon Barrio." In Alfred W. McCoy and Edilberto C. de Jesus, eds., *Philippine Social History: Global Trade and Local Transformations*, 91–129. Quezon City: Ateneo de Manila University Press, 1982.

*Feilübin huaqiao Shanju gongsuo ban Zhonghua chongren yiyuan yu luojian jinian kan*. Manila: Zhonghua Shanghui Chubanbu, 1956.

*Feilübin huaqiao mingren shilüe*. Shanghai: Shangwu Yinshuguan, 1931.

Felix, Alfonso, Jr. "The Economic Background." In Alfonso Felix Jr., ed., *The Chinese in the Philippines, 1770–1898*, 18–44. Manila: Solidaridad Publishing House, 1975.

———. "The Economic Development of the Philippines in the Second Half of the Eighteenth Century." *Philippine Studies* 11 (1963), 195–231.

———. "The Role of the Chinese in the Philippine Domestic Economy (1550–1770)." In Alfonso Felix Jr., ed., *The Chinese in the Philippines, 1570–1770*, 175–210. Manila: Solidaridad Publishing House, 1966.

Felix, Alfonso, Jr., ed. *The Chinese in the Philippines, 1570–1770*. Manila: Solidaridad Publishing House, 1966.

———. *The Chinese in the Philippines, 1770–1898*. Manila: Solidaridad Publishing House, 1975.

Feng Ziyou. *Geming yishi*. 5 vols. Taipei: Shangwu Yinshuguan, 1965.

———. *Huaqiao geming kaiguo shi*. Shanghai: Shangwu Yinshuguan, 1947.

———. *Huaqiao geming zuzhi shihua*. Taipei: Zhengzhong Shuju, 1954.

Fenner, Bruce L. *Cebu under the Spanish Flag (1521–1896): An Economic and Social History.* Cebu City: San Carlos Publications, 1985.

Feuchtwang, Stephan. "School Temple and City God." In G. William Skinner, ed., *The City in Late Imperial China*, 581–608. Stanford: Stanford University Press, 1977.

Fewsmith, Joseph. *Party, State, and Local Elites in Republican China.* Honolulu: University of Hawai'i Press, 1985.

Folsom, Kenneth. *Friends, Guests, and Colleagues: The Mu-fu System in the Late Ch'ing Period.* Berkeley: University of California Press, 1968.

Fong, Eric, and William T. Markham. "Immigration, Ethnicity, and Conflict: The California Chinese, 1849–1882." *Sociological Inquiry* 61:4 (Fall 1991), 471–490.

Forbes, W. Cameron. *The Philippine Islands.* 2 vols. Boston: Houghton Mifflin, 1928.

Fox, Robert. "Chinese Pottery in the Philippines." In Schubert S. C. Liao, ed., *Chinese Participation in Philippine Culture and Economy*, 96–114. Manila: Schubert S. C. Liao, 1964.

Freedman, Maurice. *The Chinese in South-East Asia: A Longer View.* London: China Society, 1965.

———. "The Chinese in South-East Asia: A Longer View." *Asian Review* 3:1 (1966), 24–38.

———. *Chinese Lineage and Society: Fukien and Kwangtung.* 2d ed. London: Athlone Press, 1971.

———. "Colonial Law and Chinese Society." *Journal of the Royal Anthropological Institute* 80 (1950), 97–126.

———. *Lineage Organization in Southeastern China.* London: Athlone Press, 1958.

———. *The Study of Chinese Society: Essays; Selected and Introduced by G. William Skinner.* Stanford: Stanford University Press, 1979.

Frodsham, J. D. *The First Chinese Embassy to the West: The Journals of Kuo S'ung-t'ao, Liu Hsi-hung and Chang Te-i.* Oxford: Clarendon Press, 1974.

Fukuyama, Francis. *Trust: The Social Virtues and the Creation of Prosperity.* New York: Free Press, 1995.

Geiss, James Peter. "Peking under the Ming." Ph.D. dissertation, Princeton University, 1979.

Ginsberg, Philip E. "The Chinese in the Philippine Revolution." *Asian Studies* 8:1 (1970), 143–159.

Go Bon Juan and Teresita Ang See, eds. *Heritage: A Pictorial History of the Chinese in the Philippines.* Manila: Kaisa Para Sa Kaunlaran, 1987.

Godley, Michael R. "The Late Ch'ing Courtship of the Chinese in Southeast Asia." *Journal of Asian Studies* 34:2 (1975), 361–385.

———. *The Mandarin Capitalists from Nanyang: Overseas Chinese Enterprise in the Modernization of China*. Cambridge: Cambridge University Press, 1981.

Goodman, Bryna. "The Locality as Microcosm of the Nation? Native Place Networks and Early Urban Nationalism in China." *Modern China* 21 (October 1995), 387–419.

———. *Native Place, City, and Nation: Regional Networks and Identities in Shanghai, 1853–1937*. Berkeley: University of California Press, 1995.

Goodrich, L. Carrington, ed. *Dictionary of Ming Biography, 1369–1644*. 2 vols. New York: Columbia University Press, 1976.

Greenow, L. L. "Spatial Dimension of the Credit Market in Eighteenth Century Nueva Galicia." In D. J. Robinson, ed., *Social Fabric and Spatial Structure in Colonial Latin America*, 227–279. Ann Arbor: University Microfilms International, 1979.

*Guangxu ershi sinian Zhongwai dashi huiji*. 4th ed. Taipei: Taiwan Huawen Shuju, 1968.

Guerrero, Milagros. "The Chinese in the Philippines, 1570–1770." In Alfonso Felix Jr., ed., *The Chinese in the Philippines, 1570–1770*, 15–39. Manila: Solidaridad Publishing House, 1966.

Hamilton, David. "Kuo Sung-t'ao: A Maverick Confucian." *Papers on China* 15 (1969), 1–29.

Hao Yen-p'ing. *The Commercial Revolution in Nineteenth-Century China: The Rise of Sino-Western Mercantile Capital*. Berkeley and Los Angeles: University of California Press, 1986.

———. *The Comprador in Nineteenth Century China: Bridge Between East and West*. Cambridge: Harvard University Press, 1970.

———. "A Study of the Ch'ing-liu Tang: The 'Disinterested' Scholar Official Group, 1875–1884." *Papers on China* 16 (1962): 40–65.

Heidhues, Mary Somers. "Chinese Organizations in West Borneo and Bangka: *Kongsi* and *Hui*." In David Ownby and Mary Somers Heidhues, eds., *Secret Societies Reconsidered: Perspectives on the Social History of Modern South China and Southeast Asia*, 68–88. Armonk, N.Y.: M. E. Sharpe, 1993.

———. "Chinese Settlements in Rural Southeast Asia." In Anthony Reid, ed., *Sojourners and Settlers: Histories of Southeast Asia and the Chinese: In Honour of Jennifer Cushman*, 164–182. St. Leonards, N.S.W.: Asian Studies Association of Australia in association with Allen and Unwin, 1996.

Helly, Denise, ed. *The Cuba Commission Report: A Hidden History of the Chinese in Cuba: The Original English-Language Text of 1876*. Baltimore: Johns Hopkins University Press, 1993.

Hertslet, G. E. P., ed. *Treaties &c. between Great Britain and China; and between China and Foreign Powers*. London: Harrison and Sons, 1908.

Ho Ping-ti. *Studies in the Population of China, 1386–1953*. Cambridge: Harvard University Press, 1959.

Hoadley, Mason C. "Javanese, Peranakan and Chinese Elites in Cirebon:

Changing Ethnic Boundaries." *Journal of Asian Studies* 47:3 (1988), 503–517.

Horsley, Margaret Wyant. "Sangley: The Formation of Anti-Chinese Feeling in the Philippines." Ph.D. dissertation, Columbia University, 1950.

Hsieh, Winston. *Chinese Historiography on the Revolution of 1911.* Stanford: Hoover Institution Press, 1975.

Hsu, Gideon C. T. "Jose Rizal and Sun Yat Sen: A Comparative Study." *Annals of the Philippine Chinese Historical Association* 4 (June 1973), 76–83.

————. "The Life and Work of Jose Ignacio Paua." *Annals of the Philippine Chinese Historical Association* 6 (May 1976), 44–50.

Hsü, Immanuel C. Y. *China's Entrance into the Family of Nations: The Diplomatic Phase, 1858–1880.* Cambridge: Harvard University Press, 1960.

————. *The Ili Crisis: A Study in Sino-Russian Diplomacy, 1871–1881.* Oxford: Clarendon Press, 1965.

Hsu, Madeline Yuan-yin. *Dreaming of Gold, Dreaming of Home: Transnationalism and Migration between the United States and South China, 1882–1943.* Stanford: Stanford University Press, 2000.

Hu-DeHart, Evelyn. "Chinese Coolie Labor in Cuba in the Nineteenth Century: Free Labour or Neo-Slavery?" *Slavery and Abolition* 14 (1993), 67–86.

Huang Jianchun. *Wanqing xinma huaqiao dui guojia rentong zhi yanjiu.* Taipei: Zhonghua Minguo Haiwai Huaren Yanjiu Xuehui, 1993.

————. *Xinjiapo huaqiao huidang dui Xinhai geming yingxiang zhi yan jiu.* Singapore: Xinjiapo Nanyang Xuehui, 1988.

Huang, Ray. "Lung-ch'ing and Wan-li Reigns, 1567–1620." In Frederick W. Mote and Denis Twitchett, eds., *The Ming Dynasty, 1368–1644, Part I,* 511–584. *Cambridge History of China,* vol. 7. Cambridge: Cambridge University Press, 1988.

Huang Xiaocang, ed. *Feilübin Minlila Zhonghua shanghui sanshi zhounian jinian kan.* Manila: Zhonghua Shanghui Chubanbu, 1936.

Huang Zisheng and He Sibing. *Feilübin huaqiao shi.* Guangdong: Guangdong Gaodeng Jiaoyu Chubanshe, 1987.

Hucker, Charles O. *A Dictionary of Official Titles in Imperial China.* Stanford: Stanford University Press, 1985.

Hummel, Arthur W., ed. *Eminent Chinese of the Ch'ing Period.* 2 vols. Washington, D.C.: Government Printing Office, 1943.

Hunt, Michael H. *The Making of a Special Relationship: The United States and China to 1914.* New York: Columbia University Press, 1983.

Hutchison, J. "Class and State Power in the Philippines." In Kevin Hewison, Richard Robison, and Garry Rodan, eds., *Southeast Asia in the 1990s: Authoritarianism, Democracy and Capitalism,* 193–212. Sydney: Allen and Unwin, 1993.

Irick, Robert L. *Ch'ing Policy toward the Coolie Trade, 1847–1878*. Taipei: Chinese Materials Center, 1982.

Iriye, Akira. *Across the Pacific: An Inner History of American-East Asian Relations*. Chicago: University of Chicago Press, 1992.

———. *After Imperialism: The Search for a New Order in the Far East, 1921–1931*. Chicago: Imprint Publications, 1990.

———. *From Nationalism to Internationalism: US Foreign Policy to 1914*. London: Routledge, 1977.

———. *Pacific Estrangement: Japanese and American Expansion, 1897–1911*. Cambridge: Harvard University Press, 1972.

Jagor, Feodore. *Travels in the Philippines*. London: Chapman and Hall, 1875.

Janse, Olov Robert True. "Notes on Chinese Influences in the Philippines in Pre-Spanish Times." *Harvard Journal of Asiatic Studies* 8 (1940), 34–62.

Jensen, Khin Khin Myint. *The Chinese in the Philippines during the American Regime, 1898–1946*. San Francisco: R and E Research Associates, 1975.

———. "The Chinese in the Philippines during the American Regime, 1898–1946." Ph.D. dissertation, University of Wisconsin, 1959.

Johnson, David J., Andrew J. Nathan, and Evelyn S. Rawski, eds. *Popular Culture in Late Imperial China*. Berkeley: University of California Press, 1985.

Jordana y Morera, Ramon. *Immigración China en Filipinas*. Madrid: M. G. Hernandez, 1888.

Karl, Rebecca E., and Peter Zarrow, eds. *Rethinking the 1898 Reform Period: Political and Cultural Change in Late Qing China*. Cambridge: Harvard University Press, 2002.

Karnow, Stanley. *In Our Image: America's Empire in the Philippines*. New York: Ballantine Books, 1990.

Keesing, Felix M. *The Ethnohistory of Northern Luzon*. Stanford: Stanford University Press, 1962.

Kindleberger, Charles P. *Spenders and Hoarders: The World Distribution of Spanish American Silver, 1550–1750*. Singapore: Institute of Southeast Asian Studies, 1989.

Kuhn, Philip A. *Rebellion and Its Enemies in Late Imperial China*. Cambridge: Harvard University Press, 1970.

Kumar, A. L. "Islam, the Chinese, and Indonesian Historiography—a Review Article." *Journal of Asian Studies* 46:3 (1987), 603–615.

Kwong, Peter. *Chinatown, New York: Labor and Politics, 1930–1950*. New York: Monthly Review Press, 1979.

Lamley, Harry. "Lineage Feuding in Southern Fujian and Eastern Guangdong under Qing Rule." In Jonathan Lipman and Stevan Harrell, eds., *Violence in China: Essays in Culture and Counterculture*, 27–64. Albany: State University of New York Press, 1990.

Larkin, John A. *The Pampangans: Colonial Society in a Philippine Province*. Berkeley: University of California Press, 1972.

———. *Sugar and the Origins of Modern Philippine Society.* Berkeley: University of California Press, 1993.

Lee Kam Hing and Tan Chee-Beng, eds. *The Chinese in Malaysia.* Kuala Lumpur: Oxford University Press, 2000.

Lee, Lai To. "Chinese Consular Representatives and the Straits Government in the Nineteenth Century." In Lai To Lee, ed., *Early Chinese Immigrant Societies: Case Studies from North America and British Southeast Asia,* 64–94. Singapore: Heinemann Asia, 1988.

Lee, Lai To, ed. *Early Chinese Immigrant Societies: Case Studies from North America and British Southeast Asia.* Singapore: Heinemann Asia, 1988.

Legarda, Benito, Jr. *After the Galleons: Foreign Trade, Economic Change and Entrepreneurship in the Nineteenth Century Philippines.* Madison, Wisc.: University of Wisconsin Center for Southeast Asian Studies, 1999.

———. "Foreign Trade, Economic Change, and Entrepreneurship in the Nineteenth Century Philippines." Ph.D. dissertation, Harvard University, 1955.

Leiby, John S. *Colonial Bureaucrats and the Mexican Economy: Growth of a Patrimonial State, 1763–1821.* New York: Peter Lang, 1986.

Leong, Sow-Theng. *Migration and Ethnicity in Chinese History: Hakkas, Pengmin, and Their Neighbors.* Edited by Tim Wright, with an introduction and maps by G. William Skinner. Stanford: Stanford University Press, 1997.

Levathes, Louise. *When China Ruled the Seas: The Treasure Fleet of the Dragon Throne, 1405–1433.* New York: Simon and Schuster, 1994.

Li Hongzhang. *Li Wenzhong gong quanji.* Taipei: Wenhai Chubanshe, 1962.

Li Jinming. *Mingdai haiwai maoyi shi.* Beijing: Zhongguo Shehui Kexueyuan Chubanshe, 1990.

Li Mei-p'ing. "Historical Survey of the Development of Sino-Philippine Relations." *New Age in Asia* 1:7–8 (December 1947), 16–22.

Li Qichang, ed. *Feilübin huaqiao Shanju gongsuo jiushi zhounian jinian kan.* Manila: Chinese Charitable Association, 1968.

Li Yinghui. *Huaqiao zhengce yu haiwai minzu zhuyi, 1912–1949.* Taipei: Guoshiguan, 1997.

Liang Qichao. *Yinbingshi heji.* Shanghai: Zhonghua Chubanshe, 1936.

Liao, Schubert S. C., ed. *Chinese Participation in Philippine Culture and Economy.* Manila: Schubert S. C. Liao, 1964.

Lim, Rodrigo C. *Who's Who in the Philippines* (Chinese Edition). Manila: University of the Philippines Press, 1930.

Lim, Jade Joy R. "Carlos Palanca Tan Quien-sien: A Case Study of a Chinese in the Nineteenth Century Philippines." M.A. thesis, Ateneo de Manila University, 1980.

Liu, Chi-Tien. "An Approach to the study of Early Sino-Philippine Relations." In Alfonso Felix Jr., ed., *The Chinese in the Philippines, 1570–1770,* 252–263. Manila: Solidaridad Publishing House, 1966.

———. "The Chinese Point of View: Comments on Events and Institutions."
In Alfonso Felix Jr. ed., *The Chinese in the Philippines, 1770–1898*, 18–44.
Manila: Solidaridad Publishing House, 1975.

———. *Feilübin huaqiao shihua*. Taipei: Haiwai Wenku Chubanshe, 1958.

———. "The Junk Trade Relations in the Study of Early Sino-Philippine Relations." In Alfonso Felix Jr., ed., *The Chinese in the Philippines,
1570–1770*, 263–273. Manila: Solidaridad Publishing House, 1966.

———. "Parian: The Chinese Alcaiceria in Manila during the Spanish Regime." In Alfonso Felix Jr., ed., *The Chinese in the Philippines, 1570–1770*,
277–285. Manila: Solidaridad Publishing House, 1966.

———. *Zhong-Fei guanxi shi*. Taipei: Zhengzhong Shuju, 1964.

Liu Hong. "Bridges across the Sea: Chinese Social Organizations in Southeast Asia and the Links with *Qiaoxiang*, 1900–49." In Leo Douw, Cen
Huang, and Michael R. Godley, eds., *Qiaoxiang Ties: Interdisciplinary Approaches to "Cultural Capitalism" in South China*, 87–112. London and New
York: Kegan Paul International in association with International Institute for Asian Studies, 1999.

Liu Jinzao, comp. *Qingchao xu wenxian tongkao*. 400 juan. Shanghai: Shangwu
Yinshuguan, 1935.

Liu, Xin. "Space, Mobility, and Flexibility: Chinese Villagers and Scholars
Negotiate Power at Home and Abroad." In Aihwa Ong and Donald No-
nini, eds., *Ungrounded Empires: The Cultural Politics of Modern Chinese
Transnationalism*, 103–113. New York: Routledge, 1997.

Lombard, Denys, and Jean Aubin, eds. *Asian Merchants and Businessmen in the
Indian Ocean and the China Sea*. New Delhi: Oxford University Press,
2000.

Lu Shipeng. "Xiling shiji Feilübin huaqiao zhi shangye huodong." *Dalu zazhi*
13 (1956), 356–400.

Lyman, Stanford M. *Chinese Americans*. New York: Random House, 1974.

Lynch, John. *Spanish Colonial Administration, 1782–1810: The Intendant System
in the Viceroyalty of the Rio de la Plata*. London: Greenwood, 1969.

Ma, L. Eve Armentrout. *Revolutionaries, Monarchists, and Chinatowns: Chinese
Politics in the Americas and the 1911 Revolution*. Honolulu: University of
Hawai'i Press, 1990.

———. "The Social Organization of Chinatowns in North America and
Hawaii in the 1890s." In Lai To Lee, ed., *Early Chinese Immigrant Societies:
Case Studies from North America and British Southeast Asia*, 159–185. Singa-
pore: Heinemann Asia, 1988.

Mackie J. A. C., ed. *The Chinese in Indonesia*. Honolulu: University of Hawai'i
Press, 1976.

Macleod, Murdo J. "The Primitive Nation State, Delegations of Functions,
and Results: Some Examples from Early Colonial Central America." In
Karen Spalding, ed., *Essays in the Political, Economic and Social History of*

*Colonial Latin America,* 53–68. Newark, Del.: University of Delaware Press, 1982.

———. "The Sociological Theory of Taxation and the Peasant." *Peasant Studies* 4:3 (July 1975), 2–6.

Mak Lau Fong. "Chinese Secret Societies in the Nineteenth Century Straits Settlements." In Lai To Lee, ed., *Early Chinese Immigrant Societies: Case Studies from North America and British Southeast Asia,* 230–243. Singapore: Heinemann Asia, 1988.

Mann, Susan. *Local Merchants and the Chinese Bureaucracy, 1750–1950.* Stanford: Stanford University Press, 1987.

Massey, Douglas S., Rafael Alarcon, Jorge Durand, and Humberto Gonzalez, eds. *Return to Aztlan: The Social Process of International Migration from Western Mexico.* Berkeley: University of California Press, 1987.

May, Glenn Anthony. *Social Engineering in the Philippines: The Aims, Execution and Impact of American Colonial Policy, 1900–1913.* Westport: Greenwood Publishing Group, 1980.

Mayers, W. F., ed. *Treaties between the Empire of China and Foreign Powers: Together with the Regulations for the Conduct of Foreign Trade, Conventions, Agreements, Regulation, etc.* 5th ed. Shanghai: North China Herald, 1906.

McBeath, Gerald A. *Political Integration of the Philippine Chinese.* Berkeley: Center for South and Southeast Asia Studies, University of California Press, 1973.

McCarthy, Charles J. "On the Koxinga Threat of 1662." *Philippine Studies* 18 (1970): 187–196.

———. "Slaughter of Sangleys in 1639." *Philippine Studies* 18:3 (1970), 659–667.

McCoy, Alfred W. "Introduction: The Social History of an Archipelago." In Alfred W. McCoy and Edilberto C. de Jesus, eds., *Philippine Social History: Global Trade and Local Transformations,* 1–18. Quezon City: Ateneo de Manila University Press, 1982.

McCoy, Alfred W., and Edilberto C. de Jesus, eds. *Philippine Social History: Global Trade and Local Transformations.* Quezon City: Ateneo de Manila University Press, 1982.

McKenna, Thomas M. *Muslim Rulers and Rebels: Everyday Politics and Armed Separatism in the Southern Philippines.* Berkeley: University of California Press, 1998.

McKeown, Adam. *Chinese Migrant Networks and Cultural Change: Peru, Chicago, Hawaii, 1900–1936.* Chicago: University of Chicago Press, 2001.

———. "Conceptualizing Chinese Diasporas, 1842 to 1949." *Journal of Asian Studies* 58:2 (1999), 306–337.

McLennan, Marshall S. "Changing Human Ecology on the Central Luzon Plain, Nueva Ecija, 1705–1939." In Alfred W. McCoy and Edilberto C. de

Jesus, eds., *Philippine Social History: Global Trade and Local Transforma-tions*, 57–90. Quezon City: Ateneo de Manila University Press, 1982.

Mei, June. "Socioeconomic Origins of Emigration: Guangdong to Califor-nia, 1850–1882." *Modern China* 5:4 (October 1979), 463–501.

Meskill, Johanna Menzel. *A Chinese Pioneer Family: The Lins of Wu-feng, Tai-wan, 1729–1895*. Princeton: Princeton University Press, 1979.

Moloughney, Brian, and Xia Weizhong. "Silver and the Fall of the Ming." *Pa-pers on Far Eastern History* 40 (1989), 51–78.

Murray, Dian H. "Migration, Protection, and Racketeering: The Spread of the Tiandihui within China." In David Ownby and Mary Somers Heid-hues, eds., *Secret Societies Reconsidered: Perspectives on the Social History of Modern South China and Southeast Asia*, 177–189. Armonk, N.Y.: M. E. Sharpe, 1993.

*Nanyang huaqiao kangri jiuguo yundong shimo, 1937–1942*. Taipei: Guo-shiguan, 1984.

Naquin, Susan, and Evelyn S. Rawski. *Chinese Society in the Eighteenth Century*. New Haven: Yale University Press, 1989.

Ng Chin-Keong. "Gentry-Merchants and Peasant-Peddlers—the Response of Southern Fukienese to Offshore Trading Opportunities, 1522–66." *Jour-nal of Nanyang University* 7 (1973–74): 161–173.

———. *Trade and Society: The Amoy Network on the China Coast, 1683–1735*. Singapore: Singapore University Press, 1983.

Norman, Henry. *The Peoples and Politics of the Far East: Travels and Studies in the British, French, Spanish and Portuguese Colonies, Siberia, China, Japan, Korea, Siam and Malaya*. London, T. F. Unwin, 1900.

Omohundro, John. T. *Chinese Merchant Families in Iloilo: Commerce and Kin in a Central Philippine City*. Quezon City: Ateneo de Manila University Press, 1981.

———. "Trading Patterns of Philippine Chinese: Strategies of Sojourning Middlemen." In Karl L. Hutterer, ed., *Economic Exchange and Social Inter-action in Southeast Asia: Perspectives from Prehistory, History, and Ethnogra-phy*, 113–136. Ann Arbor: Center for South and Southeast Asian Studies, University of Michigan, 1977.

Ong, Aihwa. *Flexible Citizenship: The Cultural Logics of Transnationality*. Durham: Duke University Press, 1999.

———. "On the Edge of Empires: Flexible Citizenship among Chinese in Diaspora." *Positions* 1:3 (1993), 745–778.

Ong, Aihwa, and Donald M. Nonini, eds. *Ungrounded Empires: The Cultural Politics of Modern Chinese Transnationalism*. New York: Routledge, 1997.

Owen, Norman G. *Prosperity without Progress: Manila Hemp and Material Life in the Colonial Philippines*. Berkeley: University of California Press, 1984.

Ownby, David. *Brotherhoods and Secret Societies in Early and Mid-Qing China: The Formation of a Tradition*. Stanford: Stanford University Press, 1996.

————. "Chinese Hui and the Early Modern Social Order: Evidence from Eighteenth-Century Southeast China." In David Ownby and Mary Somers Heidhues, eds., *Secret Societies Reconsidered: Perspectives on the Social History of Modern South China and Southeast Asia*, 34–67. Armonk, N.Y.: M. E. Sharpe, 1993.

————. "Communal Violence in Eighteenth Century Southeast China: The Background to the Lin Shuangwen Uprising of 1787." Ph.D. dissertation, Harvard University, 1989.

————. "The Heaven and Earth Society as Popular Religion." *Journal of Asian Studies* 54:4 (1995), 1023–1046.

————. "Introduction." In David Ownby and Mary Somers Heidhues, eds., *Secret Societies Reconsidered: Perspectives on the Social History of Modern South China and Southeast Asia*, 3–33. Armonk, N.Y.: M. E. Sharpe, 1993.

Ownby, David, and Mary Somers Heidhues, eds. *Secret Societies Reconsidered: Perspectives on the Social History of Modern South China and Southeast Asia.* Armonk, N.Y.: M. E. Sharpe, 1993.

Peng Naiyang and Li Maozhou. "Xiaoshi." In Chen Zhiping ed., *Xiaolusong huaqiao Zhongxi xuexiao wushi zhounian jinian kan,* 101–104. Manila: Anglo-Chinese School, 1949.

Phelan, J. L. *Hispanization of the Philippines: Spanish Aims and Filipino Responses, 1565–1700.* Madison, Wisc.: University of Wisconsin Press, 1959.

Philippine Chinese General Chamber of Commerce. *Feilübin Minlila Zhonghua shanghui wushi zhounian jinian kan.* Manila: Zhonghua Shanghui Chubanbu, 1955.

Philippine Islands, Census Office. *Census of the Philippines Taken under the Direction of the Philippine Commission, in the Year 1903.* 4 vols. Washington: Government Printing Office, 1905.

————. *Census of the Philippines Taken under the Direction of the Philippine Legislature, in the Year 1918.* 4 vols. Manila: Bureau of Printing, 1920–1921.

Polachek, James M. *The Inner Opium War.* Cambridge: Harvard University Press, 1992.

Ptak, Roderick, and Dietmar Rothermund, eds. *Emporia, Commodities, and Entrepreneurs in Asian Maritime Trade, c. 1400–1750.* Stuttgart: Steiner Verlag, 1991.

Purcell, Victor. *The Chinese in Malaya.* London: Oxford University Press, 1948.

————. *The Chinese in Modern Malaya.* Singapore: D. Moore, 1956.

————. *The Chinese in Southeast Asia.* 2d ed. London: Oxford University Press, 1966.

————. *South and East Asia since 1800.* Cambridge: Cambridge University Press, 1965.

Quiason, Seraphin. "The Early Philippine-China Sampan Trade." *Fookien Times Yearbook* 1966, 273–277.

———. "The Sampan Trade, 1570–1770." In Alfonso Felix Jr., ed., *The Chinese in the Philippines, 1570–1770,* 160–174. Manila: Solidaridad Publishing House, 1966.

Rankin, Mary Backus, and Joseph W. Esherick. "Concluding Remarks." In Joseph W. Esherick and Mary Backus Rankin, eds., *Chinese Local Elites and Patterns of Dominance,* 305–345. Berkeley: University of California Press, 1990.

Redding, S. Gordon. *The Spirit of Chinese Capitalism.* Berlin: Walter de Gruyter, 1990.

Reid, Anthony. "Economic and Social Change, c. 1400–1800." In Nicholas Tarling, ed., *The Cambridge History of Southeast Asia,* vol. 1: *From Early Times to c. 1800,* 460–507. Cambridge: Cambridge University Press, 1992.

———. "Entrepreneurial Minorities, Nationalism and the State." In Anthony Reid and Daniel Chirot, eds., *Essential Outsiders: Chinese and Jews in the Modern Transformation of Southeast Asia and Central Europe,* 33–73. Seattle: University of Washington Press, 1997.

———. "Flows and Seepages in the Long-Term Chinese Interaction with Southeast Asia." In Anthony Reid, ed., *Sojourners and Settlers: Histories of Southeast Asia and the Chinese: In Honour of Jennifer Cushman,* 15–49. St. Leonards, N.S.W.: Asian Studies Association of Australia in association with Allen and Unwin, 1996.

———. "The Seventeenth-Century Crisis in Southeast Asia." *Modern Asian Studies* 24:4 (1990), 639–659.

———. *Southeast Asia in the Age of Commerce, 1450–1680,* vol. 1: *The Lands Below the Winds.* New Haven: Yale University Press, 1988.

———. *Southeast Asia in the Age of Commerce, 1450–1680,* vol. 2: *Expansion and Crisis.* New Haven: Yale University Press, 1993.

———, ed. *The Last Stand of Asian Autonomies: Responses to Modernity in the Diverse States of Southeast Asia and Korea, 1750–1900.* Basingstoke, Hampshire: Palgrave Macmillan, 1997.

———. *Sojourners and Settlers: Histories of Southeast Asia and the Chinese: In Honour of Jennifer Cushman.* St. Leonards, N.S.W.: Asian Studies Association of Australia in association with Allen and Unwin, 1996.

———. *Southeast Asia in the Early Modern Era: Trade, Power, and Belief.* Ithaca, N.Y.: Cornell University Press, 1993.

Reid, Anthony, and Daniel Chirot, eds. *Essential Outsiders: Chinese and Jews in the Modern Transformation of Southeast Asia and Central Europe.* Seattle: University of Washington Press, 1997.

Rizal, José. *El Filibusterismo.* Translated by León Ma. Guerrero. 2d ed. Bloomington, Ind.: Indiana University Press, 1962.

*Rosenstock's Manila City.* Various vols. Manila: C. W. Rosenstock, 1903–1917.

Roth, Dennis Morrow. "Church Lands in the Agrarian History of the Tagalog Region." In Alfred W. McCoy and Edilberto C. de Jesus, eds., *Philippine Social History: Global Trade and Local Transformations*, 131–153. Quezon City: Ateneo de Manila University Press, 1982.

Rowe, William T. *Hankow: Commerce and Society in a Chinese City, 1796–1889.* Stanford: Stanford University Press, 1984.

———. *Hankow: Conflict and Community in a Chinese City, 1796–1895.* Stanford: Stanford University Press, 1989.

Rush, James R. *Opium to Java: Revenue Farming and Chinese Enterprise in Colonial Indonesia.* Ithaca, N.Y.: Cornell University Press, 1990.

Salmon, Claudine. "Ancestral Halls, Funeral Associations, and Attempts at Resinicization in Nineteenth Century Netherlands India." In Anthony Reid, ed., *Sojourners and Settlers: Histories of Southeast Asia and the Chinese: In Honour of Jennifer Cushman*, 183–214. St. Leonards, N.S.W.: Asian Studies Association of Australia in association with Allen and Unwin, 1996.

Sa-onoy, Modesto P. *The Chinese in Negros.* Bacolod City, Philippines: St. John's Institute and Negros Occidental Historical Commission, 1980.

Sarkisyanz, Manuel. *Rizal and Republican Spain and Other Rizalist Essays.* Manila: National Historical Institute, 1995.

Saxton, Alexander. *The Indispensable Enemy: Labor and the Anti-Chinese Movement in California.* Berkeley: University of California Press, 1971.

Schumacher, John N., ed. *The Making of a Nation: Essays on Nineteenth-Century Filipino Nationalism.* Manila: Ateneo de Manila University Press, 1996.

Schurz, William Lytle. *The Manila Galleon.* New York: Dutton, 1939.

Scott, William Henry. *Cracks in the Parchment Curtain, and Other Essays in Philippine History.* Quezon City: New Day Publishers, 1985.

———. *The Discovery of the Igorots: Spanish Contacts with the Pagans of Northern Luzon.* Revised ed. Quezon City: New Day Publishers, 1977.

———. *Looking for the Prehispanic Filipino: And Other Essays in Philippine History.* Manila: New Day Publishers, 1993.

See, Chinben. "Chinese Clanship in the Philippine Setting." *Journal of Southeast Asian Studies* 12:1 (1981), 224–246.

———. "Chinese Education and Ethnic Identity." In Theresa Carino, ed., *Chinese in the Philippines*, 32–42. Manila: China Studies Program, De La Salle University, 1985.

———. *The Chinese Immigrants: Selected Writings of Professor Chinben See.* Ed. Teresita Ang See. Manila: Kaisa Para Sa Kaunlaran and the Chinese Studies Program, De La Salle University, 1992.

———. "Chinese Organizations and Ethnic Identity in the Philippines." In Jennifer Wayne Cushman and Wang Gungwu, eds. *Changing Identities of the Southeast Asian Chinese since World War II*, 319–334. Hong Kong: Hong Kong University Press, 1988.

See, Chinben, ed. *A Bibliography of the Chinese in the Philippines.* Manila: Pagkakaisa Sa Pag-unlad, 1972.

————. *Chinese in the Philippines: A Bibliography.* Manila: Chinese Studies Program, De La Salle University, 1990.

See, Teresita Ang. "The Ethnic Chinese As Filipinos (Part II)." In Teresita Ang See, ed., *Proceedings of Conference on "The Ethnic Chinese As Filipinos."* Quezon City: Philippine Association for Chinese Studies, 1997.

————. "On Kidnapping, Elections, and the Political Position of the Chinese in the Philippines." In Teresita Ang See, ed., *Chinese in the Philippines: Problems and Perspectives*, vol. 2, 161–189. Manila: Kaisa Para Sa Kaunlaran, 1997.

See, Teresita Ang, ed. *Chinese in the Philippines: Problems and Perspectives*, vol. 2. Manila: Kaisa Para Sa Kaunlaran, 1997.

————. *Proceedings of the Conference on "The Ethnic Chinese As Filipinos."* Quezon City: Philippine Association for Chinese Studies, 1997.

————. *The Ethnic Chinese as Filipinos: Proceedings of the Third Conference on "The Ethnic Chinese as Filipinos."* Quezon City: Philippine Association for Chinese Studies, 1999.

See, Teresita Ang, and Go Bon Juan, eds. *The Ethnic Chinese in the Philippine Revolution.* Manila: Kaisa Para Sa Kaunlaran, 1996.

Shao Xunzheng et al., eds. *Zhongfa zhanzheng.* Shanghai: Xinzhi Chubanshe, 1955.

Shepherd, John Robert. *Statecraft and Political Economy on the Taiwan Frontier, 1600–1800.* Stanford: Stanford University Press, 1993.

Shi Zhenmin. "Feilübin huaren wenhua de chixu: zongqin yu tingxiang zuzhi zai haiwai de yanbian." *Bulletin of the Institute of Ethnology, Academia Sinica* 42 (1976): 119–206.

Simoniya, N. A. *Overseas Chinese in Southeast Asia: A Russian Study.* Data paper no. 45. Ithaca, N.Y.: Southeast Asian Program, Department of Far Eastern Studies, Cornell University, 1961.

Skinner, G. William. "The Chinese of Java." In Morton H. Fried, ed., *Colloquium on Overseas Chinese*, 3–16. New York: International Secretariat, Institute of Pacific Relations, 1958.

————. *Chinese Society in Thailand: An Analytical History.* Ithaca, N.Y.: Cornell University Press, 1957.

————. "Creolized Chinese Societies in Southeast Asia." In Anthony Reid, ed., *Sojourners and Settlers: Histories of Southeast Asia and the Chinese: In Honour of Jennifer Cushman*, 51–93. St. Leonards, N.S.W.: Asian Studies Association of Australia in association with Allen and Unwin, 1996.

————. *Leadership and Power in the Chinese Community of Thailand.* Ithaca, N.Y.: Cornell University Press, 1958.

————. *Report on the Chinese in Southeast Asia, December 1950.* Ithaca, N.Y.: Cornell University Press, 1951.

Skinner, G. William, ed. *The City in Late Imperial China.* Stanford: Stanford University Press, 1977.

Skinner, G. William, and Mark Elvin, eds. *The Chinese City between Two Worlds.* Stanford: Stanford University Press, 1974.

Spalding, Karen, ed. *Essays in the Political, Economic and Social History of Colonial Latin America.* Newark, Del.: University of Delaware Press, 1982.

Spence, Jonathan D. *Chinese Roundabout: Essays in History and Culture.* New York: W. W. Norton and Co., 1992.

————. *The Gate of Heavenly Peace: The Chinese and Their Revolution, 1895–1980.* New York: Viking Press, 1981.

Spence, Jonathan, and John E. Wills Jr., eds. *From Ming to Ch'ing: Conquest, Region and Continuity in Seventeenth Century China.* New Haven: Yale University Press, 1979.

Stanley, Peter. *A Nation in the Making: The Philippines and the United States, 1899–1931.* Cambridge: Harvard University Press, 1974.

Suryadinata, Leo, ed. *Ethnic Chinese as Southeast Asians.* New York: St. Martin's Press, 1997.

Szonyi, Michael. "The Graveyard of Huang Xiulang: Early Twentieth Century Perspectives on the Role of Overseas Chinese in Chinese Modernization." *Asian and Pacific Migration Journal* 10:1 (2001), 81–98.

Tan, Antonio S. *The Chinese in the Philippines during the Japanese Occupation, 1942–1945.* Quezon City: University of the Philippines Press, 1981.

————. *The Chinese in the Philippines, 1898–1935: A Study of Their National Awakening.* Quezon City: R. P. Garcia Publishing Co., 1972.

————. "The Chinese in the Philippines and the Chinese Revolution of 1911." *Asian Studies* 8:1 (April 1970), 160–185.

————. *The Chinese Mestizo and the Formation of the Filipino Nationality.* Quezon City: Asian Center, University of the Philippines, 1984.

————. "Chinese Mestizos and the Formation of Filipino Nationality." In Theresa Carino, ed., *Chinese in the Philippines,* 50–63. Manila: China Studies Program, De La Salle University, 1985.

Tan Chee-Beng and Zhang Xiaojun, eds. *Bibliography of Studies on Fujian with Special Reference to Minnan.* Hong Kong: Hong Kong Institute of Asia-Pacific Studies, 1999.

Tarling, Nicholas, ed. *The Cambridge History of Southeast Asia,* vol. 1: *From Early Times to c. 1800.* Cambridge: Cambridge University Press, 1992.

TePaske, John J. "New World Silver, Castile, and the Philippines, 1590–1800." In John. F. Richards, ed., *Precious Metals in the Later Medieval and Early Modern Worlds,* 425–445. Durham: Carolina Academic Press, 1983.

Tilly, Charles. "Reflections on the History of European State-Making." In Charles Tilly, ed., *The Formation of National States in Western Europe,* 3–83. Princeton: Princeton University Press, 1975.

Tilly, Charles, and C. H. Brown. "On Uprooting, Kinship and the Auspices of Migration." *Journal of Comparative Sociology* 5 (1984), 141–164.

Tracy, J. D., ed. *The Rise of Merchant Empires: Long Distance Trade in the Early Modern World.* Cambridge: Cambridge University Press, 1990.

Trocki, Carl A. "Boundaries and Transgressions: Chinese Enterprise in Eighteenth and Nineteenth Century Southeast Asia." In Aihwa Ong and Donald Nonini, eds., *Ungrounded Empires: The Cultural Politics of Modern Chinese Transnationalism,* 61–83. New York: Routledge, 1997.

———. *Opium and Empire: Chinese Society in Colonial Singapore.* Ithaca, N.Y.: Cornell University Press, 1990.

———. *Prince of Pirates: The Temenggongs and the Development of Johor and Singapore, 1784–1885.* Singapore: Singapore University Press, 1979.

———. "The Rise and Fall of the Ngee Heng Kongsi." In David Ownby and Mary Somers Heidhues, eds., *Secret Societies Reconsidered: Perspectives on the Social History of Modern South China and Southeast Asia,* 89–119. Armonk, N.Y.: M. E. Sharpe, 1993.

Tsai, Henry Shih-shan. *China and the Overseas Chinese in the United States, 1868–1911.* Fayetteville: University of Arkansas Press, 1983.

———. *The Chinese Experience in America.* Bloomington: Indiana University Press, 1986.

United States Philippine Commission. *Official Gazette.* Manila: Bureau of Printing, December 14, 1910.

———. *Report of the Philippine Commission to the President, 1900.* 4 vols. Washington, D.C.: Government Printing Office, 1900.

———. *Report of the Philippine Commission to the President, 1901.* 3 vols. Washington, D.C.: Government Printing Office, 1901–1902.

———. *Report of the Philippine Commission to the President, 1906.* 4 parts. Washington, D.C.: Government Printing Office, 1907.

United States, War Department. *Annual Report of Major-General Arthur MacArthur, U.S. Army, Commanding Division of the Philippines, Military Governor in the Philippine Islands, May 5 to October 1, 1900.* 2 vols. Manila: Bureau of Printing, 1900.

———. *Annual Report of Major-General Arthur MacArthur, U.S. Army, Commanding Division of the Philippines, Military Governor in the Philippine Islands, October 1, 1900 to July 4, 1901.* 2 vols. Manila: Bureau of Printing, 1901.

———. *Annual Report of Major-General E. S. Otis, Military Governor of the Philippine Islands Covering the Period from August 29, 1898 to August 31, 1899.* 3 parts. Washington, D.C.: Government Printing Office, 1899.

———. *Annual Report of Major-General E. S. Otis, Military Governor of the Philippine Islands Covering the Period from June 1898 to August 1899.* Manila: Bureau of Printing, 1899.

———. *Annual Report of Major-General E. S. Otis, U.S. Army, Commanding Division of the Philippines, Military Governor in the Philippine Islands, September*

*1, 1899 to May 5, 1900.* Washington, D.C.: Government Printing Office, 1900.

―――. "Report of the Military Governor of the Philippine Islands on Civil Affairs, 1900." In *Report of the War Department, 1900.* Washington D.C.: Government Printing Office, 1901.

―――. *Report of the Special Mission to the Philippine Islands to the Secretary of War.* Washington, D.C.: Government Printing Office, 1922.

United States, War Department, Bureau of Insular Affairs. *Bureau of Insular Affairs, Record Group 350.* Washington, D.C.: National Archives and Record Service.

United States, War Department, Bureau of Insular Affairs, United States Philippine Commission. *Report of the Philippine Commission to the Secretary of War, 1900–1915.* 32 vols. Washington, D.C.: Government Printing Office, 1901–1916.

University of the Philippines, Institute of Asian Studies. *Chinos Manila. I.A.S. Project 102.* Quezon City: University of the Philippines Press, 1965.

―――. *Chinos Provincias. I.A.S. Project 103.* Quezon City: University of the Philippines Press, 1965.

―――. *Index for Chinos Manila and Chinos Provincias.* Manila: University of the Philippines Press, 1965.

Van Der Sprenkel, Sybille. "Urban Social Control." In G. William Skinner, ed., *The City in Late Imperial China,* 609–632. Stanford: Stanford University Press, 1977.

Von Glahn, Richard. *The Country of Streams and Grottoes: Expansion, Settlement, and the Civilizing of the Sichuan Frontier in Song Times.* Cambridge: Harvard University Press, 1987.

―――. *Fountain of Fortune: Money and Monetary Policy in China, 1000–1700.* Berkeley: University of California Press, 1996.

Wakeman, Frederic, Jr. "The Secret Societies of Kwangtung, 1800–1856." In Jean Chesneaux, ed., *Popular Movements and Secret Societies in China, 1840–1950,* 29–48. Stanford: Stanford University Press, 1972.

Wang Guanhua. "Chinese Emigrants and Government Policy Adjustments in the Late Qing: The Cases of Chinese Laborers in Cuba and Peru." *Twenty-First Century* 44 (December 1997), 47–57.

―――. *In Search of Justice: The 1905–1906 Chinese Anti-American Boycott.* Cambridge: Harvard East Asian Monographs, Harvard University Press, 2001.

Wang Gungwu. "Among Non-Chinese." *Daedalus* 120:2 (1991), 135–155.

―――. *China and the Chinese Overseas.* Singapore: Times Academic Press, 1991.

―――. *The Chinese Minority in Southeast Asia.* Singapore: Southeast Asian Studies Programme, Nanyang University, 1978.

————. *The Chineseness of China: Selected Essays.* Hong Kong: Oxford University Press, 1991.

————. *Community and Nation: China, Southeast Asia, and Australia.* Kensington, Australia: Asian Studies Association of Australia in association with Allen and Unwin, 1992.

————. *Community and Nation: Essays on Southeast Asia and the Chinese.* Selected by Anthony Reid. Singapore: Published for the Asian Studies Association of Australia by Heinemann Asia, 1981.

————. *The Culture of Chinese Merchants.* North York, Ont.: University of Toronto–York University Joint Centre for Asia Pacific Studies, 1990.

————. "The Limits of Nanyang Chinese Nationalism, 1912–1937. In C. D. Cowan and O. W. Wolters, eds., *Southeast Asian History and Historiography: Essays Presented to D. G. Hall,* 405–423. Ithaca, N.Y.: Cornell University Press, 1976.

————. "Merchants without Empire: The Hokkien Sojourning Communities." In J. D. Tracy, ed., *The Rise of Merchant Empires: Long Distance Trade in the Early Modern World,* 400–421. Cambridge: Cambridge University Press, 1990.

————. *Nanhai maoyi yu nanyang huaren.* Hong Kong: Zhonghua Shuju Xianggang Fenju, 1988.

————. *The Nanhai Trade: The Early History of Chinese Trade in the South China Sea.* Singapore: Times Academic Press, 1998.

————. *A Short History of the Nanyang Chinese.* Singapore: D. Moore for Eastern University Press, 1959.

————. "Sojourning: The Chinese Experience in Southeast Asia." In Anthony Reid, ed., *Sojourners and Settlers: Histories of Southeast Asia and the Chinese: In Honour of Jennifer Cushman,* 1–14. St. Leonards, N.S.W.: Asian Studies Association of Australia in association with Allen and Unwin, 1996.

————, ed. *Global History and Migrations.* Boulder, Colo.: Westview Press, 1997.

Wang, Sing-wu. *The Organization of Chinese Emigration, 1848–1888. With Special Reference to Chinese Emigration to Australia.* San Francisco: Chinese Materials Center, 1978.

Wang Teh-ming. "Sino-Filipino Historico-Cultural Relations." *Philippine Social Sciences and Humanities Review* 39 (1959), 277–471.

Wang Yanwei and Wang Liang, comps. *Qingji waijiao shiliao.* Taipei: Wenhai Chubanshe, 1963.

Watson, James L. *Emigration and the Chinese Lineage: The Mans in Hong Kong and London.* Berkeley: University of California Press, 1975.

————. "Standardizing the Gods: The Promotion of T'ien Hou ('Empress of Heaven') Along the South China Coast, 960–1960." In David Johnson, Andrew J. Nathan, and Evelyn S. Rawski, eds., *Popular Culture in Late Imperial China,* 292–324. Berkeley: University of California Press, 1985.

Watt, John R. *The District Magistrate in Late Imperial China*. New York: Columbia University Press, 1972.

Weightman, George. "The American Colonial Policy toward the Chinese: A Legacy and a Problem for the Commonwealth." *Filipinas* 7 (Fall 1986): 29–43.

———. "Community Organization of Chinese Living in Manila." *Philippine Social Sciences and Humanities Review* 19 (March 1954), 24–39.

———. "The Philippine Chinese: A Cultural History of a Marginal Trading Community." Ph.D. dissertation, Cornell University, 1960.

Weisblatt, Franz J., ed. *Who's Who in the Philippines*. Vol. 1 (1936–1937). Manila: McCullough, 1937.

———. *Who's Who in the Philippines:* A Biographical Dictionary of Notable Living Men of the Philippine Islands. Manila: Ramon Roces, 1940.

Welch, Richard E., Jr. *Response to Imperialism: The United States and the Philippine-American War, 1899–1902*. Chapel Hill: University of North Carolina Press, 1979.

Whipple, A. B. C. *The Challenge*. New York: Quill, 1987.

Wickberg, Edgar. "Anti-Sinicism and Chinese Identity Options in the Philippines." In Anthony Reid and Daniel Chirot, eds., *Essential Outsiders: Chinese and Jews in the Modern Transformation of Southeast Asia and Central Europe*, 153–183. Seattle: University of Washington Press, 1997.

———. *The Chinese in Philippine Life, 1850–1898*. 1965. Republished edition. Honolulu: University of Hawai'i Press, 2001.

———. "The Chinese Mestizo in Philippine History." *Journal of Southeast Asian History* 5:1 (1964), 62–100.

———. "Early Chinese Economic Influence in the Philippines." *Pacific Affairs* 25:3 (1962), 275–285.

Williams, Lea E. *Overseas Chinese Nationalism: The Genesis of the Pan-Chinese Movement in Indonesia, 1900–1916*. Glencoe, Ill.: Free Press, 1960.

Willmott, Donald E. *The Chinese of Semarang: A Changing Minority Community in Indonesia*. Ithaca, N.Y.: Cornell University Press, 1960.

Wills, John E., Jr. "Maritime China from Wang Chih to Shih Lang: Themes in Peripheral History." In Jonathan Spence and John E. Wills, Jr., eds., *From Ming to Ch'ing: Conquest, Region and Continuity in Seventeenth Century China*, 201–238. New Haven: Yale University Press, 1979.

Wilson, Andrew R. "Ambition and Identity: China and the Chinese in the Colonial Philippines." Ph.D. dissertation, Harvard University, 1998.

———. "Carlos Palanca Chen Qianshan: Crisis and Elite Activism in the Philippine-Chinese Community, 1896–1899." *Papers on Chinese History* 5 (1996), 59–78.

———. "Zhang Zhidong and the Manila Consulate-General: A Study in Methods and Motives." *Papers on Chinese History* 3 (1994), 116–134.

Wong, Bernard. *A Chinese American Community: Ethnicity and Survival Strategies.* Singapore: Chopmen Enterprises, 1979.

Wong, K. Scott. "Cultural Defenders and Brokers: Chinese Responses to the Anti-Chinese Movement." In K. Scott Wong and Sucheng Chan, eds., *Claiming America: Constructing Chinese American Identities during the Exclusion Era,* 3–39. Philadelphia: Temple University Press, 1998.

Wong, K. Scott, and Sucheng Chan, eds. *Claiming America: Constructing Chinese American Identities during the Exclusion Era.* Philadelphia: Temple University Press, 1998.

Wong, Kwok-chu. "The Americans in Chinese Business in the Philippines, 1920–1941." *Bulletin of the American Historical Collection* 22:3 (1994), 113–122.

———. *The Chinese in the Philippine Economy, 1898–1941.* Quezon City: Ateneo de Manila University Press, 1999.

Wu Ching-hong. "A Study of References to the Philippines in Chinese Sources from Earliest Times to the Ming Dynasty." *Philippine Social Sciences and Humanities Review* 24 (1959), 1–181.

Wu Jianxiong. *Haiwai yimin yu Huaren shehui.* Taipei: Yunchen Wenhua Shiye Gufen Gongsi, 1993.

Yan Wenqu, "Sanshi nianlai feidao huaqiao baozhi shiye." In *Xiaolusong huaqiao Zhongxi xuexiao sanshi zhounian jinian kan,* chapter 39. Manila: Anglo-Chinese School, 1929.

Yanai Kenji. "Hi-to shinajin no chiho hatten ni tsuite." *Nanpo minzoku* 7 (1942), 1–28.

———. "Ma-ni-ra no Tondo-ku no shinjin no hatten." *Minamia Ajiya gakuho* 2 (1943), 35–64.

Yeh, Wen-Hsin, ed. *Becoming Chinese: Passages to Modernity and Beyond.* Berkeley: University of California Press, 2000.

Yen, Ching-hwang. "Ch'ing Sale of Honours and the Chinese Leadership in Singapore and Malaya, 1877–1912." *Journal of Southeast Asian Studies* 1:2 (September 1970), 20–32.

———. *Class Structure and Social Mobility in the Chinese Community in Singapore and Malaya, 1800–1911.* Adelaide: University of Adelaide, Centre for Asian Studies, 1983.

———. *Community and Politics: The Chinese in Colonial Singapore and Malaysia.* Singapore: Times Academic Press, 1995.

———. *Coolies and Mandarins: China's Protection of the Overseas Chinese during the Late Ch'ing Period, 1851–1911.* Singapore: Singapore University Press, 1985.

———. *Haiwai huaren shi yanjiu.* Singapore: Xinjiapo Yazhou Yanjiu Xuehui, 1992.

———. *The Overseas Chinese and the 1911 Revolution, with Special Reference to Singapore and Malaya.* Kuala Lumpur: Oxford University Press, 1976.

―――. "Overseas Chinese Nationalism in Singapore and Malaya, 1877–1912." *Modern Asian Studies* 16:3 (1982), 397–425.

―――. *The Role of the Overseas Chinese in the 1911 Revolution*. Singapore: Chopmen Enterprises, 1978.

―――. *A Social History of the Chinese in Singapore and Malaya, 1800–1911*. Singapore: Oxford University Press, 1986.

―――. *Studies in Modern Overseas Chinese History*. Singapore: Times Academic Press, 1995.

―――. *Xing, Ma Huaren yu Xinhai geming*. Trans. Li Enhan. Taipei: Lianjing Chuban Shiye Gongsi, 1982.

Yi Jingxian, "Wushi nianlai huaqiao guoyu yundong." In Chen Zhiping, ed., *Xiaolusong huaqiao Zhongxi xuexiao wushi zhounian jinian kan*, 287–288. Manila: Anglo-Chinese School, 1949.

Yong, C. F. *Chinese Leadership and Power in Colonial Singapore*. Singapore: Times Academic Press, 1994.

―――. *Tan Kah-kee: The Making of an Overseas Chinese Legend*. Singapore: Oxford University Press, 1987.

Yong, C. F., and R. B. McKenna. *The Kuomintang Movement in British Malaya, 1912–1949*. Singapore: Singapore University Press, 1990.

Yu Heping. *Jindai Zhongguo shangren*. Guangdong: Guangdong Renmin Chubanshe, 1996.

―――. *Shanghui yu Zhongguo zaoqi xiandahua*. Taipei: Dongda Tushu Gufen Yuxian Gongsi, 1995.

Zaide, Gregorio F. "Chinese General in the Philippine Revolution." In Schubert S. C. Liao, ed., *Chinese Participation in Philippine Culture and Economy*, 120–137. Manila: Schubert S. C. Liao, 1964.

―――. "The Economic Development of the Philippines and the Contributions of Foreigners." *Far Eastern Economic Review* 19:1 (1955), 13–15.

―――. *Manila during the Revolutionary Period*. Manila: National Historical Commission, 1973.

―――. *Philippine History: Development of Our Nation*. Manila: Bookman, 1961.

―――. *Philippine Political and Cultural History*. 2 vols. Manila: Philippine Education Company, 1949.

―――. *The Philippines since Pre-Spanish Times*. Manila: R. P. Garcia, 1949.

―――, ed. *Documentary Sources of Philippine History*. 12 vols. Manila: National Book Store, 1990.

Zarco, Ricardo M. "The Chinese Family Structure." In Alfonso Felix Jr., ed., *The Chinese in the Philippines, 1770–1898*, 211–222. Manila: Solidaridad Publishing House, 1975.

―――. "The Philippine Chinese and Opium Addiction." In Alfonso Felix Jr., ed., *The Chinese in the Philippines, 1770–1898*, 96–109. Manila: Solidaridad Publishing House, 1975.

Zelin, Madeline. "The Rise and Fall of the Fu-Rong Salt-Yard Elite: Merchant

Dominance in Late Qing China." In Joseph W. Esherick and Mary Backus Rankin, eds., *Chinese Local Elites and Patterns of Dominance*, 82–109. Berkeley: University of California Press, 1990.

Zeng Shaocong. *Dong yanghang luyimin: Ming-Qing haiyang yimin Taiwan yu Feilübin de bijiao yanjiu.* Nanchang: Jiangxi Gaoxiao Chubanshe, 1998.

Zhang Cunwu, Zhu Hongyuan, and Pan Luli, eds. *Feilübin huaqiao huaren fangwen jilu.* Taipei: Jinshisuo, 1996.

Zhang Xin. *Social Transformation in Modern China: The State and Local Elites in Henan, 1900–1937.* Cambridge: Cambridge University Press, 2000.

Zhang Yinhuan. *Sanzhou riji.* 8 juan. Shanghai: Shanghai Guji Chubanshe, 1995 and 1999.

Zhang Zhidong. *Zhang Wenxiang gong quanji.* 228 juan. Taipei: Wenhai Chubanshe, 1963.

———. *Zhang Wenxiang gong sigao.* Beijing: Wenhua Zhai, 1920.

Zhao Lingyang et al. *Ming shilu zhong zhi Dongnanya shiliao.* 2 vols. Hong Kong: Hsüeh-tsin Press, 1968 and 1976.

Zheng Guanying. *Chen Qianshan.* Taipei: Haiwai Wenku Chubanshe, 1954.

*Zhongguo Guomindang nianjian.* Nanjing: Zhongyang Zuzhibu, 1934.

*Zhongguo Guomindang yu huaqiao xianqu bian, 1908–1945.* Taipei: Wenshizhe Chubanshe, 1984.

*Zhong-Mei guanxi shiliao.* Vols. 1–8. Taipei: Jinshisuo, 1968; 1988–1990.

Zhongshan Daxue Dongnanya Lishi Yanjiusuo, ed. *Huaqiao huaren lishi luncong.* Guangdong: Zhongshan Daxue Dongnanya Lishi Yanjiusuo, 1985.

———. *Zhongguo guji zhong youguan Feilübin ziliao huibian.* Beijing,: Zhonghua Shuju, 1980.

Zhou Nanjing. *Feilübin yu huaren.* Ed. Go Bon Juan. Manila: Kaisa Para Sa Kaunlaran, 1993.

Zhou Nanjing et al.. *Shijie huaqiao huaren cidian.* Beijing: Beijing Daxue Chubanshe, 1993.

Zhuang Guotu, Zhao Wenliu, Tanaka Kyoko, and Cen Huang, eds. *Zhongguo qiaoxiang yanjiu.* Xiamen: Xiamen Daxue Chubanshe, 2000.

Zuniga, J. M. *Status of the Philippines in 1800.* Trans. Viante del Carmen. Manila: Filipiniana Book Guild, 1973.

# Index

# About the Author

ANDREW R. WILSON is associate professor of strategy at the U.S. Naval War College in Newport, Rhode Island, where he lectures on military history and strategic theory. He holds a Ph.D. from Harvard University in History and East Asian languages. Prior to joining the War College faculty, Dr. Wilson taught courses on modern Chinese history and the history of Chinese emigration at Wellesley College and Harvard University. In addition to his work on overseas Chinese communities, he has published articles on Sun Tzu's *Art of War,* Chinese military history, and contemporary Chinese sea power. He is the editor of *The Chinese in the Caribbean,* a collection of essays, and is presently working on a new annotated translation of *Art of War.*

Production Notes for Wilson/*Ambition and Identity*

Cover design by Santos Barbasa Jr.

Text design University of Hawai'i Press production staff using
Caslon 224 and New Baskerville.

Composition by Binghamton Valley Composition in QuarkXPress.

Printing and binding by The Maple-Vail Book Manufacturing Group.

Printed on 60 lb. Text White Opaque, 426 ppi